TRUSTEESHIP IN CHANGE

Contributors

Terry L. Anderson
Peter M. Booth
Richmond L. Clow
David H. Getches
Theodore S. Jojola
Laura Kirwan
Diane L. Krahe
Lawrence M. Lesko
Daniel McCool
Alan G. McQuillan
Imre Sutton
Renée G. Thakali
Katherine Weist
Michelle A. Mestrovich, cartographer

TRUSTEESHIP IN CHANGE

TOWARD TRIBAL AUTONOMY IN RESOURCE MANAGEMENT

EDITED BY

RICHMOND L. CLOW & IMRE SUTTON

FOREWORD BY DAVID H. GETCHES

UNIVERSITY PRESS OF COLORADO

Published by the University Press of Colorado
5589 Arapahoe Avenue, Suite 206C
Boulder, Colorado 80303

Printed in the United States of America

The University Press of Colorado is a cooperative publishing enterprise supported, in part, by Adams State College, Colorado State University, Fort Lewis College, Mesa State College, Metropolitan State College of Denver, University of Colorado, University of Northern Colorado, University of Southern Colorado, and Western State College of Colorado.

The paper used in this publication meets the minimum requirements of the American National Standard for Information Sciences—Permanence of Paper for Printed Library Materials. ANSI Z39.48-1992

Library of Congress Cataloging-in-Publication Data

Trusteeship in change : toward tribal autonomy in resource management /
Richmond L. Clow & Imre Sutton editors ; with a foreword by David H. Getches.
p. cm.
Includes bibliographical references and index.
ISBN 0-87081-622-5 (hardback : alk. paper) — ISBN 0-87081-650-0 (pbk.: alk. paper)
1. Indians of North America—Politics and government. 2. Indians of North America—Government relations. 3. Indians of North America—Legal status, laws, etc. 4. Self-determination, National—United States. 5. Indigenous peoples—United States—Ecology. 6. Land tenure—Government policy—United States. 7. Water rights—Government policy—United States. 8. Natural resources management areas—United States. 9. Conservation of natural resources—United States. 10. United States. Bureau of Indian Affairs. I. Sutton, Imre, 1928– II. Clow, Richmond L. III. Title.

E98.T77 T78 2001
333.7'0973—dc21

2001002412

Jacket design by Laura Furney
Text design by Daniel Pratt

10 09 08 07 06 05 04 03 02 01 10 9 8 7 6 5 4 3 2 1

to
My daughter, Catherine Clow

and
My grandson, Aaron [Sutton] Meek

and the
children and grandchildren
of our contributors

Contents

Part II: Tribalism: Encouraging Indian Participation

Part III: Self-Determination: Pursuing Indigenous and Multiagency Management

Figures

Tables

Foreword

David H. Getches

In the long run, American Indian tribes must stake the future well-being of their economies and cultures on their lands. This truth is nothing new, but it takes on fresh vitality in an era when the opportunities for anchoring tribal land and resource use to an ethic of sustainability have never been better. Efforts to achieve this goal, however, may be frustrated as tribes feel the centripetal forces of non-Indian proximity to and involvement on their reservations.

In the minds of many Americans, the mention of Indian reservation economies conjures a vision of windfall profits from casinos plunked down in unlikely spots. Two realities, most poignant in light of this book's theme, defy that vision. One is that only the luckiest tribes have locations that enable them to run profitable casinos. The other is that even fewer tribes will enjoy the heyday of Indian gambling for long. Plainly, when states decide to allow gambling everywhere, most tribes will lose their present advantage of limited competition. These realities renew the necessity for tribes to focus on how to ensure the permanent tenure and productivity of their homelands.

This can be the moment in history when tribes seize greater control of what is theirs and prevent it from slipping away. If the exhilaration of gaming revenue is ephemeral, it at least provides the wherewithal for many tribes to buy back lands historically lost in flurries of misguided federal policies, and it funds technical assistance needed for sophisticated resource planning and management.

Moreover, the ideal of more intensive exercise of tribal proprietorship and sovereignty provides a model for the tribes not fortunate enough to benefit from the current surge of gambling income and, significantly, for the federal "trustee" whose mandate historically has been vague. Indeed, it may be time to reform the nature of the trust responsibility of the federal government to tribes. Most trusts, such as those held by banks under carefully drafted legal documents, are designed to accomplish a particular purpose, with the trustee playing a special role designed to serve the needs of the beneficiary as well as commercial or familial motives.

For tribal leaders, government officials, and anyone concerned with Indian policy past and present, this book can provoke creativity in redefining a federal trust responsibility aimed at enhancing the sustainability of the tribal land and resource base. The authors blend historical experiences—some grim, some satisfying—with diverse ideas on why some approaches succeeded and others either fizzled or produced downright disastrous consequences. Whatever may separate the perspectives of individual authors, there is remarkable agreement among them that successful resource management on reservations is linked to Indian control. They also concur that federal agencies can support and stimulate tribal resource management goals or can hamper and even destroy resources, not to mention tribal governing institutions and traditions.

The accounts and individual conclusions in the chapters that follow, therefore, can inform the work of reforming a federal trust relation. The stories told in this book resonate with ill-fated attempts to impose national policies on Indian reservations. Dividing up tribal lands and parceling them out to individual farmers seemed wholesome and progressive in the nation's homesteading era. But the allotment policy was devastating for tribal land bases and political structures and an economic failure for the individual allottees. As the nation haltingly groped toward a public land forest policy, it forced "expertise" on tribes that resulted in deforesting once-rich reservation timberlands. Many more stories could be told. In wartime, Indian resources were conscripted, with helium seized without fair compensation and uranium gouged out of the land, leaving the Indians with tragic environmental and health effects.

Even attempts to "conserve" Indian resources faltered. In the era when conservation meant development of resources for productive use, dams were thrown across rivers, variously dewatering or flooding Indian homelands. Tribal communities were destroyed, and some of the most fertile reservation lands were inundated. "Indian irrigation projects" ended up aiding non-Indian farming more than Indian agriculture. More recently, the popular notion of conservation as preservation has been embodied in laws like the Endangered Species Act. Noble as its goals may be, the act has had perverse effects on tribes. With some species like the Pacific salmon, driven to the brink of extinction by the excesses of the larger society's dam construction, pollution, and overfishing, tribes were told there were insufficient fish for their traditional uses. Moreover, if Indians—unable to fish—wanted to farm, develop businesses, or cut timber from their lands to survive, they would be restricted by the act's strict protections for habitats of species endangered by their neighbors' past exploitation.

The dilemma of perennially resource-dependent Native Americans is hard for non-Natives to understand. An oil company's ad showing a mournful Indian shedding a tear as pollution desecrates his land fixes a romantic image of the nation's original environmentalist. But the stereotype does not fit with a tribe's efforts to negotiate exceptions to the Endangered Species Act to enable logging. Those who understand a bit about Native history and culture, however, see no contradiction in the Indian's desire to develop an economy based on natural resources any more than they would eschew the Indian's desire to kill a deer to feed the family. For many tribal peoples, a sense of mutuality and interdependence between humans and the rest of nature ensures that resources will be treated with stewardship. Used, to be sure, but used thoughtfully, gratefully, and in ways that preserve their availability so future generations can endure on the land.

The coalescence of reverence for the land and use of natural resources is comprehended in the emerging ideal of sustainability, which posits a more comprehensive vision of conservation. A vision that comports with the commitment to the permanent interconnection with the land best characterizes most Native philosophy. The linkage of sustainable modern economies to careful stewardship of resources first captured international understanding with the United Nation's Brundtland Commission report, *Our Common Future,* in the 1980s. Sustainability has now become the touchstone of the locally based collaborative efforts widely used in the United States to solve resource issues in sensible and sensitive ways. The rhetoric of sustainability has not yet been fully embraced at the national level.

An essential part of sustainability is the engagement of the people of a place in determining how best to conserve and use resources. This demands new concepts of governance—new at least to the historically top-down structures of state and federal establishments. Tribes are, by contrast, well situated for governing sustainably. They are close to the ground, close to the people. Many are culturally and spiritually committed to walking lightly on the land, using resources with a consciousness of the need to give back, and to thinking intergenerationally. Tribes are also equipped with sovereignty predating that of the United States itself, ownership of a respectable land and resource base, and the latter-day legal credentials to regulate and protect their own environment.

Yet tribes need protection against states that would extend control into Indian country. And they often need expertise that is either too expensive or too specialized for them to hire when dealing with other governments and with powerful economic interests. The role of a trustee for tribes, then, could include at a minimum firm legal protections for the integrity of the land base and for the tribes' sovereign prerogatives and access to first-rate technical assistance.

As many of the chapters of this book corroborate, the ability of tribes to protect or use resources wisely has always depended on the mood swings of national policy. Typically, an ambitious congressional or executive policy, often specific to land or resources, has been imposed on tribes. Usually, that policy has emulated directions of social or natural resource policy in the dominant society. Tribes have shown an impressive resilience to policies that eroded their land bases and experimented with and sometimes wasted their natural resources. The great Indian law scholar Felix Cohen wrote that these extensions of national policy to Indian country have made the Indian like the miner's canary, marking the shift from fresh air to poison gas in our national culture.

For about forty years the announced Indian policy of both Congress and the executive has been rather stable. The prolonged period of "self-determination" policy has allowed important tribal advances in economic development and self-governance. More than ever, tribes are capable of influencing national policies that affect them. But a new challenge confronts the tribes, and it has begun to affect profoundly their ability to exercise self-determination over the land and resources within their boundaries. The U.S. Supreme Court has begun to tie tribal sovereignty—such as the power to zone lands and even to adjudicate conflicts—within reservations to land ownership, limiting tribal authority in many cases to tribal members. A short but pernicious line of cases has begun to threaten tribal control of land and resources. Tribes are being told that, unlike any other kind of sovereign, they cannot control the activities of noncitizens within their boundaries unless the land where the activities take place is Indian owned or the activity is under a contract. This coincides with the greatest period of economic expansion ever in Indian country, a time when the growth of trade and commerce excites a related need to regulate, tax, and mediate disputes arising out of these activities. At stake is the tribes' ability to ensure wise use and protection of the land, water, wildlife, and cultural resources of their reservations.

Although the trend in Supreme Court decisions may pass, tribes cannot count on rehabilitating their governments and economies and reclaiming their resources after the Court eventually realizes the error of its ways or Congress finally puts the Court in check. Now they must consider palliatives. These include consolidating tribal ownership and exercising tribal authority to restrict and to limit by contract non-Indian presence and ownership within their territory. To do this, the trustee's assistance and cooperation in finding lawful methods, getting funding for land purchases, and strengthening tribal institutions—like courts and planning and regulatory agencies—will be critical.

Implicit in the quest for effective tribal efforts to achieve sustainability in the use of tribal resources is tribal control. That, in turn, depends on the support of a federal trustee who can help to balance the political and economic scales. Where tribes have financial resources, this means finding the best professional and technical assistance. Where tribes lack funds, the trustee should fill the gap. In all cases the trustee can undergird tribal initiatives to exercise sovereignty and stanch the attempts of other governments and non-Indian interests that resist that sovereignty.

This book provides ample evidence of the need for trusteeship to allow tribal resource stewardship to flourish. It is up to those who would have tribes chart a path to sustainable resource governance to learn from the lessons the authors provide and to revitalize a trust relationship that supports effective tribal resource sovereignty.

—David H. Getches
Raphael J. Moses Professor of Natural Resources Law,
University of Colorado, Boulder

Preface and Acknowledgments

Our association began when Imre Sutton encouraged Richmond L. Clow to write an article for an earlier symposium, published in 1991. After exchanging letters and many phone calls, they charted a path toward a book on the tribes and reservation resource management. We knew it would not be the first attempt to examine Indians and the environment, but we hoped our particular approach and choice of contributors would create a distinctive book, one critical of government and tribal decisions but with a balanced view of the successes and failures in Indian Country resource management. Our critics and readers will determine if we achieved our goal of providing balance, even though we admit to some bias.

Both of us have published in the Indian field—Clow as a historian, Sutton as a geographer. We have tried to put our collective experiences as professors and researchers together in this volume. As a historian, Clow's interests reflect in part not just Native American history but environmental and Western history. As a geographer, Sutton's interest in conservation and Indian lands stems from the time he worked for the U.S. Forest Service, encountering Zuni Indians fighting forest fires 600 miles from their reservation. None of this experience exonerates us from omissions, errors, and other inadequacies that befall editors. We alone are responsible.

In this symposium we collectively explore the background, continuum, and contemporary circumstances of environmental management of trust resources. We have chosen case studies that cut across Indian Country; although most chapters focus on reservation resource management, a few also explore tribal rights and options to resources and environments that today are part of the public domain or private holdings. Our objectives are to disseminate knowledge, offer critical judgments, but not to propose policy. When we enlisted independent scholars with expertise in specific fields of inquiry such as forestry, history, planning, and water resources, we emphasized to them, as we now do to you the readers, that this is not an *in-house* or sponsored publication. To be sure, we gained considerable hindsight by reexamining such notable works as the *Problem of Indian Administration* (1928) and *The Indian: America's Unfinished Business* (1966)*—two important reports on the status of the tribes, including their resource bases. Only the staff members of the U.S. Forest Service, as insiders, deal directly with agency policy in their discussion of Indian traditional knowledge and the Kaibab National Forest (Chapter 11). All the contributors were asked to be eclectic in developing their chosen topic, discussing not only the Bureau of Indian Affairs but other agencies and factors that have abetted or frustrated the conservation and management of trust resources.

As discussions ensued chapter by chapter, we came to recognize that today the trusteeship of tribal resources has diffused among several federal agencies, and many of the positive changes in environmental policy on tribal lands and former aboriginal lands have emanated from such agencies as the National Park Service, U.S. Forest Service, and others since the passage of the Indian Self-Determination and Educational Assistance Act in 1975. In recent years, a number of resource agencies such as the Army Corps of Engineers and the Environmental Protection Agency have identified areas of responsibility to the tribes. We approached this multiple agency perspective with some caution, since it is no secret that many federal agencies often enter into conflicts of interest where tribal resources are the concern.

Although we do not deny some bias in the interpretation of many past events in the environmental management of tribal resources, it is our hope that no one persuasion has consumed the intent of this book. Although this book is mostly environmental history, certain events and ideas have necessitated one author and not another to focus on the documentary evidence; other authors have explored an ethnohistorical approach to define the factors, explaining why some tribes have rejected or accepted the conservation goals of the Indian Bureau and the participation of other agencies. We did not ask each author to couch discussions in terms of the dichotomy between conservation and environmentalism, and in fact in most chapters, where applicable, authors have treated conservation and environmentalism as a continuum in the quest to improve man's utilization of resources.

Each author had free expression, and method and philosophy were theirs. We encouraged all authors to turn to pertinent Indian observations that might bear on their subject. In fact, we sought the assistance of several Indian scholars who made manuscripts and publications available, and we would like to thank especially Dr. Holly YoungBear-Tibbetts of the College of the Menominee Nation, Keshena (Wisconsin); Bryan Marozas of the Bureau of Indian Affairs,

*See #5 in the bibliographical note, p. 323.

Albuquerque; and Ward Churchill of the Ethnic Studies Department, University of Colorado, Boulder. Size limitations for this book precluded the development of chapters on wildlife, fisheries, mining, and hazardous waste management. Finally, we did not choose a proactive position as editors, yet our collective efforts should not be characterized as armchair.*

In addition to our contributors, who have given considerable time, thought, and energy to this project for which we thank them immensely, we also want to acknowledge with thanks and appreciation the many persons who have provided counsel and assistance as this book progressed. To those who read earlier drafts of chapters or provided advice, materials, and other forms of assistance: Professor Richard Sattler, an anthropologist in the Native American Studies Department, University of Montana; geography colleagues Professors Stephen Jett, University of California, Davis, and David J. Wishart, University of Nebraska–Lincoln; E. Richard Hart of Hart West and Associates, Seattle (WA); T. J. Ferguson, Institute of the NorthAmerican West, Tucson (AZ); the U.S. Army Corps of Engineers: Peggy O'Bryan, Missouri River Division, Omaha; Tom O'Hara, Omaha District; and Conrad Weiser, Pittsburgh District—for researching and sending materials on Garrison Dam and Kinzua Dam. To the Associated Press/Wideworld Photo Service for use of a photograph of Fort Berthold tribal members and the Secretary of the Interior signing a contract in 1948; to the Arizona Historical Society for historic photos of the Tohono O'odham (Papago) Reservation; to the American Indian Studies Center, UCLA, for reprinting Figure 7.3; and to the Menominee Nation for forestry photographs. Thanks also to Regina Eastmann, director of the Interlibrary Loan Office of Pomona Public Library, for acquisition of the historic photo of Ute hunters; and Roy's Photo Lab, Fullerton.

We warmly thank Michelle A. Mestrovich for her considerable computer interpretative and cartographic skills; all of the maps were designed by Imre Sutton except those for Chapter 8, which Diane L. Krahe designed, and all maps and diagrams were rendered by Michelle. We also thank Jill Kinyon of the Native American Studies Department at the University of Montana for typing and other secretarial assistance. A special note of appreciation to David H. Getches for agreeing to write a foreword. Last but not least we wish to thank Darrin Pratt, director, Laura Furney, editorial and production manager, and the staff at the University Press of Colorado (UPC); Dr. Richard Ellis, member and chair of the Editorial Board of UPC; and former director Luther Wilson; also much thanks for the diligent copyediting by Cheryl Carnahan and to reviewer Lynn A. Robbins, who encouraged us to expand our discussions to include many other government agencies that today participate in tribal resource management. Both editors wish to acknowledge the assistance and use of facilities

*See #6 and #12 in the bibliographical notes, pp. 323–324, 325.

at our respective campuses—the University of Montana, Missoula, and California State University, Fullerton. For the latter, the Interlibrary Loan Office and its director, Nancy Caudill, are to be thanked for so many favors in the course of developing this book. Additionally, generous use of Western State University School of Law Library, Fullerton, is much appreciated.

—Richmond L. Clow, Missoula, MT
Imre Sutton, Fullerton, CA
May 2001

A Note on Tribal Names, Toponyms, and Spellings

As much as we have been able, name choices and spellings reflect current practices and options (e.g., Tohono O'odham vs. Papago, Yakama vs. Yakima). We utilize Indian, Native American, and indigenous to mean the same thing in context. From time to time we may slip into the usage of one term more than another—for example, Bear Lodge vs. Devil's Tower.

Contributors

Terry L. Anderson is executive director, Political Economy Research Center, Bozeman, MT 59718-6827; senior fellow at the Hoover Institution, Stanford University; and professor of economics, Montana State University. His work has helped launch the idea of free market environmentalism and has prompted public debate over the balance between markets and government in managing natural resources. He is the author or editor of twenty-one books, including *Sovereign Nations or Reservations: An Economic History of American Indians* (1995) and (coauthor with Donal Leal) *Enviro-Capitalists: Doing Good While Doing Well* (1997). He has published eclectically in the *Journal of Economics and Sociology,* the *Wall Street Journal, Christian Science Monitor,* as well as *Fly Fisherman.* He has been a visiting scholar at Oxford University, the University of Basel, and Cornell University Law School. He was awarded a Fulbright Research Fellowship to Canterbury University and was a National Fellow at the Hoover Institution.

Peter MacMillan Booth, member of a fifth-generation western family, graduated with a B.A. from the University of Texas and an M.A. from the University of Arizona and completed his Ph.D. at Purdue University—all in history. He prepared his dissertation, "The Creation of a Nation: The Tohono O'odham From 1900 to 1937," under the supervision of Professors Donald Parman and Raymond DeMallie. He pursues his focus on American Indian and American Southwest history as a museum professional, first at the Arizona Historical Society and now at the Desert Caballeros Western Museum in Wickenburg, AZ 85390.

Richmond L. Clow is professor of Native American studies at the University of Montana, Missoula, MT 59812-2664. He is coauthor (with James J. Lopach and Margery Hunter Brown) of *Tribal Government Today: Politics on Montana Indian Reservations* (1990, 1998). He has also authored numerous articles on tribal issues.

David H. Getches is the Raphael J. Moses Professor of Natural Resources Law, University of Colorado School of Law, Boulder, CO 80309-0401. He has authored *Water Law* (1984) and numerous legal articles on Indian law and coauthored (with Charles F. Wilkinson and Robert A. Williams Jr.) *Cases and Materials on Federal Indian Law* (1998), which is in its 4th edition. He is former executive director, Department of Natural Resources, state of Colorado.

Theodore S. Jojola is professor of community and regional planning and former acting director of the program at the University of New Mexico, Albuquerque, NM 59831. He holds a B.A. in architecture, M.A. in city planning, and a Ph.D. in political science. He served as a legal-historical researcher for the Institute for the Development of Indian Law in Washington, D.C., and as series editor for *Public Policy Impact on American Indian Development* and *Pueblo Style and Regional Architecture* (Van Nostrand Reinhold, 1980). As the former director of Native American Studies, Institute for Native American Development at UNM, he participated in the publication of *Irredeemable America* (1985) and contributed a chapter to *Making the Invisible: Insurgent Planning Histories* (1998). His publications include *Memoirs of an American Indian House: The Impact of Cross-National Housing Programs on Two Reservations* (1976) and articles in *Antipodes* and other journals. He is a member of the Isleta Pueblo (NM).

Laura Kirwan holds a J.D. and an M.P.A. from the University of Utah. She is currently an attorney with the Utah State Institutional Trust Lands Administration.

Diane L. Krahe began her career as a print journalist in Washington, DC, and Virginia. She holds a masters in environmental studies from the University of Montana and is currently a doctoral candidate in American history at Washington State University, Pullman, WA 99163, where she teaches history. Her dissertation investigates the role "wilderness" has played in the twentieth-century struggles of a number of Indian tribes to retain (and reclaim) sovereignty over their reservation lands.

Lawrence M. Lesko is the tribal liaison-archaeologist at Kaibab National Forest, Williams, AZ 86046. His responsibilities include the determination, planning, and management of cultural heritage resources on the forest as claimed by various Indian communities—for example, Hopi, Havasupai, Yavapai-Piute.

Daniel McCool is professor of political science and director, American West Center, University of Utah, Salt Lake City, UT 84112. He is the author of *Command of the Waters: Iron Triangles, Federal Water Development, and Indian Water* (1987) and numerous articles on Indian water in journals and symposia. He coauthored *Staking Out the Terrain: Power Differentials Among Natural Resource Management Agencies* (1985) and is currently working on a book on Indian water settlements.

Alan G. McQuillan is professor of forest management, University of Montana, Missoula, MT 59812, where he teaches timber management and ethics and management of public lands. He served as director of the School of Forestry's Wilderness Institute from 1989 to 1996. His publications include (coedited with A. Preston) *Globally and Locally: Seeking a Middle Path to Sustainable Development* (1998) and numerous articles on forestry, ethics, aesthetics, and planning in such journals as the *Journal of Forestry, Forest Science,* and *Environmental Ethics.* He also served as an expert witness for the Quinault in the case of *Helen Mitchell et al. v. U.S.* and the Menominee in a congressional reference case regarding forest mismanagement.

Imre Sutton is Professor Emeritus of geography, California State University, Fullerton, CA 92834, where he taught conservation, law and environment, and water resources planning. He was a founding member, instructor, and director of the Environmental Studies graduate program at CSUF. He authored *Indian Land Tenure* (1975) and edited *Irredeemable America: The Indians' Estate and Land Claims* (1985). He has also edited symposia "Land Tenure in the West," "California Indian Research," "The Political Geography of Indian Country," and "The Continuing Saga of Indian Land Claims" and has published numerous articles on Indian land in the *American Indian Culture and Research Journal, Geographical Review,* and other journals.

Renée G. Thakali is employed by the U.S. Forest Service, currently serving as the Prairie Parkland coordinator, Midewin National Tallgrass Prairie, Wilmington, Il 60481. She is the former district ranger, Tusayan Ranger District, Kaibab National Forest. She is a member of the Pit River Band of California Indians.

Katherine Weist is professor emeritus of anthropology at the University of Montana, Missoula, MT 59812. Over the years Dr. Weist has had an active research interest in human relocation subsequent to the development of dams and has published on such in the *Journal of Refugee Studies*. She is currently working with the Peace Corps in South Africa.

Cartographer Michelle A. Mestrovich holds a masters in industrial arts and a graduate certificate in cartography from California State University, Long Beach. She has worked as a GIS programmer. She was the cartographer for Sherna B. Gluck's *An American Feminist in Palestine: The Intifada Years* (1994) and for the symposium "The Continuing Saga of Indian Land Claims," in Imre Sutton, ed., *American Indian Culture and Research Journal* (2000). She is currently a GIS programmer analyst for the County of Sonoma (CA), Geographic Information Systems Department.

Prologue

Tribes, Trusteeship, and Resource Management

Richmond L. Clow and Imre Sutton

> Our tradition of stewardship continues to guide the natural resource management philosophy of the White Mountain Apache Tribe. Our lands were severely damaged due to mismanagement by the Department of the Interior from the time the reservation was first established in 1871. We have since regained managerial control of our lands and are now in the process of repairing the extensive damages that were done to our grazing lands, forest, and riparian areas.
> (Ronnie Lupe, Chairman)[1]

White Mountain's Apache Chairman Ronnie Lupe's remarks addressed to a congressional committee do not speak well of the trustee's responsibilities for the care of tribal resources. The White Mountain Apache are not alone in their criticism of long-term government stewardship of the environmental affairs of Native Americans. At times benign and well-intentioned, more often inept, even unconscionable policies characterize the history of Indian land administration. Yet in all fairness, the demands of special interests such as mining companies, as well as the general citizenry, have accounted for many ill-conceived and ineffective environmental schemes. The Bureau of Indian Affairs (BIA), the *designated* trustee agency, and some other agencies newly created after 1900, although both pragmatic and altruistic in their goals, often have demonstrated an insensitivity to tribal wishes and needs by pushing ahead without consideration of cultural differences, not just among the tribes but between the tribes and the majority of this country.

Although the BIA has made many efforts, past and present, to ovecome this image of a less than effective environmental manager, we must query whether this agency as trustee has done enough on behalf of the conservation and management

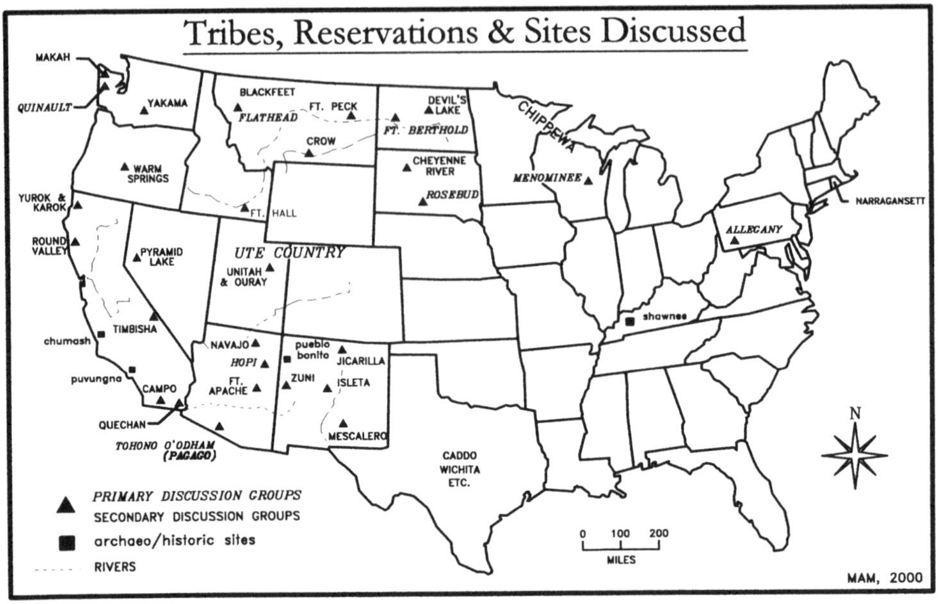

Fig. P.1 Tribes, Reservations, and Sites Discussed. Several tribes or reservations form the focus (primary discussion groups) of chapters; other Indian groups (secondary discussions) are included in broader comments within some chapters. A number of archaeological or historical sites are also discussed. Locations are inexact because of map scale.

of reservation resources. In addition, we seek to ascertain the contributions other federal, tribal, as well as state agencies have made to tribal resource management. A corollary question asks: How have the BIA and other agencies assisted tribes toward autonomous resource management? Case studies cut across Indian Country (Fig. P.1), providing lengthy discussions of the Flathead, Menominee, Quinault, Rosebud, and others and shorter commentaries on other tribes, such as the Mescalero, Navajo, Shawnee, and Yakama.

Trusteeship and Resource Management

Trusteeship predicates that the United States would dominate reservation resource management.[2] From early nationhood the federal government assumed plenary authority over Indian affairs to diminish or dismiss any attempts by states or other political entities to intervene or dominate over the tribes and their lands. This fiduciary relationship arises when the government takes control over the natural resources and property of the Indians.[3] In fact, as environmental lawyer Lynn Fuller notes in a study of Navajo range conservation, "The government's trust responsibility *mandates* that the BIA actively prevent the Navajo Tribe from wasting its range resources." If we hazard to generalize from these remarks, the government's intervention in tribal resource management may be perceived as a good thing or not because "the trust responsibility was intended to protect the sovereignty of tribes by preserving the integrity of their lands and resources."

Protecting sovereignty and intervening in resource management may well create tension and lead to tribal rejection of the trustee's efforts. The Navajo brought suit against the United States for alleged violations of the trust responsibility to Navajo rangelands through overgrazing. The court sustained the government's position that the Navajo had strongly encouraged unrestricted grazing and invoked intense opposition to stock reduction programs.[4]

Two interrelated concerns need to be addressed in understanding trusteeship: (1) the nature and effectiveness of the trusteeship and (2) the effect of a conflict of interest between government mandates and tribal cultural values and between agencies that interact with the tribes. Discussions of the role of the BIA—the agency most responsible for trust resources decisions from the mid-nineteenth century to the present—explore the efficacy of that agency's environmental management approach. Because of the diffusion of the trusteeship among other agencies, their entry into many contemporary evaluations draws attention to a great many conflicts of interest and the fact that a number of agencies in recent years have sought to overcome their past image of hostility toward or indifference to tribal wishes and expectations of the responsibilities of the government. The effectiveness of trustee management does depend in part upon how conflicts of interest, which inevitably intervene, work against the establishment or success of resource management programs.

The Consultation Factor

A controversial element in tribal resource management is the way the government consults with the tribes. A considerable list of statutory provisions authorizes deliberation; nonetheless, the efficacy of consultation has been called into question.[5] In 1994 President William Clinton reaffirmed an earlier policy issuing a government-to-government memorandum that reads: "Each executive department and agency shall consult, to the greatest extent practicable, and to the extent permitted by law, with tribal governments prior to taking actions that affect federally recognized tribal governments. All such consultations are to be open and candid so that all interested parties may evaluate for themselves the potential impact of relevant proposals."[6]

As a rule, litigation over the interpretation of consultation language found in the National Environmental Policy Act (NEPA), the American Indian Religious Freedom Act (AIRFA), and the National Historic Preservation Act (NHPA) has been a mixed blessing. Working for or against the tribes, we generally have witnessed a judicial erosion of tribal sovereignty.[7] The president's memorandum directs agencies to "undertake activities . . . in a knowledgeable, sensitive manner respectful of tribal sovereignty."[8] Despite this consultation order, government agency and tribal interests are often in conflict and thus affect resource management decisions. As attorney Derek Haskew notes, "Perhaps it is axiomatic . . . that Native Americans' interests do not necessarily coincide with those of the federal government."[9] Haskew further remarks that "a divergence of interest between tribes and the federal government gives rise to what in other contexts would be a conflict of interest: the federal government must make impartial decisions regarding interests for which, as trustee, it must also be the zealous defender."[10]

The Role of Other Agencies

Whether the BIA or the Congress has been openly invited to assist the tribes, the federal government nonetheless has played a varying although not always welcome role in the conservation of tribal resources; for example, the U.S. Department of Agriculture entered into Indian forestry in the early part of the twentieth century, and during the New Deal of the 1930s the Soil Conservation Service (now the Natural Resources Conservation Service [NRCS]) played a major role in enabling Indians to improve farm and range lands.[11] Since the 1960s the Environmental Protection Agency (EPA) has advocated tribal immunity from state intervention in environmental affairs on reservations. When we revisit Indian forestry, the BIA and the Forest Service parted company over management policies and practices. On the other hand, the NRCS has remained a staunch supporter of soil and moisture management of trust land resources. In recent years the EPA has created an office of Indian affairs and has championed some tribes in their litigation—for example, in *Washington Department of Ecology v. EPA* and others.[12]

Recent federal legislation has also given Indians more muscle, but tribes may become reluctant to assume authority over some resource management when litigation works against them. For example, the Confederated Salish and Kootenai Tribes of Montana (Flathead Indian Reservation) invoked the Clean Water Act (§ 518), which grants regulatory authority over water quality standards on reservations to tribal governments; the EPA actually intervened, and the court ultimately argued that the authority must fall within the scope of the tribe's inherent sovereign powers.[13] Of course, other legislation may be more clear-cut, as in the instance of the executive order that provides federal actions on behalf of minorities, including Indians,[14] and the Indian Environmental General Assistance Program Act of 1992, which provides grants to tribes and intertribal consortia to develop a capacity to administer environmental regulatory programs delegated by the EPA.[15]

Unfortunately, a number of field agencies have functioned to the detriment of the interests of some tribes. Michael Lawson, in *Dammed Indians,* wrote that both the Bureau of Reclamation and the Army Corps of Engineers, which directed the construction, supported upper Missouri River dams that ultimately led to the inundation of tribal lands on several reservations.[16] In 1971 attorney

Reid Chambers claimed conflict of interest has existed between agencies that are part of the same department (e.g., Interior) and yet have different management agendas.[17]

The Bureau of Land Management (BLM) has also found itself at odds with Indians. In the 1960s the BLM initiated a program to eradicate pinon pine (piñon juniper) on public lands in Nevada but within the traditional territory of Western Shoshone, who considered those lands theirs. This vegetation association or ecozone was a mainstay to those Indians as they moved into the Great Basin, and they have regarded pinon pine as a resource that represented " 'an environmental amenity' whose value extended far beyond economic considerations that might otherwise be debatable."[18] Litigation pursued, and the Ninth Circuit Court of Appeals in 1983 declared that the Western Shoshone still held aboriginal title to the land, forcing the BLM to reduce the scope of its pinon pine eradication. The advent of the provisions of NEPA now forces the BLM to consider Shoshone cultural heritage in the development of land management policies.[19]

In response to the 1994 presidential government-to-government memorandum, the Army Corps of Engineers began to conduct workshops and collect data to "assess the scope, extent and quality of Corps-tribal interactions."[20] The corps identified that "a conflict exists between the Corps' multistage execution of its water resource missions and its obligations, as a Federal agency, to honor the commitments made to Federally Recognized Tribes in treaties, statutes, administrative orders, and court cases. . . . The Corps has an obligation to reconcile these conflicts as they arise."[21] The corps further reported that the "failure to recognize and reconcile these conflicts was a repetitive theme of the workshops." Among important issues has been the protection of traditional cultural properties and practices relative to NAGPRA. Among policy concerns was to "establish a Civil Works policy on consultation with Indian tribes."[22]

An example of the corps' favorable response under newer guidelines was its action regarding the negative impact of the King River Reservoir in Virginia.[23] The reservoir would have inundated 1,526 acres lying between the Mattaponi and Pamunkey Indian Reservations. Both tribes are recognized by the state of Virginia. The ecological consequences would have altered diverse wetlands and uplands, including the habitat of the shad. Both tribes complained that the reservoir would inundate traditional lands and thus affect tribal lifeways that included fishing, farming, and hunting, as well as worship. Archaeological and sacred sites were also identified for the area. The corps' response noted that the "reservoir would destroy their [Indian] way of life . . . [and] their subsistence shad fishery and hatchery operation would be lost or irreparably harmed by changes in salinity."[24] The EPA, in its analysis of the project, "extensively addressed the intricate relationship between the local ecology and the Mattaponi under the rubric of *environmental justice*"[25] (emphasis added). As in other instances, it was found that "key components of *identifying and addressing concerns, in consultation with the affected communities,* have yet to be completed"[26] (emphasis in the original). In 1999 the Army Corps of Engineers rejected the project, arguing among other factors that the future water demand calling for the reservoir was overstated and that the reservoir would not be in the public interest. Not all environmental projects involving present or former tribal lands have turned out so favorable to Indians, yet this example does credit the Army Corps of Engineers with considerable sensitivity to tribal needs.[27]

The Antiquities Act of 1906 ordered the National Park Service to manage Indian ruins that became the initial land body of national monuments. Earlier, the same agency had disregarded or rejected living tribes occupying lands that became included in monuments and parks. Indian displacement from Yosemite and Mesa Verde was prominent; however, the recent debate over granting the Timbisha occupancy rights within Death Valley National Park ultimately led to a favorable resolution.[28] On the other hand, in 1999 officials from Wupatki National Monument in northern Arizona began prohibiting the Hopi from capturing golden eaglets within the park, contending that eagle taking violated federal laws that banned the removal of wildlife from national parks.[29]

It is not unusual for tribes to approach other agencies, such as the Administration for Native Americans (ANA), for grants and services. In 1956 Alfred Left Hand Bull, a member of the Rosebud Sioux Tribe, observed that "it's bad enough that there is no motivation in the Indians to become interested in raising cattle. Some who have the spark of such a motivation are hampered and discouraged because of the stiff or tough [BIA] regulations."[30] Thirty-five years later Gregg Bourland, chairman of the Cheyenne River Sioux Tribe, noted that "[the ANA] has consistently increased the ability of many tribes to further their struggle for self-sufficiency . . . without imposing unnecessary and restrictive policies."[31] And Michael Pablo, chairman of the Confederated Salish and Kootenai Tribes of Montana, concurred that "the ANA is more than just a model of an effective government agency. . . . It is also a key player in the renaissance of Indian Self-Determination."[32] These statements raise questions about the long-term performance of the *designated* trustee and the increasing role being played by other agencies on behalf of American Indians, demonstrating strong support to renew legislation in the early 1990s.

Trusteeship also extends to Congress and federal courts. Vine Deloria Jr. and David E. Wilkins emphasized the political importance, for example, of the plenary powers of Congress as demonstrated by the Committees on Indian Affairs, commenting to a Senate committee that Congress

> Also has oversight responsibility for operation of programs of all other federal agencies with programs affecting Indians. . . . It is charged with dealing with matters related to tribal and individual lands, the government's trust responsibilities, Indian claims, and

> *natural resources*. . . . In short, this committee . . . is charged with an enormous task: the oversight of Congress's continuing historical, constitutional and legislative obligations to over five hundred tribal and Alaska-native polities.[33]

Factoring in the Objectives of Conservationists and Environmentalists

Besides public land officials' ambivalence, conservationists and environmentalists have not always supported tribes. Conservation organizations have their own agendas that may or may not coincide with Indian management plans. The Sierra Club, Friends of the Earth, and other groups have joined the Klallam Indians of the Olympic Peninsula (Washington) seeking the removal of the Elwha Dam that has reduced fisheries for decades.[34] On the other hand, when the Havasupai sought an additional 185,000-acre land restoration adjacent to their reservation in northern Arizona in the 1970s, the Sierra Club, Friends of the Earth, the Wilderness Society, and the National Parks and Conservation Association, among others, represented the opposition. According to Keller and Turek, "Environmental arguments ran from relevant to trivial to derogatory. . . . The NPCA . . . condemned a 'Havasupai land grab' . . . the *New York Times* accused the Havasupai of a 'raid' on public land." The authors reported that many environmentalists saw land transfers to the tribes as precedents for additional losses of parkland. The Association for American Indian Affairs was the most effective proponent, whereas the NPS maintained a low profile.[35]

Alaskan Inuit (Eskimo) leaders and environmentalists began to consider one another as allies following the discovery of oil on the North Slope of Alaska. Both opposed the state of Alaska and the oil industry.[36] The Miccosukees of south Florida have sought to establish stronger water quality standards for the Everglades, a position not supported by politicians or environmentalists. The problem is phosphorous runoff from sugar farms. In 1999 the EPA approved the tribal petition to establish legal limits ten times lower than concentrations found in the region.[37]

On the other hand, not only did the Forest Service object to turning over part of the Kit Carson National Forest for the restoration of Blue Lake to the Taos Pueblo, but so did conservationists, who did not believe the Indians had the necessary experience to manage forestlands. Conservation groups also failed to support Indian goals, as in the case of the protection and exclusive use of Mt. Graham in Arizona. Similarly, the Nature Conservancy, subsequent to buying 400 acres of land on the White Earth Indian Reservation (MN), turned it over to the state of Minnesota, and when confronted by the tribe, which sought "collaborative ventures," seemed to shun the tribe as marginal to its efforts.[38] Yet conservationists did sustain Indian rights to sacred ground within the Six Rivers National Forest in northern California.[39]

Conservation organizations have political power to influence legislation. As a result, Indians have been allied selectively to the current environmental movement but remain skeptical of the hidden agendas of conservation. Historian David Lewis comments that "in recent years, tribal development and land use has put some Indians at odds with environmentalists. This fascinating turn of events emerges as modern Indians begin placing needs over older cultural regulatory patterns, shattering white stereotypes of Indians as the original conservationists."[40] In defense of their perspective, he adds "they were careful students of their functional environments, bound by material and cultural needs and constraints, striving for maximum sustained yield, not maximum production."[41]

Identifying Issues and Concerns

Why is there continual concern over the status and condition of American Indian tribes and their lands? According to law professor Charles F. Wilkinson, "The reservation system is essential to the preservation of Indian culture," distinct from the majority. Wilkinson is concerned with the stability and viability of the legal foundation sustaining the trust status of tribes and their lands.[42] A corollary is that any long-term preservation of tribal culture depends as much on the tribal conservation and management of trust lands and traditional aboriginal areas as it does on the foundation of law and justice. That is, environment and institutions are of equal importance.

Tribes' dependence on a resource base and territorial locus requires a new era of tribal resource management that should contribute toward strengthening tribes and their reservations.[43] To sustain tribal autonomy, neither the legal system nor environmental management can ever hope to achieve such a goal alone: *law and environment must interact favorably and consistently.* To date, the legal system, despite its flaws and contradictions, has more often championed and supported Indian communities than has environmental management, which has only recently become proactively Indian.[44] The history of Indian affairs tells us that the reservation system is both law and geography and that the survival of Indian tribes predicates the continuance of Indian Country as a durable *place* as well as *institution* in which to live and be Indian.

Conservation and Environmentalism

Over the last one hundred years, Americans have become more aware of the importance of the conservation and environmental movements and the role each has played in resource planning and management. From its inception in the late nineteenth century, the conservation movement has stressed the importance of ongoing efficient utilization of resources to ensure economic self-sufficiency and multiple uses of resources, as well as preservation. Broad conservation principles have always embraced total environments or ecosystems (defined in the glossary), even though in its narrower interpretation conservation efforts have focused on specific resources—forests, parklands and wilderness, soil, water, and other resources. Also, early conservationists such as George Perkins Marsh and John Muir made important literary contributions to the movement but were less proactive than environmentalists today.

By the 1970s the nation had moved toward the implementation of a broader environmental policy; thus began the environmental movement as a logical continuum of conservation. This movement has made the public aware that efficient utilization of resources does not always guarantee a community's well-being by warning that unchecked dumping of toxic wastes and uncontrolled emissions create lasting social, health, and economic disasters.

In part, the movement has merged the resource emphasis of conservation with concerns for total environmental management and has sought to bridge wild, rural, and urban environmental concerns, as in water and air resource management. Also, environmentalism has more boldly embraced the preservation ethic.

Today, environmental issues not only transcend the concern for efficient utilization of resources but also embrace a holistic view of environmental management. For tribes, the need is to balance developmental goals on and off trust lands to protect surrounding areas beyond the reservation where tribal cultural sites are found. Since resource conservation and environmental concerns *do* transcend natural and cultural boundaries and potentially touch many resources and peoples, important questions need be asked: How have reservation Indian communities received and benefited from these movements? In what ways would conservation and environmental management abet the social, political, and cultural conservation of Native Americans as reflected in the variable roles of the tribes, the trustee—that is, the United States—and the states?

Perceptions and Misperceptions

Several popular perceptions generally suggest how the public perceives the Indian situation. One contends that if the general populace is at all aware of Indians and knows of the existence of reservations, it presumes that the federal trustee to date has administered to *all* the basic needs of Indians resident on trust lands and that conservation has been a working principle on reservations since its inception at the turn of the twentieth century. This implies that the trustee long ago assumed responsibility for the development and management as well as conservation of reservation resources. Shall the populace assume, then, that the conservation and environmental movements have embraced tribal lands with the same rigor and commitment as they have the public and private lands of this nation? Knowledgeable and observant Americans are not so naive as to make such broad assumptions.

The perception is that the conservation and environmental movements benefited everyone and that reservation residents would have been especially supportive of the goals of these movements. Frequently, the contrary has been true: reservation management decisions have provided many tribal residents with a minimal living standard because too often these resources have been developed by non-Indian lessees, who have been the beneficiaries of conservation or environmental management, or reservation resources have been inadequately developed under the aegis of the trustee. In its defense, the Indian Bureau does seek more funds than Congress and the president have been willing to grant.[45]

In other words, tribes have made sacrifices by watching their traditional lands be ceded to the public domain or diminished after the establishment of reservations in the name of the conservation movement. A century ago, Congress authorized President Theodore Roosevelt to sever nearly all of the Uintah and Ouray Reservation's forested lands from the Northern Utes and transfer them to the Uintah National Forest. Two days before his second term ended, the "conservationist" president issued eight executive orders severing tribal timbered lands that lay adjacent to national forests, citing the need to protect the watershed, but his successor restored these lands to their tribal owners.[46]

It is also true that National Park Service ideology regarding untrammeled wilderness ultimately led to a policy of displacing Indians who resided within park boundaries.[47] Yosemite and Yellowstone have led the list of parks from which Indians were dislocated at one time. And in recent memory, tribes have continued to sacrifice their resources for the greater cause of conservation. During the 1950s reservation residents, mostly member tribes of the Lakota Nation living along the Missouri River, witnessed the condemnation and flooding of their river-bottom lands and the destruction of many tribal communities, all in the name of flood control.[48] Even though Indian communities in the Great Plains, in the Allegheny River Valley in Pennsylvania and New York, and along the Columbia River in Oregon and Washington were paid for lands inundated by Kinzua Dam and the Dalles Dam, respectively, the loss was inexplicable in terms of the goals of conservation.[49]

As these examples illustrate, the conservation movement has not always been kind to tribal populations, and any research attempting to explain reservation resource conservation and environmental concerns must consider a variety of factors. These include the singular role of the United States as trustee in managing tribal and individual Indian resources, the application of environmental standards, tribal rights to make conservation and environmental decisions, and the long-term effects of such decisions that may be contrary to the worldviews of many Indian communities. For example, Northern Ute "ideology of water is based upon Northern Ute views of nature and power," which stem from their animate belief in the physical environment that contrasts with their white neighbors' view of water as resource in the irrigation project.[50] The Navajo opposed the 1930s policy to reduce the size of their flocks of sheep despite the government's claim that the decision was reasonable to stop soil erosion.[51] The inclusion of these factors reveals the importance of studying conservation and environmental questions as part of an integrated relationship among people, culture, and physical environment.[52]

Indians as Environmentalists

Tribal resource management in the face of scarcity is not new.[53] As with other indigenous peoples of the world, Indian cultures have always possessed a capacity to perceive and evaluate the environment whether in times of scarcity or plenty. Indians have addressed the question of tribal traditional knowledge of nature, a sense of environmental ethics in terms of resource exploitation, and similar themes. N. Scott Momaday, a Kiowa author, spoke of "appropriateness" in man's relationship to the environment and the need to understand tribal conception of what is appropriate, especially in a moral sense, in dealing with or utilizing the environment.[54] Many Indians see themselves as part of, not separate from, nature. In fact, the perception of the Indian as environmentalist—the *ecological Indian*—may today overshadow a better understanding of their variable involvement in environmental management.[55]

Corollary questions to these broad-based ones about how conservation has benefited the tribes ask, What aspects of indigenous perception of nature and utilization of resources have provided a basis for reception of government conservation goals and efforts? Why have many tribes supported, rejected, or been indifferent to the trustee's efforts to establish conservation goals on their reservations? How much of this debate over the ecological Indian is germane to the discussion of the trustee's responsibilities to manage Indian environments? We believe the larger theme—the pros and cons of the ecological Indian—although a fascinating debate that we embrace but only as observers, is its own intellectual arena. On the other hand, insights as provided by Cronon, Krech, White, and others cause us to want to draw attention to the fact that many Indians—communities as well as individuals—prefer to be perceived as ecological, for it abets their causes. Other Indians, however, offer no apology for seeking to enter into mining leases. In fact, they might even contend that they learned such behavior from the majority culture.[56]

Yet numerous examples reveal that a number of tribes have been involved in resource decisions. On the Quileute Reservation situated on Washington's Olympic peninsular coast, tribal hunters and fishermen witnessed the loss of one resource after another. The sea otter was all but gone from the Quileute coastal shores by the 1880s. They killed their last California gray whale in 1904. To preserve salmon from the same fate, the Quileute refused to trade salmon to outsiders as early as 1881. They prevented overfishing by removing "the weirs from the river in order that the fish they did not need could go upstream."[57] To the south of the Quileute, the Quinault enacted model salmon conservation regulations for tribal members in 1907. Tribal regulations required "a seventy-five-foot open channel between nets and a Sunday closure while [the] State of Washington regulations required neither." Even the state of

Washington conceded the importance of the Quinault regulations in 1912, declaring that the Quinault had the "best fish protection of any river in the state of Washington."[58]

Prior to the creation of reservations, tribal communities practiced some form of resource management. The intensity and goals of pre-reservation tribal management and the resource focus of the tribe's manipulation of the landscape differed among tribal cultures and from that of the newcomers. Yet certain Indian communities have informed us in words, deeds, rituals, or daily experiences, as well as through ethnographic study, how indigenous America perceived (and still perceives) nature and the cosmos.

Although differences abound, the long-standing consensus has been that Indians perceive the landscape at a level generally not well understood by post-Europeans. Not all scholars would concur in characterizing Indians as the first ecologists, yet with limited resources and technology their ancestors peopled this continent and sustained extreme hardship. They endured in part because they were at one with nature and subordinated themselves as part of nature. The specific ecologies and lifestyles of the tribes and bands evolved over long periods of time, and native practices of land tenure and territoriality reflected this intimate relationship among tribe, culture, and nature.[59] Contrary views today argue that Native American utilization of the environment has never been quite so ecological as this idyllic view and that Indians did exploit resources to their near extinction.[60]

With Euro-American exploitation of forests, waters, and lands and the loss of Native territoriality and subsequent confinement to reservations, the tribal resource base considerably narrowed and hence was limited in both geography and ecology.[61] Tribesmen—hunting-and-gathering tribes—were especially precluded from any continuing success in the utilization of traditional resources. For a time agrarian tribes as in the American South pursued their sustenance base until dispossessed of their farmlands. It is correct to implicate the white man in drastically altering the Indian's perception of environment by enforcing the restrictions of reservation life and then proceeding to exploit not only former tribal habitats but also the reserved tracts set aside for the tribes.

Despite the existence of historical traditional resource use practices, it was clear from the onset that tribal cultures and the federal government and citizens of individual states were on an early ecological collision course because their differing environmental values and images, concepts of resources, ideas of property and land tenure, management techniques, and "mutually exclusive relationships to the same" resources made conflict inevitable.[62] Anthropologist Morton Fried observed that "it is in the struggle over systems of tenure and ownership that the contest between social systems for the control of an area is to be understood."[63] It is difficult to separate the perception of the landscape by any one culture or people from their ecology and territoriality. Dispossession of land

Fig. P.2 Range on the Blackfeet Indian Reservation (Montana). Range is the most ubiquitous resource of Indian trust lands. On many reservations tribal grazing enterprises exist, for other grazing associations have divided the range into management units. Of 1.5 million acres on the Blackfeet, about 41 percent are used for grazing. Photo by Imre Sutton.

predicated the displacement of traditional environmental relations and loss of traditional membership in nature.[64]

A Brief Geography of Tribal Resources

Resources and environments of tribal concern include trust lands on and off reservations and certain traditional aboriginal areas such as sacred places found on public or private lands.[65] Trust lands exist in more half of U.S. states, whereas nonreservation areas and sites of cultural heritage may be found in every state. Although the majority of the reservations lie in the arid-semiarid West, there are reservations in the humid Northeast and South, as well as in Alaska. Several tribes hold important forest resources—for example, the Quinault, Menominee, White Mountain Apache—and others such as the Osage and Blackfeet possess oil reserves. Coal and uranium are found on the Navajo Indian Reservation. The largest single on-reservation resource is grazing land with a wide range of browsable cover and carrying capacity (Fig. P.2). The greatest area of concern off-reservation is in the West because of the hundreds of square miles of federal public lands, where a number of tribes and individual Indian families still exercise treaty rights to hunt or fish and maintain cultural sites.

Despite litigation and controversial judicial decisions, tribes enjoy the protection of water rights within the major watersheds such as the Colorado, Columbia, and Missouri River systems, although water supplies are less developed on numerous reservations. The agricultural resource of reservations within every natural region of the nation is highly variable, yet often it is the deficiency of water, not the soil, as well as complexities of land tenure that determine levels of production.

Today, in states as far apart as Connecticut and California, location has become a resource: tribes within easy commuting distance of metropolitan areas have entered into the casino business with considerable success. Tribal autonomy also abets Indian gaming even in less dynamic locations.

Reservation Environments and the Role of the Trustee

In disregard of tribal resource practices, the United States, acting as trustee over tribal lands and resources, initiated its own reservation resource management programs, frequently without tribal consent. Treaties provided an early source of federal obligations, whereas Congress enacted statutes to initiate reservation resource conservation or environmental programs.[66] Since the United States preempted states from having jurisdiction over tribes and their reservations, the federal government created the Office (later the Bureau) of Indian Affairs to administer this trust relationship, and it became the primary agency directing reservation resource management until after World War II. The BIA was legislatively charged with helping tribes and individual tribesmen sustain a livelihood on both tribal and allotted lands. By the late nineteenth century and in compliance with congressional policy, the BIA began to issue land allotments in severalty, issued fee patents to individual Indians, supervised Indian and non-Indian agricultural and grazing enterprises on trust lands, constructed irrigation projects, and administered mining leases.

These resource management activities were undertaken philosophically to fulfill the nation's policy of making the Indians self-supporting members of U.S. society and to manage reservation resources for the benefit of tribal owners.[67] Against this administrative historical background, reservation resource management has evolved through three phases, each overlapping the next: (1) trusteeship: balancing realty and resource management, (2) tribalism: encouraging Indian participation, and (3) self-determination: pursuing indigenous and multiagency management.

The first phase began almost as soon as the Indian Office was established in 1849 and might be characterized by contradicting resource strategies reflecting the dilemma between the nation's Indian policy, rooted in ideological beliefs of cultural transformation and not sound land use practices. On one hand, from the 1880s on, tribal lands were allotted, which led to the creation of unmanageable tracts followed by infamous leasing legislation that encouraged Indians to stop utilizing land and permit non-Indians to take over; on the other hand, a forestry program was imposed to preserve reservation timberlands.

The second phase of reservation resource management began as an attempt to reform policy, and although some progress occurred, World War II interrupted many resource management reforms on reservations. The third phase of reservation resource management coincided with the environmental movement that began in the late 1960s and has been accompanied by increasing tribal participation in reservation resource and environmental projects, in part inspired by the policy of self-determination.[68] In this same period, tribes have reasserted claims to nonreservation lands and cultural sites. To be sure, some policy factors as well as management concerns of one phase have also occurred in another phase—for example, tribal hunting and fishing on former ancestral lands that today are part of the public domain continues to be an issue between some tribes and public land agencies.

Trusteeship in the Early Years

When the conservation movement began in the last decades of the nineteenth century, the United States had embarked on a resource management blunder in the cause of "civilizing" Indians. In the push to make them yeoman farmers, the national assimilation goal took precedent over efforts to conserve resources for land utilization. Reservation allotment programs, pursuant to the General Allotment Act of 1887, reduced and fragmented tribal land bases and associated resources. Allotment created other resource management problems that made further environmental decisions more difficult for the remaining lands. Indian timberlands were clear-cut to make fields ready for farming. Allotment would also handicap sustainable forestry programs on reservations because forests spread across multiple jurisdictions beyond either tribal or federal control. Not only were poorly arable forest soils exploited, but arid grazing lands were also plowed, exposing both habitats to the forces of soil erosion. The opening of reservations to non-Indian homesteaders further aggravated environmental conditions by not only reducing the availability of acreage for tribal use but often displacing tribes from the best cultivable acreage.

Because allotment divided vast tribal acreage, Indian land use vitally altered native ecology. First, it reduced the acreage for subsistence; second, it presumed that rural people who had not embraced farming in the past would easily take to being agrarian—a serious flaw in U.S. understanding of many Indian communities. This first phrase of reservation resource management sought to implement the allotment and leasing programs accompanied by the concomitant diminishment of so-called surplus acreage. In short, there was little evidence of proactive conservation except for forestry and irrigation projects that had to struggle against allotment and leasing trends.[69] At the same time, cooperative agreements were made between federal agencies, but these short-lived arrangements did not bring other federal agencies into long-term and meaningful face-to-face relations with tribal residents.

Newly created resource agencies were a response to the conservation movement and included the Forest Service, National Park Service, and the Soil Conservation Service, which were most involved in developing new resource management practices. They had their own agendas, and it would take years before many of them would be responsive to tribal resource needs. One might presume that the establishment of the trusteeship over the tribes precluded the need for any additional articulation of the preservation of living Indians and their lands. Perhaps there was some historical presumption that because conservation predicates trusteeship (stewardship) of the environment, the BIA as the trustee represented a parallel concept. Aside from a few individuals, those who evoked the early conservation ethic were different from those who espoused the cause of the Indian. The Indian was not then perceived as an ecologist. Indeed, early National Park policies that embraced the most pristine view of wilderness did not champion the idea that tribes whose past homelands lay within the borders of new parks should be allowed to remain and continue their using resources in national parks.

The New Deal and Its Precursors

Despite its contradictions, when *The Problem of Indian Administration* (also known as the Meriam Report) was published in 1928, it urged reforms in Indian affairs. The study concluded that after tribal resources were reduced through land allotment, heirship land sales, and leasing, "the Indian Service has rendered much valuable service in *conserving* Indian property."[70]

Instead of addressing the application and efficacy of conservation practices on tribal lands, this statement essentially reflects the ability of the BIA to preserve tribal lands from sale in the face of allotment. The study praised the forestry program, however, for being staffed by "many excellent men" who practiced "selective logging on several of the jurisdictions[, which] seems specially worthy of commendation." On a negative note, the Meriam Report was critical of the Indian Service for not employing workers with technical skills. This was especially true of individuals hired as farmers who were supposed to be able to teach farming methods and develop conservation practices.[71] In addition, the report recommended that the BIA secure the services of livestock personnel with college training. In fact, with regard to tribal range management, the report also recommended the establishment of a division of planning and development.[72]

The New Deal of the 1930s inaugurated national conservation programs that cut across executive departments, whose objectives included conserving soil, forests, and wildlife. When New Deal funds became available for conservation purposes, Commissioner of Indian Affairs John Collier sought specialists from other agencies, especially the Department of Agriculture, to provide expertise for the fledgling reservation Civilian Conservation Corps–Indian Division (CCC-ID) projects.[73] That represented only the beginning. Collier then asked Hugh H. Bennett (later director of the Soil Conservation Service) to conduct a study of soil erosion on the Navajo Reservation. From Bennett's 1933 Navajo study came the Mexican Springs Demonstration Area, where 43,000 acres of the reservation were placed under specific scientific control. This work gave birth to the Soil Erosion Service of the Department of the Interior, which was later renamed the Soil Conservation Service and was transferred to the Department of Agriculture in 1935.[74]

Other New Deal relations forged between agencies included a legislative relationship among the BIA, the Bureau of Fisheries, and the Bureau of Biological Survey, which was "authorized jointly to prepare plans for the better protection of the wild-life resources, including fish, migratory waterfowl and upland game birds, game animals and fur-bearing animals, upon all the Indian reservations and unallotted Indian lands coming under the supervision of the Federal Government."[75] Thus with the New Deal and following World War II, conservation was in place, even if budget constraints and policy shifts detoured or slowed environmental progress. During these prewar years a few tribes began to assume some management responsibilities, but generally tribal leadership in resource management awaited future national policies that encouraged more tribal autonomy.

Tribal Proactive Management

Prior to the new ecology age of the 1960s, new ideas and philosophy invigorated the third reservation resource management era. The publication of Rachel Carson's *Silent Spring,* warning of the dangers of chemical insecticides to public health, is often considered a beginning point that initiated the era of environmentalism.[76] The creation of the EPA closely followed. President Richard M. Nixon encouraged tribal participation in resource issues in his 1970 Indian policy of self-determination, and President Ronald Reagan's 1983 policy statement encouraged government-to-government relations.[77]

To correct wrongs, many tribes successfully pursued litigation against the United States for mismanagement of tribal resources following the Menominee Indians of Wisconsin's 1935 suit against the United States for improper handling of tribal stumpage.[78] Postwar resource claims, along with aboriginal land claims settlements derived from awards handed down by the Indian Claims Commission,[79] provided many tribes with monetary resources to abet their own planning process and pre-dates the policy of self-determination. For example, based on a $7 million land claim, the Southern Utes drafted a planning document with specific resource goals that included a land consolidation project, increased agricultural production involving development of 4,000 irrigable acres, and increased reservation livestock production "through better range management and improvement practices developed by trained Southern Ute stockmen." The document also placed tribal "timber revenues on a sustained-yield basis" and involved Ute people in resource management decisions.[80]

Other tribes also began to assert more autonomy in management. The Puyallup contracted for the development of a planning model, which has stimulated the application of conservation principles, and the Warm Springs tribes contracted with Oregon State University to utilize claims award monies to develop long-range environmental planning.[81] When the Zuni won a land claims judgment in the mid–1980s, Zuni leaders created a reservation developmental plan.[82] No doubt, evidence suggests that pan-Indian organizations such as the All-Indian Pueblos Housing Authority and the Council of Energy Resource Tribes have contributed to greater application of conservation and environmental measures on reservations.

The advent of greater tribal resource and environmental planning accompanied the national policy of tribal self-determination. As a result, other federal agencies have also cooperated with tribal governments, which has allowed for greater tribal participation in the ongoing planning process. For example, the ANA, an office in the Department of Health and Human Services, has independently funded various tribes for resource development and related environmental goals. For another example, in 1984 William Ruckelshaus, administrator of the EPA, announced that his agency supported tribal self-government by taking the first step "toward more cooperative and productive working relations between the Federal and tribal governments."[83] From that point in time, tribal governments entered into more government-to-government agreements. Subsequent to these actions, the EPA soon established an Office of Indian Affairs and has thereafter asserted its role as *the* federal agency representing environmental affairs on reservations. Both the Forest Service and the National Park Service have more recently created Indian affairs liaisons.

National environmental goals underwent dynamic change during the end of the 1960s and throughout the 1970s, yet tribal populations and resources were not always the beneficiaries of the era's environmental reforms. Since around 1980 conservation, or in current parlance, environmentalism, has been asserted in terms of improving conditions on reservations, but the rhetoric has not always translated into action. The *Survey of American Indian Environmental Protection Needs on Reservation Lands: 1986* reveals the gap between words and actions. Tribes suffered from poor "water quality, inadequate solid waste management and disposal, hazardous waste management and disposal, sewage treatment." Tribal leaders expressed additional environmental concerns, including "land use, air quality management, erosion, and nuclear waste/radiation."[84] Politics in other forms has influenced or affected the implementation of environmental programs on reservations.

In recent years, states and local governments have asserted authority over certain tribal land use zoning and environmental regulations. States have not always been successful yet have created separation in environmental management on a number of reservations. States rarely interfere with federal public purposes; however, prevailing state laws do govern most wildlife, and private inholdings may be subject to county or tribal planning authority, depending on one's interpretation of jurisdiction. Moreover, most law-and-order matters are retained by state and local governments, although differences do exist among the various public land agencies. How do Indian trust lands square with this general perspective? In what ways do law-and-order matters interact with environmental issues on reservations and on former aboriginal lands? These and other issues continue to concern tribes as they seek to find ways to embrace resource management in the era of self-determination.

References

1. Ronnie Lupe, Chairman, White Mountain Apache Tribe, [statement before] U.S. Cong., Senate Committee on Environment and Public Works, Subcommittee on Drinking Water, Fisheries, and Wildlife, 104th Cong., 1995; quoted in David H. Getches, Charles F. Wilkinson, and Robert A. Williams Jr., *Cases and Materials on Federal Indian Law,* 4th ed. (St. Paul: West, 1998): 731.
2. The editors are aware of the role of several eastern states that assumed jurisdiction over tribal lands and resources; see, for example, Laurence M. Hauptman, *Conspiracy of Interests: Iroquois Dispossession and the Rise of New York State* (Syracuse: Syracuse University Press, 1999). Historical studies cut across the time period of this book: Lawrence F. Schmechebier, *Office of Indian Affairs: History, Activities, and Organization,* Service Monograph 48 (Baltimore: Brookings Institution for Government Research, 1927); Kirke Kickingbird and Karen Ducheneaux, *One Hundred Million Acres* (New York: Macmillan, 1973); Francis Paul Prucha, *The Great Father: The United States Government and the American Indians,* abridged ed. (Lincoln: University of Nebraska Press, 1986); Fergus M. Bordewich, *Killing the White Man's Indian: Reinventing Native Americans at the End of the Twentieth Century* (New York: Doubleday, 1996).
3. See Getches, Wilkinson, and Williams, *Cases and Materials on Federal Indian Law,* pp. 305–372; Charles F. Wilkinson, *American Indians, Time and the Law (*New Haven: Yale University Press, 1987); Mary Christina Wood, "Indian Land and the Promise of Native Sovereignty: The Trust Doctrine Revisited," *Utah Law Review* (1994): 1471.
4. Lynn Fuller, "Desertification on the Navajo Reservation: A Legal and Historical Analysis," *Stanford Environmental Law Journal,* 8 (1989): 229–291, quote on p. 276, emphasis added. Fuller observes, "Although the trust responsibility was intended to protect the sovereignty of tribes by preserving the integrity of their lands and resources, there is a fundamental tension between these two concepts. Nowhere is this tension more evident than in the context of the Navajo desertification problem" (p. 276). See also *Navajo Tribe v. U.S.,* 9 Ct. Cl. 336 (1986). William Graf, a physical geographer, noted that the Navajos were correct when they asserted that climatic variation accounted for increased sedimentation in the Colorado River, not overgrazing by their sheep. See "Science, Public Policy, and Western American Rivers," *Transactions, Inst. of British Geographers,* 17 (1992): 10–11.

5. Derek C. Haskew, "Federal Consultation With Indian Tribes: The Foundation of Enlightened Policy Decisions, or Another Badge of Shame?" *American Indian Law Review,* 24:1 (1999–2000): 21–74.
6. President William J. Clinton, "Government-to-Government Relations With Native American Tribal Governments: Memorandum for the Heads of Executive Departments and Agencies" (Washington, DC: White House, April 29, 1994).
7. Haskew, "Federal Consultation," p. 34.
8. Quoted in ibid., p. 40.
9. Ibid., p. 55.
10. Ibid.
11. For a general account of agencies and Indian resources, see Theodore W. Taylor, *American Indian Policy* (Mt. Airy, MD: Lomond, 1983), and the older volume by Henry W. Hough, *Development of Indian Resources,* the Indian Community Action Program (Denver: World, 1967).
12. Imre Sutton, "Preface to Indian Country: Geography and Law," *American Indian Culture and Research Journal,* 15:2 (1991): 3–36; *Washington Dept. of Ecology v. EPA,* 752 F 2d 1465 (9th Cir. 1985).
13. Clean Water Act, and *Montana v. EPA,* 137 F 3d 1135 (9th Cir. 1998), cert. denied 119 S. Ct. 275 (1998). Cf. Regina Cutler, "To Clear the Muddy Water: Trust Regulatory Authority Under Sec. 518 of the Clean Water Act," *Environmental Law,* 29:3 (1999): 721–742.
14. Executive Order 12898, "Federal Actions to Address Environmental Justice in Minority Populations and Low-Income Population," February 11, 1994. See *U.S. Code—Congressional and Administrative News,* 103rd Cong., 2d sess., 1994; §6–606 applies to Native Americans but only to federally recognized tribes.
15. Indian Environmental General Assistance Program Act, 1992; 42 *USC* 43686, 106 Stat 3258, part of PL 102–497, 102nd Cong.
16. Michael Lawson, *Dammed Indians: The Pick-Sloan Plan and the Missouri River Sioux, 1944–1980* (Norman: University of Oklahoma Press, 1982); see also J. C. Carroll, "Dams and Damage: the Ojibway, the U.S. and the Mississippi Headwaters Reservoirs," *Minnesota History,* 52:1 (1990): 3–15.
17. Reid Chambers, "Discharge of the Federal Trust Responsibility to Enforce Claims of Indian Tribes: Case Studies of Bureaucratic Conflict of Interest," *Amer. Ind. Law Newsletter,* 4:16 (1971): 1–20. See also William R. Coffeen, "The Effects of the Central Arizona Project on the Fort McDowell Indian Community," *Ethnohistory,* 19:4 (1972): 345–377.
18. Richard O. Clemmer, "The Pinon Pine: Western Shoshone Indians vs. the Bureau of Land Management," *Environmental Review,* 9:2 (1985): 131–149; quote on p. 131.
19. Ibid.
20. See Native American Inter-governmental Relations Task Force, *Assessment of Corps/Tribal Intergovernmental Relations,* Interim Report, IWR Report 96-R-6 (Washington, DC: U.S. Army Engineers, Hq., Civil Works Directorate, 1994): v.
21. Ibid., p. vii.
22. Ibid., p. x.
23. This discussion of the Mattaponi is based on Barry E. Hill and Nicolas Targ, "The Link Between Protecting Natural Resources and the Issue of Environmental Justice," *Boston Coll. Environmental Affairs Law Review,* 28:1 (2000): 1–37.

24. Ibid., pp. 29, 31.
25. Ibid., p. 32.
26. Ibid.
27. Ibid., pp. 35–36.
28. 34 *Stat.* 225 (1906). Cf. Mark Spence, "Dispossessing the Wilderness: Yosemite Indians and the National Park Ideal, 1864–1930," *Pacific Historical Review,* 65 (February 1996): 27–59; also Bruce J. Noble Jr., "A Legacy of Distrust: The Ute Mountain Utes and the Boundaries of Mesa Verde National Park," *Colorado Heritage* [Journal of the Colorado Historical Society] (summer 1995): 32–42; Stephen Crum, "A Tripartite State of Affairs: The Timbisha Shoshone Tribe, the National Park Service, and the Bureau of Indian Affairs, 1933–1994," *American Indian Culture and Research Journal,* 22:1 (1998): 117–136; for a general discussion of NPS policies and practices, see Robert H. Keller and Michael F. Turek, *American Indians and National Parks* (Tucson: University of Arizona Press, 1998). Steven Haberfeld, in "Government-to-Government Negotiations: How the Timbisha Shoshone Got Its Land Back," *American Indian Culture and Research Journal,* 24:4 (2000): 127–165, reports that the Timbisha were influential in the creation of the Alliance to Protect Native Rights in National Parks, which went on "to promote the idea that NPS should have a national Indian policy and that a cross-section of tribes should be involved with NPS in formulating it" (p. 140).
29. Mario Gonzalez and Elizabeth Cook-Lynn, *The Politics of Hallowed Ground: Wounded Knee and the Struggle for Indian Sovereignty* (Urbana: University of Illinois Press, 1999): 227.
30. Alfred Left Hand Bull, Rosebud Sioux Indian Reservation, addressing a Subcommittee on Indian Affairs; U.S. House of Representatives, *Sioux Indian Tribes, North and South Dakota,* Hearings before the Subcommittee on Indian Affairs, 84th Cong., 1st sess., pursuant to H. Res. 30 to authorize investigations into any matter within its jurisdiction (Washington, DC: Government Printing Office (GPO), 1956): 139.
31. Gregg Bourland, chair, Cheyenne R. Sioux Tribe, [comments in] "Reauthorization of Native American Programs Act—Administration for Native Americans," Hearings before Select Committee of Indian Affairs, U.S. Senate, 102nd Cong., 1st sess. (Washington, DC: GPO, 1991): 318.
32. Michael T. Pablo, chair, Confederated Salish and Kootenai Tribes of the Flathead, [comments in] ibid., p. 328.
33. Vine Deloria Jr. and David E. Wilkins, *Tribes, Treaties, and Constitutional Tribulations* (Austin: University of Texas Press, 1999): 48, emphasis added.
34. Keller and Turek, *American Indians and National Parks,* pp. 103–104.
35. Ibid., quote on pp. 165–166.
36. Theodore Catton, *Inhabited Wilderness: Indians, Eskimos and National Parks in Alaska* (Albuquerque: University of New Mexico Press, 1997): 194.
37. Tim Padgett, "Last Stand: Battling Both Polluters and Conservationists, the Miccosukees Aim to Save Their Everglades Home," *Time* (July 5, 1999): 60–61.
38. Donald L. Parman, *Indians and the American West* (Bloomington: Indiana University Press, 1994): 153; Dean B. Suagee, "Tribal Voices in Historic Preservation: Sacred Landscapes, Cross-Cultural Bridges, and Common Ground," *Vermont Law Review,* 21 (1996): 145–224, quote on p. 167; see also Andrew Gulliford, *Sacred Objects and Sacred Places: Preserving Tribal Traditions* (Boulder: University Press of Colorado,

2000): 131–135; Winona LaDuke, *All Our Relations: Native Struggles for Land and Life* (Cambridge: South End, 1999): 131.

39. *Northwest Indian Cemetery Protective Assn. v. Peterson,* 795 F. 2d 688 (1986); *Lyng v. Northwest Indian Cemetery Protective Assn.,* 108 S. Ct. 1319 (1988). Cf. discussion in Getches, Wilkinson, and Williams, *Cases and Materials on Federal Indian Law,* pp. 754–768.
40. David Rich Lewis, "Environmental Issues," in *Native America in the Twentieth Century: An Encyclopedia,* ed. Mary Davis (New York: Garland, 1994): 187–190, quote on p. 190.
41. Ibid.
42. Charles F. Wilkinson, "Shall the Islands Be Preserved?" *The American West, the Magazine of Western History,* 16:3 (1979): 33–69, quote on p. 69; for a revised statement see Wilkinson, *The Eagle Bird: Mapping a New West* (New York: Pantheon, 1992): chapter 3. Wilkinson refers to tribes living on reservations as a "measured separatism." Cf. Wilkinson, *American Indians, Time, and the Law* (New Haven: Yale University Press, 1987): 14–19. See also Glossary.
43. David H. Getches, "A Philosophy of Permanence: The Indians' Legacy for the West," *Journal of the West,* 29:3 (1990): 54–68.
44. A recent general survey is "Developing Resources on American Indian Lands," *Natural Resources and Environment,* 7:4 (1993); see also David R. Lewis, "Native Americans and the Environment: A Survey of Twentieth-Century Issues," *American Indian Qtly,* 19:3 (1995): 423–450.
45. "Native Americans' Future: Do U.S. Policies Block Opportunities for Progress," *CQ Researcher,* 6:26 (July 12, 1996): 601–624. The BIA budget is normally dumped in with those for the National Park Service, Forest Service, and Bureau of Land Management; all must compete nearly equally.
46. J. P. Kinney, *A Continent Lost, A Civilization Won: Indian Land Tenure in America* (Baltimore: John Hopkins University Press, 1937): 275–278.
47. Spence, "Dispossessing the Wilderness."
48. For the Great Plains, see Lawson, *Dammed Indians*; in general, Imre Sutton, *Indian Land Tenure: Bibliographical Essays and a Guide to the Literature* (New York: Clearwater, 1975): 166–171.
49. A. E. Morgan, *Dams and Other Disasters: A Century of the Army Corps of Engineers in Civil Works* (Boston: Porter Sargent, 1971): 166–168, 170; Jack Hunt, "Land Tenure and Economic Development on the Warm Springs Indian Reservation," *Journal of the West,* 9:1 (1970): 93–109.
50. Joanna Lynne Endter, "Cultural Ideologies and the Political Economy of Water in the United States West: Northern Ute Indians and Rural Mormons in the Uintah Basin, Utah," Ph.D. diss., University of California, Irvine, 1987, pp. 231–232.
51. George A. Boyce, *When Navajos Had Too Many Sheep: The 1940s* (San Francisco: Indian Historian Press, 1974); cf., Leonard S. Fonaroff, "Aid and the Indian: A Case Study of Faulty Communication," *California Geographer,* 5 (1964): 57–68; see also Ronald Takaki, *A Different Mirror: A History of Multicultural America* (Boston: Little, Brown, 1993): 24l–242; Edward H. Spicer, "Sheepmen and Technicians: A Program of Soil Conservation on the Navajo IR," in *Human Problems in Technological Change: A Casebook,* ed. Spicer (New York: Russell Sage Foundation, 1952): 185–208; Richard White, *The Roots of Dependency: Subsistence, Environment and Social*

Change Among the Choctaws, Pawnees and Navajos (Lincoln: University of Nebraska Press, 1983): 250–264. White reports the observations made then by Commissioner John Collier "that down there on the Colorado River is the biggest, most expensive dam in the world; the Boulder Dam . . . will be filled up with your fine agricultural soil in no great number of years if we do not stop erosion on the Navajo reservation" (p. 258). It was determined later that stock reduction was unnecessary, since scientists determined that silt settlement was not caused by overgrazing but was mostly the result of drought, and the Navajos understood this from living in the area so long.

52. Interestingly, there are parallels in earlier efforts of BIA doctors to impose science on Indians to overcome Indian trachoma. See Todd Benson, "Blinded by Science: American Indians, the Office of Indian Affairs, and the Federal Campaign Against Trachoma, 1924–1927," in the symposium "Disease, Health, and Survival Among Native Americans," eds. Clifford E. Trafzer and Diane Weiner, *American Indian Culture and Research Journal,* 23:3 (1999): 119–142. Benson concludes: "The racial beliefs which had been used originally to justify the tarsectomy [a surgical process] now provided . . . OIA physicians, when confronted with evidence of the campaign's failure, with an airtight alibi. Indian peoples' supposed backwardness . . . now could be used to absolve OIA physicians from any blame" (p. 135). Just as there was concern for non-Indian resources—the erosion that would allegedly engulf Lake Mead behind Hoover Dam—there was fear that non-Indians would become infected because the sale of surplus lands subsequent to allotment to individual Indians had brought countless non-Indians into nearly daily contact with potential trachoma victims on reservations (p. 121).
53. Nancy M. William and Eugene S. Hunn, eds., *Resource Managers: North American and Australian Hunter-Gatherers,* Selected Symposia No. 67, American Association for the Advancement of Sciences (Boulder: Westview, 1982): 7; Thomas C. Blackburn and Kat Anderson, eds., *Before the Wilderness: Environmental Management by Native Californians,* Anthropological Papers No. 40 (Menlo Park, CA: Ballena, 1993): 15–16.
54. N. Scott Momaday, "Native American Attitudes to the Environment," in *Seeing With a Native Eye: Essays on Native American Religion,* ed. W. H. Capps (New York: Harper and Row, 1976): 79–85.
55. Cf. Shepard Krech III, *The Ecological Indian: Myth and History* (New York: W. W. Norton, 1999).
56. Besides ibid., see Richard White and William Cronon, "Ecological Change and Indian-White Relations," in *History of Indian-White Relations,* ed. Wilcomb E. Washburn, vol. 4 of *Handbook of North American Indians* (Washington, DC: Smithsonian Institution, 1988): 417–429. Note that a number of studies explore the contribution of Indians to the conservation movement; see George L. Cornell, "The Influence of Native Americans on Modern Conservationists," *Environmental Review,* 9:2 (1985): 104–117.
57. Bruce Brown, *Mountains in the Clouds: The Search for the Wild Salmon* (New York: Simon and Schuster, 1982): 138–139.
58. Ibid., p. 139. Since 1995 the Columbia River Inter-Tribal Fish Commission has proposed a tribal salmon restoration plan within that watershed. Thus salmon fishing continues to represent an issue of tribal resource management in the Pacific Northwest. See Melissa Powers, "The Spirit of the Salmon: How the Tribal Restora-

tion Plan Could Restore Columbia Basin Salmon," *Environmental Law,* 30:4 (2000): 867–910.

59. J. Baird Callicott, "Traditional American Indian and Western European Attitudes Toward Nature: An Overview," *Environmental Ethics,* 4:4 (1982): 293–318; Christopher Vecsey and Robert W. Venables, eds., *American Indian Environments: Ecological Issues in Native American History* (Syracuse: Syracuse University Press, 1980). See also Blackburn and Anderson, comps. and eds., *Before the Wilderness*; and Robert Boyd, ed., *Indians, Fire and the Land in the Pacific Northwest* (Corvallis: Oregon State University Press, 1999).
60. Cf. the approach of Krech, *The Ecological Indian.*
61. For a comparison of tribal versus reservation territory, see Raymond White, *Luiseño Social Organization, University of California Publications in American Archaeology and Ethnology,* 48:2 (1963): 91–94.
62. Beverly Smaby, "The Mormons and the Indians: Conflicting Ecological Systems in the Great Basin," *American Studies,* 16 (spring 1975): 35–48.
63. Morton H. Fried, "Land Tenure, Geography, and Ecology in the Contact of Cultures," *Journal of Economics and Sociology*, XI (1952): 302–303.
64. Richard McCabe and Thomas R. McCabe, "Of Slings and Arrows: An Historical Retrospection," in *White-Tailed Deer: Ecology and Management,* a Wildlife Management Institute book, ed. Lowell K. Halls (Harrisburg, PA: Stackpole, 1984): 19–72. Although Indians seemed to have been prudent in their hunt for deer, the authors query: "If Indians were 'ecological heros' [sic], why did they so readily abandon their ecological principles and spiritual values and ultimately dispossess themselves of their successful primitive lifestyles by becoming enthusiastic accomplices in the fur trade?" (p. 57).
65. For a general geography, see Klaus Frantz, *Indian Reservations in the United States: Territory, Sovereignty, and Socioeconomic Change,* Geography Research Paper 242 (Chicago: University of Chicago Press, 1999).
66. Felix Cohen, *Handbook of Federal Indian Law,* Rennard Strickland, editor-in-chief (Charlottesville, VA: Michie, Bobbs-Merrill, 1982 ed.): 673–674.
67. Lawrence F. Schmeckebier, *The Office of Indian Affairs: History, Activities, and Organization, Service Monograph 48* (Baltimore: Brookings Institution for Government Research, 1927; reprint, New York: AMS, 1972): chapter 2.
68. Cf. Taylor, *American Indian Policy,* and Stephen Cornell and Joseph P. Kalt, eds., *What Can Tribes Do: Strategies and Institutions in American Indian Economic Development,* American Indian Manual and Handbook Series no. 4 (Los Angeles: American Indian Studies Center, UCLA, 1992). Several aspects of tribal initiative in environmental management are discussed in Tracy J. Andrews and Castle McLaughlin, eds., "Farming and Ranching in Reservation Economies," *American Indian Culture and Research Journal,* 22:3 (1998): 1–222.
69. U.S. National Resources Board, *Indian Land Tenure, Economic Status and Population Trends,* Report 10, Land Planning Committee (Washington, DC: GPO, 1935).
70. Lewis Meriam et al., *The Problem of Indian Administration: Studies in Administration* (Baltimore: Brookings Institution for Government Research, 1928; Johnson reprint, 1971): 18, emphasis added.
71. Ibid., pp. 14–15, 504–507.
72. Ibid., pp. 518, 540. For critical comments on the efficacy of the Meriam Report, see Francis Paul Prucha, *The Great Father: The United States Government and the Ameri-*

can Indians, abridged ed. (Lincoln: University of Nebraska Press, 1986): 278–279, 315–316.

73. Donald Parman, *The Navajos and the New Deal* (New Haven: Yale University Press, 1976): 36–37.
74. Harper, *The Indian and the Land,* p. 9.
75. 48 *U.S. Stat.* 401–402, "To Promote the Conservation of Wildlife, Fish, and Game" (1934).
76. Rachel Carson, *Silent Spring* (Boston: Houghton Mifflin, 1962); Petulla, *American Environmental History,* p. 376.
77. Alvin M. Josephy Jr., *Red Power: The American Indians' Fight for Freedom* (New York: McGraw-Hill, 1971): 223–242. The Indian Self-Determination and Education Act was passed in 1975; Americans for Indian Opportunity, *Survey of American Indian Environmental Protection Needs on Reservation Lands: 1986,* Submitted to the Environmental Protection Agency, September 1986, p. ii.
78. Nicholas C. Peroff, *Menominee Drums: Tribal Termination and Restoration, 1954–1974* (Norman: University of Oklahoma Press, 1982): 53; *Menominee Tribe v. U.S.,* 119 Ct. Cl., 832, 391 U.S., 404 (1968). The Menominee brought additional resource management claims. Unfortunately, prior to the Kennedy administration, Congress enacted legislation seeking to terminate the trust status of many tribes, including the Menominee. The issues in litigation bore significantly on the survival of the Menominee timber industry. The Menominee as well as several other tribes were restored to trust status many years later. See Nancy O. Lurie, "Menominee Termination: From Reservation to Colony," *Human Organization,* 31:3 (1969): 257–269.
79. See Imre Sutton, ed., *Irredeemable America: The Indians' Estate and Land Claims* (Albuquerque: University of New Mexico Press, 1985).
80. *Progress: A Report by the Southern Ute Tribe* (Ignacio, CO: January 1, 1958): 3–4.
81. See Hunt, "Land Tenure." A comprehensive management report to the Warm Springs tribes was prepared by faculty of Oregon State University and other persons. Sutton had an opportunity to examine the proposals on the reservation while a faculty member, 1962–1964.
82. E. Richard Hart, ed., in *Zuni and the Courts: A Struggle for Sovereign Land Rights* (Lawrence: University Press of Kansas, 1995), reports on the Zuni Land Conservation Act of 1990, which resulted from tribal litigation over land losses and on the plan for the use of judgment funds; pp. 308–318.
83. Americans for Indian Opportunity, p. ii; Taylor, in *American Indian Policy,* summarizes many of the conservation services to the tribes by other federal agencies such as the Fish and Wildlife Service, Housing and Urban Development, ANA, and others; chapter 3.
84. Americans for Indian Opportunity, p. v. Many tribal resource management programs are summarized in Veronica E. Velarde Tiller, ed. and comp., *Tiller's Guide to Indian Country* (Albuquerque: BowArrow, 1996).

TRUSTEESHIP IN CHANGE

I

TRUSTEESHIP

Balancing Realty and Resource Management

Introduction

For the period from the 1880s to the 1920s, real estate management overwhelmed resource management. Preoccupation with record keeping, especially after the initiation of land allotment, required the trustee to produce reservation maps and update heirship land and sales.[1] Additionally, non-Indian land leasing consumed considerable administrative time and effort. Moreover, the government often sought to adjust its cadastral records to reflect favorably the intrusion of non-Indian newcomers who sought to settle any surplus lands. After tribal lands were divided into allotments, what Michael Lawson notes became true: "The selling and leasing of allotted lands and inherited interests gradually turned the Indian office into a giant real-estate and banking enterprise."[2]

This was also a period when tribes were generally excluded from resource management decisions. Once on a reservation, the trustees had the task of getting many tribes to accept the conditions of reservation life, but they also intervened in tribal resource decisions. Whenever the trustee did not make decisions, the states too often were ready to assume control to the exclusion of the tribes. Although individuals and groups supportive of the Indians' cause spoke about their material plight and state of health,[3] the trustee was not ready to contemplate any special land-based programs. Prior to the late 1870s, conservation concerns were few and often relegated to armchair advice. When conservation emerged as a national concern in the early 1890s, the U.S. Congress focused on the public domain of the West with its wilderness, parklands, forests, and waters. Conservationists saw the general populace eager and able to reconfigure the western landscape into productive farms and ranches and to exploit forests and mines. As a result, conservation efforts on reservations were an afterthought.

Many tribes did not adjust to reservation life. Subsequent to dispossession and dislocation, some tribes sustained traditional rights to hunt and fish on former aboriginal territory. Others struggled to continue hunting and fishing, often in defiance of federal authority. It was first a matter of survival, then a political statement.[4] The Northern Ute pursued subsistence hunting out of need and because of their understanding of treaty provisions. Few tribes would have the option to sustain traditional subsistence beyond the limits of reservations, and if recorded, accounts of their fate would parallel what happened to the Utes. Early state conservation statutes infringed on the inherent off-reservation hunting rights of Utes and other tribes. Because treaties frequently were silent on the question of tribal off-reservation hunting and in the absence of federal wildlife legislation, state agencies asserted that tribal hunters came under game laws, setting the stage for state-tribal hunting conflicts.

To be sure, other tribes when left to themselves even after their displacement by treaties and other means also had to contend with competition for game by nearby and even distant tribes, which were also hard-pressed by the entry of settlers and others into their territories. For example, when the Pawnee attempted to continue hunting and farming, they were raided again and again by other, stronger tribes—the Lakota in this instance.[5]

Indian hunting or fishing on ceded lands is more than a historical event; it is very real today, and tribes enter into conflict with federal, state, or local authorities and private landowners over the issue. In 1995, in *Crow Tribe of Indians v. Repsis,* the U.S. Court of Appeals (10th Circuit) rejected the tribe's complaint that it still possessed aboriginal hunting rights on public lands. The state of Wyoming had arrested and convicted a tribal member for killing elk on federal lands in that state. The court ruled that the Indians only had a temporary right to hunt on unoccupied lands, and thus the tribe was subject to state game laws. The court argued that the creation of a national forest resulted in the occupation of ceded lands, terminating the meaning of "unoccupied" in such a treaty. In general, treaty provisos were worded thusly: tribes had the right to hunt on "unoccupied lands of the U.S. so long as game might be found . . . and as long as peace subsists among the white and Indians on the borders of the hunting districts."[6] As discussed in Part III, states contend that they may regulate off-reservation treaty hunting and fishing rights in the interest of conservation if and when such regulations do not discriminate against the tribes and are reasonable for conservation. Clow's historical review of the plight of Ute hunters, despite treaty provisions that permitted the survival of hunting and fishing rights off-reservation, has a contemporary ring and will be reviewed in the introduction to Part III with a focus on current efforts to establish principles of comanagement of public and common property resources on ceded lands.[7]

Off-reservation hunting and fishing also extends to the seas. The federal government regulates territorial waters through the National Marine Fisheries Service. Beyond national limits, international conventions govern many species of wildlife. When the gray whale (*Eschrichtius robustus*) was taken off the endangered species list in 1994, the Makah tribe of the Olympic Peninsula (Washington) received a favorable response from the International Whaling Commission to return to whaling. The U.S. government backed the tribal request. In spring 1999 an exclusion zone of 500 yards was delimited around each whaling canoe, and the U.S. Coast Guard intervened to protect tribal whaling rights. When the tribe returned to the sea, it was again met by protesters. In early June a Federal District Court ruled that the National Marine Fisheries Service erred in granting the Makah the right to hunt whales within territorial waters. The court contended that the environmental assessment was "slanted in favor of finding that the Makah whaling proposal would not significantly affect the environment." Environmentalists believed they had won a victory, but the tribe deems the setback as temporary. This controversy between environmentalists and the Makah continued when in spring 2000 the tribal return to whaling was protested by antiwhaling environmentalists.[8]

Past events do not completely explain away the demise of tribes at the time of the coming of Americans into their territories. Those tribes that "accepted" their fate and others that continued to resist the inevitable ultimately relocated and consolidated their settlement on smaller tracts, where the government made minimal efforts to supply food and other commodities. But changes in reservation environment, including reduced acreage and loss of superior soil (e.g., bottomlands) for horticulture, severely limited the free choice of a means to subsist and made many tribes quickly dependent on the government. But even after farming got under way, with surprisingly bountiful harvests on some reservations but not everywhere and not in every year, Indians were reported hunting some distance from reservations. Even today some tribes continue to hunt and fish off-reservation—for example, as sustained by case law, tribes of the Columbia River Valley continue to pursue traditional harvests despite a long history of opposition.[9]

Reservation policies and the politics of altruism soon ushered in land allotment and set the stage for making farmers of Indians, but the trustee did not sustain many existing Indian farming communities. The land policy took more from the Indians than it gave back. Soon, better lands were transferred to homesteaders; allotments quickly became encumbered by inheritance policies in each state and were sold.[10] Many Indians stopped farming; others never attempted to farm. One elderly tribal leader—Jane Penn—in Southern California spoke of the government's gesture of giving families orchard trees but no information to prepare Indian orchardists for the white-dominated marketplace.[11]

It is instructive that a considerable portion of reservation lands lack quality soil (i.e., classes I, II, and III in the Soil Conservation Service scheme);[12] where better soil exists, some of that land passed from Indian hands through lease and sale to non-Indians. Field observers would surely note that better soils may well lay under natural vegetation that has never been cleared but may from time to time be grazed by livestock. Of course, the success of Indian agriculture was something less than an edaphic issue and more one of water supply, for the bulk of reservation lands lie in the arid-semiarid western states.[13] Thus government assistance in Indian farming had to ride tandem with parallel water developments.

Efforts to establish farming on reservations, often assisted by "skilled" and "informed" personnel hired by the Indian Bureau, got under way without any real scientific or practical know-how. The farming policy commenced as early as land allotment, which, although begun decades before the passage of the General Allotment Act of 1887, moved rapidly thereafter and introduced farmer-teachers to many tribes.[14] Much of what was identified as conservation exchanged hands from relatively uneducated farmer-teachers to countless nonfarming Indians, who knew even less about soil and crop cultivation.

During the late nineteenth and early twentieth centuries, federal land allotment policy ran counter to the era's conservationists, who demanded better use of the soil, careful forestry practices, and alternative farming practices on arid lands.[15] As the allotment disaster persisted, successful resource management became even more crucial if tribesmen were to become self-supporting citizens on their remaining reservation lands. It is ironic that the trustee was out of touch with economic realities by persisting in its zeal to assimilate the Indian as a social goal even when his environmental base continued to limit his opportunity to sustain himself even as a member of a tribe resident on a reservation. Not to minimize the non-Indian presence within reservations, in poor economic times trust lands leased or owned by non-Indian farmers often lay idle.

Legislative efforts to assist the Bureau of Indian Affairs (BIA) in managing tribal resources have been ambivalent in many instances. For example, the general leasing of tribal lands and individual allotments, which began with the passage of the 1891 leasing act, represented both the good and the bad of the nineteenth-century conservation movement for reservation communities. After reservation lands were allotted, many of the new allottees were unable to farm or ranch simply because they did not have the funds necessary to begin an operation; others were physically unable to farm, and often lacked specific skills or orientation to agriculture. Despite a number of valid reasons for not farming, the result was that both reservation-allotted and tribally owned lands remained non- or underproductive, a situation that ran counter to the conservation movement's ideology of efficiency. If tribesmen did not farm their lands, then the general public would have an opportunity. In 1901 Commissioner of Indian Affairs William A. Jones explained that with the passage of the legislation, "Congress had in view the best interests of the Indians as well as the people at large. The act seems to be in entire harmony with the uniform [conservation] policy of Congress to encourage the development and utilization of all of our general resources."[16]

Although the 1891 law required tribal consent, it made both tribal and allotted acreage and resources—including soil, range, coal, oil, and natural gas—available for non-Indian exploitation. That was the evil of the era's conservation-utilization ideology, but the benefit was, supporters argued, that tribes would receive ongoing revenues and individual Indians would bring in some income from those resources as long as lessees followed conservation practices. This rarely occurred because a dynamic yet negative relationship exists between lessors and lessees. Since lessees do not own the land, they tend to overwork lease properties, taking quick profits by overstocking rangelands and practicing poor farming methods, both depleting soils and encouraging soil erosion. Then at the end of the lease, lessees have too often refused to reclaim or return property they leased to its original state. Moreover, income per acre leased was almost always below market.

Since most reservations lie in the arid-semiarid West, irrigation became the first conservation concern the government provided to tribes to promote individual Indian industry, sustain the tribes on the land, and develop reservation economics. As early as the 1860s, the Indian Service (BIA) assisted in the construction of irrigation works long before the passage of the Reclamation Act of 1902. Ultimately, reservation irrigation projects were intended to "restore water to Indians who have been deprived of it and to place water on the land of other Indians in order to increase its productivity."[17] Many early efforts to harness water supply, build channels, and the like, however, met with the frustrations of soil alkalinity or sterility. For example, the Indian Service was unsuccessful in developing and maintaining irrigation works on the Colorado River Indian Reservation.[18] After the Reclamation Service was established, the Indian Service entered in a cooperative agreement in 1907 for the construction of large irrigation projects on the Flathead, Blackfeet, Fort Peck, Pima, and Yuma Reservations.[19]

Against this historical record of Indian Service efforts to develop Indian farming, Terry Anderson in Chapter 2 succinctly outlines the role Indian land tenure has played in agricultural production on trust lands. His analysis emphasizes institutional factors that affect environmental factors in the utilization and management of tribal resources. The author's analysis measures the impact of land tenure using cross-sectional data from large western reservations. His interpretation of the evidence suggests that BIA trusteeship, by raising the costs of organizing agricultural productivity, has thwarted production and thus discouraged sustainable reservation economic development. Citing tribal examples of indigenous success in resource management, he asserts that "sustainable conservation accompanies an institutional evolution driven from the bottom up by the special circumstances of each tribe and reservation." This theme tends to be repeated in several other chapters, emphasizing again and again that in part because of shifting government policies, officials continue to lose sight of the

Fig. I.1 Agriculture on the Colorado River Indian Reservation (Arizona). Irrigated agriculture is the mainstay of tribal income. The tribes (Mohave, Chemehuevi, Hopi, and Navajo) operate a 6,700-acre farm and lease other acreage. In the 1990s more than 80,000 acres were under irrigation. These Indians hold a vital allocation to Colorado River water, seen in a canal in the foreground. Photo by Imre Sutton.

important lessons learned by early ethnographers such as Edward Hall who worked in the field with the tribes in the 1930s.[20]

In the final quarter of the twentieth century, numerous tribes expanded tribal agriculture. For example, the Colorado River Indian Reservation, Arizona, operates a 6,700-acre farm (Fig. I.1) while leasing other acreage, as do many tribes as well as individuals, to non-Indians. Most of the cultivable land on the Crow Indian Reservation, Montana, is leased (Fig. I.2). The White Mountain Apache (Fort Apache Indian Reservation, Arizona), for example, maintain a 900-acre irrigation farm mainly to produce alfalfa for the tribe's successful cattle industry.[21]

As for the development of water, the construction of dams and efforts at reclamation (irrigation) on Indian lands began even before federal surveys of western rivers but ultimately depended on innovations in hydroengineering that came with the establishment of federal water responsibilities. The *Winters* decision declared that the tribes possessed an original reserved water right based on the fact that the establishment of reservations in the drylands predicated water

Fig. I.2 Farming on the Crow Indian Reservation (Montana). An allotted reservation, most of the cultivable land is leased to non-Indians who were dry farming around 150,000 acres and irrigating another 30,000 in the 1990s. In that period more than 30 percent of the land was held by non-Indians. The site of the photograph is just west of the Little Bighorn National Battlefield Monument. Photo by Imre Sutton.

allocation for Indians to pursue farming, the goal of land allotment and strengthening tribal conservation programs.[22]

Indian Service performance in the construction and management of Indian water systems has a mixed record, but the development of larger schemes tended to rely on the capacity and assistance of other agencies. The Bureau of Reclamation and the Army Corps of Engineers have worked on-reservation, but neither has championed the Indians' cause; in recent years they have implemented cooperative efforts with tribes. Katherine Weist's study of the "Iron Triangle" in regard to water developments on Indian lands reveals much about the projects sought to enhance both rural and urban growth and that tribal lands were often in the backwash of these developments.

Many tribes were less often beneficiaries of these vast river basin construction schemes, although others—for example, tribes adjacent to the Colorado River or its tributaries—have benefited from the impoundment of their water rights and from flood control. Inundation of Indian lands is seen by some observers as a necessary evil accompanying major water project development.

Others speak less charitably of either politicians or water planners. Indian lands have often been perceived as "national sacrifice areas" so that greater resource developments can be achieved for the public at large.[23]

The study of dams on Indian lands (Chapter 3) examines not the laudatory or minor gains of small and large water projects by the Indian Irrigation Service but rather evaluates the social impact of these water resource developments by other agencies on the loss of Indian lands and the problems of resettlement, destruction of sacred ground, and dislocation in terms of community and towns. Despite payment for these losses, tribes have become embittered by government deals. The treatment of many tribes is well documented for projects in the Missouri River Valley[24] and for many projects from Kinzua Dam, which floods lands of the Cornerplanter Indian Reservation (Pennsylvania) and the Allegany Indian Reservation (Pennsylvania–New York), and the El Capitán Dam on the Capitán Grande Indian Reservation in Southern California.[25] Many tribes have made the best of being displaced, as did the several tribes in the Dalles area of the Columbia River who relocated to the Warm Springs Indian Reservation (Oregon) and eventually utilized claims payments for resource development of their lands.[26] Interestingly, a few tribes have more recently taken advantage of reservoir sites to establish tourist attractions, including the Chemehuevi casino on Lake Havasu, a reservoir on the lower Colorado River.

The trustee's management of nineteenth-century tribal forests followed a similar pattern. Instead of turning to tribal forested lands to search for water to abet the irrigation of allotments, tribal forestlands were themselves frequently allotted to individual tribesmen, yet they could only be cut for agricultural purposes. As a result, early logging efforts focused on clearing allotments for agricultural operations.[27] With the introduction of forest management principles, the Indian Service entered into a cooperative agreement with the Forest Service in 1907, seeking forestry expertise to manage tribal forests.

In 1909 Congress appropriated $100,000 to the Department of the Interior "to make investigations on Indian reservations and take measure for the purpose of preserving living and growing timber, and removing dead timber, standing or fallen; to advise the Indians as to the proper care of forests and to conduct such timber operations and sales of timber as may be deemed advisable and provided by law."[28] With this appropriation, the Indian Service severed its cooperative agreement with the Forest Service and organized its own conservation-resource-oriented forestry program. Indian Service foresters advocated ongoing trust status and even land consolidation to improve tribal forests, which was philosophically opposed to those individuals who favored forced tribal farming, assimilation of Indians, and removal of trust status from their lands.[29]

The stories of farming and forestry share the theme of outside management, even though land allotment had divided thousands of forested acres and encouraged individuals to clear timber to attempt to farm smaller parcels. Often forests remained in tribal tenure, although for years the trustee claimed that timber belonged to the United States, not the tribes. Alan McQuillan suggests that Indian forestry evolved ahead of, alongside, but too often behind general forest conservation in this country. Controversy over the ecological and operational values of selective cutting versus clear-cutting stalled progress for long periods of time. At a later date, controversy arose over a dichotomous management philosophy that set off sustained-yield timber management from multiple uses of forests but ultimately led to a common goal of ecomanagement for both Indian and public forests. McQuillan focuses his discussion of Indian forestry on the Quinault and the Menominee, the latter having recently established timber harvest instruction, a degree program in their Sustainable Development Institute. Such a program is enabled by a grant from the U.S. Department of Agriculture.[30]

In the early decades, a rivalry evolved between the fledgling Forest Service and the forestry division of the Indian Office. Ultimately, a well-trained forester and effective administrator, J. P. Kinney, established a management program that embraced both conservation and economics even during the 1920s. Unlike agriculture, observers of Indian forestry note some success stories but must also lament the abject failures and disappointments. In recent times forestry, mainly a tribal responsibility, has exhibited some successes on a handful of reservations such as the Hupa (California), Quinault (Washington), Menominee (Wisconsin), and Warm Springs (Oregon).

These chapters on the changing responsibilities of trusteeship represent studies that span the period from the treaty years to the present. We sought representative studies that illustrate trustee control and cut across resources as well as time—wild game and tribal hunting, agriculture, forestry, and water development. These studies identify some of the foundations for changes in official policy; they point to weaknesses, flaws and misperceptions, strengths and gains. Conservation at the hands of the Bureau of Indian Affairs administration followed, paralleled, and even initiated the implementation of a conservation project.

References

1. The graphic presentation of dispossession and diminishment of tribal holdings may be found in C. C. Royce, comp., *Indian Land Cessions in the United States,* 18th Annual Report, 1896–97, pt. 2, *Bureau of American Ethnography* (Washington, DC: Government Printing Office (GPO), 1899): 521–997; in Sam B. Hilliard, comp., "Indian Land Cessions," map supplement to *Annals, Association of American Geographers,* 62:2 (1972); and in Imre Sutton, ed., *Irredeemable America: The Indians' Estate and Land Claims* (Albuquerque: University of New Mexico Press, 1985). For an interpretation of map classifications in Indian affairs: Sutton, "The Cartographic Factor in Indian Land Tenure: Some Examples from Southern California," *American*

Indian Culture and Research Journal, 12:2 (1988): 53–80. See also Wilcomb E. Washburn, ed., *The Indian and the White Man* (New York: Anchor Books, Doubleday, 1964); Sutton, *Indian Land Tenure: Bibliographical Essays and a Guide to the Literature* (New York: Clearwater, 1975); Francis P. Prucha, *A Bibliographical Guide to the History of Indian-White Relations in the United States* (Chicago: University of Chicago Press, 1977); Prucha, *American Indian Treaties: The History of a Political Anomaly* (Berkeley: University of California Press, 1994).

2. Michael L. Lawson, "The Fractionated Estate: The Problem of American Indian Heirship," *South Dakota History,* 21:1 (1991): 1–42, quote on p. 13.
3. See, for example, Helen Hunt Jackson, *A Century of Dishonor: A Sketch of the United States Government's Dealings With Some of the Indian Tribes* (1881; reprinted by Harpers, New York, 1965, A. F. Rolle, ed.); also the various publications of the Indian Rights Association (Philadelphia).
4. For a detailed historical reconstruction of the conflicts between Indians and non-Indian miners, hunters, and others in Alaska, see Donald C. Mitchell, *Sold American: The Story of Alaska Natives and Their Land, 1867–1959* (Hanover, NH: University Press of New England, 1997). Mitchell recounts how efforts to set aside and establish reservations, which were supportive of indigenous land rights and would permit the continuance of hunting and trapping on aboriginal lands, were frustrated by commercial interests. He also reports, however, that from the time of Theodore Roosevelt, the setting aside of reserves and promulgating open and closed seasons for the conservation of wildlife in Alaska also worked hardship on the native population. Such contradictions between conservation policy and practice were not uncommon then or now.
5. Richard White, in *The Roots of Dependency: Subsistence, Environment, and Social Change Among Choctaws, Pawnees, and Navajos* (Lincoln: University of Nebraska Press, 1983), discusses the Pawnee in transition; chapters 6–9.
6. See *Crow Tribe of Indians v. Repsis,* 73 Fed. 3d., 982 (1995); see also "Treaty With the Crow Indians," 15 *Stat.* 649 (1868). See also the discussion of *United States v. Hugs,* 109 Fed. 3d., 1375 (9th Circuit 1997). Crow members Frank and William Hugs were arrested in connection with "taking, attempting to take, and purchasing eagles in violation of the Bald and Golden Eagle Protection Act" [16 U.S.C. §§ 668–6684 (1994)]. The Ninth Circuit upheld their conviction in 1997. See Matthew Perkins, "The Federal Indian Trust Doctrine and the Bald and Golden Eagle Protection Act: Could Application of the Doctrine Alter the Outcome in *U.S. v. Hugs*?" *Environmental Law,* 30:3 (2000): 701–727. Indian hunting of wildlife is just one of many issues involving tribes and states in the arena of conservation and resource management.
7. See, for example, Ed Goodman, "Protecting Habitat for Off-Reservation Tribal Hunting and Fishing Rights: Tribal Comanagement as a Reserved Right," *Environmental Law,* 30:2 (2000): 279–361; Kari Krogseng, "Minnesota v. Mille Lacs Band of Chippewa Indians," *Ecology Law Qtly.,* 27:3 (2000): 771–797. These cases consider the "reserved" rights of tribes to participate as comanagers on public lands and with common property, which states contend fall within their environmental jurisdiction.
8. See Kim Murphy, "Makah Finally Gets Its Whale," *Los Angeles Times* (May 18, 1999): A18; and "Tribal Whale Hunt Begins Amid Protests," *Los Angeles Times* (April 18, 2000): A21. Cf. Murphy, "Ruling Allowing Whale Hunts by Makah Tribe Rejected," *Los Angeles Times* (June 6, 2000): A18, quote on p. 18. See also Murphy,

"Lifestyle in Hunters' Cross Hairs," *Los Angeles Times* (October 7, 1999): A1, 18, which reports indigenous subsistence and commercial fishing in Alaska. In that state the Department of the Interior has had to intervene to protect the rights of Alaskan Natives to fish along federal waterways. What in part aggravated the fishing preference issue was that Alaska had enacted legislation that granted preference to Natives on federal lands, but the Alaska Supreme Court declared the act unconstitutional in 1989. Thus the entry of the federal government in subsequent years.

9. Fay G. Cohen, *Treaties on Trial: The Continuing Controversy Over Northwest Indian Fishing Rights* (Seattle: University of Washington Press, 1986); David H. Getches, Charles F. Wilkinson, and Robert A. Williams Jr., *Cases and Materials on Federal Indian Law,* 3d ed. (St. Paul: West, 1993): chapter 13.
10. Leonard A. Carlson, *Indians, Bureaucrats, and Land: The Dawes Act and the Decline of Indian Farming* (Westport, CT: Greenwood, 1981).
11. Jane Penn of the Morongo Indian Reservation (IR) (California) told Imre Sutton about the prejudices in the marketing of Indian fruit and the discouragement that ensued. Imre Sutton, "Land Tenure and Changing Occupance on Indian Reservations in Southern California," Ph.D. diss. in geography, University of California at Los Angeles, 1964. Remnants of those orchards still stand on the Morongo IR about 80 miles east of Los Angeles.
12. Gary A. Klee, *Conservation of Natural Resources* (Englewood Cliffs, NJ: Prentice-Hall, 1991): chapters 3 and 4.
13. See Klaus Frantz, *Indian Reservations in the United States,* Geography Research Paper 242 (Chicago: University of Chicago Press, 1999): figure 8.1, p. 209; cf. Harold Dregne, "Desertification of Arid Lands," *Economic Geography,* 53 (1977): 322.
14. Carlson, *Indians, Bureaucrats.*
15. Joseph M. Petulla, *American Environmental History: The Exploitation and Conservation of Natural Resources* (San Francisco: Boyd and Fraser, 1977): 220–235.
16. U.S. Congress, Senate, *Leasing of Indian Lands,* 57th Cong., lst sess., 1902, Serial 4234, p. 32.
17. Lawrence F. Schmeckebier, *The Office of Indian Affairs: History, Activities, and Organization, Service Monograph 48* (Baltimore: Brookings Institution for Government Research, 1927; reprint, New York: AMS, 1972): 237.
18. Cf. Ann Caylor, " 'A Promise Long Deferred': Federal Reclamation on the Colorado River Indian Reservation," *Pacific Historical Review,* 69:2 (2000): 193–213; see also Dwight Lomayesva, "The Adaptation of Hopi and Navajo Colonists on the Colorado River Indian Reservation," Masters in Social Science, California State University, Fullerton, 1980. Sutton's graduate student included an account of the significant agrarian input of the Japanese Americans who were relocated to the reservation (Poston) during World War II and the legacy of their efforts to irrigate desert lands.
19. On the Winters doctrine see Daniel McCool, "Watering the Reservation: American Indians and Their Water," in *Environmental Politics and Policy in the West,* ed. Zachary A. Smith (Dubuque, IA: Kendall-Hunt, 1993): 219–236; *Winters v. U.S.,* 207 U.S., 564 (1908]).
20. Cf. Edward Hall, *West of the Thirties: Discoveries Among the Navajo and Hopi* (New York: Doubleday, 1994).
21. For a comprehensive survey of economic activity on Indian reservations, see Veronica E. Velarde Tiller, ed. and comp., *Tiller's Guide to Indian Country: Economic Profiles of*

American Indian Reservations (Albuquerque: BowArrow, 1996). Some data for both photos (Figs. I.1 and I.2) come from Tiller, pp. 200–201, 400–401.

22. See Daniel McCool, *Command of the Waters: Iron Triangles, Federal Water Development, and Indian Water* (Berkeley: University of California Press, 1987).
23. Historically, dams and subsequent inundation of tribal lands showed little more respect for archaeological resources. Independent field scholars, with or without support, sought to recover such resources even as dams were being planned and constructed. Even for a project the size of Hoover Dam, archaeologists had an uphill struggle, for upstream of Boulder Canyon, the site of Hoover Dam, were remnants of early pueblo construction, and although at least one structure was dismantled and reconstructed on a site near Overton (Nevada), archaeological research in the reservoir area had to cease before complete salvage was possible. See Imre Sutton, "Geographical Aspects of Construction Planning: *Hoover Dam Revisited*," *Journal of the West,* 7:3 (1968): 301–344. The development of emergency or salvage archaeology drew attention to the need to incorporate such efforts into water resource planning.
24. Michael Lawson, *The Dammed Indians: The Pick-Sloan Plan and the Missouri River Sioux, 1944–1980* (Norman: University of Oklahoma Press, 1982).
25. A brief review of dams on Indian lands with an accompanying map appears in Imre Sutton, *Indian Land Tenure* (New York: Clearwater, 1975): 166–171. For a newer work that examines the impact of dams on Indian ecology, see Roberta Ulrich, *Empty Nest: Indians, Dams, and the Columbia River* (Corvallis: Oregon State University Press, 1999).
26. Jack Hunt, "Land Tenure and Economic Development of the Warm Springs Indian Reservation [Oregon]," *Journal of the West,* 9:1 (1970): 93–109. Several departments at Oregon State University participated in the resource data gathering and assessment for the Warm Springs IR, and the project was winding down about the time Imre Sutton joined the faculty in 1962.
27. Schmeckebier, *The Office of Indian Affairs,* p. 185.
28. 35 *U.S. Stat.* 51 (1908); quote on p. 51.
29. Alan S. Newell, Richmond L. Clow, and Richard N. Ellis, *A Forest in Trust: Three-quarters of a Century of Indian Forestry, 1910–1986,* for Bureau of Indian Affairs, Litigation Support Services (Missoula: Historical Research Associates, 1986): chapter 2, p. 7.
30. Kinney wrote his own account of Indian forestry: *Indian Forest and Range: A History of the Administration and Conservation of the Redman's Heritage* (Washington, DC: Forestry Enterprises, 1950); Menominee Nation, *Sustainable Development Institute, Annual Report FY 99* (courtesy, Dr. Holly Youngbear-Tibbetts, dean and director, Keshena, Wisconsin).

CHAPTER 1

Colorado Game Laws and the Dispossession of the Inherent Hunting Right of the White River and Uncompahgre Utes

RICHMOND L. CLOW

Tribal Hunting Rights and Colorado's Increasing Restriction

Nineteenth-century state game laws restricted hunting activities to protect game animals from perceived exploitation. Typical state legislation of this era included closed seasons, buck-only hunts, and bag limits. On either an emotional or a philosophical plane, most Americans supported these restrictive measures. One exception was tribal hunters who claimed these early conservation statutes infringed on their inherent off-reservation hunting rights. Treaties frequently were silent on the question of tribal off-reservation hunting, and in the absence of federal wildlife legislation state agencies asserted that tribal hunters came under game laws, setting the stage for state-tribal hunting conflicts.

Representative of many nineteenth-century conservation game wars was the two-decade battle between Colorado game wardens who argued that White River and Uncompahgre Utes' mule deer hunts violated state law. The Colorado General Assembly fired the initial shot, enacting the state's first game law in 1877, and creating a closed hunting season from January 1 to September 1 of each year for all species. The legislation permitted limited subsistence hunting only "for food; and then only when necessary for immediate use, governed in amount and quantity by the reasonable necessities of the person or persons killing such animal."[1]

Unlike the Colorado Assembly, which pushed legislation to limit mule deer hunting, Ute hunters practiced efficiency, attempting to maximize productivity without waste. This required picking an optimal opportunity to hunt by techniques that produced the greatest return for their efforts, and the methods upset many local whites. After passage of the 1877 game act, Ute hunters frequently found themselves at odds with state authorities, especially since Utes used deer as a tribal staple and a market commodity and Ute hunting practices offended many local whites.

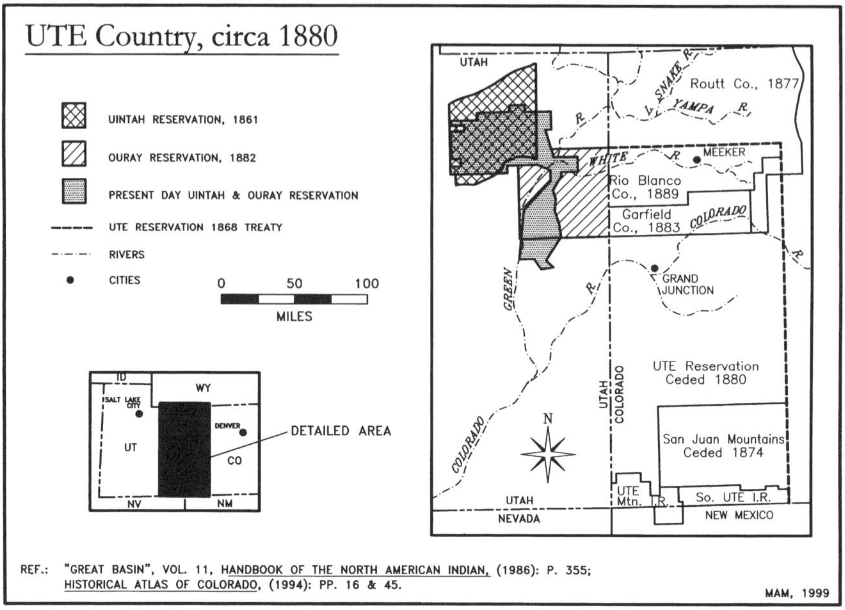

Fig. 1.1 Ute Country, circa 1880. Ute Indians displaced from northern Colorado were resettled on a portion of their aboriginal territory in northeastern Utah.

Deer hunting not only provided large quantities of protein for the Utes, but they also sold hides and meat in a developing market. After the 1873–1874 Brunot mineral agreement, tribal hunters sold deer meat to local Colorado miners. As their hunting territory decreased and markets for deer increased, Utes employed fire to drive deer for easier killing. Captain Francis J. Dodge reported in 1879 that many Utes were at Middle Park and North Park, setting fires and killing deer for hides. He added, "The charge of killing game out of season . . . seems well founded."[2] The campaign against Ute deer hunting had begun.

The Meeker Massacre in 1879, not deer hunting, pushed the United States to move the White River Utes from the White River Agency in northwest Colorado to the Uintah Reservation in Utah the next year. The Uncompahgre band left Colorado in 1881 but settled on the adjacent Ouray Reservation (Fig. 1.1).[3] Now in Utah, state authorities had reason to believe the former Colorado tribesmen would not continue to hunt in Colorado. The Utes disappointed Colorado officials. From Utah, the White River and Uncompahgre Utes returned to northwest Colorado for fall mule deer hunts. Ute hunters claimed they had an inherent tribal hunting right, noting that state regulations did not restrict their hunting rights on ceded land.

White River (Parusanuch and Yamparka Utes) and Uncompahgre (Taviwach Utes) hunting rights were property privileges that originated in their tribe's sovereignty. As a sovereign, the Utes possessed an inherent aboriginal right to hunt on their former Colorado territories, and this right was not dependent on treaty recognition or a congressional act. That original right remained with the Utes until they either discarded or ceded their hunting privilege or the United States "extinguished [that right] by statute."[4] Since Congress never terminated that natural right and the Utes had not ceded that entitlement, the Utes maintained their access to deer on ceded lands in Colorado after the White River and Uncompahgre Utes removed to Utah.

Treaties and agreements reported little about inherent hunting rights despite the importance of hunting to the Ute economy. The 1863 Tabeguache Treaty recognized the band's hunting privilege, noting that they had "an exclusive right to the following described country [in Colorado] as their lands and hunting-grounds."[5] The 1863 treaty language was important because the document acknowledged that land and hunting activities were separate and at the same time established similar boundaries for both activities. The subsequent treaty of 1868 reduced Ute lands to the western third of Colorado (15 million acres) and created the Los Pinos Agency and White River Agency but was silent on their inherent hunting right.[6] By the same token, the Utes reserved for themselves "all of the Bear River and White River District, generally conceded to be the best game country in the Union."[7]

Six years later Felix Brunot, chairman of the Board of Indian Commissioners, negotiated for the San Juan Mountains in southwest Colorado. The signatory Utes maintained their inherent hunting rights on ceded lands through a hunting provision that stated "the United States shall permit the Ute Indians to hunt upon said lands so long as the game lasts and the Indians are at peace with the white people."[8] Following the Meeker Massacre, White River and Uncompahgre Utes relocated to the Uintah and Ouray Reservations in Utah. Despite ceding lands and leaving Colorado, as stipulated in the Ute Agreement of 1880, the tribesmen claimed they retained inherent hunting privileges on the former lands. Utes argued that the 1880 agreement preserved their Colorado hunting privileges where the fifth condition stipulated "all provisions of the . . . [previous treaties and agreements] not altered by this agreement shall continue in force."[9] The inherent right of a sovereign preserved Ute ongoing off-reservation hunting rights even after their removal from northwest Colorado.

After their removal to Utah, the White River and Uncompahgre returned to hunt in northwest Colorado but modified their hunting techniques. Instead of several hunts per year, they usually made one extended late summer–early fall hunt, killing a large number of deer, and then returned to Utah. They also stopped using fires to drive deer, likely to minimize detection. Nonetheless, tribal hunters continued to kill a large number of animals, although the harvest would not

Fig. 1.2 Ute Indian Hunters in Colorado. Two Ute deer hunters posed for a photographer despite the fact that Colorado officials sought to arrest Ute Indians caught hunting off their reservation lands (in Utah). Photo by Summer W. Matteson ("Red Man and White Man in Colorado's Hunting Fields," *Outing,* vol. 38 [1901]: 32). Courtesy, Interlibrary Loan Office, Pomona Public Library, California.

threaten total mule deer numbers. Despite that reality, tribal hunts still offended both state officials' sense of control over the animals and conservation-minded individuals who had a strong sense that Ute hunting practices were lawless or illegal (Fig. 1.2).

On the other hand, the Uintah and Ouray Indian agents acquiesced to Ute inherent Colorado hunting rights when they issued hunting passes permitting the tribesmen to return to northwest Colorado to hunt in Garfield, Rio Blanco, and Routt Counties. Local stockmen opposed these Ute hunting excursions, claiming that the Ute stole cattle, killed elk and deer only for the hides, and burned the grasslands that deprived cattlemen of winter ranges. Whites often made these allegations to stop Ute fall hunting expeditions from Utah that clashed with settlers' use of the public range.[10]

In early 1885 local whites complained to Colorado Governor Benjamin H. Eaton that Utes had crossed into western Colorado to hunt. On behalf of the Garfield County Commissioners and the General Assembly of Colorado, Eaton asked Secretary of the Interior Henry M. Teller to end the Ute hunting trips because they were "taking advantage of that provision of the [1880] treaty allowing them to hunt a portion of the year at the old White River Agency."[11] Secretary Teller ordered Utah Indian agents to stop issuing hunting passes and added that the Utes must stop returning to their old hunting camps.[12] Teller's mandate had no effect. The agent and even his clerk continued to issue "loosely worded permits to Indians to leave their reservation on pretence of hunting and fishing."[13]

Besides seasonal tribal hunters from Utah reservations, the presence of several small permanent Ute settlements in northwest Colorado aggravated the situation. One group resided on the White River close to Douglas Creek near the Colorado-Utah border; a second band, led by the Uncompahgre Colorow and White River Colorow, remained near the former White River Agency, herding stock on public lands and hunting game. These Utes defied orders to return to Utah, claiming that the 1880 Ute Commission granted them permission to stay and that they had also retained hunting rights by terms of the 1874 Brunot Agreement.[14]

In 1887 Colorado restricted the open elk season from October 1 to January 1 and the deer and antelope season from September 1 to December 1.[15] In August of that year Joe Burgett, the first Garfield County state game warden, obtained arrest warrants for twelve Utes living with White River Colorow for hunting before the season opened.[16] While serving the warrants, Burgett's posse fired on the Ute camp, and after the shooting ended the game warden confiscated 5,000 pounds of dried meat the Utes had obtained before the state hunting season had opened.[17] The war over inherent tribal rights and Colorado game conservation law had escalated.

The attack on Colorow's camp did not end the seasonal Ute hunts. Uintah and Ouray Indian agent W. G. Swanson defended the White River and Uncompahgre hunting rights, claiming they had the same privileges as whites to hunt on public lands. He added that "an agreement with them in 1873 grants them the privilege to hunt on the public domain in the State of Colorado."[18] Even more important, inadequate beef rations forced agent T. A. Burns to issue hunting passes the following year. He concluded, "We were out of Beef at the Agency—hence their desire to obtain meat on the hunt."[19]

As long as the Utes remained peacefully, the tribesmen believed they maintained their inherent hunting privileges. Either to force a confrontation or because they did not understand Ute hunting methods, local Colorado residents described Ute hunting trips as military expeditions or willful ventures of destruction to slaughter animals and simply leave the carcasses to rot.[20] In reality, large kill sites represented both efficient hunting methods and months of meat for the hunters and their kin. Although Ute hunting parties posed no threat to local residents,[21] Routt County residents claimed in 1889 that "Ute Indians [were] shooting game and killing cattle."[22] Based more on fear than reality, local whites threatened to attack Ute hunters.[23]

Rumors of indiscriminate kills became truth in the local press as soon as the Ute fall hunting parties entered Colorado.[24] These local accounts became the evidence state leaders used to try to end Ute hunts. In August 1889, as Utes traveled to the headwaters of the White River, Colorado Governor Job A. Cooper telegraphed President Grover Cleveland, claiming Ute hunters "are invading Routt Co. Colo. and committing depredns [sic] annoying citizens."[25] To end this problem, the governor asked Cleveland to revoke the Utes' hunting permits.[26]

These charges forced the U.S. Army to send 2nd Lieutenant Samuel A. Smoke to investigate the Ute hunts. Smoke interviewed J. H. Fisher, cashier of the First National Bank of Glenwood Springs, Colorado, who reported four or five Ute hunters going to the White River Plateau. Former postmaster J. L. Clark informed Smoke that Utes hunted every summer on the Tampa Plateau and other parts of Routt County. After completing his investigation, Smoke found no evidence that Ute hunters wantonly massacred wildlife.[27] The stories did not end with Smoke's denial of Ute game massacres. In fall of 1890 John W. Lowell, a Lily, Colorado, rancher, claimed large numbers of Utes were "slaughtering the deer by the thousands. In many cases they take only the hides, leaving the carcasses to rot." Lowell added, "They come from both the Uintah and Ouray agencies, and are not only more bold in their demeanor, but have come further east into Colorado than any year before since old Colorow and his band were driven out of the State." Lowell concluded, "If not compelled to leave promptly they will destroy more game in the next thirty days than has been killed by all the white settlers in the county in the last year."[28]

Lowell's powerful claims were not true but were fuel for trouble. To prevent a conflict, Uintah agent Robert Waugh ordered the tribesmen back to the reservation.[29] At the same time, the army dispatched 1st Lieutenant Alfred B. Johnson from Fort Logan, Colorado, to find the truth. Johnson traveled to the Lily Park Horse Ranch, at the junction of the Little Snake and Yampa Rivers, and questioned Lowell. Johnson reported that the Utes had been near the ranch for ten days prior to the deer migration from the mountains, and he claimed that "these Indians have killed at least 3,000 deer, almost all of which were skinned and left upon the ranges to decompose." Then the Utes left for Utah, scattering at least 300 mares but committing no depredations.[30]

Upon the conclusion of Johnson's damaging investigation, Uintah and Ouray agent Waugh initiated his own inquiry, which vindicated the Utes. Waugh sent Ouray Agency police chief John McAndrews to Colorado, and he discovered that the Utes had built a hunting camp in southwest Routt County, where they traded with Lowell, and that he had also given them permission to hunt. McAndrews refuted Lowell and Johnson's claim, reporting that the Utes had "killed a great many deer but in every instance they had taken all the meat found nothing left but back bone even had taken feet and head in many instances."[31]

McAndrews told Waugh that "there is a rule among the Indians, not to kill deer indiscriminately old & young but to spare the young and does for future killings."[32] This practice of selective killing while hunting efficiently reflected the Utes' desire to hunt for the maximum without waste to maintain animals for future kills.

Indian Inspector Arthur Tinker lent further support to the Utes during his November 1890 survey. Tinker interviewed several cowboys who reported that Utes had shot "some game, but they did not see a single carcass left to decay." Instead of being ill-tempered, Tinker discovered that the Utes "were well disposed and peaceful." When Tinker quizzed the Utes, they told him "they were out hunting and did kill some game, but no meat was allowed to spoil[, but] . . . when the white men kill a deer, they take only the hind quarters and the skin, and leave the fore quarters on the ground to decay." The Utes added, "They seldom kill any thing but bucks, as they are larger, the skins are much better." Based on his inquiry, Tinker refuted Lowell's claims and concluded that the Utes did not understand why Lowell had made his false charges.[33]

Indian Service Efforts to Enforce a Hunting Ban

Although McAndrews and Tinker absolved the Utes of indiscriminate killing, acting commissioner of Indian affairs R. V. Belt ordered Uintah agent Robert Waugh to comply with Secretary Teller's 1885 off-reservation hunting ban. Belt assumed that the secretary's order had eliminated tribal inherent off-reservation hunting rights because "even if they had [hunting rights] the Secretary of the Interior has decided that the privilege of hunting outside of existing reservations . . . is the right to merely kill such game as may be necessary to supply the needs of the Indians." As a result, Belt reasoned that the Utes "have no treaty stipulations which can be construed as guaranteeing them the right to hunt outside of their reservation." At the same time he utilized Johnson's dubious 1890 report claiming Utes had lost their hunting right by slaughtering "wild animals in vast numbers for the hides only, and the abandonment of the carcasses without attempting to make use of them, is as much a violation of the treaty as an absolute prohibition on the part of the United States against the exercise of such privilege would be."[34]

Belt refuted the tribesmen's hunting claims, declaring that "the Indians . . . have no right to go into Colorado, or elsewhere outside of their reservation for the purpose of hunting, and they are liable to arrest and prosecution for violation of the laws of the State or Territory in which offenses may be committed." He concluded that "they may hunt as much as they choose within the limits of their own reservation, but they must not go beyond it for that purpose." He then ordered agent Waugh to "give no permits to any of your Indians to leave the reservation for such purpose."[35]

Belt's attempt to end White River and Uncompahgre Utes' off-reservation hunting trips failed. Ute hunters returned to Colorado in November 1891.

Game warden Eugene Taylor reported the Indians camping for four weeks between the White River and the Bear River and that they killed between "two to three thousand does and fawns. The bucks not averaging more than one in twenty." Taylor added that when "I find a party who have just arrived and attempt to send them back without an opportunity to hunt they at once understand the Game Laws and are only going to kill bucks."[36]

As a result of Taylor's complaints, Commissioner of Indian Affairs Thomas J. Morgan ordered agent Waugh to investigate Ute off-reservation hunting practices. Waugh interviewed local residents during the holidays and discovered "that the preponderance of testimony . . . is against the wanton and indiscriminate killing of deer for hides only, or any species of violence or depredations."[37] Rancher Joseph L. Still never saw the Utes kill does or fawns or take only deer hides.[38] Likewise, A. C. Hatch never found doe and fawn carcasses, only buck carcasses where the Utes hunted. Hatch explained the large animal kills, stating that "deer were very plentiful at that time and many white men were slaughtering them for the hides."[39] Waugh questioned United States Deputy Thomas H. Horn, who had traveled from the White River to the Ashley Valley, the region where the alleged slaughters had occurred. Horn stated, "I saw at least two hundred live deer on my trip . . . but did not see one carcass." Horn added that no ranchmen along the way reported any depredations.[40] Likewise, the Utes were "emphatic in their denials of any disturbance, any killing for hides only, or any violence . . . and that they were told that there was no objection to their hunting."[41]

Waugh freed the Utes from any indiscriminate deer slaughters and instead directed his inquiry toward local Colorado residents. He concluded that people were not opposed to the Ute hunts, otherwise the task of keeping them in Utah would be easier. In fact, game warden Taylor even gave one Ute a hunting permit. The Utes' desire to hunt for subsistence, coupled with their conviction of an inherent right to hunt, made it difficult to end their Colorado expeditions. Waugh opposed the hunts because trips exhausted the horses, and he feared the Utes' hunting would create more trouble because they did not observe state game laws.[42]

Trouble aside, the Utes entered northwest Colorado in the fall of 1892,[43] and Colorado Governor John L. Routt informed warden Morgan that a small band was killing game out of season.[44] Waugh refuted the governor's claim, reporting that Utes from the Uintah and Ouray Reservation had not committed any game depredations.[45] He added that "no one has [a] keener sense of the liability of trouble in connection with Indians hunting in Colorado than myself."[46] The following year a local rancher M. C. Portis claimed Utes moved their annual hunt to the headwaters of Roan Creek, Salt Creek, and Salt West—all near the Colorado-Utah border. Portis declared that territory as his home range and reported that Utes were "hunting and killing game contrary to the law of Colorado."[47] Uintah agent Major James Randlett discredited these rumors, writing that "reports from Colorado last year and [the] year before regarding slaughter of deer by indians [sic] of these agencies were false."[48]

In fact, Randlett discovered that Uncompahgre Utes never hunted on Roan Creek in 1893 but traveled directly east of the Ouray Reservation to Colorado where ranchers were friendly. Likewise, White River Utes entered the state along the Bear or Yampa Rivers. Even though the Utes were not in the vicinity of the alleged depredations, Randlett reported that in years past, he "had this matter to investigate and report upon, and have sent officers of this command over the ground where the deer slaughters were claimed to have been made for the purpose of obtaining reliable knowledge in the premises." He added "that the reports as published and circulated through the newspapers of the country were false; no evidence of ruthless slaughter has been found, no carcasses left upon the ground."[49]

Several factors explain this contradiction. First, local ranchers opposed the Ute hunting expeditions because the hunters competed with the ranchers for available grass, water, and wildlife resources. Blaming the Utes for an alleged deer slaughter forced local law enforcement officials to consider removing Ute hunters and thereby preserve these resources for local ranchers. Second, when white hunters slaughtered animals for hides, it was expedient to blame Ute hunters. Third, these fabricated stories illustrated the extent to which conservation-oriented state residents failed to understand Ute hunting practices in their arguments to end Ute Colorado deer hunts. As long as the Utes claimed an inherent sovereign right to hunt and hunted for maximum return, conflict was inevitable. Despite the potential for trouble, Randlett noted that the Utes "have never shown any disposition to make trouble about it." Hoping to prevent the crisis from escalating, he warned the Utes to remain in Utah, but the tribal hunters defended their decision, claiming "the U.S. government should protect them in their right to hunt upon the lands they gave up in Colorado."[50]

Unable to convince the Utes to stop their fall hunts in Colorado, in fall of 1895 Randlett asked General Alexander M. McCooke, commander of the Department of Arizona, for his opinion of the Ute's treaty rights. After reviewing Ute statutes and treaties, McCooke claimed the Utes had a right to hunt in Colorado, and this "legal right was recorded in the Statutes at large and that it was so guaranteed that he had no authority to alter or abrogate it."[51] McCooke's opinion only encouraged the Utes to hunt in Colorado.

When the 1895 Ute hunting season began, Randlett was confident that whites would start trouble because the Utes had remained peaceful during the past ten years of harassment. Randlett observed that "this great outcry against the wanton destruction of game is the same as has been made every Autumn the past ten years. I dare say it is just as unjustifiable now as it has invariably been in past years." The officer noted, "They will bring home for winter food the meat of the game they kill. They will put the hides to profit in the same way as other hunters do." Randlett concluded that the reason for this conflict "is there are too many Indian hunters to suit the interests of the white hunters on the ground."[52]

Tribal-State Hunting Conflicts Widespread in the West

By the end of the nineteenth century, tribal-state off-reservation hunting conflicts were familiar in the American West. For example, Bannock hunters left Idaho and entered Wyoming to hunt, and that dispute reached the United States Supreme Court in 1896. The court eliminated inherent Bannock off-reservation hunting rights in *Ward v. Race Horse,* claiming the creation of the state of Wyoming terminated tribal off-reservation hunting rights. The court ruled that tribesmen possessed off-reservation hunting rights on unoccupied lands until "the necessities of civilization did not require otherwise." Since western states entered the Union as equal members with other states, that equality gave each state the power to regulate game laws against tribal hunters and their hunting rights.[53]

Instead of litigating Ute off-reservation hunting rights, Commissioner of Indian Affairs William A. Jones and Uintah Indian agent William A. Beck decided that the *Race Horse* ruling applied to the Utes' inherent rights and ordered them to end their Colorado hunting trips in 1897. This administrative decision not only violated inherent tribal hunting rights, but now the Indian Service was cooperating with the state to terminate inherent Ute off-reservation hunting privileges. To illustrate this state-federal concurrence, Beck convened a council at Whiterocks where Colorado and Utah game officials informed the Utes to follow state game laws; if they failed to do so, state officials would arrest them.[54]

The Ute hunters refused to accept this threat, even though the 1897 Colorado hunting regulations were more strict than past laws. The season began August 1 and ended November 1, and each hunter was limited to only antlered animals and was restricted to one deer or elk or antelope.[55] Still, the Utes returned to Colorado to hunt in the fall of 1897,[56] but they heeded the game official's warnings by altering their past hunting patterns. Ungutsheone Starr and Snake Pete went to the Little Snake River and constructed protected hunting camps at higher elevations, away from any water, to make it harder to detect their presence. As soon as they began hunting, game warden W. R. Wilcox determined they were violating Colorado game laws, and the state game commissioner ordered that the Utes be arrested.[57]

To carry out the arrests, Wilcox assembled a citizens' posse on the morning of October 24, 1897, to accompany him to one camp. The Utes claimed the posse entered their camp with guns pointed at them, a fact the game warden dismissed. The Utes refused to surrender, and tempers flared. Quickly, deputy game wardens fired their weapons, killing two and wounding two other Ute hunters. The posse then retreated, and the Utes struck camp and returned to Utah without further repercussions or legal action.[58]

The skirmish was the culmination of a resource management conflict between the Utes and the state of Colorado over tribal access to mule deer. The tribesmen claimed an inherent property claim to hunt animals in Colorado, whereas the state asserted the sole privilege to control the disposition of all the animals, an authority superior to that of the tribe. Now Colorado's decision to use force to end the Utes' subsistence and market hunts escalated this resource conflict.[59] Ute hunters did not return to Colorado the following year, and the lack of deer created hardships at their Utah homes. Without deer, the Utes had fewer hides to sell and less venison to consume. Those shortages forced the hunters to ask the Uintah and Ouray agent for beef and flour, increasing their dependency on the United States.[60] The loss of one fall Colorado deer hunt deprived the White River and Uncompahgre Utes of a large portion of their self-sufficiency and independence. Sowawick, a leader of the White River Utes, asked for permission to return to Colorado to hunt deer in the summer of 1899.[61] The agent refused his request, and the White River Utes announced their intention to return to Colorado in early August.[62]

The White River Utes' decision to return to Colorado forced the agent to convene a tribal council in late July 1899. Old Tabby, a non-Colorado Ute, opposed Sowawick's decision to continue hunting in Colorado.[63] Sowawick and his followers took a hard line. He declared that "white people all the time get after Indian for killing deer. Deer don't belong to white men. They run wild in the mountains and don't belong to any one. . . . Deer are as much Indians as white man's." Speaking for the White River Utes, he stated that they would stay if all the whites left the Ashley Valley to make room for more deer.[64]

The council revealed the value the White River Utes placed on maintaining their inherent right to hunt deer herds, and Ute hunters left the Uintah Reservation in late September 1899 to hunt in Colorado.[65] Secretary of War Elisha Root immediately ordered the commander, Department of the Colorado, to prevent any disgruntled Utes from entering Colorado and "killing game in violation of the State law."[66] Instead of going to Garfield or Routt Counties, 200 tribesmen entered Rio Blanco County in early November 1899 and began hunting on Duck Creek, where a local game warden reported Utes "slaughtering game for hides."[67] Uintah agent H. P. Myton sent the agency police to the Ute hunting camp, and the police escorted the hunters back to the reservation. Myton refuted the sensational animal slaughter stories and reported that the Utes "do not kill game for the hides because they are too hungry." He added that he did not "believe Colorado game wardens are very truthful. I prefer to believe Indians."[68]

The Ute hunters returned to Colorado the following fall, and the agency police again escorted them back to the reservation. At the same time, sensational but spurious stories filled local papers. Myton blamed Colorado game wardens for manufacturing these lies, claiming once they heard of a few Utes hunting in the state, the wardens "immediately get to the nearest telegraph office and give the Associated Press the information that hundreds of Indians are slaughtering thousands of deer and elk for their hides, leaving the carcasses on the ground to rot." That simply was not true because "the Ute Indians need meat too badly to leave any of it on the ground to rot." To end the yellow journalism and potential conflict, Myton suggested that the wardens call him, and he would escort the hunters home.[69]

As the Utes moved toward their off-reservation hunting territories in 1900, Colorado Governor Charles S. Thomas wired the secretary of the interior that Utes had crossed the state line and reported that the agent was either negligent or privy to the invasion.[70] As usual, Myton sent the agency police to the Ute camps as soon as he heard they were in Colorado. The agent discovered that no more than twenty-five Utes had hunted in Rio Blanco County and that the local game wardens had told them to hunt at that location. In fact, a tribal policeman reported that one deputy warden even hunted with the Utes, and at no time did a game warden order the hunters to leave.[71]

The long history of sensational stories of Ute deer slaughters prodded outdoor writers to investigate. One author, Sumner W. Matteson, writing for *Outing,* traveled to Colorado at the turn of the twentieth century. Upon his arrival he interviewed individuals who made conservation a moral issue, informing him that "our game would be safe if only the Ute Indians could be kept in their reservations." Yet Matteson observed "ranchmen and pothunters . . . slaughtering large numbers in a single day, and if questioned, they credit two each to every member of the family or party, regardless of who may actually have done the killing." On the other hand, Matteson discovered that the Utes "killed large quantities of game, yet when it comes to needless waste of hides and meat, cruel neglect of wounded animals, and wilful [sic] violation of game laws, civil and moral, the Indian has a clean record as compared with the white man."[72]

Ute Hunting and Increased Law Enforcement

By now both Ute hunting practices and inherent hunting rights had become secondary concerns, as state and federal officials simply wanted to end the tribesmen's Colorado hunts. Uintah agent Myton took the lead and urged state officials to begin arresting tribal hunters. Myton hoped "the Colorado authorities would arrest some of the Indians, and punish them according to law, and that is what I have continually told the Indians would happen to them, but as it never does happen they begin to think I lie about it."[73] The agent suggested that the wardens should "lock all of them up."[74] Myton added that if "Colorado authorities make an example of a few of them," they would stop hunting.[75]

Myton's actions compromised Ute hunting rights and ensured that the 1901 Colorado Ute hunting season would be difficult. Not only did Myton's arrest position encourage conflict, but the state restricted the possession limit to only two bucks in 1899, thus ensuring that Ute hunters would violate the law.[76] As the local newspapers printed stories of indiscriminate slaughters of game animals, game wardens patrolled the Utah-Colorado border, threatening to kill Utes for crossing. Under these conditions, Myton refused to issue permits to the Utes, hoping to prevent trouble.[77]

With neither agency permits nor state licenses, Ute hunters entered Colorado and confronted restrictive game laws and law-abiding game wardens. In 1901 the Utes hunted past October 15, the end of the hunting season. Following Myton's suggestion, game warden George W. Fravert "arrested Eggelston, three Indians, three women and one boy, charging them with killing deer unlawfully in Rio Blanco County." The accused were brought to trial in Meeker, Colorado, without an interpreter, and a jury acquitted them at ten o'clock that night.[78] Two reasons explained the acquittal: local citizens either believed Utes had rights to hunt, or local citizens had also killed in excess of state game limits and released fellow violators.

After their release the Utes returned to jail, having no other place to sleep. Then "at 1 o'clock in the morning the deputy game warden woke the Indians and told them he was going to take them to the Agency." Instead he took them to the railroad station, and when the Utes discovered they had been tricked, they dropped their possessions and scattered. The game warden recaptured Eggleston, an elderly Ute, and took him to Glenwood Springs, Colorado. The Utes' property was either destroyed or stolen in this melee.[79]

Although Myton encouraged game wardens to arrest Ute hunters, he demanded fair treatment, which they did not receive. Myton discovered that "game wardens took the Indians from this country without any process of law." Since Eggleston's civil rights had been violated, Myton requested that the commissioner of Indian affairs seek assistance from the U.S. district attorney of Colorado for Eggleston's release. Myton added that "suit should be brought against the game warden to make him pay Eggleston and the other Indians damages."[80]

Warden Fravet's handling of Eggleston angered local Meeker, Colorado, residents.[81] Quickly, a citizen's group petitioned Justice Skankland, claiming the Ute hunting party was "held here in Meeker for nearly a week on a charge of violating the game laws." The citizen's petition continued: "On Saturday this case was tried and after a fair and impartial hearing before a jury the Utes were acquitted. This prosecution and trial was generally acquiesced in by our people." After the acquittal warden Fravert,

> With malice, cupidity and avarice in his soul . . . in violation of law and justice, took said Indians past and away from the nearest Justice, with the avowed intentions of taking said Indians before some Justice who did not know the foregoing facts, in the hope that the Indians, being unable to speak English, he, the said Fravert, could

> get an illegal and dishonest decision, without a fair trial, and thus deprive said Indians of their property to his own advantage.[82]

The Meeker citizens wanted the court to refuse Fravert's request for a warrant and release Eggleston.

There was also support for the Utes outside of Colorado. Abiel Leonard from Salt Lake City defended Ute hunting rights claiming "it was promised them that they should hunt deer in western Colorado for a definite number of years. Now that privilege is denied them by the Colorado state authorities."[83] Even agent Myton, who was responsible for encouraging the arrests, accused game wardens of "playing politics in this matter." He added that if Colorado offices would "cease trying to be sensational, we will get along much better and accomplish more."[84]

Since Eggleston was a ward Indian, the Department of the Interior asked the Department of Justice to obtain his release.[85] Acting Secretary of the Interior F. L. Campbell warned Governor Omman that "if game wardens are persecuting Indians, as appears in Eggleston's case, [the] matter will be fully investigated by that Department and this, and all necessary legal steps taken to put a stop to their illegal acts and to protect Indians."[86] U.S. Attorney for Colorado Earl M. Cranston obtained Eggleston's release from jail, but he was unable to return Eggleston's property. The state maintained possession of Eggleston's guns, and Colorado State Attorney Edward Taylor claimed Eggleston would have to return to identify his property. That would provide the state with an opportunity to issue a summons in the state's $600 civil suit against Eggleston.[87]

Despite the disastrous hunting season of 1901, Utes continued hunting in Colorado for several more years because their need for venison outweighed the threat of arrest and loss of property. They continued to hunt, claiming their inherent sovereign rights guaranteed them Colorado hunting privileges before they ever moved to Utah, and that was a powerful Ute argument. In 1904 Uintah and Ouray agent Captain Chalmers G. Hall reported that "no matter what means are used to prevent their going there, they will invariably enter by a round-a-bout way to gain their winter hunting." To end Ute hunts, Hall recommended an examination of their treaty right claim to hunt in Colorado and, if no right existed, to advise them to stop trespassing.[88]

Ward v. Race Horse and the Decline of Tribal Hunting in Colorado

Force was not necessary, as the Utes eventually stopped their Colorado deer hunts after the turn of the twentieth century. After decades of trouble, a majority of the White River Utes shunned Colorado and moved their fall hunts to Wyoming, and only a small group of Uncompahgres continued to hunt in Colorado. These hunters often avoided detection because their numbers were small. Uintah and Ouray supervisor William Rosenkrans was partially responsible for the reduced number of hunters by 1914. He convinced White River

Utes to stop traveling to Wyoming because of the rising costs, which included the high purchase price of a state hunting license and the great wear on their horses.[89]

Although fewer Utes hunted off the reservation, as late as 1914 White River and Uncompahgre Utes maintained "a firm belief that they have the right to hunt deer in the vicinity of Meeker and Douglas Creek, in Colorado." The Utes defended "their right upon promises which they claim were made to them by the [Ute] Commission [of 1880] which arranged with the Indians for their transfer from the Meeker district to this [Uintah and Ouray] reservation, and they claim that the [Ute] Commission verbally promised them that they should always have the right to hunt deer in Colorado."[90]

Nearly three decades of state-Ute conflict over northwest Colorado deer herds ended in 1915 when the White Mountain and Uncompahgre Utes ceased their Colorado hunts. At that point the Utes stopped exercising, but did not relinquish, their inherent right to hunt off-reservation in Colorado. The barriers thwarting Ute hunting included enforcement of state game conservation laws and U.S. encroachment against Ute inherent hunting rights by applying the Supreme Court's defense of state game laws in *Ward v. Race Horse* to Utes, which denied Ute hunters their inherent hunting rights. Nor was this an isolated state-tribal resource management conflict. Throughout the American West, late nineteenth and early twentieth century state game legislation came between tribal hunters and their animal property. These property clashes extended to other resources as well, restricting tribal access to subsistence and denying tribes their cultural callings, crafts, and professions. Hence the importance of tribal-state resource management conflicts to all.

References

1. Keith G. Hay, Gilbert N. Hunter, and Larry Robbins, *Big Game Management in Colorado, 1949–1958, a Ten Year Survey of Applied Big Game Management,* Technical Bulletin No. 8 (Denver: State of Colorado, Department of Game and Fish, December 1961): 9. See also *General Laws, State of Colorado* (1877): 484–485.
2. U.S. Congress, *Ute Indians in Colorado,* Senate Executive Document No. 31, 46th Cong., 2d sess, serial 1882 (1880): 16, 59, 60, 64, 67, 106, 124–125, 143–145, 149; quote on p. 106.
3. Sumner Matteson, "Red Man and White Man in Colorado's Hunting Fields," *Outing,* 38 (1901): 32; Joseph G. Jorgensen, *The Sun Dance Religion: Power for the Powerless* (Chicago: University of Chicago Press, 1972): 48–49.
4. F. Cohen, *Handbook of Federal Indian Law,* ed. Rennard Strickland (Charlottesville: Mickie Bobbs Merrill, 1982 ed.): 442–443.
5. 13 *Stat.* 673.
6. Donald Callaway, Joel Janetski, and Omer C. Stewart, "Ute," in *Great Basin,* ed. Warren L. D'Azevedo, vol. 11, *Handbook of North American Indians* (Washington, DC: Smithsonian Institution, 1986): 355.
7. Matteson, "Red Man and White Man," p. 32.

8. 18 *Stat.* (pt. 3): 37.
9. 21 *Stat.* 201.
10. Ora Brooks Peake, *The Colorado Range Cattle Industry* (Glendale, CA: Arthur H. Clark, 1937): 50–51.
11. Benjamin H. Eaton to Henry M. Teller, Washington, DC, February 12, 1885, 4580–1887, Letters Received by the Office of Indian Affairs, 1881–1907, RG [record group] 75, NA [National Archives].
12. H. M. Teller to James F. Gardner, February 17, 1885, 4580–1887, Letters Received by the Office of Indian Affairs, 1881–1907, RG 75, NA.
13. John T. Wallace to the Attorney General, October 23, 1886, 4580–1887, Letters Received by the Office of Indian Affairs, 1881–1907, RG 75, NA.
14. Annual Report of the Commissioner of Indian Affairs, *House Executive Document,* no. 1, 50th Cong., 1st sess., serial 2542 (1887): 77.
15. Matteson, "Red Man and White Man," p. 29.
16. Annual Report, 1887, pp. 76–78; Wilson Rockwell, *The Utes: A Forgotten People* (Denver: Sage, 1956): 182–183.
17. Annual Report, 1887, p. 80.
18. W. G. Swanson to Major Chaffee, November 12, 1888, 29793–1888, Letters Received by the Office of Indian Affairs, 1881–1907, RG 75, NA.
19. T. A. Burns to John H. Oberly, February 7, 1889, 4562–1889, Letters Received by the Office of Indian Affairs, 1881–1907, RG 75, NA.
20. Peake, *Colorado Range Cattle Industry,* pp. 48–52.
21. George Crook to Adjutant General, telegram, August 25, 1889, 24009–1889, Letters Received by the Office of Indian Affairs, 1881–1907, RG 75, NA.
22. R. Williams, Assistant Adjutant General to Adjutant General, telegram, August 23, 1889, 24218–1889, Letters Received by the Office of Indian Affairs, 1881–1907, RG 75, NA.
23. Acting Adjutant General Thomas Ward to Commanding General, Division of the Missouri, telegram, August 21, 1889, Letters Received by the Office of Indian Affairs, 1881–1907, RG 75, NA.
24. Peake, *Colorado Range Cattle Industry,* pp. 48–52. Peake's notes provide a sampling of newspapers stories. Also see Rockwell, *The Utes,* pp. 188–189, for a later yearly sampling of Ute hunting stories from the *Craig Courier.*
25. Governor of Colorado to the President, telegram, August 23, 1889, 23582–1889, Letters Received by the Office of Indian Affairs, 1881–1907, RG 75, NA.
26. R. Williams, Assistant Adjutant General to Adjutant General of the United States, telegram, August 24, 1889, 24008–1889, Letters Received by the Office of Indian Affairs, 1881–1907, RG 75, NA.
27. 2nd Lieutenant Samuel A. Smoke to Assistant Adjutant General, August 24, 1889, 25147–1889, Letters Received by the Office of Indian Affairs, 1881–1907, RG 75, NA.
28. John W. Lowell to Job A. Cooper, Governor, October 15, 1890, 32861–1889, Letters Received by the Office of Indian Affairs, 1881–1907, RG 75, NA.
29. Robert Waugh to the CIA, telegram, October 31, 1890, 33623–1890, Letters Received by the Office of Indian Affairs, 1881–1907, RG 75, NA.
30. A. B. Johnson to the Post Adjutant, November 6, 1890, 35736–1890, Letters Received by the Office of Indian Affairs, 1881–1907, RG 75, NA.

31. John McAndrews to Robert Waugh, November 7, 1890, 36252–1890, Letters Received by the Office of Indian Affairs, 1881–1907, RG 75, NA.
32. Robert Waugh to T. J. Morgan, November 14, 1890, 36252–1890, Letters Received by the Office of Indian Affairs, 1881–1907, RG 75, NA.
33. Arthur A. Tinker, Uintah and Ouray, Inspection, November 22, 1890, Reports of Inspection of the Field Jurisdictions of the Office of Indian Affairs, 1873–1900, roll 54, M1070, pp. 12–13.
34. R. V. Belt to Robert Waugh, November 20, 1890, 35736–1890, Letters Received by the Office of Indian Affairs, 1881–1907, RG 75, NA.
35. Ibid.
36. Eugene Taylor to Gordan Land, November 3, 1891, 15281–1892, Letters Received by the Office of Indian Affairs, 1881–1907, RG 75, NA.
37. Robert Waugh to T. J. Morgan, April 15, 1892, 15281–1892, Letters Received by the Office of Indian Affairs, 1881–1907, RG 75, NA.
38. Affidavit, Joseph L. Still, January 1, 1892, 15281–1892, Letters Received by the Office of Indian Affairs, 1881–1907, RG 75, NA.
39. Affidavit, A. C. Hatch, January 2, 1892, 15281–1892, Letters Received by the Office of Indian Affairs, 1881–1907, RG 75, NA.
40. Affidavit, Thomas H. Horn, December 31, 1891, 15281–1892, Letters Received by the Office of Indian Affairs, 1881–1907, RG 75, NA.
41. Robert Waugh to T. J. Morgan, April 15, 1892, 15281–1892, Letters Received by the Office of Indian Affairs, 1881–1907, RG 75, NA.
42. Ibid.
43. Robert Waugh to Commissioner of Indian Affairs Morgan, telegram, November 9, 1892, 40340–1892, Letters Received by the Office of Indian Affairs, 1881–1907, RG 75, NA.
44. John L. Routt to Commissioner of Indian Affairs, telegram, July 21, 1892, 26250–1892, Letters Received by the Office of Indian Affairs, 1881–1907, RG 75, NA.
45. Robert Waugh to T. J. Morgan, July 30, 1892, 28702–1892, Letters Received by the Office of Indian Affairs, 1881–1907, RG 75, NA.
46. Robert Waugh to T. J. Morgan, telegram, November 17, 1892, 41297–1892, Letters Received by the Office of Indian Affairs, 1881–1907, RG 75, NA.
47. M. C. Portis to Governor Waite, July 29, 1893, 31501–1893, Letters Received by the Office of Indian Affairs, 1881–1907, RG 75, NA.
48. J. Randlett to Commissioner of Indian Affairs, telegram, August 11, 1893, 29969–1893, Letters Received by the Office of Indian Affairs, 1881–1907, RG 75, NA.
49. James Randlett to General A. McCook, August 15, 1893, 31501–1893, Letters Received by the Office of Indian Affairs, 1881–1907, RG 75, NA.
50. Ibid.
51. James Randlett to Adjutant General, Department of Colorado, October 24, 1895, 44923–1895, Letters Received by the Office of Indian Affairs, 1881–1907, RG 75, NA.
52. Ibid.
53. *Ward v. Race Horse,* 163 U.S. 509 (1896); see also Cohen, *Handbook of Federal Indian Law,* pp. 469ff.
54. Report of a Commission Appointed by the Governor of Colorado to Investigate the Killing of Indians, October 24, 1897, 22877–1897, Letters Received by the Office of Indian Affairs, 1881–1907, RG 75, NA.

55. Matteson, "Red Man and White Man," p. 29.
56. *The Fifteenth Annual Report of the Executive Committee of the Indian Rights Association,* for the Year ending December 13, 1897 (Philadelphia: Office of the Indian Rights Association, 1898): 40–41.
57. Report of a Commission . . . Killing of Indians.
58. *Fifteenth Annual Report of the Executive Committee,* pp. 40–41; Rockwell, *The Utes.*
59. Report of a Commission . . . Killing of Indians, pp. 40–41. The Indian Rights Association entered the discussion arguing that the United States had to intervene and had only two options for ending this dilemma: one, negotiate a revision of state laws granting an exception for Indian hunters; two, purchase tribes' hunting rights.
60. E. R. Harper to Commissioner of Indian Affairs, July 27, 1899, 36981–1899, Letters Received by the Office of Indian Affairs, 1881–1907, RG 75, NA. Richard White developed this relationship between access to resources and tribal independence in *The Roots of Dependency: Subsistence, Environment, and Social Change Among the Choctaws, Pawnees, and Navajos* (Lincoln: University of Nebraska Press, 1983).
61. H. P. Myton to the Commissioner of Indian Affairs, July 10, 1899, 33990–1899, Letters Received by the Office of Indian Affairs, 1881–1907, RG 75, NA.
62. H. P. Myton to Commissioner of Indian Affairs, telegram, July 17, 1899, 33991–1899, Letters Received by the Office of Indian Affairs, 1881–1907, RG 75, NA.
63. E. R. Harper to Commissioner of Indian Affairs, July 27, 1899, 36981–1899, Letters Received by the Office of Indian Affairs, 1881–1907, RG 75, NA.
64. *Daily Tribune,* Salt Lake City, Utah (July 31, 1899).
65. H. P. Myton to Secretary of the Interior, telegram, September 23, 1899, 45514–1899, Letters Received by the Office of Indian Affairs, 1881–1907, RG 75, NA.
66. Elisha Root to Secretary of the Interior, October 13, 1899, 49560–1899, Letters Received by the Office of Indian Affairs, 1881–1907, RG 75, NA.
67. Charles S. Thomas to Secretary of the Interior, telegram, November 11, 1899, 54373–1899, Letters Received by the Office of Indian Affairs, 1881–1907, RG 75, NA.
68. H. P. Myton to Commissioner of Indian Affairs, telegram, November 14, 1899, 54573–1899, Letters Received by the Office of Indian Affairs, 1881–1907, RG 75, NA.
69. H. P. Myton to the Commissioner of Indian Affairs, September 29, 1900, 49157–1900, Letters Received by the Office of Indian Affairs, 1881–1907, RG 75, NA.
70. Charles S. Thomas to Secretary of the Interior, telegram, October 15, 1900, 51230–1900, Letters Received by the Office of Indian Affairs, 1881–1907, RG 75, NA.
71. H. P. Myton to the Commissioner of Indian Affairs, November 5, 1900, 55714–1900, Letters Received by the Office of Indian Affairs, 1881–1907, RG 75, NA.
72. Matteson, "Red Man and White Man," pp. 30–31.
73. H. P. Myton to the Commissioner of Indian Affairs, November 5, 1900, 55714–1900, Letters Received by the Office of Indian Affairs, 1881–1907, RG 75, NA.
74. H. P. Myton to Commissioner of Indian Affairs, telegram, October 16, 1900, 51263–1900, Letters Received by the Office of Indian Affairs, 1881–1907, RG 75, NA.
75. H. P. Myton to Commissioner of Indian Affairs, telegram, October 23, 1900, 52480–1900, Letters Received by the Office of Indian Affairs, 1881–1907, RG 75, NA. Although Myton encouraged the state to prosecute Ute hunters for violating games laws, he wrote the "Atty Gen'l of Colorado to day, asking him if it were legal for an Indian to kill a Deer with horns in the open season. I want to know if the Indians had

the same rights as a White man in this respect." H. P. Myton to Commissioner of Indian Affairs, September 27, 1901, 54554–1900, Letters Received by the Office of Indian Affairs, 1881–1907, RG 75, NA.

76. Matteson, "Red Man and White Man," pp. 29–30.
77. H. P. Myton to Commissioner of Indian Affairs, telegram, October 23, 1900, 52480–1900, Letters Received by the Office of Indian Affairs, 1881–1907, RG 75, NA.
78. H. P. Myton to the Commissioner of Indian Affairs, October 21, 1901, 61440–1901, Letters Received by the Office of Indian Affairs, 1881–1907, RG 75, NA.
79. Ibid.
80. Ibid.
81. H. P. Myton to Commissioner of Indian Affairs, telegram, October 21, 1901, 58735–1901, Letters Received by the Office of Indian Affairs, 1881–1907, RG 75, NA.
82. To Justice Skankland, Esq., J. P., and whomever it may concern, 61440–1901, Letters Received by the Office of Indian Affairs, 1881–1907, RG 75, NA.
83. Abiel Leonard to Bishop H.Y. Satterlee, October 29, 1901, 68825–1901, Letters Received by the Office of Indian Affairs, 1881–1907, RG 75, NA.
84. H. P. Myton to Commissioner of Indian Affairs, December 21, 1901, 74251–1901, Letters Received by the Office of Indian Affairs, 1881–1907, RG 75, NA.
85. F. L. Campbell to the Attorney General of the United States, October 23, 1901, 61440–1901, Letters Received by the Office of Indian Affairs, 1881–1907, RG 75, NA.
86. F. L. Campbell to James B. Orman, telegram, October 23, 1901, 61440–1901, Letters Received by the Office of Indian Affairs, 1881–1907, RG 75, NA.
87. Earl M. Cranston to the Attorney General, June 21, 1902, 41811–1902, Letters Received by the Office of Indian Affairs, 1881–1907, RG 75, NA.
88. C. G. Hall to Commissioner of Indian Affairs, December 12, 1904, 88835–1904, Letters Received by the Office of Indian Affairs, 1881–1907, RG 75, NA.
89. William Rosenkrans to Commissioner of Indian Affairs, November 19, 1914, Uintah and Ouray, 110006-14-115, Central Classified Files, RG 75, NA.
90. Ibid.

Chapter 2

Land Tenure and Agricultural Productivity in Indian Country

Terry L. Anderson

Although generally endowed with abundant land, coal, oil, and amenity resources, American Indians have not been able to capitalize on their resources and therefore remain at the bottom of the economic ladder. The 1990 census showed that 22 percent of Indian households on reservations had incomes of less than $5,000 per year, compared with 6 percent for the overall U.S. population. At the other end of the income distribution, only 8 percent of reservation households had incomes greater than $35,000, compared with 18 percent for the nation as a whole. In 1990, 31 percent of Indian households received public assistance income, and 23 percent were below the poverty line.

Traditional explanations for the lack of economic growth among Indians have focused on insufficient access to capital markets, low levels of education, and cultural constraints. Hence government policies to alleviate poverty have focused on standard economic development strategies. These have included attempts to augment both the physical and human capital stocks, with little discernable impact on economic development. Efforts have also been made to acquire additional tribal land and to litigate or negotiate water rights disputes in the hope that more resources will enhance the economic base.

Because none of these traditional development approaches has been effective, economists have begun to look at the underlying cultural, political, and legal institutions that determine incentives of individuals and groups on reservations.[1] One of the first studies to do this considered Indian cattle ranching efficiency. After considering typical economic variables that might affect efficiency, Ronald Trosper concluded that "land tenure and other institutional problems underlie Indian difficulties attaining the operating scale of whites in ranching" and called for further research to "investigate the nature of these relationships rather than focus upon Indian abilities and goals."[2] To date, however, few have answered Trosper's call.

To do so requires considering the institutional milieu that has developed on reservations since their establishment. Once Indians were relegated to reservations, the white man's government assumed the role of trustee for the Indian wards, with the Bureau of Indian Affairs (BIA) acting as the government's agent. Initial federal policies were aimed at assimilating the Indians into an agrarian economy by allotting parcels of land to individual Indians in an attempt to develop private ownership on reservations. Later policies, however, halted the privatization process and locked reservation lands into a complex mosaic of land tenure that significantly affects productivity.

This chapter examines the importance of land tenure arrangements to sustainable resource use. It begins with a brief history of Indian institutions from pre-Columbian times to the reservation era in an effort to show that land tenure has always been an important part of Indian culture. It then turns to an empirical analysis that considers how land tenure and especially federal government trust constraints influence agricultural productivity. This analysis measures the impact of land tenure using cross-sectional data from large western reservations. The data suggest that trusteeship under the BIA raises the costs of organizing agricultural productivity sufficiently to thwart production and discourage sustainable economic development. The concluding section suggests that land tenure and trusteeship may also explain why other resources, from minerals to wild animals, are not generating much economic return on most reservations.

Pre-Reservation Land and Water Rights

Where resources were abundant, Indians acted rationally, worrying little about who owned the resources and using them extensively. It was common for Indians such as the Choctaw, Iroquois, and Pawnee to clear land for farming by cutting and burning forests. Once cleared, fields were farmed extensively until soil fertility was depleted; then they cleared new lands and started the process again.[3] From New England to the Southwest, wherever Indian populations were dense and farming was intense, deforestation was common. Indeed, the mysterious departure of the Anasazi from the canyons of southeastern Utah in the thirteenth century may have been caused by the depletion of wood supplies used for fuel.[4]

When land became more scarce and required investments to maintain productivity, however, ownership and use changed markedly. Because agricultural land required investments and boundaries could be easily marked, exclusive land use privileges evolved. Unlike private land ownership as we know it today, these property rights were usually held by families or clans rather than individuals. But they still provided the incentive for sustainable use.

For example, families among the Mahican Indians in the Northeast possessed hereditary rights to use well-defined tracts of garden land along the rivers. Europeans recognized this ownership, and deeds of white settlers indicate that they often approached lineage leaders to purchase this land. Prior to European contact, other Indian tribes recognized Mahican ownership of these lands by not trespassing.[5] Away from the rivers, however, where the value of land for crops was low, it was not worth establishing ownership. As one historian put it, "No one would consider laying out a garden in the rocky hinterlands."[6]

In the Southeast, where Indians engaged in settled agriculture, private ownership of land was common. "The Creek town is typical of the economic and social life of the populous tribes of the Southeast," wrote historian Angie Debo. "Each family gathered the produce of its own plot and placed it in its own storehouse. Each also contributed voluntarily to a public store which was kept in a large building in the field and was used under the direction of the town chief for public needs."[7]

The Omaha tribe in what is now Nebraska cultivated private garden patches along streams. Plots were allocated on the basis of occupancy, and "as long as a tract was cultivated by a family no one molested the crops or intruded on the ground."[8] When the Omaha obtained the horse, as did other Plains Indians, they became more nomadic, abandoning most crop cultivation. Their tradition of private garden plots, however, carried over into the reservation era when the tribe again allotted land to families and clans.

The Havasupai in the Southwest also considered ownership of farmland private as long as it was in use, and the Hopi Indians assigned to the various matrilineal clans of the village exclusive rights to the fields. According to Edward Kennard, "Each clan allotment was marked by boundary stones, set up at the corners of the fields, with symbols of the clans painted on them."[9] Another anthropologist noted that clan lands were marked "by numerous boundary stones . . . placed at the corners and junction points [and] engraved on their faces with symbols of the appropriate clan."[10] The clan allotments were usually assigned to the women and became associated with a specific household through inheritance. To spread the risk associated with lack of rain or sudden flooding, each clan generally had plots in more than one location: "Dispersal of the lands of each clan over a number of sites is of very great practical importance since it reduces the risk of crop failure; where one group of fields may be washed out there remains the chance that the others may be spared."[11]

The Hopi and Zuni branches of the Pueblo Indians living in the Colorado River watershed also developed property rights reflecting their environment and production techniques. The Hopi made use of periodic flooding of their lands during the summer months by building small stone walls to check the water flow, thereby increasing soil moisture but preventing flooding of crops. Because flood control and irrigation systems required extensive capital investment and provided economies of scale, construction was communal. Where water flowed constantly from springs on family-owned land and required little or no investment, water rights were privately owned. Florence Ellis wrote of the Isleta:

> Technically the irrigated farmlands belonged to the Pueblo as a whole. Through assignment by the Isleta governor, an individual usually obtained a single acre of land [and the necessary water rights], but if the governor or his captains found that the assignee left the land within a year or did not farm it, the plot and accompanying water rights were returned to Pueblo possession and reassigned.[12]

Fruit and nut trees, which required long-term investment and care, were privately owned and usually inherited.[13] "So important were the piñon resources that groves of trees were considered family property in several locations" within the Great Basin area of the West, said an anthropologist.[14] In one case a Northern Paiute reflected that his father had "paid a horse for a certain piñon-nut range," suggesting that the property rights were valuable and tradable.[15]

Among Indians in California, families owned piñon, mesquite, screw-bean trees, and a few wild-seed patches, with ownership "marked off by lines of rocks."[16] Although permission to gather food was sometimes given during times of abundance, trespass was not tolerated, with "the owner rebuking him [the trespasser] with such words as, 'Don't pick pine nuts here! They are not yours, but mine.' "[17] Noted conservationist John Muir reported that the owner of a piñon tree killed a white man for felling his tree.[18] Contrary to popular myths that precontact Indians did not understand the idea of land ownership and based their conservation practices on a reverence for nature, the anthropological data document that land tenure systems were an integral part of sustainable resource use. Prior to European contact, Indian land tenure systems varied considerably, "ranging from completely or almost completely communal systems to systems hardly less individualistic than our own with its core of fee simple tenure."[19] The degree of private ownership reflected the scarcity of land and the difficulty or ease of defining and enforcing rights. Julian H. Steward concluded that "truly communal property was scant" among American Indians.[20]

The Reservation Era

After Indians were placed on reservations but before the bureaucratic controls on land tenure became effective, Indians were mostly left to their own devices. Without abundant buffalo, tribes had little choice but to provide for themselves with the resources at hand. To do so required institutional changes compatible with settled agriculture rather than those that had evolved for the nomadic buffalo hunters. As Alvin Josephy noted, "Particularly those who had traditionally been nomadic hunters and gatherers, could not or would not become farmers overnight; they had neither the cultural background nor the necessary training."[21] Similarly, Douglas Hurt argued that "only the most agricultural tribes, such as the Cherokee, showed much aptitude and success in farming once removed west of the Mississippi River. The tribes that had no agricultural traditions, such as the Sioux, found the sedentary farming life culturally unacceptable."[22] Where there was an agricultural tradition, "The Indian concept of land tenure enabled various villages to make the best possible use of the [reservation] land in order to meet their own specific needs."[23]

A combination of necessity and a prior tradition of agricultural practices, however, made the transition easier than might have been expected. Leonard Carlson observed:

> Once a tribe was confined to a reservation, it needed to find a land tenure system suitable to the new environment. On the closed reservations, the system that evolved was one of use rights. Typically, the [BIA] agent and members of a tribe recognized individual's title to animals and, where farming was practiced, a family's claim to the land it worked. . . . What is remarkable is how similar this system of land tenure was to that which existed among agricultural tribes before being confined to reservations.[24]

Under the new tenure arrangements, reservation Indians were discovering how to farm in their new economic environment. Given their agricultural heritage and their experience with trading, it is not surprising that the Five Civilized Tribes adapted first. Thomas Wessel found that by 1877 these tribes "produced over 69 percent of the wheat grown on Indian reservations, 81 percent of the corn, and over 43 percent of the vegetables."[25]

Many other tribes, including some of the more nomadic, also adopted land tenure systems compatible with agricultural production. According to Carlson, the Santee Sioux, the Yakima, and the Flathead "all had recognized individual property rights in land before allotment."[26] The Sioux bands on the eastern edge of the Plains came from an agricultural heritage and were able to adapt quickly to the nomadic horse culture. Carlson found that the Yankton Dakota (Sioux) Indians, whose reservation was established in the late 1850s, experienced a "growth of farming by individual Indians so that by 1878 farming was conducted by 'each man to himself on his own plot of ground.' "[27] Acreage cultivated by all Indians except those in the Five Civilized Tribes

> Rose from less than 117,267 acres in 1875 to 379,974 acres by 1896. Similarly, a five-year moving average of the output of grain . . . shows that Indian grain output also grew . . . by 5.5 percent per year from 1875 to 1895 and by 3.1 percent for the whole period from 1875 to 1904. . . . These data show that after 1875, many Indians who were members of tribes without extensive agricultural traditions did try to become farmers.[28]

The 1900 U.S. Census concluded that "notwithstanding the numerous difficulties, there has been steady progress toward civilization in the past decade on most reservations. A number of tribes are now peaceable, self-supporting agriculturists, wearing citizens' clothing, and able to speak the English language."[29]

Indian cattle ranching also evolved to enable them to make what they could from their limited land resources. Given the economies of scale in grazing and a tradition of private ownership of horses, it made sense to have individual ownership of the livestock and common ownership of the land. As a result, Carlson found that on the Blackfeet Reservation in Montana "the tradition of individual ownership was so well established that Indians resisted government efforts to establish common herds from 1910 to 1920." He quotes from John C. Ewers who reported that "the fullbloods, who had always considered livestock in terms of individual possession, showed little interest in the tribal herd. They acted as if it belonged to someone else."[30] The 1900 U.S.Census stated that Indians on the Standing Rock Reservation "have begun to realize that their support must come from their cattle, and they give them great care, stock raising being even now their principal pursuit, although most of them grow a few small crops in addition to cutting large quantities of wild grass."[31] Carlson concluded that "the average number of head per family ranged from 16 to nearly 40. These figures do not indicate that Indian cattlemen were self-sufficient but they do indicate a healthy beginning."[32]

This evidence confirms that the Indians who adapted to the often harsh conditions of the Plains and to the introduction of the horse were equally capable of adapting to agriculture on reservations. Certainly, there was resistance to agriculture, but as Ralph Linton noted, "It is an open question how far this resistance stemmed from the aboriginal culture and how far from the fact that most of the lands assigned in severalty were unsuited for farming and insufficient in amount to support individual families."[33] Unfortunately, the bottom-up Indian adaptation that started soon after reservations were established came to an abrupt halt with the Allotment Act of 1887.

The Reservation Tenure Mosaic

After an initial period of bottom-up adaptation, the federal government took control from the top and played a pivotal role in molding land institutions. Under a guardianship model, the federal government tried to correct what it saw as imperfections in the institutional structure on Indian reservations. Reformers saw allotment of small parcels of land to individual Indians as the only way to "Americanize" the Indian. If Indians were to be Americanized, the "friends of the Indian" thought they would have to abandon their communal way of life: "What the allotment debaters meant by communism was that title to the land was dependent on its use and occupancy. They meant vaguely the cooperatives and clannishness—the strong communal sense—of barbaric life."[34] Overcoming this communism meant adopting a system of private property rights on reservations similar to that evolving at the time under the Homestead Act.

On February 8, 1887, the General Allotment Act, also known as the Dawes Act, was passed, giving the president of the United States authority to assign parcels of land on reservations to individual Indians. Although a few tribes were exempted from the legislation, most found themselves with the head of the household being assigned 160 acres. Once allotted, the lands were originally to be held in trust by the federal government for twenty-five years, at the end of which time the Indian was to receive full fee simple title to the land. A 1906 amendment to the act authorized the secretary of interior to issue fee patents immediately if any Indian was deemed "competent and capable of managing his or her affairs." Fred McChesney described the government's "radical switch" from its paternalistic role. "From 1913 to 1920 issuance of fee patents became the top priority of the Indian Office. Between 1917 and 1920 [just three years], there were 10,956 patents issued, compared with 9,894 issued between 1906 and 1916 [ten years]."[35]

When fee simple title to allotted lands or surplus lands (those left after all individual Indians got their 160 acres) passed to individuals, the land was no longer considered "Indian land"—even if it was owned by an Indian. Hence the total amount of Indian land declined dramatically as fee simple patents were issued. Measured in terms of privatization, the General Allotment Act was incredibly effective; measured in terms of Indian ownership, however, it was a disaster. According to Wilcomb Washburn, "About 60 percent of this land passed out of Indian hands."[36]

Allotments ended in 1934 with the Indian Reorganization Act (IRA), with which the federal government locked into place a mosaic of land tenure that plagued reservation agricultural productivity. To stop the hemorrhage of Indian lands into private lands, the IRA locked allotted but unreleased lands and tribal lands into a perpetual trust status with the federal government as the trustee.

Between 1890 and 1933, Indian lands held in trust by the federal government declined from 104.3 million acres to 52.7 million acres. Of more than 54 million acres of Indian land in 1987, 77 percent was tribal trust, 20 percent was individual trust, and 2 percent was government owned.[37] In the set of thirty-nine large reservations discussed later, 47 percent of reservation acreage is in fee simple ownership (owned by either Indians or non-Indians) not subject to BIA or tribal authority. The data in Table 2.1 show the number of total reservation acres (Indian Country), as well as the number of acres of tribal trust, individual trust, and fee simple land for these thirty-nine large reservations.

The Legacy of Allotment

The result of this top-down history of land tenure evolution is a mosaic of ownership that fits into three basic tenure categories: (1) *fee simple,* under which individual Indians and non-Indians own the land, can determine its use, and can transfer it to new owners without BIA supervision; (2) *individual trust,* under which land has been allotted to individual Indians but remains held in

Table 2.1—Acreage in Various Ownership Classifications for Selected Reservations

State / *Reservation*	*Total*[a]	*Tribal Trust*[b]	*Individual Trust*[c]	*Fee Simple*
Washington				
Colville	1,367,761	1,028,339	39,940	299,475
Yakama	1,402,469	918,544	222,937	260,965
Oregon				
Umatilla	174,800	19,273	68,612	86,792
Warm Springs	659,012	587,794	51,105	15,441
Idaho				
Fort Hall	522,600	269,655	220,313	0
Coeur d'Alene	345,750	22,470	39,237	284,043
Nez Perce	805,815	36,949	47,244	721,612
Montana				
Blackfeet	1,546,950	312,879	628,822	605,113
Crow	2,347,177	414,263	1,095,373	836,140
Flathead	1,287,941	609,365	42,640	635,213
Rocky Boys	127,235	108,325	0	18,910
Fort Peck	2,162,288	395,703	510,093	1,246,492
Northern Cheyenne	471,415	321,363	115,585	34,466
Wyoming				
Wind River	2,195,940	1,794,758	93,413	306,473
North Dakota				
Fort Berthold	797,505	70,997	351,469	374,875
Standing Rock	2,306,098	356,037	441,211	1,508,850
Fort Totten	255,203	16,228	36,635	202,172
South Dakota				
Cheyenne River	2,872,342	959,687	444,901	1,435,993
Crow Creek	310,293	65,018	60,425	184,850
Lower Brule	245,956	106,135	22,597	112,694
Pine Ridge	2,779,200	708,559	1,070,058	998,263
Rosebud Sioux	1,624,202[d]	529,575	429,575	664,631
Yankton	406,045	16,706	19,852	369,487
Sisseton	978,465	17,544	90,518	870,112
Nebraska				
Omaha	186,591	9,596	17,196	159,799
Santee	111,844	6,943	2,415	102,486
Winnebago	111,876	4,321	23,282	84,273
Kansas				
Kickapoo	13,696	3,659	3,124	6,913
Arizona				
Colorado River	269,918[d]	264,048	5,870	0
Gila River	347,474	269,128	97,642	18
Nevada				
Duck Valley	286,816[d]	289,819	0	0
Walker River	323,406	313,690	8,572	8,572
Utah				
Goshute	109,293[d]	109,133	80	0

continued on next page

Table 2.1—*continued*

State *Reservation*	*Total*[a]	*Tribal Trust*[b]	*Individual Trust*[c]	*Fee Simple*
Utah (contd.)				
Uintah and Ouray	4,337,393	1,007,278	14,318	3,375,795
New Mexico				
Isleta Pueblo	211,981	211,037	0	36
Colorado				
Southern Ute	629,313	307,562	2,408	316,241
Ute Mountain	579,073	307,562	8,578	0
Oklahoma				
Osage	1,435,114	734	168,119	1,264,895
Minnesota				
Fond Du Lac	78,958	4,701	16,185	57,947

Notes: [a]Total acres are estimated from reservation maps using a computerized planimeter. For reservations where all land is held in trust, total acres are calculated as the sum of tribal and individual trust.

[b]Tribal trust and individual trust acreages are taken from the U.S. Department of Interior, Bureau of Indian Affairs (1987) Natural Resources Information Service (NRIS) data.

[c]Fee simple lands are the difference between total acres and total NRIS acres.

[d]In cases where there is no fee simple ownership, total acreage is calculated as the NRIS estimate of total Indian land. Total acres do not necessarily equal the sum of the three classes of ownership because government and other owners are not included.

trust by the BIA as a check on individual decisions; and (3) *tribal trust,* under which land is owned by the tribe but held in trust by the BIA as a check on tribal decisions. Because these three tenure arrangements have very different implications for agricultural productivity, they offer an opportunity for measuring the impact of ownership institutions on reservations.

Contrary to the notion that reservations belong to Indian tribes, much of the land is privately owned in fee simple tenure nearly identical to private land outside the reservation. This fee simple land owned by both Indians and non-Indians provides a benchmark against which we can measure the impact of alternative institutions on agricultural productivity. Fee simple lands do not fall under the trust authority of the BIA and hence are essentially the same as fee simple lands outside Indian Country.[38] These lands can be freely alienated by sale or inheritance to either Indians or non-Indians, thus substantially reducing control by the tribe or the Bureau of Indian Affairs. As the data in Table 2.1 show, fee simple lands constitute a substantial fraction of Indian Country.

Fee simple land tenure is a norm against which other tenures were measured because fee simple landowners have nearly exclusive use rights and face the fewest constraints on alienation. Furthermore, because the land can be sold or otherwise encumbered, fee simple ownership allows the landowner to use land as collateral in the capital market. With fewer constraints on contracting, land thus owned is subject to lower costs of organizing inputs compared with other land tenures. Fee simple owners will therefore likely employ the optimal amounts of land, labor, and capital and maximize the net value of output.

In contrast to fee simple land owned by both Indians and non-Indians, Indian land includes only that portion of the reservation owned by the tribe or individual Indians but held in trust by the Bureau of Indian Affairs. Generally, under its trust authority the BIA grants or denies permission to change land use, approves lease arrangements, and agrees to capital improvements. The question addressed here is whether this added layer of bureaucracy inhibits productivity.

Allotment had three major effects on reservation land tenure. First, it broke up contiguous tribal land holdings by allocating land to individual Indians and allowing settlement of tribal lands by non-Indians. Second, as whites settled tribal lands and individual allottees gained fee simple title to their allotments, land owned in fee simple became interspersed with land held under trusteeship. Third, when the allotment policy ended in 1934, more than 10 million allotted acres—nearly 20 percent of total Indian lands—were left in the peculiar legal status of individual trust, meaning they were owned by individual Indians but held in trust by the BIA. Because the 1934 act prevented the alienation of trust land, these allotments could not be sold out of trust status, taxed, or subjected to legal encumbrance such as liens or mortgages.

Trust status complicates land use decisions in many ways. First, it restricts the way individual trust lands can be passed on to heirs. Under the 1887 Allotment Act, if an allottee died before obtaining fee title, the allotment could not be willed but had to pass to the heirs according to the rules of inheritance in the state where the land was located. Whereas this was changed later to allow estate inheritance through a will, the will may be set aside if the decedent's family is not included.[39] Because of these heirship provisions, reservation allotments are held by so many owners in common that the Indians are helpless to make effective use of their property. By 1960, 12 million acres of allotted lands were in heirship status, with half of that owned by six or more heirs. As ownership becomes more divided, the costs of coordinating production and selling or leasing land increase dramatically.[40] The story one allottee told the House Committee on Interior and Insular Affairs is illustrative of the problems that arise with fractionation:

> My sister's allotment was 80 acres. She dies and my dad, a white man, was willed the land. He dies and all his children fell heir. His share was 13440/20160. We had that probated in court—four children share is 960/20160, and cousins one share 270/20160, one share 305/20160, five shares 128/20160, one share 320/20160, one share 140/20160, seven shares 35/20160 and these last seven are no

> relation only that this man was once a brother-in-law and they are the ones that won't sign so that we can have a 100 percent signers [the requirement for sale or lease of allotments].[41]

Land ownership record keeping becomes more complicated each day because of the heirship problem, as this BIA report suggests:

> There are over 200,000 surface tracts of individually owned trust land with an average tract ownership of ten undivided interest owners. This means there are over 2,000,000 separate undivided interests to keep track of. Ownership in some tracts is so complicated that owners own an undivided interest in which the common denominator is in the quintillionths. If such tracts were leased, some undivided-interest owners would receive a fraction of a penny. This kind of ownership either makes it impossible to develop such tracts or severely restricts the development since all owners have to be contacted.[42]

These heirship restrictions generally mean that each allotment is inherited by a large number of individuals, each of whom has a share in land use decisions. This in turn makes it difficult to establish who will manage the land and fractionates the returns to such an extent that each heir has little incentive to monitor management. As Ethel Williams observed, "Unless this pattern can be reversed, all Indian allotments inevitably will have an astronomical number of owners."[43]

Tribal trust lands differ from individual trust lands because title is held by an organized tribe subject to allocation by the tribal governing unit and to the trust authority of the federal government.[44] Management of tribal lands varies considerably by reservation depending on the collective decisionmaking mechanism used by the tribe. In most cases a tribal council is the general governing body that ultimately decides how tribal lands will be used. How well these councils enhance the welfare of Indians depends mostly on constitutional and cultural constraints. This fractionation problem applies equally to tribally owned lands unless tribal governance structures can overcome the problems of collective management.

Trust status reduces the ability of individuals and tribes to alienate their land, which in turn reduces the efficiency of use for several reasons. First and perhaps most important, the restriction on alienation or other encumbrances constrains the use of land as collateral in the capital market. Banks making loans cannot easily sell the land to collect on defaulted loans, and even the government cannot take the land in return for delinquent taxes. Given the constraints on alienation, the capital deficiency recognized by Trosper is more appropriately viewed as the result of trust restrictions.[45]

Second, the cost of alienating land also prevents the land from being held in its optimal configuration, thus lowering the value of the land and agricultural productivity. When allotments were made, they tended to be small, usually less than 320 acres. In nearly all types of modern agriculture, this parcel size is too small for optimal use with other inputs. In Montana, for instance, members of the Blackfeet Tribe were allotted 320 acres. Today in this region the average farm is greater than 1,500 acres. When ownership patterns do not coincide with the optimal size production unit, lease or sale is required to consolidate land holdings into the appropriate configuration. If parcels could be bought, sold, or leased, this problem would be overcome through market transactions, but restrictions on alienation inhibit such exchanges. Fee simple land can be easily alienated, but the BIA must supervise and approve all leases of Indian land, thus raising the costs of organizing optimal farming units. Because allotments were generally small compared with today's optimal farm size, the scale of farming on restricted fee lands will be too small, thus reducing output per acre.[46]

Tribal trust tenure also constrains organizing inputs and restricts agricultural productivity relative to fee simple lands. As with individual trust lands, it is difficult to use tribal lands as collateral in capital markets except through federal government programs where eligibility for loans is generally less restrictive than in commercial credit markets. The collateral problem, however, is likely to be less severe for tribes than for individuals because tribes often have other alienable resources they can use as collateral.

More crucial to productivity on tribal trust lands is the extent to which tribal governance structures are able to prevent the power of tribal government from being used to encourage wealth transfers as opposed to enhanced productivity. Instead of maximizing the income stream from tribal lands, government officials could allow political patronage to determine land use. For example, Gary Libecap and Ronald Johnson concluded that the politics of the Navajo Tribal Council and its grazing committees have essentially legislated "a common property condition for the range" wherein access is open to all tribal members and overuse occurs.[47]

The general hypothesis tested here is that, all else equal, the gross value of agricultural output per acre will be lower for individual trust and tribal trust land relative to fee simple land because tenure constraints influence the costs of organizing agricultural production.[48] Because the costs of organizing production under fee simple tenure are lower than under individual or tribal trust tenure, fee simple owner's choice of a land, labor, and capital mix is taken as approximately optimal.

In general, trust lands tend to be used in relatively low-valued uses, such as grazing, rather than in higher-valued uses such as row crops, small grains, and horticulture. The 1987 *Natural Resources Information System* summary for all reservations showed that 82 percent of Indian land was in grazing earning $3.48 per acre. In contrast, 1 percent was in row crops earning $380 per acre, 2 percent in small grains earning $91 per acre, 1 percent in forage-hay-pasture earning $145 per acre, and 0.10 percent in horticulture earning $497 per acre.[49]

A more systematic test of the impact of tenure was conducted using data from the BIA's *Natural Resource Information System.* This source contains information on acres devoted to a variety of land use classes, acres under Indian and non-Indian management, land quality, and value of products grown on Indian land for a large number of reservations. By combining these data for 1987 with data from the 1987 U.S. Agricultural Census for counties encompassing the reservations, we can compare agricultural output for Indian trust land with fee simple land for thirty-nine large western reservations.[50] The estimate of the value of agricultural output from Indian land includes row crops, small grains, forage-hay-pasture, horticulture, native hay, and grazing. To obtain per acre value, this total value is divided by Indian acres with agricultural potential.[51]

The data in Table 2.2 compare the value of output per acre for individual trust and tribal trust land with the value per acre of cultivated crops (excluding grazing and cattle production) grown on all farms in surrounding counties. The latter was used because the BIA collects no data for fee simple land on reservations. Therefore a weighted average for all private farms in the counties encompassing the reservation is used as a proxy for fee simple lands on reservations.[52] The ratio of trust land output to fee simple land output shows that on average, trust lands are about half as productive as fee simple lands, and the difference is statistically significant.[53]

The extent to which the value of reservation output declines as the fraction of the reservation land subject to trust constraints rises was determined using regression analysis.[54] Controlling for other variables, the per-acre value of agricultural output was found to be 85 to 90 percent lower on tribal trust land than on fee simple land and 30 to 40 percent lower on individual trust land than on fee simple land.[55] Collective management of tribal trust land need not reduce productivity if tribal governance structures can prevent "those who exercise the legitimate powers of government from using that power to transfer wealth."[56] The data suggest, however, that tribal governments are not able to constrain the transfer power.

The Impact of Trusteeship on Other Resources

Further support for the conclusion that trust tenure raises the costs of organizing inputs and reduces resource productivity is provided by Matthew Krepps's study of American Indian forestry. He hypothesized that tribal control of Indian forestry resources would result in higher worker productivity, lower costs, and higher incomes relative to BIA control because tribal control "shifts the onus of accountability for tribal forestry onto the tribes themselves without necessitating any increase in federal appropriations."[57] Indians can obtain control of their forestry resource through P.L. 638, the Indian Self-Determination and Education Assistance Act passed by Congress in 1975. This law allows

Table 2.2—Average Value of Agricultural Output Per Acre, 1987

State *Reservation*	*County Value*	*Trust Value*	*Ratio of Trust Value to County Value*
Washington			
Colville	$ 292.19	$ 7.15	0.02
Yakama	857.45	24.72	0.03
Oregon			
Umatilla	143.36	43.06	0.30
Warm Springs	174.36	2.01	0.01
Idaho			
Fort Hall	132.64	102.79	0.77
Coeur d'Alene	115.80	203.05	1.75
Nez Perce	101.53	87.40	0.79
Montana			
Blackfeet	45.10	11.61	0.26
Crow	46.17	22.06	0.48
Flathead	44.69	9.46	0.21
Rocky Boys	39.54	19.64	0.50
Fort Peck	27.33	13.80	0.50
Northern Cheyenne	40.41	7.50	0.19
Wyoming			
Wind River	54.80	3.76	0.07
North Dakota			
Fort Berthold	28.83	16.52	0.57
Standing Rock	18.49	19.86	1.07
Fort Totten	41.00	15.22	0.37
South Dakota			
Cheyenne River	21.21	0.00	0.00
Crow Creek	39.35	39.68	1.01
Lower Brule	38.80	39.26	1.01
Pine Ridge	28.32	10.12	0.36
Rosebud Sioux	24.92	11.19	0.45
Yankton	45.50	42.93	0.94
Sisseton	53.01	37.22	0.70
Nebraska			
Omaha	100.23	156.34	1.55
Santee	38.99	35.73	0.92
Winnebago	97.79	154.86	1.58
Kansas			
Kickapoo	98.16	47.75	0.49
Arizona			
Colorado River	1,152.61	266.83	0.23
Gila River	577.00	239.90	0.42
Nevada			
Duck Valley	95.09	6.06	0.06
Walker River	94.18	3.77	0.04
Utah			
Goshute	37.39	1.71	0.05

continued on next page

Table 2.2—*continued*

State / *Reservation*	*County Value*	*Trust Value*	*Ratio of Trust Value to County Value*
Utah (contd.)			
Uintah-Ouray	24.04	8.02	0.33
New Mexico			
Isleta Pueblo	163.94	4.85	0.03
Colorado			
Southern Ute	21.02	17.72	0.84
Oklahoma			
Osage	18.47	30.63	1.66
Minnesota			
Fond Du Lac	25.99	12.58	0.48
n	39	39	39
Mean	130.18	45.57	0.54
Standard Deviation	230.83	67.29	0.49

Source: The values were calculated by using a weighted average of average cropland value per acre for the counties encompassing each reservation. Cropland values and cropland acreage for the counties were taken from the U.S. Bureau of the Census (1989). The weights for each county value were the percentage of the reservation acreage found in a given county.

tribes to contract with the government to undertake responsibility for tribal operations formerly under control of the BIA as trustee. As Krepps stated, "By participating in the 638 program, a tribe takes over one or more of these aspects itself and receives the concomitant funding to dispense as it sees fit in the task."[58]

In the case of tribal forestry, Krepps found that forty-nine of seventy-five tribes in his sample participated in the 638 forestry program, in some cases to the extent of taking total control of tribal forestry. Participation in this program has led to the replacement of 4,000 BIA forestry workers with tribal workers and, not surprisingly, has generated opposition to the program within the bureaucracy.[59]

The impact of tribal control on forest productivity was measured using regression analysis to account for differences between the annual harvest level and the annual allowable cut (AAC).[60] Krepps believes the extent to which the annual harvest level is less than the AAC depends on "four primary factors: the amount of timber available for sale, the maintenance efforts of low-skilled workers, the marketing efforts of high-skilled workers, and the internal rate of time preference . . . of the forest's owner."[61] His statistical analysis shows that the addition of "tribal high-skilled labor" increased harvest by 24,000 board feet (bf) per worker per year, whereas the addition of "BIA high-skilled labor" reduced harvest by 14,000 bf per worker per year. Whereas additional "BIA low-skilled labor" increased harvest by 40 bf per year per worker, additional "tribal low-skilled labor" was 75 percent more effective. "This differential labor productivity provides a compelling rebuttal of the argument that tribes cannot manage their own resources."[62]

The Krepps data support the agricultural results regarding individual control relative to tribal control. In his estimates of annual harvest relative to AAC, Krepps finds that a larger percentage of allottee ownership increased harvest by "1.34 million bf per year given the AAC and the degree of tribal involvement."[63] This result is consistent with the hypothesis that accountability matters in that individual allottees have more incentive to manage their forests efficiently.[64] Accountability is a key to productivity, and accountability is difficult to obtain under the trusteeship of a large federal bureaucracy.

Another important resource on many western reservations is coal reserves, which again are held in trust by the federal government. The Crow Tribe, for example, is one of the largest owners of coal reserves in the world, with a total value estimated at $26,820,779,087, or $3,283,000 per capita, in 1988. Yet these assets earn only about $3 million annually for an appalling rate of return of 0.01 percent per annum.[65] Whereas this abysmal rate of return cannot be definitively tied to federal trusteeship, we must ask whether more direct control by the tribe might not generate more wealth from the asset.

Conservation Native American Style

Reflecting on the history of Indian institutions, it is clear that indigenous people in North America demonstrated a remarkable ability to adapt. Necessity was no less the mother of invention for institutions than for technology, and American Indians rose to the challenge of getting the incentives right in a variety of ways. Their institutional responses may not have always followed the prescriptions of modern private property, although property ownership was not alien to Indians. They relied on many informal rules that provided positive rewards and negative penalties for individuals who failed to conserve resources.

Once relegated to reservations and left to their own devices, there is good evidence that Indians hammered out institutions that promoted agricultural productivity. Although their technology was meager and their land base small relative to the vast territories taken by white men, they were able to begin producing crops and livestock for subsistence and markets. This productivity was a direct result of successful institutional innovation that started from the bottom up, utilizing traditional systems of property ownership and land tenure. When the bottom-up evolution was replaced with top-down institutional imperialism from Washington, reservations were left with a land tenure mosaic not conducive to sustainable agricultural productivity. The net result is that Indian lands are far less productive than fee simple land in or around reservations.

Although fee simple lands are much more productive, it does not follow that privatization is the only way to encourage sustainable land use. Some tribes such as the White Mountain Apache in Arizona, for example, are successfully managing tribally owned timber, wildlife, and recreational assets with institutions consistent with their culture and resource base.[66] The lesson, therefore, is not that all reservation assets should be privatized, although that might work in some cases; rather, the lesson is that sustainable conservation accompanies an institutional evolution driven from the bottom up by the special circumstances of each tribe and reservation.

References

1. See James Lopach, Margery H. Brown, and Richmond L. Clow, *Tribal Government: Politics on Montana Indian Reservations* (Boulder: Westview, 1990); Terry L. Anderson, *Property Rights and Indian Economies* (Lanham, MD: Rowman and Littlefield, 1995).
2. Ronald L. Trosper, "American Indian Relative Ranching Efficiency," *American Economic Review,* 68:4 (1978): 503–516, quote on p. 514.
3. Richard White and William Cronon, "Ecological Change and Indian-White Relations," in Wilcomb E. Washburn, ed., *History of Indian-White Relations,* vol. 4 of *Handbook of North American Indians* (Washington, DC: Smithsonian Institution, 1988): 417–429, quote on pp. 419–421.
4. J. Richard Ambler, *The Anasazi* (Flagstaff: Museum of Northern Arizona, 1989).
5. Ted J. Brasser, "Riding on the Frontier's Crest: Mahican Indian Culture and Culture Change," Ethnology Division, Paper 13 (Ottawa: National Museums of Canada, 1974): 14.
6. Ibid., p. 7.
7. Angie Debo, *A History of the Indians of the United States* (Norman: University of Oklahoma Press, 1970): 13–14.
8. Alice C. Fletcher and Francis LaFlesche, *The Omaha Tribe,* 2 vols. (Lincoln: University of Nebraska Press, 1992 [1911]): 269.
9. Edward A. Kennard, "Hopi Economy and Subsistence," in Alfonso Ortiz, ed., *Southwest,* vol. 9 of *Handbook of North American Indians* (Washington, DC: Smithsonian Institution, 1979): 554.
10. C. Daryll Forde, "Hopi Agriculture and Land Ownership," *Journal of the Royal Anthropological Institute of Great Britain and Ireland,* 61 (1931): 357–405, quote on p. 367.
11. Ibid., p. 369. Forde offers an extensive discussion of Hopi agriculture and land ownership.
12. Florence H. Ellis, "Isleta Pueblo," in Ortiz, ed., *The Southwest,* vol. 9 of *Handbook of North American Indians* (Washington, DC: Smithsonian Institution, 1979): 351–365, quote on p. 355.
13. See Kennard, "Hopi Economy," pp. 554–557, and Forde, "Hopi Agriculture," for details.
14. Catherine S. Fowler, "Subsistence," in Warren L. D'Azevedo, ed., *The Great Basin,* vol. 11 of *Handbook of North American Indians* (Washington, DC: Smithsonian Institution, 1986): 64–97, quote on p. 65.
15. Julian H. Steward, "Cultural Element Distributions, XIII: Nevada Shoshone," *Anthropological Records,* 42:2 (1941): 209–360, quote on p. 240.
16. Robert H. Lowie, "Ethnographic Notes on the Washo," *Univ. of Calif. Publs. in American Archaeology and Ethnology,* 36:5 (1939): 301–351, quote on p. 303.

17. Ibid.
18. Muir reported in Julian H. Steward, *Ethnography of the Owens Valley Paiute, University of Calif. Publs. in American Archaeology and Ethnology,* 33:3 (1933): 233–350, quote on p. 305. Lowie, "Ethnographic Notes," provides a more complete discussion of property rights for piñon trees.
19. John M. Copper, "Indian Land Tenure Systems," in *Indians of the United States,* Contributions by Members of the Delegation, and by Advisers to the Policy Board of the National Indian Institute, for the Second Inter-American Conference on Indian Life (Cuzco, Peru, 1949): 1.
20. Julian H. Steward, *Basin-Plateau Aboriginal Sociopolitical Groups,* Smithsonian Institution, Bureau of American Ethnology, *Bulletin,* 120 (Washington, DC: Government Printing Office (GPO), 1938): 253.
21. Alvin M. Josephy Jr., *The Indian Heritage of America* (New York: Bantam, 1968): 351.
22. Douglas F. Hurt, *Indian Agriculture in America: Prehistory to the Present* (Lawrence: Kansas University Press, 1987): 230.
23. Ibid., p. 75.
24. Leonard A. Carlson, "Learning to Farm: Indian Land Tenure and Farming Before the Dawes Act," in Terry L. Anderson, ed., *Property Rights and Indian Economies* (Lanham, MD: Rowman and Littlefield, 1992): 73.
25. Thomas R. Wessel, "Agriculture, Indians, and American History," *Agricultural History,* 50 (1976): 9–20, quote on p. 17.
26. Carlson, "Learning to Farm," p. 74.
27. Ibid., p. 73.
28. Ibid., p. 75.
29. U.S. Bureau of the Census, *Twelfth Census of the United States, 1900,* vol. 5, *Agriculture* (Washington, DC: GPO, 1900): 717.
30. Carlson, "Learning to Farm," p. 74.
31. U.S. Bureau of the Census, *Twelfth Census,* p. 722.
32. Leonard A. Carlson, *Indians, Bureaucrats, and the Land: The Dawes Act and the Decline of Indian Farming* (Westport, CT: Greenwood, 1981): 123.
33. Ralph M. Linton, "Land Tenure in Aboriginal America," in Oliver LaFarge, ed., *The Changing Indian* (Norman: University of Oklahoma Press, 1942): 54.
34. D. S. Otis, "History of the Allotment Policy," in *Readjustments of Indian Affairs,* Hearings before the Committee on Indian Affairs, House, 73rd Cong., 2d sess. (Washington, DC: GPO), reprinted as F. P. Prucha, ed., *The Dawes Act and the Allotment of Indian Lands* (Norman: University of Oklahoma Press, 1973): 11–12.
35. Fred S. McChesney, "Government as Definer of Property Rights: Indian Lands, Ethnic Externalities, and Bureaucratic Budgets," in Anderson, ed., *Property Rights and Indian Economies,* p. 114.
36. Wilcomb E. Washburn, *Red Man's Land/White Man's Law* (New York: Charles Scribner's Sons, 1971): 145.
37. These percentages were calculated from U.S. Department of the Interior, Bureau of Indian Affairs (1987) data that showed 54,339,757 acres of Indian land, 42,104,294 acres of tribally owned trust land, 10,621,712 acres of individually owned trust land, and 1,191,562 acres of government land. An additional 422,189 acres were unclassified as to ownership status.

38. *Essentially* is used because the tribes do have limited regulatory power within the reservation, even for fee lands. Such authority has become more of an issue in recent years as tribes have claimed additional land and use rights. Twenty years ago bureau and tribal concern was solely with trust lands; reservation boundaries were of little concern. Granting of recent tribal claims to territorial rights for such use as fishing and hunting, however, has increased the interest of tribes in control of land for certain uses extending to the reservation border and sometimes beyond. [Editors' note: See also Chapter 9.]
39. 25 *U.S.C.A.*, § 348, 373 (1964). For a more complete discussion of heirship, see Ethel J. Williams, "Too Little Land, Too Many Heirs—The Indian Heirship Land Problem," *Washington Law Review,* 46 (1970–1971): 709–744. Because fee simple lands are not subject to these heirship rules and tribal trust lands cannot be willed, heirship problems are not present with these two tenures.
40. For a discussion of regulations regarding leasing under heirship, see 25 *CFR* [Code of Federal Regulations], chapter 1 (4-1-89 ed.): 162. [Editors' note: For a more recent evaluation of the heirship problem vis-à-vis the Land Consolidation Act of 1982, see Michelle M. Lindo, "*Youpee v. Babbitt*—The Indian Land Inheritance Problem Revisited," *American Indian Law Review,* 22:1 (1997): 223–246.]
41. U.S. Congress, House, Committee on Interior and Insular Affairs, *Indian Heirship Land Study,* parts 1 and 2, 86th Cong., 2d sess. (Washington, DC: GPO, 1960): 463.
42. U.S. Department of the Interior, Bureau of Indian Affairs, *Natural Resources Information System* (Washington, DC: GPO, 1987): 104.
43. Williams, "Too Little Land," pp. 710–711.
44. There are minor exceptions in cases where tribes have purchased fee simple land, especially outside the reservation. In general, however, when the tribe purchases fee simple land, the land is placed into trust status.
45. Trosper, "American Indian Relative Ranching Efficiency." Indeed, the capital problem seems serious. Conversations with Bureau of Indian Affairs officials, Indians, and business owners indicate that local banks tend to completely avoid Indian farmers with trust lands because their land cannot be used to cover defaults on loans.
46. For a detailed discussion of the relationship between output and tenure and the empirical estimates, see Terry L. Anderson and Dean Lueck, "Agricultural Development and Land Tenure in Indian Country," in Anderson, ed., *Property Rights and Indian Economies,* pp. 147–166.
47. Gary D. Libecap and Ronald N. Johnson, "Legislating Commons: The Navaho Tribal Council and the Navaho Range," *Economic Inquiry,* 18 (1980): 69–86, quote on p. 83. Other variables might impact productivity of tribal land. If a tribe had a history of agriculture and the associated land tenure institutions, it is more likely that land will be put to productive use. Also, if the tribal population is small relative to the number of tribally controlled acres, tribal council decisions will have a greater impact per capita and therefore are more likely to be scrutinized by members, thus leading to more productive land use. Proxies for these were included in the empirical estimates.
48. Note that the analysis uses gross value. The net rental value of land will also be reduced, but available data do not allow a test of this hypothesis.
49. U.S. Department of the Interior, *Natural Resources,* p. 50; U.S. Bureau of the Census, *U.S. Agricultural Census 1987* (Washington, DC: GPO, 1987).

51. These data were taken from part 6 and part 2, respectively, of U.S. Department of the Interior, *Natural Resources,* for each reservation. The reason for using acres with agricultural potential rather than the actual acres in production is that some acres are idle or "underemployed" because of trust constraints. If Indians are able to overcome the higher costs inherent in trust constraints, output per acre should be similar to fee simple land. Using potential acres recognizes that trust constraints can keep land underemployed or out of production.
52. The weights were the estimated percentage of the reservation within each county.
53. Given the mean of 0.54 and the standard deviation of 0.495, the hypothesis that trust land and private land are equally productive can be rejected at the 99 percent confidence level.
54. For a complete discussion of the other variables used in the statistical analysis, see Anderson and Lueck, "Agricultural Development," pp. 446–447.
55. For details of this regression analysis, see ibid., pp. 446–448.
56. Stephen Cornell and Joseph A. Kalt, *What Can Tribes Do? Strategies and Institutions in American Indian Economic Development* (Los Angeles: University of California, American Indian Studies Center, 1992): 25.
57. Matthew B. Krepps, "Can Tribes Manage Their Own Resources? The 638 Program and American Indian Forestry," in S. Cornell and J. Kalt, eds., *What Can Tribes Do?* (Los Angeles: University of California, American Indian Studies Center, 1992): 181–182.
58. Ibid., p. 181.
59. Ibid., p. 182.
60. Annual allowable cut is a measure of the annual harvest rate that can be sustained from a forest given biological constraints such as tree growth rate, current and expected future timber prices, and interest rates. For further discussion, see ibid., p. 184.
61. Ibid., p. 185.
62. Ibid., p. 188.
63. Ibid., p. 189.
64. Ibid., p. 186. Krepps attributes this higher rate of harvest to the possibility that "individuals' rates of time preference do not include the full consideration of descendants that may characterize tribal decision makers." Unfortunately, his data do not allow a separation of these two hypotheses.
65. Stephen Cornell and Joseph A. Kalt, "Culture and Institutions as Public Goods: American Indian Economic Development as a Problem of Collective Action," in Anderson, ed., *Property Rights and Indian Economies,* p. 224.
66. For details, see Terry L. Anderson, "Conservation—Native American Style," *PERC Policy Series,* PS-6 (Bozeman, MT: Political Economy Research Center, 1997).

CHAPTER 3

For the Public Good: Native Americans, Hydroelectric Dams, and the Iron Triangle

KATHERINE WEIST

Marc Reisner's *Cadillac Desert* contains a photograph of the chairman of the Fort Berthold Indian Tribal Business Council wiping the tears from his eyes as the U.S. secretary of the interior signs an agreement authorizing the flooding of over 152,000 acres of prime reservation land by the Garrison Dam reservoir (see Fig. 3.1).[1] This photograph, frequently reproduced in books about Indian-white relations or Indian resources, symbolizes not only the deep grief felt with the loss of resources and culture by native peoples but also their impotence in the face of powerful government agencies and national and local interest groups.[2] The sad reality of this frequently reproduced scene was that conservation arguments, based on the greater good for the majority, were employed to justify the flooding of these tribal lands and accompanying resources. Although the photograph was taken in 1948, the grief and impotence go back centuries and extend to the present day.

This chapter examines the loss of Native American resources through conservation programs that relied on the construction of large dams on rivers throughout North America to transform those waters into managed resources. By so doing, tribal groups were denied access to and control over their riverine resources, which were essential to their physical and cultural well-being. My focus is not on who has rights to waters flowing through Indian lands or on the legal machinations of government agencies in taking over lands guaranteed by treaties but on the destruction of Indian resources by dams, the protests enacted by Native Americans to prevent their destruction, the effects of dams on Native American lifeways, and the larger conservation and political contexts in which dams are justified and authorized. My analysis entails a historical perspective to ascertain changes in these processes.

Fig. 3.1 Tribal Members and Secretary of the Interior Sign Contract, 1948. George Gillette (*left*), then chairman of the Fort Berthold Indian Tribal Business Council, covers his face as he weeps in the office of Secretary of the Interior J. A. Krug in Washington, D.C., May 20, 1948. Krug is signing a contract whereby the tribe is selling 155,000 acres of its reservation for the Garrison Dam project. Gillette then said: "The members of the Tribal Council sign this contract with heavy hearts . . . right now the future does not look good for us." © AP/Wide World Photos; used with permission of the copyright owner.

Damming the Indians

In November 1994 Hydro-Quebec of Canada announced that it had put the second phase of the massive James Bay hydroelectric dam project "on ice." Undoubtedly, vigorous protests by the James Bay Cree, Inuit, and the international environmental community influenced Hydro-Quebec's decision. The first segment of the project, the LaGrande Project—built to utilize the rivers of the sub-Arctic for hydroelectric power and completed in 1979—destroyed the nesting areas of the Hudson Bay geese, wiped out a herd of 10,000 caribou, put methylmercury into the food chain, reduced Cree hunting grounds by 4,000 square miles, and opened the area to other development projects such as timber, mining, and tourism.[3] When the Cree learned of Hydro-Quebec's plans to build more dams, they immediately set in motion legal actions and drew upon their established networks to engage in a worldwide protest that, at least for the time being, has been successful.[4]

Although the Cree protests attracted recent international attention to the impact of dams on native peoples, dams have had direct and indirect consequences on the resources and cultures of North American Indians for well over a century. Some of the first large dams to affect native peoples in the United States were built in Minnesota between 1882 and 1910 by the Army Corps of Engineers. The Leech Lake, Winnibigoshish, and Pokegama Dam reservoirs in particular flooded the wild rice–collecting areas of the village-dwelling Ojibway Indians to provide steady water resources to businesses in Minneapolis and improve downstream navigation on the Mississippi River.[5]

Since at least the early eighteenth century, the Ojibway have resided in the Minnesota lake region, subsisting on the seasonal abundance of fish, deer, berries, and vegetable gardens. Of special significance to their lifeway was wild rice, which was and remains central to their everyday cuisine, ceremonial and ritual offerings, and medicinal practices.[6] The Ojibway, especially the Pillager's Band at Leech Lake Reservation, protested that the reservoirs destroyed not only the wild rice but a whole way of life. As Flatmouth, chief of the Pillager Band, proclaimed in 1883, "No one that comes here and stops for a while can know how important this is to us. When our lands were given to us by the Great Father we could do something, but if these dams are made we will all be destroyed."[7]

After four years of protests, Congress awarded the bands $150,000 in compensation in 1886, although it took thirty-four years for them to receive most of this settlement. Dissatisfied with the settlement, the Ojibway pressed their claims and finally received additional compensation of $3,390,288 in 1985. According to Jane L. Carroll, however, the Ojibway remain vigilant over the Corps' management of the reservoirs.[8] Thus the battle between the Ojibway, protecting their wild rice, and downstream resource users continues.

Other Native Americans decried similar losses of natural resources and culture for over a century throughout the United States and Canada as white settlers, industry, agriculture, and shipping interests expanded their political, economic, and ecological dominance. Although the direct effects of dams and reservoirs on Native lifeways are dramatic and far-reaching, the indirect repercussions can entail enormous changes as well. For example, the construction of a series of hydroelectric dams on the Columbia River and the accompanying "take areas" for storing irrigation water transformed the river from a free-flowing one to a series of reservoirs. The dams and reservoirs destroyed fish migratory patterns and spawning and fishing sites, which in turn forced the Indians, who were dependent on fish for a major portion of their subsistence, to switch from dip nets to gill nets. The use of gill nets, however, was prohibited by Oregon and Washington.[9] Although the resulting conflict during the mid-1960s between Indians asserting their treaty rights and non-Indian fishermen and government officials is more complex than this, dams played an indirect role in setting the stage for the "fishing rights controversy."

Kerr Dam, built in the late 1930s on the Confederated Salish-Kootenai Reservation, is part of the long-term process by which non-Indians appropriated Indian lands and resources for the benefit of outside interests, expansion, development, and conservation. The construction of the dam destroyed a sacred waterfall and fishing site on the reservation to provide electricity to growing white communities. Of little concern was the Indians' use of these resources. The Bureau of Indian Affairs (BIA) denied the tribes permission to hire a lawyer to defend their rights and ignored tribal sovereignty until the tribes gained assistance from John Collier's Indian Defense Fund.[10] Eventually, the tribes received rent of $140,000 a year, and more recently they renegotiated their settlement to $9 million a year for thirty years, after which they will take direct control in 2015.[11]

The construction of the Yellowtail Dam, located on the Bighorn River in the southern section of the Crow Reservation and built to increase the irrigation capabilities of off-reservation farmers, indirectly impacted the Crow of Montana and the Arapaho and Shoshone of Wyoming. The Bureau of Reclamation began construction of the Yellowtail Dam in 1961 after years of negotiations with the Crow for 6,000–7,000 acres of land.[12] Difficulties arose over compensation for the land, and the contestants litigated for fifteen years with the Crow, who in 1963 received the $5 million they had initially requested. According to Richard Berkman and W. Kip Viscusi, conflicts between the Bureau of Reclamation and the Crow continued even after the dam was constructed because the bureau sold water from the reservoir to large corporations, with the revenues going to the federal government rather than to the Crow.[13] The damming of the Bighorn River also affected the Arapaho and Shoshone on the Wind River Reservation who live upstream from the dam but were never consulted about the disposal of water, which would have flowed through their reservation. The Wind River tribes protested, but no settlement had been reached when Berkman and Viscusi's book was published in 1973.[14]

Even when not built on or near reservations, dams can produce negative impacts on Indian tribes. For example, the massive efforts to reduce the Navajo sheep herds because of overgrazing, which had been occurring since the 1890s, became a serious problem for the federal government only when it feared sedimentation along the Colorado River would cause siltation problems for Hoover (Boulder) Dam.[15] For this and other reasons, the government instituted the Navajo stock reduction program, leading to the anger and hardship the Navajo still feel today.

More examples of the impacts of dams on tribes and their resources can be cited. Of particular note are the Pyramid Lake Paiutes,[16] the Fort McDowell Yavapai,[17] the Missouri River Sioux,[18] the Papagos (Tohono O'odham) of Sil Murk village,[19] the Tuscarora of upstate New York,[20] and the Stoney, Cree, and Métis of Canada,[21] to name a few.[22]

In every case conservation conflicts erupted among tribes, government agencies, and off-reservation/downstream resource users, raising questions about the basic principles governing resource use and the justifications given for the loss of tribal resources. Detailed analysis focuses on the construction of the Garrison Dam in North Dakota and Kinzua Dam in northern Pennsylvania to explore the specific contexts in which conflicts and their resolution occurred.

The Garrison Dam

The settlement, farming, and industrial developments of the arid West posed continual predicaments for the white migrants to the area. The rivers, especially the Missouri, possess vital resources for irrigation and to some degree for navigation. To extract as many benefits as possible from the Missouri and its tributaries, the Army Corps of Engineers and the Bureau of Reclamation built six multipurpose dams on the river between the late 1930s and early 1960s to provide irrigation, hydroelectric power, and recreation opportunities; to control flooding; and to improve the depth of the water level downstream for barge traffic.[23] Frequently referred to as the Pick-Sloan Plan, after Colonel Lewis A. Pick of the Army Corps of Engineers and William Sloan of the Bureau of Reclamation, these dams have been scrutinized recently by historians and economists.[24] Michael Lawson, in *Dammed Indians,* details the history of the catastrophic effects these dams had on the Sioux Indians. According to him the dams' take areas destroyed 550,000 acres of tribal land in South and North Dakota and dislocated more than 900 Indian families.[25] Although the dams were disastrous to all the tribes, the Garrison Dam was most destructive to the Three Affiliated Tribes of the Fort Berthold Reservation in North Dakota (Figure 3.2).

The 1851 Fort Laramie Treaty created the Fort Berthold Reservation, home to the Three Affiliated Tribes of the Mandan, Hidatsa, and Arikara. Over the years, subsequent treaties reduced the reservation to 580,000 acres in south-central North Dakota.[26] These matrilineal, village-dwelling tribes—who had lived along the Missouri River for over 700 years—farmed the rich river bottoms, sheltered their domesticated animals among the groves of trees, collected firewood, hunted wild game, and gathered berries and medicinal herbs. Before the construction of the Garrison Dam, these farmers and herdsmen were independent and self-sufficient, although relatively isolated and poor. Most of the reservation was allotted between 1890 and 1929, with many allotments severely fragmented and the best farmland on the prairie located a short distance from the river owned by non-Indians who had homesteaded there when the government opened up the reservation in the early 1900s.[27]

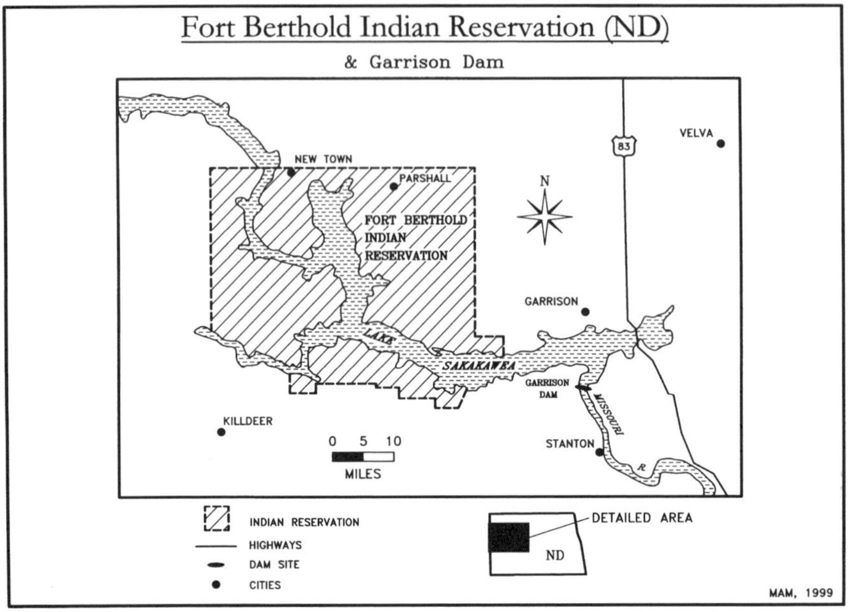

Fig. 3.2 Fort Berthold Indian Reservation and Garrison Dam (North Dakota). Garrison Dam, a project of the Army Corps of Engineers for the upper Missouri River, inundated more than 150,000 acres of the Fort Berthold Indian Reservation.

The Three Affiliated Tribes began protesting the dam in 1943 with a tribal council resolution to the BIA, voicing their opposition. As one man put it, "This land is our home, our people are buried in the hills of our lands. We are opposed to leaving our homes."[28] The BIA rebuffed their petition, and in 1945 the agency concluded that it was too late to halt construction.[29] The tribes' efforts to hire a lawyer to defend their position and an engineer to find an alternative site were dismissed without close study. The Army Corp of Engineers attempted to find lieu lands to replace in size and quality those to be flooded, but none could be found.[30] Only in 1947 did the tribes begin serious negotiations for a cash settlement. The federal government awarded the tribes $5,105,625 for relocation costs—building new houses or relocating old ones—and the acquisition of new lands. An additional $7.5 million was distributed to settle all claims and rights tribal members might have against the federal government.[31] Many people accrued no tangible assets because of the per capita distribution of the settlements.

Tribal members today equate the relocation of 90 percent of the reservation population between 1951 and 1954 with the smallpox epidemics of the nineteenth century and their disastrous consequences.[32] The reservoir flooded over 150,000 acres, including the tribes' rich bottom farmland; their sources of wood, water, and shelter; and the basic reservation infrastructure of schools, roads, the major bridge spanning the Missouri, cemeteries, and the agency town of Elbowoods. Leaving their nucleated villages, they moved up onto the flat, treeless prairie onto individual allotments distant from towns and clan members. Many people lacked electricity, and wells dried up, requiring the hauling of water. The area was unsuited to dry-land farming, and few had the capital to become ranchers.

Given the way the reservoir flooded, the reservation was divided into five segments with no roads or bridges linking them. New Town, located at the northern end of the reservation, became the new agency town and was inaccessible to many tribal members.

Because of a public disagreement between Crow Flies High, a leader of a tribal faction that opposed the dam's construction, and Colonel Pick, the latter ensured that the final agreement denied the tribes access to the reservoir's shoreline for all purposes, including rights to irrigation waters, royalties from any subsurface minerals found within the reservoir area, and the small amount of electricity the tribes requested for their own development.[33] Thus the Three Affiliated Tribes quickly moved from a state of self-sufficiency to one dependent on welfare and commodities and entered a condition today labeled "underdevelopment" because of the need by the dominant society to "develop" and control the Missouri River waters.

The Pick-Sloan Plan was lauded in 1944 as the savior to the semiarid prairie states. According to the Bureau of Reclamation:

> Every water resource and all feasible beneficial uses of water, such as aids to navigation, flood control, the irrigation of land, the producing of power, the restoration of surface and groundwater levels and of domestic and municipal water supplies, the abatement of stream pollution, silt control, fish and wildlife preservation, and recreation, were taken into account in an effort to formulate a basin-wide plan most likely to yield the greatest good to the greatest number of people.[34]

The lands to be flooded were determined by the bureau to be of little agricultural value and "insignificant compared with the area to be benefited."[35]

In the face of their misery and loss of resources, the Bureau of Indian Affairs, as stated in its Missouri River Basin Investigations Staff reports, viewed the flooding of the reservation as positive for the Three Affiliated Tribes. Although special problems would be associated with land appraisals, removal costs, and the development of residual lands, long-term benefits would be derived from the Indians' increased incorporation into the dominant society. In particular:

> The Indian Bureau is attempting to see the Indian and to see him whole, a member of a changing society derived from primitive status, which is slowly but steadily merging with the total population. Resource development is viewed from the standpoint of enlarging the Indians' opportunities for economic and social growth towards self-dependence, absorption into the body politic, and release from governmental guardianship and supervision.[36]

Isolation rather than assimilation became their reality. Federal policy at the time, however, stressed reservation termination and urban relocation, and after being so rudely dealt with over the Garrison Dam, tribal members feared termination with each new piece of legislation.[37]

The Pick-Sloan Plan was a compromise between two powerful government agencies, the Army Corps of Engineers and the Bureau of Reclamation. Other local and regional parties contended for control of the water and electricity, whether for irrigation, flood control, or navigation on the lower reaches of the Missouri. The governors and farmers of the upper basin states sought expanded irrigation systems; the lower basin residents sought flood control and navigational stability.[38] Still others sought a unified Missouri Valley Authority, similar to the Tennessee Valley Authority (TVA).[39] In all the wrangling that ensued, seldom were the Indians' interests considered, except to make sure they received compensation for their loss of land.[40] What Michael Welsh refers to as the "iron triangle" of water interests, government agencies, and state and federal legislators effectively worked against Indian interests and resources.[41]

Contradictions and conflicts permeated the process at all levels. According to tribal chairman Wilbur D. Wilkinson's testimony before the U.S. Senate's 1991 hearings to redress the inequities of the Garrison Dam agreement, the Three Affiliated Tribes contended that no one consulted them when the Garrison Dam plans were developed, and construction of the dam began before a settlement with the tribes was reached. As he said, "The trust-ward relationship created by the treaties between the Three Affiliated Tribes and the United States worked to the detriment of the tribes, wherein the trustee, the United States, acting on behalf of the tribe, reduced their land holdings by 11.857 million acres, allegedly for 'the public good.'"[42] Lands guaranteed to the Indians by treaties were taken for nontribal purposes. They were denied access to what should have been tribally owned resources, such as water, reservoir shorelines, and minerals. The army asked native soldiers, recently returned from fighting in World War II, to relinquish their land and houses and move to inhospitable locations. The Bureau of Indian Affairs, mandated to protect their interests, in fact assisted those agencies planning to usurp tribal resources.[43] The ethic of conservation through the "wise use" of water resources in fact brought loss and years of dependency for the Three Affiliated Tribes.

Kinzua Dam

The building of the Kinzua Dam on the Allegheny River in northern Pennsylvania by the Army Corps of Engineers followed much the same process as the Garrison Dam a decade earlier. The Kinzua reservoir ultimately flooded 9,000 acres of Seneca lands of both the Cornplanter Reserve in Pennsylvania and the Allegany Reservation in New York–Pennsylvania, destroyed sacred sites—including the grave of Seneca religious prophet Handsome Lake—and prime farming land, and forced the relocation of 550 Senecas. The idea for the dam began in 1908 but only gained popularity in 1956; construction began in 1960, and the dam's reservoir was filled in 1966. Desire for the dam came from downstream residents seeking flood control in the Ohio River Valley and from Pittsburgh businessmen who wanted a constant water flow for their factories. According to Laurence Hauptman, a near-total lack of concern for the Seneca emerged at every stage of the project[44] (Figure 3.3).

The Seneca Nation, a division of the League of the Iroquois, signed away portions of their territory in New York state by way of the treaty process during the eighteenth century and eventually resided on the Allegany Reservation in western New York. The reservation, situated on both sides of the Allegheny River, is 42 miles long and at least half a mile wide on both sides of the river. During their pre-reservation days, the Seneca lived in compact matrilineal villages, but with reservation settlement families spread out along the river bottoms where they planted their crops, hunted animals, and collected fruits and herbs. Over time many Seneca, like their white neighbors, took up wage labor.

The Seneca enacted diverse strategies to fight dam construction. First, they sought recourse through the courts based on their rights to the land as integral to their treaty rights. Every court from the Federal District Court to the U.S. Supreme Court denied their petitions. The courts cited the doctrine of plenary power that allowed Congress to sever unilaterally treaty guarantees.[45]

Second, they received assistance from the Quakers, a religious denomination long associated with the Seneca, from the Indian Rights Association and the governor of New York. Most noted was the eloquent plea by the literary critic, Edmund Wilson, in his book *Apologies to the Iroquois.*[46]

With the assistance of the Quakers, the Seneca hired Arthur E. Morgan, the innovative planner and first administrator of the TVA, to find a better dam site. Morgan found a location that would hold more water and protect Seneca land. Although the Army Corps of Engineers studied the plan, they rejected it as too expensive, too large, and too disruptive to too many non-Indians.[47]

The Army Corps of Engineers broke ground for the dam in 1960, and the reservoir was filled in 1966, with the removal of the Senecas occurring between 1964 and 1966. When the Senecas realized they could not halt the construction, they attempted to attain the best settlement they could. In August 1964, President Lyndon Johnson signed into law an appropriation of $12,128,917.[48] Many

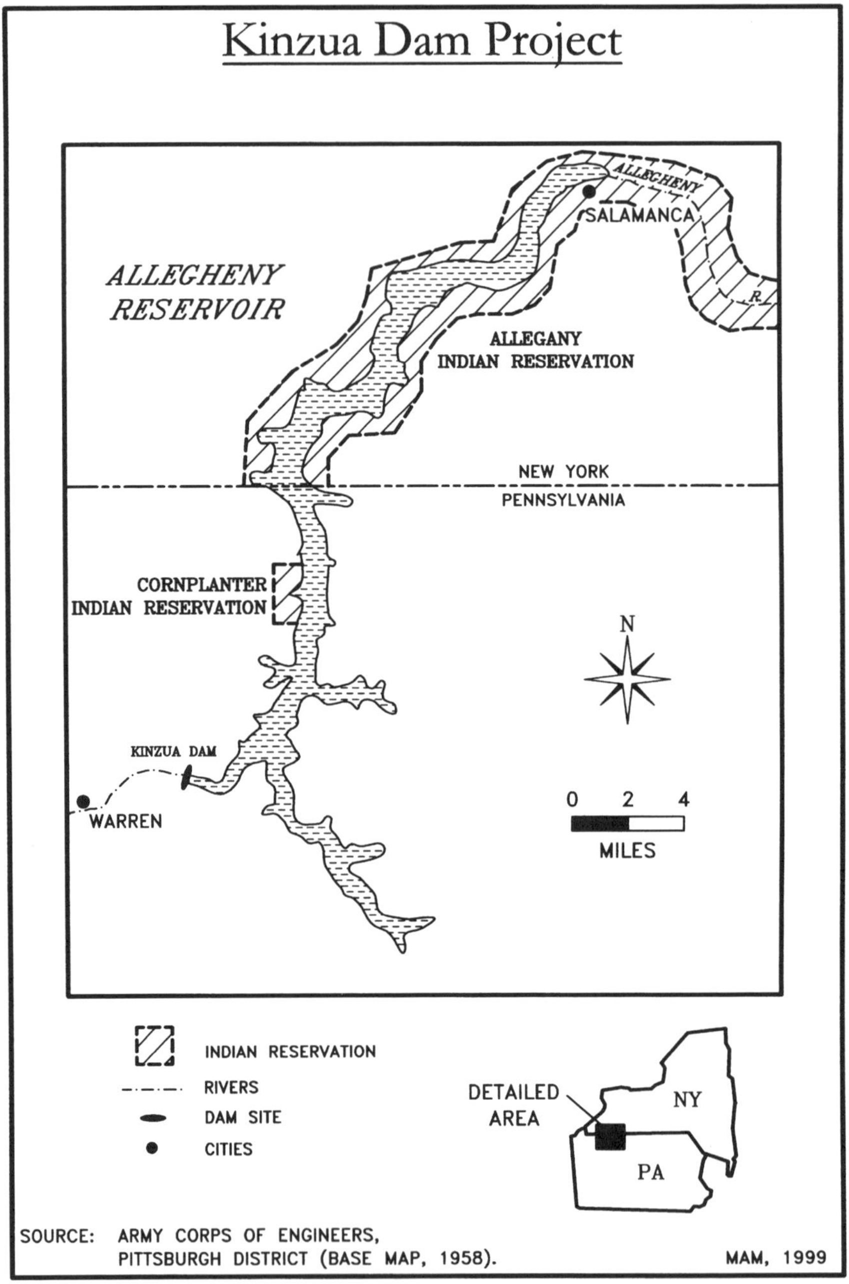

Fig. 3.3 Kinzua Dam Project (Pennsylvania/New York). Kinzua Dam, a project of the Army Corps of Engineers located on the Allegheny River in the upper watershed of the Ohio River system, inundated lands of both the Cornplanter and the Seneca Indians.

Senecas had only two months from the time they received the money to the time they had to move. Many built new houses constructed by the Seneca Nation Housing Enterprises, which bought building materials in bulk and by December had either built or was in the process of building 102 houses for the relocatees.[49]

The people moved to one of two locations—Jimersontown, a suburb of the town of Salamanca, or Steamburg, the new location of the Longhouse religion and thus the village of many elderly Seneca. Given the distance of 12 miles between the two locations, communication is difficult, especially for older tribal members. Jimersontown offered more wage employment and today is the location of the tribal center, schools, museum, library, and tribal offices. The tribe authorized the expenditure of the compensation monies to build tribal houses, improve basic infrastructure, and invest in education and tribal development projects.[50]

Like the Three Affiliated Tribes, Seneca of all ages underwent massive trauma with removal.[51] They abandoned their agricultural subsistence economy along the river and moved their scattered settlements to compact villages and towns. Removal forced them from their traditional life along the Allegheny River, their source of medicinal plants and spirituality.[52] The reservoir destroyed schools, and over 3,000 graves had to be removed. The inundation of the Cornplanter Track and the Coldspring Longhouse, the ceremonial center of the Handsome Lake religion, caused particular anguish. Because of the geographic nature of the reservation, little land was available for relocation, so the Senecas moved into closer proximity with each other. Old neighbors and some kin were separated, and nonkin moved closer together. As the Seneca population expanded, young people left the reservation because of the lack of available house plots.

Similar to the Garrison Dam, myriad political and economic interests created the Kinzua Dam. Hauptman, in *Iroquois Struggle for Survival,*[53] details the political inputs that brought the dam into being from government officials and agencies, congressmen, and local—especially downstream—beneficiaries seeking flood control and the "Pittsburgh renaissance."[54] He describes these forces as forming an "iron triangle," with congressmen looking for votes at the apex, beneficiaries (local users and lobbyists) looking for federal subsidies on the right-hand corner, and federal agencies, seeking to justify their existence, forming the left-hand corner.[55] Little thought or interest was given to Seneca rights or needs or the repercussions of their removal on their culture and society.

Maurice Goddard, the Pennsylvania secretary for forests and waters, stated the usual justification for the dam: "To date this will mean that some of our people may have to give up homes and land, in accordance with law, for the common good of the majority . . . in the march of civilization and progress, there must be sacrifice of a few for the protection and well-being of the many."[56] Besides justifying the construction of the Kinzua Dam's reservoir for the conservation needs of flood control and economic development, politicians in the late 1950s and early 1960s linked these needs with Cold War fears based on the premise of "safeguarding our economy and way of life."[57] Development projects such as dams were seen as upholding national security interests to protect Americans from attacks by outsiders.

Assimilationist and racist attitudes permeated the advice given to policymakers. In 1956 John Hamlin, executive assistant to President Dwight Eisenhower, wrote a memorandum to the president in which he outlined the "Indian Problem" as one associated with the lack of assimilation:

> It seems to be probable that the two kinds of culture cannot co-exist intimately indefinitely. The less competitive culture would have to adapt or die out, if it could not be effectively insulated geographically or otherwise. This may seem a hard conclusion, but it is probably a manifestation of that harsh law of nature, the survival of the fittest. . . . Subsidizing of the backward group by the productive one is a possible temporary palliative and it is temporarily acceptable if the surplus of the productive group is considerable. But it is costly; it seems unfair to the productive people; and it aggravates the problem and postpones the solution. The backward population becomes constantly larger and poorer as it relies on primitive means of production, and hence more reliant, more costly, and more frustrated.[58]

Similar to the situation with the Three Affiliated Tribes, the BIA was virtually absent in the litigation and removal process. The Seneca, unlike the Three Affiliated Tribes, have a closer Indian-state relationship with the state of New York since the founding of that state in 1777.[59] Since 1848 the Seneca have governed themselves under a constitution, and the Nation claims ownership over all the tribal land.[60] Thus the BIA has less jurisdiction over the Seneca compared with most other tribal groups. Furthermore, the U.S. government encouraged at this time the termination of BIA services to Indian communities with the relocation of Indians to cities.

Evaluating a summary report published by the Department of the Interior for the years 1953–1960, Hauptman notes that the BIA merited the least amount of space and was the last subject reviewed. Reclamation and hydroelectric power developments received the highest priority.[61] Native peoples—who lost land, other resources, and a way of life—and the federal agency designated to represent them were conspicuously absent from the iron triangle of local interests, politicians, and federal agencies that fought for and controlled the Garrison and Kinzua Dams.

Conclusion

River basin systems—viewed by nonnative peoples as sources of destruction through flooding or of "progress" with the generation of power—have been utilized by native peoples for subsistence, shelter, navigation, and spirituality for millennia. Over the last century, however, native riverine communities and resources have been extensively demolished by large dams constructed for their conservation benefits to white communities, businesses, and politicians. Given the pervasive belief that native peoples either would or should assimilate or that their small populations and needs were irrelevant, serious considerations of the effects of dams on native lifeways have not been forthcoming until recently. Comparative analysis reveals that over the last century, in both the United States and Canada, significant similarities exist in the processes by which native rights and resources were abrogated by powerful agencies and interests.

Reservoirs create less diverse ecosystems by flooding valuable resources and making tribal access more difficult. All of the tribes protested and fought for their resources through the court systems, their legislative representatives, Indian agencies, and powerful individuals. All considered the loss of resources devastating to the continuity of their way of life, the integrity of their culture, their subsistence, and their spiritual relationship with their environment. All fought for their land, not for monetary compensation. As a Cree trapper expressed when asked how much money he would need to make up for the damages the James Bay Project would cause: "It can never be that there will be enough money to help pay for what I get from trapping. I do not think in terms of money. I think more often of the land because the land is something you will have for a long time. That is why we call our traplines, our land, a garden."[62]

A memorial to Congress drawn up by the tribal council of the Three Affiliated Tribes in 1943 expressed the same sentiments: "We have permanently located on these lands, and our forefathers also have lived on these grounds and it is the hopes and plans to have our children and their children to occupy this land continually forever; and money or exchange for other land will not compensate us for the land, landmarks, and sentimental attachments."[63]

Even with the loss of land, the compensation offered usually did not come close to the value of the land, and in no instance was land equal in quality offered in exchange for the land lost. All of the tribes underwent major social, economic, and psychological restructuring. Families of the Three Affiliated Tribes were removed to isolated homes without adequate facilities and were separated from clansmen. The Seneca were crowded into an even smaller reservation, one inadequate for future generations.

The agencies responsible for planning the construction of the dams gave both the native peoples and the public at large two justifications for the tribal removals and loss of resources. First, the dam projects were presented as essential for the "public" good. Translated this means the larger population, region, or even the nation was of higher priority than Indian resources, well-being, or culture. That is, the conservation of resources requires the more "efficient" utilization of these resources, especially for the promotion of large-scale economic development[64] and not necessarily for the benefit of grassroots users—in this case, native peoples. For example, the judgment of the Quebec Court of Appeals, in its justification for ruling against the James Bay Cree, stated: "It is, then, the general and public interest of the people of Quebec which is opposed to the interests of about 2,000 of its inhabitants. We believe that these two interests cannot be compared at this stage of the proceedings."[65] In a slightly less dogmatic stance but with the same message, Pennsylvania governor Lawrence exclaimed at the dedication ceremony of the Kinzua Dam that the project "will some day stand as a living, useful reminder of the first lesson of good government—the needs of human welfare come first and those needs can be answered when we work together and meet the challenge willingly."[66] These sentiments must have sounded very ironic to the Seneca.

Second, the loss of native resources was proffered as beneficial for their future well-being. As stated in the 1948 Missouri River Basin Investigations report on the Pick-Sloan Plan: "Indian life on the reservations has inevitably been channeled toward the essentially undemocratic controls of the 'Agency,' rather than outwards to the surrounding society with which the Indian people should become associated in the long sweep of cultural amalgamation."[67] This report goes on to enumerate the exciting benefits the Three Affiliated Tribes will reap from the destruction of their old agency town of Elbowoods and the establishment of a new type of tribal-federal relationship.

All of the tribes were caught in an iron triangle of vote-seeking politicians, federal agencies, and business, farming, and water interests. As river basin projects attract greater scholarly analysis, the political intent of the construction of large-scale dams becomes more obvious. Thayer Scudder, an authority on international basin development schemes, recently stated, "In some cases political considerations play a major role (perhaps even *the* major role) in decisions to proceed with or expand river basin initiatives."[68] Both Lawson's work on the Pick-Sloan Plan and Hauptman's on the Kinzua Dam demonstrate the political role federal agencies and politicians had in controlling the decisions to build the dams. As James Waldram describes for the Cree of Manitoba, they were "mere pawns in the hydro game."[69]

Within the larger political context, the BIA stands out as a weak agency—plagued by lack of funds, in contention with other Department of the Interior agencies, and with continually shifting policy directions. Like most agencies the BIA was unsuited to undertake the relocation process, one it foresaw as resulting in greater assimilation. Advocation of Indian resources and cultures was not a priority. Waldram, in his analysis of the effects of dams on two communities of Cree in Manitoba, found the Canadian Department of Indian Affairs took a passive role as well.[70] Although many historians, anthropologists, and others accuse the BIA of bureaucratic ineptitude in handling Indian affairs and in fact this is true, analysis of the process by which dams are constructed demonstrates that other federal agencies and interests are more powerful in determining policy.

Waldram, in his conclusion to his book-length study of hydroelectric development in western Canada, states that the land and resource alienation incurred by hydroelectric dams is very similar to the treaty process and goes far beyond the appeal to the "common good."[71] Specific similarities are the lack of communication with native peoples directly affected, the plans are presented as a fait accompli, and formal commissions—frequently with no authority to render judgments—are convened to negotiate the settlement. Promises are made at that time that are later revoked or "not remembered." Frequently, disagreement over the agreements continue for years, and in some cases the tribes are able to reopen their cases.[72]

Recent protests by the James Bay Cree suggest that native peoples are finally succeeding in halting the destruction of their lands, resources, and livelihoods. The old conservation ethic of greater "efficiency" of resource use is being called into question with respect to who makes decisions, for what ends, and for whose benefit. A new environmental ethic that acknowledges the value of man-land relationships and the rights of native peoples as sovereign entities is finding favor with the general public. Recently enacted laws in the United States help to protect sacred sites and can be used in the court system. Native peoples are becoming more sophisticated in their use of the media and protest strategies, and it is hoped that a tribal chairman will never again cry as tribal resources are summarily signed away. But as Waldram reminds us, the hydro groups are becoming more sophisticated as well.[73]

References

1. Marc Reisner, *Cadillac Desert: The American West and Its Disappearing Water* (New York: Viking, 1986).
2. Edgar S. Cahn, ed., *Our Brother's Keeper: The Indian in White America* (New York: New Community Press, 1969); Arthur E. Morgan, *Dams and Other Disasters: A Century of the Army Corps of Engineers in Civil Works* (Boston: Porter Sargent, 1971); Peter Iverson, ed., *The Plains Indians of the Twentieth Century* (Norman: University of Oklahoma Press, 1985); Richard White and William Cronon, "Ecological Change and Indian-White Relations," in *The History of Indian-White Relations,* ed. Wilcomb E. Washburn, vol. 4 of *Handbook of North American Indians* (Washington, DC: Smithsonian Institution, 1988): 417–429; Marjane Ambler, *Breaking the Iron Bonds: Indian Control of Energy Development* (Lawrence: University Press of Kansas, 1990).
3. Katherine Weist, "Development Refugees: Africans, Indians and the Big Dams," *Journal of Refugee Studies,* 8:2 (1995): 163–184.
4. Ward Churchill, *Struggle for the Land: Indigenous Resistance to Genocide, Ecocide and Expropriation in Contemporary North America* (Monore, MA: Common Courage, 1993); Terry Turner, "The World Struggle to Save James Bay," *Northeast Indian*

Quarterly, 8:4 (1991): 55–57.

5. Jane L. Carroll, "Dams and Damages: The Ojibway, the United States and the Mississippi Headwater Reservoirs," *Minnesota History,* 52:1 (1990): 2–15.
6. Thomas Vennum Jr., *Wild Rice and the Ojibway People* (St. Paul: Minnesota Historical Society Press, 1988).
7. Carroll, "Dams and Damages," p. 3.
8. Ibid., p. 15.
9. Charles A. Hobbs, "Indian Hunting and Fishing Rights II," *George Washington Law Review,* 37 (1969): 1251–1273. Cf. Roberta Ulrich, *Empty Nets: Indians, Dams, and the Columbia River* (Corvallis: Oregon State University Press, 1999).
10. Roy Bigcrane and Thompson Smith, *Place of the Falling Water,* Native Voices Workshop, Salish Kootenai College Media Center (Pablo, MT, 1991).
11. Ibid.
12. Richard L. Berkman and W. Kip Viscusi, *Damming the West* (New York: Grossman, 1973): 165.
13. Ibid., p. 179.
14. Ibid., p. 183–184.
15. Leonard S. Fonaroff, "Conservation and Stock Reduction on the Navajo Tribal Range," *Geographical Review,* 53 (1963): 200–223. [Editors' note: It is suggested that the government exhibited more concern over erosion control on the Navajo Reservation than over the preservation of archaeological ruins in the reservoir area of future Lake Mead; see also Imre Sutton, "Geographical Aspects of Construction Planning: *Hoover Dam Revisited,*" *Journal of the West,* 7:3 (1968): 301–344.
16. Martha C. Knack and Omer C. Stewart, *As Long as the River Shall Run: An Ethnohistory of Pyramid Lake Indian Reservation* (Berkeley: University of California Press, 1984).
17. Sigrid Khera and Patricia S. Mariella, "The Fort McDowell Yavapai: A Case of Long-Term Resistance to Relocation," in Art Hansen and Anthony Oliver-Smith, eds., *Involuntary Migration and Resettlement: The Problems and Responses of Dislocated People* (Boulder: Westview, 1982): 159–177.
18. Michael L. Lawson, *Dammed Indians: The Pick-Sloan Plan and the Missouri River Sioux, 1944–1980* (Norman: University of Oklahoma Press, 1982).
19. Morgan, *Dams and Other Disasters.*
20. Churchill, *Struggle for the Land,* pp. 97–98.
21. James Waldram, *As Long as the Rivers Run: Hydroelectric Development and Native Communities in Western Canada* (Winnipeg: University of Manitoba Press, 1988).
22. Imre Sutton, in *Indian Land Tenure: Bibliographical Essays and a Guide to the Literature* (New York: Clearwater, 1976), briefly discusses most of these projects and provides a map of the location of dams on Indian reservations, pp. 166–171. (Waldman's map, "Some Dams and Indian Lands" [freely adapted from *Indian Land Tenure,* figure 8, p. 167, in Carl Waldman and Molly Braun, *Atlas of the North American Indian* (New York: Facts on File, 1986): 202], does come forward in time and has removed projected dams that have not been constructed. [Editors' note: One of the earlier projects, the El Capitán Dam in San Diego County, California, inundated the Capitán Grande Indian Reservation, displacing two villages, but the Indians ultimately received compensation—although they were obliged to permanently abandon the reservation. See Imre Sutton, "Land Tenure and Occupance Change on

Indian Reservations in Southern California," Ph.D. diss. in geography, UCLA, Los Angeles, 1964: 281–283.]

23. Lawson, *Dammed Indians,* p. 12.
24. Edward C. Cass, "Flood Control and the Corps of Engineers in the Missouri Valley, 1902–1973," *Nebraska History,* 63:1 (1982): 108–122; David C. Campbell, "The Pick-Sloan Program," *Journal of Economic Issues,* 18:2 (1984): 449–456; John Ferrell, "Developing the Missouri: South Dakota and the Pick-Sloan Plan," *South Dakota History,* 19:3 (1989): 306–341; Mark Harvey, "North Dakota, the Northern Plains, and the Missouri Valley Authority," *North Dakota History,* 59:3 (1992): 28–39; Michael Welsh, "Western Historians, the U.S. Army Corps of Engineers, and the Rivers of Empire," *North Dakota History,* 59:3 (1992): 5–12.
25. Lawson, *Dammed Indians,* p. 27.
26. Roy W. Meyer, *The Village Indians of the Upper Missouri* (Lincoln: University of Nebraska Press, 1977): 242.
27. Ambler, *Breaking the Iron Bonds,* p. 198.
28. Meyer, *The Village Indians,* p. 215.
29. Ibid., pp. 212–213.
30. Ibid., pp. 214–215.
31. Ibid., p. 218.
32. Charlotte Gilman and Mary Jean Schneider, *The Way to Independence: Memories of a Hidatsa Indian Family 1840–1920* (St. Paul: Minnesota Historical Society Press, 1987): 316–318.
33. Morgan, *Dams and Other Disasters,* pp. 45–46.
34. U.S. Congress, Senate. *Conservation, Control, and Use of Water Resources of the Missouri River Basin in Montana, Wyoming, Colorado, North Dakota, South Dakota, Nebraska, Kansas, Iowa and Missouri,* Senate Doc. 191, 78th Cong., 2d sess. (1944): 17.
35. Ibid., p. 23.
36. Missouri River Basin Investigations (MRBI), Bureau of Indian Affairs, *The Indians and the Pick-Sloan Plan* (Billings, MT: MRBI staff, Region 2, Bureau of Indian Affairs, November 1, 1948): pp. 4–5.
37. Meyer, *The Village Indians,* p. 240.
38. Ferrell, "Developing the Missouri."
39. Joseph K. Howard, Statement of Joseph Kinsey Howard, Montana, on "Missouri—Valley of Opportunity" before subcommittee of Senate Irrigation and Reclamation Committee (September 22, 1945), mimeographed; Public Affairs Institute, *The Big Missouri: Hope of Our West,* Report no. 2, June 1948 (Washington, DC: 1948).
40. Meyer, *The Village Indians,* p. 218.
41. Welsh, "Western Historians," p. 10; see also Daniel McCool, *Command of the Waters: Iron Triangles, Federal Water, Development, and Indian Water* (Berkeley: University of California Press, 1987).
42. U.S. Congress. Senate. Select Committee on Indian Affairs, *Three Affiliated Tribes and Standing Rock Sioux Tribal Equitable Compensation Act of 1991,* U.S. Senate, 102nd Cong., 1st sess., Senate Hearings (Washington, DC: 1991): pp. 43–44, quote on p. 43.
43. Ibid.
44. Laurence M. Hauptman, *The Iroquois Struggle for Survival: World War II to Red Power* (Syracuse: Syracuse University Press, 1986): 91.

45. Ibid., p. 90. Cf. *Seneca Nation of Indians v. United States,* 380 U.S. 952 (1965).
46. Edmund Wilson, *Apologies to the Iroquois* (New York: Farrar, Straus and Cudahy, 1959).
47. Hauptman, *The Iroquois Struggle,* p. 113. [Editors' note: Imre Sutton corresponded with Morgan in the early 1960s about Kinzua and later visited the dam site in 1965. He notes of Morgan that this engineer-planner was the first to conceive the idea of comprehensive river basin planning; he applied the concept to the Ohio Conservancies and then encouraged the federal government to adopt the approach for the TVA.]
48. William N. Fenton, "From Longhouse to Ranch-type House: The Second Housing Revolution of the Seneca Nation," in Elizabeth Tooker, ed., *Iroquois Culture, History, and Prehistory,* Proceedings of the 1965 Conference on Iroquois Research (Albany: New York State and Science Service, 1967): 7.
49. Ibid., p. 10.
50. Joy Ann Kolb, "Ghosts of Broken Hearts and Laws: The Allegany Seneca and the Kinzua Dam," Ph.D. diss. in anthropology, Bryn Mawr College, Bryn Mawr, Pennsylvania, 1987: 95.
51. Ibid., p. 97.
52. Laurence M. Hauptman, *Formulating American Indian Policy in New York State, 1970–1986* (Albany: State University of New York Press, 1988): 99–100.
53. Hauptman, *The Iroquois Struggle for Survival,* pp. 85–112.
54. Laurence M. Hauptman, "General John S. Bragdon, the Office of Public Works Planning, and the Decision to Build Pennsylvania's Kinzua Dam," *Pennsylvania History,* 53:3 (1986): 181–200, quote on p. 184.
55. Hauptman, *The Iroquois Struggle,* p. 95.
56. Quoted in Hauptman, "General John S. Bragdon," p. 96.
57. Ibid.
58. Quoted in Hauptman, *The Iroquois Struggle,* p. 103.
59. Hauptman, *Formulating American Indian Policy,* p. 3.
60. Confederation of American Indians, *Indian Reservations: A State and Federal Handbook* (Jefferson, NC: McFarland, 1986): 194–195.
61. Hauptman, *The Iroquois Struggle,* p. 98.
62. Quoted in Boyce Richardson, *Strangers Devour the Land* (Post Mills, VT: Chelsea Green, 1991): 121.
63. Quoted in Meyer, *The Village Indians,* p. 213.
64. Samuel Hays, *Conservation and the Gospel of Efficiency* (Cambridge, MA: Harvard University Press, 1959): 265.
65. Quoted in Richardson, *Strangers Devour the Land,* p. 301.
66. Quoted in Hauptman, *The Iroquois Struggle,* p. 121.
67. MRBI, *Indians and the Pick-Sloan Plan,* p. 9.
68. Thayer Scudder, "Recent Experiences With River Basin Development in the Tropics and Subtropics," *Natural Resources Forum,* 18:2 (1994): 101–113, quote on p. 108.
69. Waldram, *As Long as the Rivers Run,* p. 234.
70. Ibid.
71. Ibid., p. 173.
72. Ibid., pp. 171–179.
73. Ibid., p. 235.

Chapter 4

American Indian Timber Management Policy: Its Evolution in the Context of U.S. Forest History

Alan G. McQuillan

The history of timber policy on American Indian lands is inextricably linked to the general history of timber policy in the United States, particularly on public forestlands. Because timber policy on Indian lands has been largely determined by the federal government—beginning with the War Department, followed by the Department of the Interior—this is perhaps not surprising. Federal policy, however, has not developed in a vacuum. Although forestry as a professional activity was not introduced from Europe until the late nineteenth century, well before that time federal timber policy was heavily influenced by pressures for land development in the West.

Thus up until now little is uniquely "Indian" about Indian timber policy; it has grown out of an interplay of tensions within the federal government. Sometimes precedent-setting forestry legislation grew out of statutes that first applied to Indian lands. This happened in 1890, when a federal statute regarding the Menominee Indians in Wisconsin led the way for a series of laws that brought European-style forestry into the United States, and it happened again in 1934, when the Indian Reorganization Act became the first federal act mandating management of forests on the principle of sustained yield. In both cases this likely occurred because a new phase of forestry development was in the wind, and it just happened that Indian-related legislation was the first to pick up on the trend. Thus Indian forestry has sometimes led and sometimes followed other milestones in U.S. timber policy history, but it has always remained an integral part of that history.

U.S. Timber Policy Prior to the Civil War

Although the first forest regulations were home grown—in the Plymouth Colony in 1626—most timber regulation in Colonial America was imposed by Britain to protect supplies of masts for warships. Similar protectionist policies for military purposes were then pursued by the United States after independence.[1]

The legal precedent for government control of timber cutting on "public" (including Indian) lands was well established. Northern European nations had long adopted the principle that whichever nation "discovered" a "new" territory gained exclusive right to negotiate treaties with any indigenous inhabitants. By extension, when U.S. independence was established, that right was deemed transferred to the newly sovereign nation. When other land acquisitions were made (such as the Louisiana Purchase from the French in 1803), this right was acquired with the territory. Under this legal tradition, title to the land was deemed to belong to the colonial nation and not to its original inhabitants.

Explaining the moral basis of this principle, George Coggins and colleagues cite Chief Justice Marshall who, in a seminal case in 1823, opined that Indians were "fierce savages, whose occupation was war, and whose subsistence was drawn chiefly from the forest. To leave them in possession of their country was to leave the country a wilderness." As savages, they were "deemed incapable of transferring the absolute title to others."[2] The ethical assumption was that such Indians had natural rights of occupancy, but title of ownership (a legal and written right in contradistinction to natural rights) could belong only to a power that possessed written laws.

Notwithstanding the accepted right of indigenous occupants to cut wood strictly for their own needs (in accordance with John Locke's theory of natural rights), legal ownership of any trees accompanied title to the land.[3] Treaties with tribes guaranteed the Indians continuance of their right of occupancy on designated lands, but legal title to all Indian treaty lands began and remained in the name of the United States. Logically, therefore, timber on treaty lands also belonged to the United States.[4] Thus and importantly, in the eyes of the law there was no difference between Indian reservations and public domain lands in terms of title to timber—the U.S. government possessed it in both instances.

From the outset, U.S. policy was to dispose of public domain lands by sale to encourage settlement and raise revenue.[5] Under the Jeffersonian "yeoman farmer" policy, clearing forests to make room for productive agriculture was a morally commendable occupation; given the imperative of manifest destiny, popular opinion was accurately reflected by those members of Congress who believed the rush to settle the West should not be thwarted by legal or bureaucratic processes. The setters needed wood—for railroads and mining, forts and farming, ranching and construction—and there were plenty of trees on the public domain, whether cutting was legal or not.

The problems of keeping settlers and developers off public lands and keeping them from cutting the timber (until title could be formally transferred) went hand in hand. Technically, since government ownership of public timber was guaranteed under the U.S. Constitution, no statutory authority for enforcement of government property rights should have been necessary. Yet in 1807 an antitrespass act authorized the U.S. marshal to use military force to remove unauthorized settlers ("squatters") from all public domain lands (although in practice "the law did little to stop squatting").[6] In 1821 the attorney general declared that the 1807 act also provided authority to prevent timber trespass (illegal timber cutting) by use of military force.

Unlike today, there was no way to cut trees legally on public lands. The commissioner of the General Land Office sought to enforce government property rights to "every species on every acre of the public lands,"[7] but Congress was chronically ambivalent in its support of the administration. The Public Lands Committee of the House of Representatives declared in 1828 that squatting ("preemption") was inevitable and even desirable. Laws in 1830, 1841, 1854, and 1862 gradually legalized preemption in more states and under broader circumstances before it was finally prohibited in 1891.[8]

Despite willingness to part with its lands, Congress continued to pass laws purporting to protect its trees. In 1831 it strengthened the antitrespass laws, giving "its official stamp of approval of the Attorney General's interpretation of the Act of 1807 that *all* kinds of trees on *all* public lands were to be protected from trespass."[9] In 1847 Congress extended to all public lands a fine of triple stumpage value for people found cutting timber illegally. But throughout this entire period, Congress provided no funds explicitly for preventing such illegal cutting.

This ambivalence of Congress reflects its reluctance to formally admit its de facto policy of waiving its property rights in the interest of developing the West. If settlement and development were to proceed, land and timber had to be readily available. For example, farming required even more wood for fencing than it did for building construction or fuel, and "by 1850 there were about 3.2 million miles of wooden fence in the United States, enough to encircle the earth one hundred times."[10]

However slowly, concern for the future of timber supplies did emerge; an agricultural writer in 1846 warned that "the day is not far distant when we shall be as destitute of timber as many parts of Europe."[11] The extant knowledge at this time in U.S. history was that forest protection meant "no cutting of trees." Timber trespassers were said to be wasting the forest. There was as yet no thought for the European concept of forestry as a long-term agricultural activity. American people thought that once cut, a forest was simply ruined; it was gone. And since the American people's experience was with conversion of woods to farms, they had little evidence to the contrary.

With demands for resources building, Congress in 1849 created the Department of the Interior. At the same time the Office of Indian Affairs was transferred to Interior from the War Department. From this point on, much of the vacillation regarding timber protection seems to reflect the changing attitudes of the various individuals who held the office of secretary of the interior.

Initially, timber agents were appointed by the secretary to protect government trees, but when one agent took his job too seriously in 1853 and held timber trespassers in custody, political repercussions forced the secretary to abolish all timber agent positions. By 1867 a compromise had been reached regarding timber trespassers: they could escape prosecution by paying a "stumpage" tariff for timber cut, so under a worst case scenario a trespasser would have to pay the value of the timber cut, and, given lax enforcement, most of the time he would pay nothing at all. Prior to the 1870s public lands timber policy was one of extreme lenience.

Familiar Ambivalence on Indian Lands

From its outset in 1849, Interior assigned all responsibilities for Indians and reservations to the Indian Office, whose approach to timber reflected what prevailed in the public domain: officially, trees on all lands whose title was in the name of the United States belonged to the government. Still, the government's overriding moral concern was not with timber but with peopling the West with diligent yeoman farmers. On Indian lands, similarly, the proposed solution to the "Indian problem" was to turn these traditional nomads into settled farmers.

In 1853 President Pierce began the policy "of restricting the area occupied by each Indian tribe to the amount of land that was considered sufficient to meet the needs of the members of the tribe on the basis of an agricultural or a grazing economy."[12] A government "farmer" was appointed on each reservation to instruct Indians in farming techniques, and to these farmers fell the responsibility for timber matters. This policy was given a boost with passage of the General Allotment Act in 1887. The act, which granted 80- or 160-acre farming allotments to each adult Indian, was vigorously pursued despite the fact that, as a Bureau of Indian Affairs (BIA) report later stated: "Of the total land area in Indian ownership only a relatively small portion is suited to agricultural cultivation and by far the larger proportion is either forest or range land." The result was that "the Indian Service found it necessary to allot hundreds of thousands of acres of forestland, much of which was unfitted for agricultural use even when cleared of its forest growth." And despite vigorous objections by the first Indian Service forester, J. P. Kinney, around 1910, this policy continued intermittently until it was finally halted in 1934.[13]

The General Allotment Act placed Indian lands under an explicit trust management mandate—one that was extended indefinitely by the Indian Reorganization Act of 1934—and it was with this understanding that the Indian Service carried out the protection of Indian forests:

> The relationship of the Federal Government toward Indian property, both tribal and individual . . . is that of a trustee; and the Federal

> Government holds itself to the same fiduciary responsibility that would be imposed upon a trustee who had been clothed by a court with the duty of administering the property interests of a minor or other incompetent.[14]

Despite later attempts by the Justice Department to deny this trust responsibility for the management of Indian forests, the principle was upheld by the U.S. Supreme Court as recently as 1983.[15]

From the perspective of the mid-nineteenth century, since logging meant forest destruction the agency's responsibility to protect Indian forests obliged it to prevent all but minimal cutting of trees. Timber cutting was deemed permissible only when necessary to clear land for conversion to agricultural use. Clearing forests for farming and logging to meet Indians' wood needs for "school, agency, and domestic purposes" (including home building and heating) were complementary legitimate activities. But commercial logging, selling timber to lumber companies was not deemed compatible with forest protection.

This formal policy, however, did not accord with the huge demand for lumber to develop the West. Developers were just as partial to Indian timber as they were to timber on the public domain. On reservations, this policy also did not accord with the needs of Indians to raise money with which to feed and clothe themselves—having been largely deprived of traditional sources of sustenance. This was especially true in the vast majority of situations where attempts to turn the Indians into subsistence farmers (usually on land wholly unsuited for agriculture) turned into abject failures.

Consider the Menominee Indian Reservation (IR) in Wisconsin, established by a treaty in 1854.[16] Three years earlier, while laying out boundaries, the superintendent of Indian Affairs was exploring land near the center of what was to become the reservation, along with three Menominee chiefs and an interpreter. Here, deep within Indian Country (and part of the U.S. public domain at the time), the men "discovered . . . a good saw mill, with two saws and excellent fixtures, cutting twelve thousand feet of lumber per day."[17] And immediately after their reservation was established, the Menominee Indians entered into a contract with a white man named Jones to cut pine on the reservation in exchange for 100 barrels of flour monthly to the Indians.[18]

When the secretary of the interior learned about this contract in 1861, he forbid it on the grounds that his department lacked authority to permit it. Curiously, it was not inconsistent with this policy that the Menominee treaty had provided funds "to procure a suitable [white] person to attend and carry on the [Indians'] grist mill and sawmill for a period of fifteen years";[19] government responsibility extended to hiring white people to assist and educate the Indians, but the Indians were not to be allowed to help themselves by selling timber commercially.

In 1855 a subagent was appointed at Menominee, who devoted much of his time to instructing and assisting Indians in "clearing and grubbing [trees and stumps] towards preparing land for crops."[20] These crops failed in 1858 (the wheat was destroyed by smut and rust), however, and failed again in 1859.[21] Farming continued to fail, but the Menominee at least had the flour from the logging contract until that was abrogated in 1861. The following year a new agency farmer at Menominee (named Davis) reported that crop failure had been caused by the Indians having chosen to till the lightest sandy soil (because it was the easiest to work); he encouraged the Indians to move their farming onto the clay ridges, even though they were very stony and would require much patient labor. Davis also believed the best soil was in the heaviest timber, but that would be the most difficult to clear. The Indians dutifully obeyed instructions and again attempted to make farming work. By 1867, however, the Indian agents themselves were realizing that the land was not suited to agriculture, and attention shifted to finding jobs for Indians (such as working in the woods and mills).

Two years after forced termination of the first commercial logging contract, Indian agents at Menominee were telling the Washington office of the Indians' desire to sell for cash the better-quality boards they were producing at their own sawmill, but this too was denied. Interior did permit the Indians to enter into a contract with white lumbermen to remove "dead and down" timber that would otherwise have gone to rot. But the Indians were soon complaining that the lumbermen were taking green standing trees in addition to the dead and down, and when great fires raged across the reservation around 1868, the lumbermen were accused of having set them to create dead and down timber for exploitation. Interior canceled the contracts and impounded the logs cut.[22] By 1870 the Indians were living in deep poverty, disgusted and discouraged, and the school closed for lack of attendance. The agent, Army Lt. W. S. Bourne, reported that "the superintendent who located this tribe selected a poor sand barren and obliged them [the Indians] to live on it and pretend to make farms."[23]

The following year the local Indian agent succeeded in convincing the Washington office (under a new secretary of the interior) to approve selling green timber on the Menominee Reservation, under the understanding that the trees were being cut solely for purposes of clearing the better agricultural land and on the condition that white lumbermen (who encouraged drunkenness and dishonesty and generally set a bad example) would not be allowed on the reservation. The logs were to be cut and stacked by the Indians on the frozen riverbanks in winter and then sold before being floated downriver in the spring.[24] From 1871 through 1875 this new policy was remarkably successful, and it might have continued had external legal events not again brought commercial logging to a halt.

In 1872 the new secretary of the interior had approved a 10-year contract between the Indians on the La Pointe Indian Reservation (Wisconsin) and a white logger for the sale of an indeterminate amount of green pine. According to J. P. Kinney, the terms of the contract were so loose that "it was impossible to protect adequately the interests of the Indians." This led to litigation that culminated in the far-reaching Cook decision of 1874. In Kinney's words:

> In October 1873 an action was brought in the Supreme Court of the United States involving the question of the legal right of Indians to cut timber from reservations for sale. In May, 1874, the court's decision reasserted a former decision that Indians had only rights of occupancy in lands held in common, had no right to cut timber therefrom for sale and that timber so cut belonged to the United States.[25]

The crucial difference was that whereas Indians could cut timber for their own use, especially when incidental to clearing their land for farming, they had no right to cut it for sale. Thus by adhering to legal principle, Indians were deprived of one of their very few means of raising money.

The local agent at Menominee either did not know of the Cook decision or ignored it in the interest of preventing starvation, and for a while the Indians were allowed to continue cutting green timber and selling the logs to off-reservation buyers. For the 1875–1876 winter logging season, however, Menominee logging was restricted "strictly to timber that had been injured by fire, and was liable to waste unless cut."[26] If this was designed to prevent a shutdown as a result of the Cook decision it failed, because in January 1876 the secretary of the interior ordered *all* logging activity at Menominee to cease immediately. By this time the Indians had already cut over 13 million board feet of logs that winter, which they had sold for an average price of over six dollars per thousand board feet—a substantial revenue ($78,000) of which they were henceforth deprived. After Congress passed emergency legislation to authorize sale of those logs already cut and stacked but not yet sold, the Menominee ignored Washington again and resumed cutting dead and down timber the following winter. As Kinney remarked: "The Indians were often in a pitiable condition, with their local agents unable to do anything for their relief. It is no wonder that they winked at infractions of the letter of the law."[27] But blatant continuation of Menominee logging "aroused a storm of protest and from autumn 1877 to that of 1881 no cutting for sale purposes was reported."[28]

Thus, as we have seen, government ambivalence and social pressures affected conditions similarly on public domain and Indian lands. Local needs for wood conflicted with Washington-level efforts to enforce legal rights to government property. If the secretary of the interior appears to have been taking a hard-line approach on reservations in the late 1870s in the wake of the Cook decision, that is also explainable by changes in the broader political climate of the decade.

The Emerging Concept of Forestry

Up to and even beyond this time, the American experience with forests was that timber cutting and conversion of land to farming went hand in hand, the general opinion being that once cut or burned, forests were simply gone. The approach to forest protection—when any was implemented—was militaristic and simple: prevent people from cutting trees. This approach continued for years; for example, in 1879, shortly after the establishment of a new military post at Hell Gate Pass in Montana, Edgar Ford mapped out the Fort Missoula Timber Reserve of 1,577 acres in the hitherto unsurveyed Pattee Canyon.[29] As any military officer knew, one could not run a fort without proper provision for a timber supply, and this was achieved by preventing unsanctioned cutting within the reserve. Forest protection as prevention from cutting was easily understood, and as evidenced by the Cook decision, this view was shared by the Supreme Court in the protection of American Indian forests.

Although the word *forestry* had still not appeared in a U.S. dictionary by 1880,[30] the first significant stirring of American concern for forestry—as continual production of timber through regulation (as opposed to prohibition) of tree cutting—occurred in 1864 when George Perkins Marsh published his famous book *Man and Nature: Or, Physical Geography as Modified by Human Action*.[31] One-third of this voluminous work was devoted to forests. As a utilitarian and a Calvinist, Marsh was concerned with preventing waste. Marsh was perplexed by the destruction of forests he had seen as a child in Vermont, and as a U.S. diplomat stationed in Rome he was motivated by his realization that empires (such as the Roman Empire) had been lost by squandering natural resources. Unlike the recently deceased Thoreau, Marsh viewed forest protection as a strictly practical rather than romantic endeavor. In Europe Marsh saw the devastation of French forests that followed the sweeping away of the old punitive forest code during the Revolution, and he witnessed the revival of French forest regulation in the 1860s. He admired the Prussian approach to forest regulation that had been in place for over a century and also saw the problems created by the absence of forest regulations in Turkey.[32] Marsh was regarded as an important influence by virtually all the major figures who contributed to the birth of American forestry between the 1870s and the turn of the twentieth century.

One of these was Franklin Hough, who through his involvement with census taking learned of drastic declines in lumber production in the Northeast. In 1873 Hough presented a paper "On the Duty of Governments in the Preservation of Forests" and convinced the American Association for the Advancement of Science to appoint a committee to report on the subject to President Grant. This led to a position for Hough in the office of the commissioner of agriculture as the nation's first forestry agent. Here he wrote a 650-page report criticizing the government's ineffective control of timber abuse. Because he was in Agriculture and not in the Interior Department, Hough's role was purely advisory, but his Division of Forestry became an important part of a movement to introduce European and particularly Prussian forestry practice into the United States. Hough's division was eventually headed by the famous Prussian-born forester Bernard Fernow in 1886.[33]

In 1875 John Warner started the American Forestry Association, and in 1882 he organized (with Hough and Fernow) the First American Forest Congress.[34] By 1879 there was sufficient disgruntlement with the lack of an effective timber policy to cause Congress to create a Public Land Commission to at least review the situation. This resulted in a comprehensive report by the director of the arboretum at Harvard University, Charles Sprague Sargent.[35] Forestry journals sprang up: *The American Journal of Forestry, Forestry Bulletin, Forest and Stream, Garden and Forests, Forest Leaves, The Forester,* and *American Forests,* and other publications such as *Century Magazine* and *Atlantic Monthly* also took up the cause.

But if the birth of professional forestry was in the wind, it had yet not taken hold in congressional lands policy. Some change, however, was discernable. In 1871 Congress provided $5,000 annually for forest protection of naval reserves, and the next year it appropriated $10,000 for the protection of timber in the public domain—the same year it reserved Yellowstone "as a public park or pleasuring ground for the benefit and enjoyment of the people." But still there was no policy on those public forestlands that were physically unsuited for conversion to agriculture, although in 1874 the commissioner of public lands complained to Congress about the lack of a policy for properly disposing of similar "pine lands." Rather than allow timber depredation, he wanted to sell the pine lands for their appraised value.[36] In 1876 a forest reserves bill was introduced in the House, but no action was taken. Ambivalence and timber depredation continued.

In 1877 the Interior Department was awakened by the appointment of German-born Carl Schurz as secretary of the interior. Schurz was a hard-liner who immediately "hired special agents to halt timber thievery," reinstituting the position of timber agents that had been abolished over twenty years earlier.[37] Under Schurz, Indian reservations like Menominee were finally forced to discontinue logging to comply belatedly with the 1874 Cook decision.

In Congress new moves were afoot to address the problem of timber depredation on the public domain. Although once again they largely failed in this purpose, two important acts were passed in 1878: the Free Timber Act and the Timber and Stone Act. The Free Timber Act allowed trees to be cut on land that had been filed on for mining, but its larger effect was to underscore the illegality of cutting on the remaining public lands (well over 99 percent of the total).[38]

Secretary Schurz took the act seriously and intended to enforce it, but he met with the usual opposition from timber interests and their supporters in Congress. Schurz also recommended that timber (but not the land it grew on) should be sold in a regulated manner that might "result in the maintenance and reproduction of the forest." Congress, however, took a different approach with the Timber and Stone Act. This act allowed outright sale, at $2.50 per acre, of public timberlands unsuited for agriculture or other purposes. When passed, the act applied only on the Pacific Coast, but in 1892 it was extended nationwide, and by 1924, 12.7 million acres had been disposed of under this law. Although each purchaser was supposedly limited to 160 acres, the ubiquitous use of "dummy entrymen" allowed lumber barons to accumulate vast acreages.[39]

Four years after passage of these acts Schurz was replaced by Henry Teller, a secretary sympathetic to western timber interests, and "from 1882 to 1885 lumbermen in Montana [and elsewhere] went about their business untroubled by agents or edicts." This was also the year logging resumed on the Menominee Indian Reservation. As K. Ross Toole commented, "Not only was Teller a Westerner, he was also a mine owner and had served as legal counsel for several Western railroads." Teller, a supporter of lumbering, lost no time in ordering "Commissioner of Indian Affairs Hiram Price to initiate 'dead and down' logging at select reservations in 1882."[40]

But things changed yet again in 1885, when conservation-minded President Cleveland appointed a similarly minded Lucius Lamar as secretary of the interior. Lamar's land commissioner, William Sparks, reported timber depredations on the public domain that were "universal, flagrant and limitless," and lawsuits were filed against the "bold, defiant, and persistent depredators on the public domain." The suits against the largest lumber barons dragged on until World War I and were eventually settled with little ado.[41]

After 1882, with white lumbermen again afoot on the Indian reservations, not surprisingly new allegations were leveled that green timber was being intentionally burned to create dead and down. In 1888 the attorney general issued the opinion that even "the dead and fallen timber that is not needed or used for improvements, agricultural purposes, or fuel by the Indians is the property of the United States."[42]

Once again logging was forced to cease, but this time the commissioner of Indian Affairs asked Congress to remedy the situation, and in 1889 it passed the Dead and Down Act.[43] The act applied to all Indian reservations, but logging was restricted to dead or fallen trees that had not been deliberately killed by use of fire.

Then in 1890, with the voices of Fernow and all the others pushing for legally sanctioned forestry ringing in its ears, as well as support from Wisconsin lumbermen and the Menominee Indians themselves, Congress passed an act that was precedent setting even though it applied only to the Menominee Reservation.[44] The act legalized the program that had been established on the Menominee Reservation in the 1870s, prior to the Cook decision. It authorized the Indian Office to supervise commercial logging of up to 20 million board feet of timber annually—either green or dead and down—provided the Indians themselves carried out the logging and banked the logs on streams, where they could be sold. Only Indians were to be employed "as far as practicable," and one-fifth of the proceeds "were to be used by the Secretary of the Interior for the benefit of the Indians, at his discretion, and four-fifths were to be deposited in the United States Treasury at 5 percent interest, to be paid to the Indians per capita, or be expended for their benefit under direction of the Secretary."[45]

This was important legislation in three ways: it helped to alleviate the desperate poverty of the Menominee Indians by allowing them to sell logs from green timber; it also established the precedent that proceeds from the sale of tribal timber should legally accrue to the Indians. And it was the first law in the nation that provided for the management of any "public" forestlands for economic purposes, authorizing the regulated sale of timber growing on lands of the United States without sale of the land itself.

Although regulations pursuant to this act were approved in January 1891, the program did not develop as hoped. Despite attempts to employ only Indian workers, white loggers were engaged, and a congressional report later found this "resulted in the introduction of intoxicating liquors upon the reservation, the demoralizing of the men, and the debauching of the women."[46] In addition, although a large proportion of the standing trees were hardwood, in practice only coniferous trees could be cut because only conifer logs would float on the river (hardwoods were too heavy), and among the conifers only the pine could be cut because the hemlock was not worth anything in the markets. The operation was therefore rather restricted, but its timing had historic importance, coming as it did in 1890—the year that perhaps best dates the movement of U.S. timber policy inexorably in the direction of professional forestry practice.

The advent of professional forestry notwithstanding, the traditional, militaristic approach to forest protection was slow to die. With its long tradition of preventing cutting on military reserves, there was good reason to associate the military with protecting forests. Moreover, this approach had gained support from the Romantic movement, led by the likes of Sierra Club cofounder John Muir. As Alfred Runte stated, "Military tenets of strictness and discipline coincided perfectly with preservationists' own assumptions that only rigid standards of protection would save the national parks." Recall that Yellowstone Park had been administered by the War Department from 1883, and when Yosemite—set aside for the state in 1864—was designated a national park in 1890, it also came under military protection.[47] Similarly, members of the 4th Cavalry rode in to protect the newly created Sequoia and General Grant National Parks in

1891. A Special Commission of the National Academy of Sciences in 1897 stated that the duties of forest officers "are essentially military in character and should be regulated for the present on military principles," and even forestry advocate Bernhard Fernow called for the training of forest officers at the West Point Military Academy.[48] Indeed, the Cavalry had long had the job of protecting Indian reservations and the forests on them.

Forestry Gains Ground

Fast on the heels of the 1889 act that allowed Indians generally to cut dead and down timber and the 1890 act that allowed the Menominee to cut green timber as well, Congress (perhaps inadvertently) in 1891 passed the famous act that allowed the president to establish forest reserves on the public domain. The act slipped through Congress late at night at the insistence of the protectionist-minded secretary of the interior, John Noble, and it marked the beginning of the series of forest reserves that became the National Forest System.[49]

Then, after years of wrangling, Congress passed the 1897 act that became the Organic Act of the Forest Service. The 1891 act had not authorized any cutting of trees whatsoever, and Congress refused to authorize regulated sales of green timber on forest reserves. The 1897 act recorded a compromise, allowing the sale of "carefully designat[ed] dead or *matured* timber . . . for the sole purpose of preserving the living and growing timber."[50] Pushed by the proforestry contingent, Congress was coming around to the view that some cutting of live trees would not devastate the forest, and similar language specifying which trees could be cut was incorporated in the next successful Menominee act in 1908. By restricting harvest to only the dead, down, or fully "ripened" green trees, it was thought one would not damage the growing capacity of the forest, and one would be obeying a moral imperative (or so it seemed) to not waste trees by allowing them to die and go to rot. It is evident, however, that Congress was not yet willing to endorse the likes of Fernow and Gifford Pinchot, who advocated European forestry practice along the lines of tree farming.

Angered but undaunted by congressional resistance, in 1898 the rising star of U.S. forestry, Pinchot, took over the Division of Forestry from Fernow (who departed to run the nation's first university-level forestry program at Cornell University). Although Pinchot was housed in the Department of Agriculture, he campaigned to win management authority over the forest reserves in Interior. By 1903 Pinchot's division was involved in field examinations of 20 million acres of forest reserves, and—with the vital assistance of his friend, President Theodore Roosevelt—in 1905 Congress passed the Transfer Act that gave Pinchot what he wanted by moving the reserves from Interior to Agriculture and creating the Forest Service with Pinchot as its first chief.[51] Indian forests, however, stayed under Interior.

Pinchot did not believe in restricting cutting to only those trees about to go to waste (as dictated by the 1897 Organic Act). Under the Pinchot-favored

European model, foresters could cut any and all trees necessary to secure the highest growth rate of the standing timber and to provide a high-level sustainable yield over the long run. In the 1906 *Use Book* (forerunner to the Forest Service manual), he wrote, "All timber on forest reserves which can be cut safely and for which there is actual need is for sale." Although Pinchot initially proposed selective cutting, leaving trees to provide seed for the next crop, a series of bad experiences with trees blowing down in windstorms led him eventually to adopt clear-cutting. This seemingly blatant violation of the restrictive language of the 1897 Organic Act was not seriously questioned until sixty-six years later, when litigation led to a Circuit Court decision that found most Forest Service timbering practices to be in violation of the 1897 act.[52]

Backed by Teddy Roosevelt, Pinchot's forestry and political power were on a roll, and in January 1908 he secured a cooperative agreement between the secretaries of Agriculture and Interior that "gave the Forest Service supervision over the handling of timber on Indian reservations."[53] In his autobiography, Pinchot makes plain his disgust for the way Interior's Indian Office had been handling timber affairs.[54] The feelings were mutual, and in short order he was embroiled in major disputes with the secretary of the interior over the withdrawal of public domain lands for the protection of potential water power sites, the patenting of coal claims in Alaska, and the transfer of 2.5 million acres of Indian lands to national forests, as well as over the administration of Indian timber generally. By January 1910 this led to his dismissal, but before then (and even after) his influence was enormous, and Indian lands were inevitably involved.[55]

The language of the 1897 Organic Act set the precedent for a new act specific to the Menominee Indian Reservation, passed in 1908, that authorized the cutting of the Menominee's "dead and down timber, and such fully matured and ripened green timber as the Forestry Service shall designate."[56] Passed after two years of wrangling, this new legislation provided for the same level of logging that had been established in 1890, but to alleviate the problems caused by white lumbermen, the act authorized construction of a tribal mill to convert the logs into lumber for sale on the open market (earlier tribal mills were for on-reservation-use lumber only). In deference to Pinchot, sections 1 and 5 of the act required that the U.S. Forest Service (in Agriculture, not Interior) should designate the trees for cutting. And reflecting Congress's new-found attachment to sustainable forestry, Senator Robert M. La Follette of Wisconsin, speaking for the Senate Committee on Indian Affairs, informed the Senate that the harvest would be made "in such a way that the forest will perpetuate itself."[57]

The 1908 act was restricted to Menominee lands, but a major watershed in Indian timber policy was about to be crossed: congressional authorization of forestry management on Indian reservations generally "may properly be said to have begun with passage of the act of March 3, 1909 . . . which appropriated the sum of $100,000 for forestry work on Indian reservations, and the act of June 25, 1910 . . . which authorized the sale of live timber from tribal and allotted lands under regulations to be prescribed by the Secretary of the Interior."[58] The latter act opened most Indian forests to regulated timber sales under the now accepted principles of forestry. From 1910 on, the government's fiduciary responsibility regarding Indian timberlands focused on the regulated sale of green timber under the forestry profession's principles of sustained yield, despite periods when the Indian Office dragged its heels on timber-only sales, in preference to land disposal through issuance of fee patents or "supervised sales" of timber together with the land it stood on.

Indian Forestry Comes Into Its Own

By early 1910 Pinchot had been fired as chief of the Forest Service, and Secretary of Interior Richard A. Ballinger had cancelled the cooperative agreement for Forest Service administration of Indian forests, returning authority to the Land Division of the Indian Service. Ballinger's Indian Service then asked J. P. Kinney if he would like to join, with a view to becoming its forester.[59] Kinney was educated in the European tradition of sustainable forestry as taught at Cornell and had passed the Civil Service examinations (written by Pinchot) for forest assistant and forest law examiner. At Interior, one of Kinney's first major jobs was to write regulations for the legislation just passed that allowed for regulated sale of green timber on most Indian lands. His regulations were approved in June 1911, and they anticipated the perpetual management of forests for future timber crops.[60]

Although Pinchot left the Forest Service in 1910, the "Pinchot faction" remained strong, and there was antipathy toward the Indian Service establishing its own forestry division in Interior.[61] Kinney did not become chief forester of the Indian Service but remained in the shadows behind a succession of short-lived chiefs who came to Interior from the Forest Service. At the end of 1913, during a general government retrenchment, the position of forester in the Indian Service was formally abolished. Kinney continued to hold the reigns under the titles of supervisor of forests (at least by 1914) and chief supervisor of forests (by 1918). Eventually, he became known as director of forestry (apparently not until after the Reclassification Act of 1924), and he continued to head Indian forestry until 1933—an effective and long career.[62]

The Menominee situation remained at the forefront of this important juncture in Indian timber history. Despite Ballinger's annulment in 1909 of the cooperative agreement with Pinchot's Forest Service, the 1908 law regarding the Menominee remained in force and required that Menominee trees be designated for cutting by the Forest Service. But given the strained political environment, it is hardly surprising that this arrangement did not work out. In 1912 a party from the Forest Service arrived to mark trees on the reservation, and, as a court later affirmed:

> These foresters had not been informed of the terms of the 1908 act limiting the cutting to "fully matured and ripened green timber" not in excess of 20 million feet a year. These men were under the erroneous impression that the Menominee Indian mills, which had a capacity for sawing approximately 40 million feet of timber a year, must be supplied with at least 35 million feet of green timber. The area selected by the Indian Service for such cutting constituted only about 2,300 acres. After experimentally marking the trees on a portion of the strip for an area about 100 feet wide and one and a half miles long, the markers ceased any further attempts to mark individual trees on the ground that the removal of 35 million feet on the 2,300 acres would not permit selective cutting and could only result in clear-cutting.[63]

This was effectively the end of Forest Service marking under the 1908 Menominee act. Whether the fault lay in ignorance of the law on the part of the Forest Service or was the result of the Indian Service having deliberately designated only 2,300 acres on which to mark the desired volume ("forcing" clear-cutting) remains unclear.[64] When Kinney visited the reservation for a second time in 1913, he criticized attempts at selective logging and recommended clear-cutting (with planting), and clear-cutting (although largely without planting) became the primary form of logging on the reservation until 1927—paralleling the dominant form of logging for most Western lands, public and private[65] (Figures 4.1 and 4.2).

Evolving Forestry Practice in the Twentieth Century

As noted, the development of forestry—from the Midwest to the West Coast, from the Indian Service to the Forest Service—followed somewhat similar paths. The "river-drive" logging that had characterized the late nineteenth century was slowly replaced by railroad logging. Although river logging had its problems, railroad logging had its share of problems also. Railroads were laid for logging on only a temporary basis, and given the expense, along with the cumbersome size of the steam donkeys used for yarding the logs, almost the only practical means of logging was in the form of clear-cutting.[66] This form was opposed to officially recommended forestry practice. Pinchot's 1905 *Primer of Forestry* detailed several kinds of "selective" harvesting he preferred, and the Indian Service's timber sale regulations always required selective logging, although both Pinchot and Kinney often recommended otherwise in practice.[67]

As the 1930s approached, railroad logging was giving way to the next era of technology—road logging. Since roads could be left in place and the costs of road transportation were lower, there was much greater flexibility in terms of where to log, the size of logging units, and how much timber to leave in the woods: selective logging became feasible after all. Indian Service foresters on

Fig. 4.1 Lumbering on the Menominee Indian Reservation (Wisconsin). Railroad logging and clear-cutting of all commercial trees on the Menominee Indian Reservation, Wisconsin, in 1915. Courtesy, David Grignon, Menominee Historical Archives, Menominee Nation, Keshena, Wisconsin, 1995.

Fig. 4.2 Selective Cutting on Menominee Indian Reservation. Successful practice of selective logging on the Menominee Indian Reservation, Wisconsin, begun in 1927. This picture shows the residual hardwood and conifer trees shortly after logging. Courtesy, David Grignon, Menominee Historical Archives, Menominee Nation, Keshena, Wisconsin, 1995.

the Menominee Reservation instituted successful trials with selective cutting beginning in 1927, and the Forest Service in the Lake states also began long-term monitoring of selective cutting at about that time.[68]

On the Quinault Reservation (Washington), there had been extensive clear-cutting using railroads south of the Quinault River since large-scale logging began there in 1922, but Indian Service foresters successfully instituted selective logging (using crawler tractors in place of the train-mounted steam donkeys) near Quinault Lake in 1936. They also began selective logging on the Hall Unit, closer to the south end of the reservation, in 1939; but the land was too swampy to allow use of anything but the older, heavier technology, and it was an abject failure.[69]

Although selective logging attained a fair measure of permanence in the Lake states, for a variety of reasons it did not catch on in the Pacific Northwest.[70] But there could be no return to the vast clear-cuts of the railroad logging era, and by the end of World War II it was obvious that a new direction had to be tried. The recommended solution was clear-cutting in small blocks or "staggered settings." These blocks (usually recommended at 40 acres, although often larger in practice) were designed to be small enough to achieve natural regeneration from the surrounding seed source of standing trees, and their "checkerboard" isolation was useful in preventing spread of fires.

Indian Service foresters adopted this practice on the Quinault Reservation beginning around 1950.[71] In some parts of the so-called Douglas fir region, particularly in areas of western hemlock where natural regeneration was easy to achieve, this system of staggered settings worked well enough. But in the Quinault part of the region, where the cedar component was very heavy, the new system was yet another failure. Naturally regenerated trees were stifled by vast quantities of cedar debris and underbrush and thus grew much too slowly. By the late 1950s timber values had risen so high (following the postwar baby boom) that prudent forest managers in the Northwest would not take a chance on natural regeneration. The foresters retained the patchwork quilt ("mangy dog") pattern of dispersed clear-cuts, but they adopted an almost universal practice of site preparation by controlled burning of logging slash, promptly followed by careful planting with fast-growing Douglas fir.[72] This practice created "monotonous monocultures," but as a tree farming technique it was very successful.[73] This intensive management practice was not adopted on the Quinault Reservation, however, and when the widening discrepancy between accepted practice and Quinault forestry became evident in 1971, Indian allottees filed suit and prevailed against the U.S. government for negligent mismanagement of the Indian forest.[74]

The negligent Quinault situation of the 1960s and early 1970s does not detract from the generalization that forestry practice on Indian lands was intended to keep step with professional practice. For example, when "intensive forest management" and "high-yield forestry" became the watchwords of foresters (pioneered by the Weyerhaeuser Timber Company), the BIA swiftly followed with a succession of reports titled "Potential for Intensive Timber Management" on six Northwest reservations (plus the Navajo) between 1962 and 1967.[75] Similarly, when "multiple use" became popular in this era—recognizing that forestry was more than just timber management and that the forest is valuable for a wide range of human benefits including wildlife, recreation, watershed values, and the long-contentious activity of grazing domestic livestock—the concern influenced forestry on both Forest Service and Indian lands.

The adoption of the sustained-yield policy similarly affected all forestry practice, and Indian policy set another historical precedent. Overproduction of lumber on private land had been seriously depressing market prices since before 1926, and lumbermen had begun to consider ways to curtail the rate of logging. Primary among them was the adoption of sustained-yield principles for private industry. The situation worsened after the start of the Great Depression, which led to a joint effort that produced a huge, 1,677-page *National Plan for American Forestry* in 1933. Both the Forest Service and the Indian Agency made significant contributions. The result was a general endorsement of sustained-yield principles among all major owners of forestland in the United States.[76]

Then, after several years of study, in 1934 Congress passed the Indian Reorganization Act.[77] This act accomplished many things, including ending the process of carving reservations into individual allotments, but for our purposes the most significant accomplishment is section 6, which mandated that Indian lands must be managed according to the principles of sustained yield. This was the first legislation mandating any U.S. federal agency to practice sustained-yield forestry; the next such statute was passed in 1937 and applied to revested Oregon and California railroad land managed by the Department of the Interior.[78] Even though sustained yield had been embraced by the Forest Service from the outset, the act that mandated sustained-yield management (and also multiple use) for national forests was not passed until 1960.[79] Once again a major movement in the development of U.S. forest policy, when initially sanctioned by Congress, applied (by happenstance) first on American Indian lands.

The Demise of Traditional "Prussian" Forestry

Notwithstanding the slow expansion of traditional forestry into multiple uses after World War II, the governing ethic of the profession remained intact for approximately 100 years: the Prussian model of forestry as "long-rotation agriculture" and the ideal of the perfectly regulated forest as one containing neat, uniform rows of healthy and fast-growing ("thrifty") trees continued to be the goal, even when conditions on the ground caused its attainment to fall short of the ideal. This tree farm approach to forestry had taken a long time to supplant mere lumbering as the "proper" way to operate in the woods of the United States. Thanks to the efforts of Marsh, Hough, Fernow, Pinchot, Kinney, and others, forestry Prussian style had become firmly entrenched in the United States, particularly but not exclusively in the management of government-run forests. Beginning around 1990, however (exactly 100 years after the first "forestry legislation" for the Menominee), this ideal came crashing down.

A veteran forest ecologist at the Forest Service's Pacific Northwest Experiment Station realized from his many years of experience that natural forest ecosystems were considerably more complex than traditional forestry believed managed forests ought to be. Simplification (and reductionism) had been the tendency of all forms of human activity in Western civilization during most of the twentieth century, and traditional "modernist" forestry fit this style very well.[80] Postmodern science, however, had been setting a new trend, one strongly influenced by complexity theory. Jerry Franklin's notions regarding the complexity of forests aligned with this trend; he coined the term *new forestry* and launched this concept to a receptive and ecologically conscious audience in *American Forestry* in 1989.[81]

The Forest Service was eager to improve its tarnished image with the public, as well as with ecologically minded critics within its own ranks. The shortcomings of Prussian-style forestry had become all too evident, so the Forest Service embraced "new forestry" and in 1992 officially adopted a Franklinesque ecological approach called Ecosystem Management.[82] Where multiple use had extended the range of concerns in forestry to more uses (the utilitarian word stressed by Pinchot), this new concept went beyond multiple uses to embrace in-site forest values, including spiritual and aesthetic values, the healthy functioning of natural systems, the diversity of species, the number of big trees that remain, and so on.

Private industry also moved in this direction of ecosystem management. An industry conference in Portland, Oregon, in February 1992 revealed considerable support for the concept, and many companies embraced some aspects of the trend—if only as a way to head off public criticism of tree farm forestry. State forest agencies have moved in this direction also.[83]

In the circumstances, therefore, it is unsurprising that an *American Indian Law Review* article that begins with the sentence "Since time immemorial, Indians have held the belief that Mother Earth is to be protected and revered" should go on to applaud a review team's recommendation to adopt ecosystem management "as a tool for an overall approach to protecting the health and productivity of Indian Forests."[84] This review team, called IFMAT (Indian Forest Management Assessment Team), had been formed by the Intertribal Council (ITC), the body that contracted with the secretary of the interior to conduct an independent assessment of Indian forestlands as mandated by Congress in 1990 under the National Indian Forest Resource Management Act.[85] It is perhaps also not surprising that the team of "seven well-recognized experts in the field of forestry," included the "father" of ecosystem management himself, Jerry Franklin.

Fig. 4.3 Selective Cutting on Quinault Indian Reservation (Washington). Selective logging in the Hall Unit of the Quinault Indian Reservation, 1941. This area was unsuited to selective logging, as can be seen from the poor growth of these trees photographed forty-three years later. Photo taken by Alan McQuillan, 1984.

Echoing the Forest Service's embrace of spiritual and aesthetic among other values for national forests in 1992, the law review article states, "Tribes have a vested interest in the viability of their land to provide them with economic, spiritual, and aesthetic values."[86] The IFMAT considered the importance of "maintaining desirable ecological conditions" and underscored the contribution of fires, snags (standing dead trees), and large old trees to the complex structure that comprises the forest ecosystem. The IFMAT also noted the importance of scenic beauty to tribal members. Gary Morishima, technical adviser to the Quinault Nation (and closely involved with the ITC contract), embraced the concept of ecosystem management when he stated, "Although this concept has recently become fashionable, Indian tribes had been practicing it for thousands of years before they were displaced from their territories"[87] (Figures 4.3 and 4.4).

Although it is clearly appealing to claim that Indians were on to ecosystem management first, this is in fact one more instance of Indian forest policy tracking alongside (sometimes leading, sometimes trailing) the development of American forest policy in general. One must hasten to add, however, that just because a policy is formally in place does not mean it is successfully adhered to

Fig. 4.4 Quinault Experimental Forest. This late-1930s Douglas fir plantation in the Experimental Forest, a clear-cut area of tribal land on the Quinault Indian Reservation, was ready for logging again exactly fifty years later. Intensive management like this did not become prevalent until long after World War II. Photo taken by Alan McQuillan, 1989.

or even adhered to at all. As we saw at the outset, the nineteenth-century history of timber depredation in the public domain is one wherein attempts to comply with official policy were only sporadically successful. Somewhat similarly, the on-the-ground history of forest management on Indian lands is a litany of failures, many of which have been the subject of congressional hearings and court cases.

In many instances the failure of policy has been blamed on understaffing and lack of funding for reservation forestry as a result of congressional indifference.[88] Failure has been blamed on other factors also, including the unfortunate situation wherein many thousands of acres of Indian forestlands have been fragmented into individual allotments under the General Allotment Act. Congress, however, cannot be blamed for everything. For example, it was revealed in the 1957 hearings on Quinault timber sales before the Senate Subcommittee on Indian Affairs that a shortage of funds for forest regeneration was a result of the BIA having failed to seek funding and authority for tree planting.[89] And regarding the Menominee Reservation, the tribe successfully sued the government for lost revenue resulting from Congress's failure to raise the annual cutting limit above the 20 million board feet first set in 1890, before the substantially higher sustainable-yield level of the Menominee forest was recognized. Although Congress cannot be held legally liable for its actions or inactions, the Supreme Court in 1980 found in favor of the Indians because the BIA had known of the problem but had not asked Congress to provide a remedy (despite apparent congressional willingness to provide one if requested).[90]

The Forest Service has also had its share of litigation. The conclusion is that the history of professional forestry in the United States—its evolution from the naive belief that all timber cutting resulted in forest devastation to the Prussian ideal of the perfectly regulated forest to the current paradigm of ecosystem management—is one that involves Indian forestry integrally with forestry in other sectors. I do not find evidence that the significant cultural differences between Indians and white people have produced distinctly different approaches to forestry. Perhaps in the future, with greater independence for Indian tribal forestry and correspondingly reduced involvement of the BIA, divergences will begin to occur. Of course, it is also possible that if divergence does occur,[91] "white" forest policy will then learn from "Indian" forestry so that convergence will result once again. Given the complexity of forestry management—as a cultural as well as a scientific and economic endeavor—who can say where the future will lead?

References

1. In the Massachusetts Bay Colony, anyone found guilty could be charged £100 for every tree cut that was over 24 inches in diameter at a foot above ground level—a hefty fine at that time. The last shipment of masts to Britain occurred in 1775. Samuel T. Dana, *Forest and Range Policy: Its Development in the United States* (New York: McGraw-Hill, 1956): 4–11.

2. George Coggins, Charles Wilkinson, and John Leshy, *Federal Public Land and Resources Law,* 3d ed. (New York: Foundation Press, 1993): 50–53.
3. Ibid.; Dana, *Forest and Range Policy,* p. 20. For more on the distinction between legal and natural rights see Peter Wenz, *Environmental Justice* (Albany: SUNY Press, 1988): chapter 4; Michel Foucault, *Madness and Civilization* (New York: Vintage, 1988): 55–63.
4. Although title to Indian trust lands is still held by the United States, the "pure" theory began to wane around 1907, when Senator La Follette made a historic move away from the traditional notion that Indian timber was the property of the United States, declaring: "The [Menominee] timber is the property of the Indians. Their property rights and their personal welfare are the matters for consideration" (U.S. Senate, "Cutting and Sale of Timber on Menominee Indian Reservation, Wis.," *Senate Report* 6669, 59th Cong., 2d sess. [February 14, 1907]: 1). It changed with passage of the Indian Reorganization Act in 1934. As a government report stated, "The theory that the Indians had only the right of occupancy in the lands . . . has practically been superseded by the legal theory that the Indians have a complete and indefeasible interest in the land, subject only to sovereign right of control by the Congress." Bureau of Indian Affairs, "Forest Conservation on Lands Administered by the Department of the Interior," part 2 of *A Report Prepared Pursuant to Senate Concurrent Resolution 31,* 75th Cong., 3d sess. (January 1940): 42.
5. Dana, *Forest and Range Policy,* p. 22. See also Benjamin H. Hibbard, *A History of the Public Land Policies* (Madison: University of Wisconsin Press, 1965 [1924]): chapter 4.
6. Dana, *Forest and Range Policy,* p. 25. The terms *public domain* and *public lands* were used interchangeably, p. 20.
7. Ibid., p. 51.
8. Ibid., pp. 25–27, 387.
9. Ibid., pp. 53–58, quote on p. 53; K. Ross Toole and Edward Butcher, "Timber Depredations on the Montana Public Domain, 1885–1928," *Journal of the West,* 7:3 (1968): 351–362, at p. 351.
10. Douglas MacCleery, *American Forests: A History of Resiliency and Recovery* (Durham, NC: Forest History Society, 1993): 11.
11. Ralph Hidy, Frank Hill, and Allan Nevins, *Timber and Men: The Weyerhaeuser Story* (New York: Macmillan, 1963): 125, referring to the agricultural writer Solon Robinson.
12. BIA, "Forest Conservation," pp. 40–41.
13. Ibid. Although no further allotments were made after 1934 [Editors' note: in 1959 the Agua Caliente Indians of Palm Springs, California, were allotted under special legislation], the problems of managing forest properties heavily fragmented by the allotment process continue to the present day.
14. Ibid., p. 42.
15. *United States v. Mitchell,* 463 U.S. 206 (1983) [*Mitchell II*]. The court found that although the 1887 act had not established an enforceable trust responsibility regarding forest management, such responsibility was implicit in subsequent acts that directly pertained to forestry. Cf. Darla J. Mondou, "Our Land Is What Makes Us What We Are: Timber Harvesting on Tribal Reservations After the NIFRMA," *American Indian Law Review,* 21:2 (1997): 259–296.
16. 10 *Stat.* 1064 (1852).

17. Once discovered, the white mill owners were apparently willing to sell the mill to the Indians. It was later revealed that a sawmill had been located at Keshena Falls since 1845, although whether this is the same mill is unclear. Elias Murray to Luke Lea, September 30, 1851, p. 308 of 1851 reg. copy, J. P. Kinney Papers, box 1, Minnesota Historical Society, St. Paul (MN); *Annual Report,* 1853, p. 293; *Annual Report,* 1865, p. 575. These were known as Annual—Agency—Reports of the Superintendent's Reports, but they could be the Commissioner's Reports. They are cited in an unpublished report prepared for the Menominee Nation by David Wrone (1996), pp. 85–86. [Wrone's report was prepared for use in court: Congressional Reference no. 93-649x, U.S. Court of Federal Claims, *Menominee Indian Tribe v. U.S.,* 101 Ct. Cl. 22 (1944).]
18. During the early 1850s the Rabbit Lake Band of the Chippewas of Minnesota had entered into a contract with lumbermen (unbeknownst to the Department of the Interior) to log Indian timber in exchange for "oxen, flour, pork, cook stoves and houses." J. P. Kinney, *Indian Forest and Range: A History of the Administration and Conservation of the Redman's Heritage* (Washington, DC: Forestry Enterprises, 1950): 5–6.
19. Article 3 of the Treaty of 1854, 10 *Stat.* 1064 (1854), cited in Wrone [unpublished report], p. 85.
20. Commissioner of Indian Affairs, *Annual Report,* House Executive Document, no. 1, 34th Cong., 1st sess., Serial 840 (1855): 363–364, cited by Richmond Clow in an unpublished report prepared for the Menominee Nation, 1995.
21. Commissioner of Indian Affairs, *Annual Report,* House Executive Document, no. 1, 35th Cong., 2d sess., Serial 997, (1858): 383, as cited in Clow [unpublished report], pp. 19–25. Clow cites Felix M. Keesing, *The Menomini Indians of Wisconsin: A Study of Three Centuries of Cultural Contact and Change* (Madison: University of Wisconsin Press, 1971 [1939 ed. published by the American Philosophical Society]): 168.
22. Patricia Ourada, *The Menominee Indians: A History* (Norman: University of Oklahoma Press, 1979): 145.
23. Commissioner of Indian Affairs, *Annual Report* (1870): 776, 928–929, cited in Wrone [unpublished report], p. 87.
24. Clow [unpublished report], pp. 27–28, citing *Annual Reports* of 1871 and 1872.
25. Kinney, *Forest and Range,* pp. 6–7, quote on p. 7, referring to *U.S. v. Cook,* 86 U.S. 591–592 (1873).
26. Commissioner of Indian Affairs, *Annual Report* (1876), cited by Clow [unpublished report], pp. 35–36.
27. Kinney, *Forest and Range,* p. 6.
28. J. P. Kinney, *A Continent Lost/A Civilization Won: Indian Land Tenure in America* (Baltimore: Johns Hopkins University Press, 1937): 256.
29. "Report to the President by Secretary of War George W. Murray," November 19, 1877; Executive Order of June 10, 1879; Survey Notes for Fort Missoula Timber Reserve on file at the Supervisor's Office, Lolo National Forest, Fort Missoula, MT.
30. David Clary, *Timber and the Forest Service* (Lawrence: University Press of Kansas, 1986): 6.
31. First published in 1864; see edition edited by David Lowenthal (Cambridge: Belknap Press of Harvard University Press, 1965).

32. David Lowenthal, *George Perkins Marsh: Versatile Vermonter* (New York: Columbia University Press, 1958): 252–256.
33. Frank Harmon, "Remembering Franklin B. Hough," *American Forests,* 83:1 (1977): 34–37, 52–54; Dana, *Forest and Range Policy,* pp. 80–87.
34. Ben Twight, "Bernard Fernow and Prussian Forestry in America: Building Support for Federal Forestry," *Journal of Forestry,* 88:2 (1990): 21–25; Dana, *Forest and Range Policy,* pp. 63, 87–90, 385.
35. Dana, *Forest and Range Policy,* p. 90; Stephen Fox, *The American Conservation Movement: John Muir and His Legacy* (Madison: University of Wisconsin Press, 1981): 109. Sargent's report was published as part of the tenth census in 1884.
36. Dana, *Forest and Range Policy,* pp. 58–59, 384.
37. Harmon, "Remembering Franklin B. Hough," p. 36; Dana, *Forest and Range Policy,* p. 59.
38. The Free Timber Act, "in effect, was a measure which made the cutting of timber illegal for any operation worth undertaking." Toole and Butcher, "Timber Depredations," p. 352.
39. Dana, *Forest and Range Policy,* p. 66; Charles F. Wilkinson and H. Michael Anderson, *Land and Resource Planning in the National Forests* (Covelo, CA: Island Press, 1987): 16, note 48; Hidy, Hill, and Nevins, *Timber and Men,* pp. 127–129; Hibbard, *A History of Public Land Policies,* pp. 465–470. The act also excused from prosecution any trespassers who were caught if they paid $2.50 per acre for the timber (and if they swore they had not exported any of the logs); the act was not repealed until 1955 (Dana, *Forest and Range Policy,* pp. 385, 425). Extending the Timber and Stone Act to all states in 1892 was, as Toole and Butcher ["Timber Depredations," pp. 352–54] state, "despite passage of the Forest Reserves Act in 1891, a clear indication that conservation had not yet prevailed as a dominant Congressional sentiment."
40. Clow [unpublished report], p. 37, citing *Annual Report* (1888).
41. Toole and Butcher, "Timber Depredations," pp. 354, 359–360. The authors provide ample evidence of the relationships between Western politicians and business interests. See also Dana, *Forest and Range Policy,* p. 61.
42. Clow [unpublished report], p. 38, citing *Annual Report* (1888).
43. 25 *Stat.* 673 (1889); Clow [unpublished report], p. 39; Dana, *Forest and Range Policy,* p. 386.
44. 26 *Stat.* 146 (1890); Kinney, *Forest and Range,* p. 116; Dana, *Forest and Range Policy,* p. 386; Wrone [unpublished report], pp. 96–97; Clow [unpublished report], pp. 40–41. Cf. Brian C. Hosmer, "Creating Indian Entrepreneurs: Menominees, Neopit Mills, and Timber Exploitation, 1890–1915," *American Indian Culture and Research Journal,* 15:1 (1991): 4.
45. Kinney, *Forest and Range,* p. 116.
46. U.S. Senate, "Cutting of Timber, etc., on Indian Reservations in Wisconsin," *Senate Report* 110, 60th Cong., 1st sess. (January 23, 1908): 2.
47. Alfred Runte, *Yosemite: The Embattled Wilderness* (Lincoln: University of Nebraska Press, 1990): 57–61; Runte, *National Parks: The American Experience,* 2d ed. (Lincoln: University of Nebraska Press, 1987): 98.
48. Dana, *Forest and Range Policy,* p. 110.
49. 26 *Stat.* 1095, 1103. Secretary of the Interior John Noble apparently insisted (during conference committee consideration and in violation of procedural rules) on

adding the famous forest reserves language to the 1891 act that was otherwise intended to repeal the Timber Culture Act and make other changes in timber laws. The section added by Noble (§ 24) authorized the president to make reservations of forestlands; this was the beginning of what became the National Forest System (Dana, *Forest and Range Policy,* pp. 100–101; Wilkinson and Anderson, *Land and Resource Planning,* p. 18, note 56.

50. 30 *Stat.* 34–36 (1897) (emphasis added). See Wilkinson and Anderson, *Land and Resource Planning,* p. 50.
51. 33 *Stat.* 628 (1905). See generally Wilkinson and Anderson, *Land and Resource Planning,* pp. 17–23, 46–54. The 1905 act changed the name of the Bureau of Forestry (in Agriculture) to the Forest Service, but the forest reserves were not renamed national forests until 1907 (Dana, *Forest and Range Policy,* pp. 391–392).
52. U.S. Department of Agriculture, *The Use Book* (1906 ed.), p. 35 (quoted in Wilkinson and Anderson, *Land and Resource Planning,* p. 54, note 272). *West Virginia Division of the Izaak Walton League of America v. Butz* went to court in 1972; 522 F.2d 945 (4th Cir., 1975). See *Land and Resource Planning,* pp. 20, 73.
53. Dana, *Forest and Range Policy,* p. 392.
54. Gifford Pinchot, *A Primer of Forestry* (Washington, DC: GPO, 1905): 203–209.
55. Technically, his dismissal was a result of his having improperly appealed directly to Congress without approval from his administration (Pinchot, *A Primer of Forestry,* pp. 11–13; Kinney, *Forest and Range,* pp. 120–121, 142–143; and Dana, *Forest and Range Policy,* pp. 166–168).
56. 35 *Stat.* 51 (1908), § 1.
57. U.S. Senate *Report* 110, p. 3.
58. 35 *Stat.* 783 (1909) and 36 *Stat.* 857 (1910); BIA, "Forest Conservation," pp. 38–39. Also 35 *Stat.* 783 authorized the commissioner of Indian Affairs to manage timber on Indian reservations (Dana, *Forest and Range Policy,* p. 394).
59. Kinney was approached by Charles Hauke, chief clerk of the Indian Service under Ballinger (Kinney, *Forest and Range,* pp. 83–92). Within little more than a year, Ballinger would resign under a storm of controversy (Dana, *Forest and Range Policy,* pp.169–170).
60. Kinney, *Forest and Range,* pp. 83, 87. These regulations stated in part: "Upon areas not adapted to agriculture, where the leaving of a second crop of timber is desirable, where the permanent maintenance of a woodlot is essential, and where any other conditions demand it, the merchantable trees necessary to accomplish the end view should be reserved from sale. Extensive clear cutting should be permitted only where the land will be utilized for agricultural purposes." U.S. Department of the Interior, Office of Indian Affairs, "Regulations and Instructions for Officers in Charge of Forests on Indian Reservations," approved June 9, 1911, sec. 10, p. 11. Section 27 of the regulations generally required leaving "20 to 30 percent of the merchantable stand as a basis for future timber crops" (p. 19).
61. Pointed questions were asked in the House regarding whether proposed funds were for establishing a separate "forestry service" in 1910. *Congressional Record-House,* 46, pt. 1 (1910): 119.
62. Kinney, *Forest and Range,* pp. 91–98, 259–279.
63. *Menominee Tribe v. U.S.,* 117 Ct. Cl. 442, 470 (1950), finding 22. At this time in 1912 the provisions of a 1911 act were still in force—which provided for salvaging

burned and blown-down timber—so up to 40 million board feet of timber could be marked as long as not more than 20 million of it was green.

64. Officially, the Forest Service remained obliged to carry out the marking until 1918. A history of Forest Service markings on the reservation is found in James J. Newman, "The Menominee Forest of Wisconsin: A Case History in American Forest Management," Ph.D. diss., Lansing, Michigan State University, 1967, pp. 31–36.
65. J. P. Kinney to Commissioner of Indian Affairs, thirty-five-page letter reporting on visit, December 31, 1913 (Files of the Forestry Office, Menominee Indian Nation, Keshena, WI). Between 1914 and 1926 the average rate of planting on the reservation was only 12 acres per year. Lee B. Winner and Walter J. Ridlington, "A Plan for Continuous Forest Control on the Menominee Indian Reservation" (June 1954): 134 (Files of the Forestry Office, Menominee Indian Nation).
66. "High investment railroad logging made 'clear cutting' practices economically desirable" (Winner and Ridlington, "A Plan for Continuous Forest Control," p. 4).
67. Gifford Pinchot, *A Primer of Forestry* (Washington, DC: Government Printing Office, 1905): 18–37; Kinney, *Forest and Range,* p. 19. When these regulations were revised in 1918 the language remained unchanged (p. 21), and when they were rewritten in 1920, "selective logging" remained in force for "all lands chiefly suitable for production of timber crops" (U.S. Department of the Interior, Office of Indian Affairs, *General Timber Sale Regulations* [April 10, 1920]: 2, reg. no. 10).
68. Newman, "The Menominee Forest of Wisconsin," pp. 46–50, 105–107; F. H. Eyre and W. M. Zillgitt, *Partial Cuttings in Northern Hardwoods of the Lake States: Twenty-Year Experimental Results,* Technical Bulletin no. 1076 (Washington, DC: U.S. Department of Agriculture, September 1953).
69. Alan G. McQuillan, "Regeneration Report—A Report on Timber Regeneration Management by the U.S. Bureau of Indian Affairs on the Quinault Indian Reservation, 1965–86, Part 1—Liability Report," prepared for the Quinault Allottees Association, Seattle, Washington (for use in *Mitchell v. United States,* U.S. Claims Court, September 30, 1987, 288 pp.): 60–71; John Libby, "Forest Management in Hemlock-Cedar Forests on the Quinault Indian Reservation, Washington," paper presented at U.S. Department of the Interior, BIA Area Forestry Conference, Portland, Oregon, October 17, 1955; anon, "Pictorial Exhibits Showing the Results of Selective Cutting in Contrast to Clear Cutting on the Quinault Indian Reservation, Submitted as Exhibits for the Defense in *Harvey Eastman et al. v. United States et al.,* Civil Case no. 45, U.S. District Court, Tacoma," Federal Record Center, Suitland, Maryland (1940), RG 75, Acc. 53A367, Box 1119.
70. There are a number of reasons why. One is the prevalence of western hemlock, which is easily damaged; trees intended to be left were often damaged in the logging operations and subsequently died. Another was the fact that the preferred timber species was Douglas fir, which did not regenerate well under partial shade. Still another reason was that the huge volumes of standing timber produced great quantities of logging slash that had to be burned. This burning was very difficult except in the situation of clear-cutting. Another reason was the very high value of the West Coast timber, which presented a high "opportunity cost" of leaving trees standing in the woods. Other reasons had to do with windthrow, insects, and disease.
71. McQuillan, "Regeneration Report," pp. 73–75; John Libby, "Forest Management," p. 2; Libby, "Logging by Alternate Clear-Cut Blocks as Practiced on the Quinault

Indian Reservation, 1950 to 1958" (Seattle: Federal Record Center, August 15, 1958, RG 75, 35535 S6-1249-339.4, Forestry–General Supervision Western Washington Agency).

72. The term *mangy dog* was coined apparently by Professor Barney Dowdle of the University of Washington (personal communication with Dowdle's student David Jackson, Missoula, Montana).

73. William A. Atkinson, "Another View of New Forestry," paper presented at Annual Meeting, Oregon Society of American Foresters, Eugene, Oregon, May 4, 1990; Atkinson, "Old Forestry in a New World," paper presented at the Western Forestry Conference, Western Forestry Conservation Association, Coeur D'Alene, Idaho, December 3, 1990; Chadwick D. Oliver, "Silviculture: The Next Thirty Years, the Past Thirty Years," *Journal of Forestry,* 84:4 (1986): 32–42.

74. *Mitchell v. U.S.,* U.S. Claims Court [now Federal Claims Court], docket nos. 7721–71, 773–71, 774–71, 775–71. After about twenty years the case was settled, largely in favor of the Indians, in the amount of $26.6 million (Gary S. Morishima, "From Paternalism to Self-Determination," *Journal of Forestry,* 95:11 [1997]: 4–9, quote on p. 8).

75. The subject reservations were Colville, Flathead, Navajo, Quinault, Spokane, Warm Springs, and Yakama. All were written by BIA forester Harold Weaver: "A Study of Indian Forest Programs: Bureau of Indian Affairs Dept. of the Interior" by Cornell, Howland, Hayes, and Merryfield, Engineers and Planners, October 1968, Vol. 2, Appendix 22, and Bibliography, p. 2; "Potential for Intensive Timber Management on the Quinault Indian Reservation, Washington 1976," and related correspondence dated April 21, 1965, on file at BIA Forestry Office, Hoquiam, Washington. These are, respectively. plaintiffs' exhibits DT 19.7–45 and DT 3.5–93 for *Helen Mitchell et al. v. United States,* U.S. Claims Court, at Historical Archives, Aubrey Watzek Library, Lewis and Clark College, Portland, Oregon. [DT stands for N. Dee Terry, the original expert witness in *Mitchell,* the Quinault case.]

76. U.S. Forest Service, *A National Plan for American Forestry,* 2 vols, transmitted in response to Senate Resolution 175, 72nd Cong. (Washington, DC: Government Printing Office, 1933). See also B. T. Parry, H. J. Vaux, and N. Dennis, "Changing Conceptions of Sustained-Yield Policy on the National Forests," *Journal of Forestry,* 81:3 (183): 150–154. For private industry endorsement see, for example, West Coast Lumberman's Association and Pacific Northwest Loggers Association, "A Decade of Progress in Douglas Fir Forestry" (Seattle: Joint Committee on Forest Conservation, 1943).

77. 48 *Stat.* 984, 986 (1934), § 6, reads in part: "The Secretary . . . is directed to make rules and regulations for the operation and management of Indian forestry units on the principle of sustained-yield management."

78. 50 *Stat.* 874 (1937). See also Dana, *Forest and Range Policy,* p. 410.

79. The Multiple Use–Sustained Yield Act (74 *Stat.* 215 [1960]). Although a Sustained-Yield Forest Management Act was passed in 1944 that called on the Departments of Agriculture and the Interior to establish cooperative sustained-yield units with the private sector, the act did not affect most Forest Service lands. (Dana, *Forest and Range Policy,* p. 410).

80. Alan G. McQuillan, "Cabbages and Kings: The Ethics and Aesthetics of New Forestry," *Environmental Values,* 2:3 (1993): 191–221.

81. Jerry Franklin, "Toward a New Forestry," *American Forests,* 95 (November-December 1989): 37–44.
82. F. Dale Robertson, Chief, Memo to Regional Forester and Station Directors, U.S. Forest Service, Washington, DC, June 4, 1991 (especially Attachment 1).
83. For example, the state of Montana's Department of State Lands adopted for its current management plan "alternative omega," which calls for retaining forest diversity and embraces many of the concepts of the ecosystem management approach. Ecosystem management concepts have also caught on in Canada; see, for example, D. Hopwood, "Principles and Practices of New Forestry," *Land Management Report* no. 71-ISSN (Vancouver, BC: Ministry of Forests, 1991).
84. Mondou, "Our Land Is What Makes Us," pp. 259, 277, 284–285.
85. 104 *Stat.* 4532 (1990). See generally ibid. See also Morishima, "From Paternalism," pp. 4–8; John Gordon et al., "An Independent Report on Tribal Forestry: Redefining the Government's Role," *Journal of Forestry,* 95:11 (1997): 10–14. [Gordon was lead author; other authors were Jerry F. Franklin, K. Norman Johnson, Jane Patton, Jim Sedell, John Sessions, and Ed Williston.]
86. Mondou, "Our Land Is What Makes Us," p. 264. The act itself defines the forest in terms of "an ecosystem" (p. 265, note 25).
87. Gordon et al., "An Independent Report on Tribal Forestry," p. 11; Morishima, "From Paternalism," p. 9.
88. See, for example, Kinney, *Forest and Range,* passim; U.S. Department of the Interior, BIA, "Forest Conservation," pt. 2, passim; Mondou, "Our Land Is What Makes Us," pp. 272–279; Gordon et al., "An Independent Report on Tribal Forestry."
89. U.S. Senate, "Timber Sales—Quinault Indian Reservation," Hearings before the Subcommittee on Indian Affairs of the Senate Committee on Interior and Insular Affairs, 85th Cong., 1st sess., pp. 486–487.
90. *Menominee Tribe of Indians v. United States,* 134-67-B Ct. Cl. (April 4, 1980). This decision was reversed on appeal for technical reasons (726 F.2d 718 Fed. Cir. [1984]) and was brought back to court as part of a larger "congressional reference" case. A settlement of $32 million was approved by the Court in 1998 and was later appropriated by Congress.
91. After the Indian Self-Determination Act was passed in 1975, many tribes (especially the Quinault) established their own forestry operations and began assuming tasks from the BIA (a transition that accelerated during the 1990s with the movement toward self-governance). Consequently, more intensive management of the Quinault eventually began around 1980. Despite the ongoing tendency (reflected by the National Indian Forest Resource Management Act, the ITC, and IFMAT) for Indian forest policy to become a matter more for individual tribes and less for the U.S. government, the trust responsibility for prudent management of the forest still lies squarely with the United States. To nullify this responsibility would be a mixed blessing for Indians. Indian tribes are not homogeneous, and if tribal governments were to find themselves with ultimate responsibility for forest management, they should be accountable to the Indian landowners. Yet Indians do not generally have the same legal right to sue their tribes as U.S. citizens (particularly trust beneficiaries) have to sue the United States for breach of trust. The IFMAT has recommended that federal trust oversight of Indian forestry be handed to an independent commission (Gordon et al., "An Independent Report on Tribal Forestry," p. 13). This idea has

been endorsed by Mondou, among others ("Our Land Is What Makes Us," p. 295). This question of trust responsibility will continue to pose difficult questions for Indian forestry.

II

TRIBALISM

Seeking Indian Participation

INTRODUCTION

> [Referring to submarginal lands that were unprofitable, thin-soiled, and exhausted yet returned to the tribes, Kicke Kickingbird (Kiowa) and Karen Ducheneaux (Sioux) wrote]: "A sizable portion . . . was earmarked for those people who had become experts in survival on thin soil—the American Indians. Once again, giving eroded lands to the Indians became a recognized federal policy."[1]

New Deal programs initiated several important changes in tribal resource management. First, the trustee had a newfound interest in soil, water, and timber conservation efforts. Second, the trustee made efforts to increase tribal participation in resource issues and to expand tribal sovereignty. Several years before the New Deal, certain events served as harbingers of potential change in resource management that would occur during the Roosevelt administration. In March 1927 Secretary of the Interior Hubert Work ordered an investigation of Indian Service irrigation projects. A parallel survey of tribal grazing took place in 1932. In 1928 *The Problem of Indian Administration* (also known as the Meriam Report) was published. This study urged important environmental and institutional reforms, some of which were incorporated in New Deal programs—for example, the creation of soil conservation programs and the creation of an Indian Division of the Civilian Conservation Corps (CCC-ID).[2]

Porter J. Preston from the Bureau of Reclamation and Charles A. Engle, irrigation engineer for the Office of Indian Affairs, completed their investigation of Indian irrigation projects in 1930. This was the first extensive study of reservation irrigation projects, and the conclusions revealed the extent of the resource management disaster.[3] In that year there were nearly 150 reservation irrigation projects on tribal lands. They had minimal success because of land allotment, which was followed by land leasing and sale; and most of the

Indians have also sought to recover and in their own way reinter human remains of their ancestors; the facts reveal how rarely this comes about in ways acceptable to Indians.

Unfortunately, Indians do not fully comprehend or accept post-European environmental perceptions, which too often differ from the more holistic view held by most Indian cultures. Although tribes will make a claim to certain specific places—for example, sacred sites—they generally reveal greater concern for larger geographic entities for multiple reasons. For example, efforts to delimit specific sacred places that they may be clearly designated for protection while surrounding areas are left open for various other land uses frustrate the native view that the entire environment is sacred.[3]

In all fairness, the federal government has not totally ignored complaints and concerns. Not only has Congress amended the National Historic Preservation Act (NHPA) to embrace the protection of Indian historical and cultural resources, but it enacted the American Indian Religious Freedom Act (AIRFA). Pursuant to the NHPA, most states have provided in law the procedures and regulations that seek to extend protection to Indian cultural resources. As for AIRFA, although the goal to preserve the Indians' right to traditional worship has been enabled, the act essentially avoids specific protection for land and cultural resources.[4]

Congress also passed the Native American Graves Protection and Repatriation Act (NAGPRA), a beneficial statute that has yet to prove truly worthy. It is evident that whereas some tribes have invoked the law with beneficial results whereby they have gained access or exclusive use to burial sites, others have rejected the proviso in section 3(c) of the act that mandates that judically established (adjudicated) boundaries of the Indian Claims Commission must be applied to any tribal claim to cultural resources on lands other than those held in trust. Tribes contend that they should have the option to determine their traditional boundaries in any effort to sustain a claim for cultural resource sites on former tribal lands. Efforts have been made to convince Congress to either modify the wording or remove it from the act. Two environmental specialists, Jhon Goes in Center (Oglala Lakota Nation) and Bryan Marozas (Ojibway), have strongly urged Congress to amend the act to include, among other elements, "tribally defined aboriginal territories (including traditional land use areas, originally occupied lands, historic resource use areas)," as well as "tribal ceded lands." Their ultimate point is, "Rather than removing provisions for utilizing spatial information from the process of determining cultural affiliation, we would suggest enhancing Section 3(c) of NAGPRA beyond the existing legislative requirements so that tribal communities are actually provided with functional data."[5]

Protection of Native American cultural resources on public land has come under closer scrutiny in recent years.[6] The Environmental Protection Agency individuals who farmed reservation irrigable lands in the twentieth century were non-Indian. If non-Indians did not farm the land, it frequently remained idle because the high cost of irrigation farming prohibited many tribesmen from starting irrigation operations. Vacant lands on a project created high operation and maintenance costs that were assessed against lands being utilized. When Indians did farm, their crop value from irrigation projects was $21 per acre, compared with $40 per acre for non-Indians. Preston and Engle attributed this disparity to the absence of trained employees to provide advice and assistance to tribal farmers. Finally, when the real water shortage in the West was considered, reservation irrigation work projects cost the tribes more than the benefits they received.[4]

Despite that warning, little changed for decades in the operations of Indian irrigation projects. In other words, tribal agricultural resources continued to be managed more for the benefit of non-Indians than for allottees, their families, and their heirs. For example, from the turn of the century to the early 1960s in Southern California, the Bureau of Indian Affairs (BIA) had invested at least $1 million in irrigation and related water works on a dozen or more small reservations, but to what avail? Although a handful of allotments were being cultivated by Indians in 1961–1962, a considerable amount of allotted acreage remained unused—vacant allotted acreage had never been cleared of native vegetation, was underutilized, or else was utilized either under lease or through ownership by non-Indians.[5]

Larry A. DiMatteo and Michael J. Meagher revisited many older irrigation projects in 1997 and condemned them as "a testament to the failure of federal Indian policy to assimilate Native Americans."[6] Although water development then, as now, constituted a conservation endeavor, what was foremost in the minds of policymakers was to assimilate the tribes through conversion to farming.

Conservation meant nothing more than perhaps to protect Indian water rights subsequent to the landmark decision in *Winters v. United States.* The irrigation projects were not an early trustee policy toward the *conservation* of reservation resources. Assimilation and conservation might have been good partners for those Indians willing to embrace an economy they had less, if any, experience with had the Indian Office placed more emphasis on land and water management as well as technical assistance rather than base the success of the projects on the evidence of Indian assimilation.

A similar resource story came from a complimentary range management study. Indian Service foresters were the best conservationists at that time; therefore, they assumed supervision of reservation grazing operations in 1932. Two years later Lee Muck, Percy E. Melis, and George M. Nyce prepared the first assessment of tribal grazing lands, concluding that reservation lands located in the Great Plains and the Southwest were overgrazed, contributing to severe soil

Fig II.1 Portable water pumping on the Flathead Indian Reservation, Montana. Not all areas on Indian reservations can be integrated into a major water delivery system. Presumed to be a marginal means, portable pumps are also flexible. Courtesy of the Confederated Salish and Kootenai Tribes Natural Resources Department, Water Rights Administration Program, Pablo (MT), n.d.

erosion. This study was a prelude to subsequent New Deal conservation studies and programs and set the stage for the second phase of reservation resource conservation practices.[7]

Since soil conservation was seen as the solution to many reservation social problems, greater emphasis was placed on implementing programs that focused on cultivable lands and range. Allan Harper, senior field representative of the Indian Service, set the tone for the era's conservation programs when he wrote, "There is the problem of conservation, i.e., the problem of repairing the damage done to his [the Indian's] lands through overgrazing and bad agronomic practice; and the preservation of his land upon a permanent, reliable basis." He added, "This problem, as affecting Indian lands, is but a segment of the larger nation-wide problem of conservation—overwhelming in proportions and utterly imperative of this generation's attention."[8]

Because of the extensive areas of soil erosion found on lands throughout the nation, soil conservation became a national emergency. Public concern with soil conservation emerged as a national issue because of the magnitude of the Dust Bowl, and tribal lands were part of the eroded regions. For example, the

South Dakota State Planning Board reported that "soil erosion is a general problem affecting much of South Dakota's farm area. It constitutes a problem for the Indian population as well, as a large part of Indian land lies within the dust-bowl region."[9] Soil conservation, then, became one of the building blocks for the nation's Indian policy of self-sufficiency.

Many tribes resisted conservation efforts. It is one thing to have appropriate conservation skills, another to know the ways of Indians and how to overcome their reluctance and distrust. Allan Harper, director of Technical Cooperation–Bureau of Indian Affairs (TC-BIA) in 1937, stated, "In the first year's work . . . it was found that technically correct erosion control and land use programs, in order to be effective, had to be adapted to the ability of the Indian land owners to carry them out."[10] Historian Rebekah Davis also recounted that the tribes initially had little to say over use and development and that "new organizational systems for decision making on the reservations [made decisions] without consulting tribal members." As a result, "Tribal members were alienated from the planning process and from their land; this alienation led to abuse and neglect of the reservations' natural resources."[11]

For the tribes, a bigger issue was a stake in sovereignty. Thus they resisted efforts to establish irrigation systems and management plans for forests. Several tribes flouted authority by continuing lumbering during the years when the government sought either to put a halt to some practices or to install measures of conservation such as selective cutting. The government was sending mixed signals to American Indians: "You are sovereign, but the trustee makes resource decisions." Perhaps the classic case was that of the Navajo. As historian Richard White recounts the plight of the Navajos, who became vulnerable after defeat in the 1860s, the loss of range and water rights weakened their economy,

> But not until the 1930s did they become dependent. Disaster, when it came to the Navajos, arrived as it so often did for American Indian peoples, in the guise of reform. In a relatively few years and in the name of conservation and self-determination, they were stripped of their stock and made largely dependent on wages and various public programs for their living. It was a blow that they stagger from still.[12]

As the Indian New Deal evolved, other land and conservation agencies were beginning to break the BIA's hold over reservation resource management. For example, the Soil Conservation Service began to deal singularly with tribal populations. That agency organized the planning unit known as the TC-BIA, which began to "prepare plans for proper land use and conservation for the Indian Service."[13] Subsequent to the establishment of field offices of the Soil Conservation Service, soil conservationists encouraged individual Indian allottees to enter into soil conservation contracts, which then provided continuity in practice and advice.[14]

Traditional cultural forces within given tribes tended to resist many, if not most, changes imposed from without. Indians often opposed each other because some individuals and groups stood for change by recognizing reality while others held on to whatever advantages they presumed would survive into the reservation era. Some tribes also sought newer approaches and were encouraged—especially in the era of the Indian Reorganization Act (IRA), with direct support from John Collier—to try innovative means to improve land utilization techniques. If we translate some of these experiences into the present day, we know that many tribes have embraced the environmental era by creating conservation codes that have considerable holistic intent—that is, they deal with the entire reservation environment and seek balanced utilization—even though the courts have time and again denied efforts to include non-Indian land utilization within tribal environmental regulations.

Indian opposition to government conservation efforts continued even after passage of the Indian Reorganization Act of 1934 that held promise of shifting management from the trustee to the tribes.[15] The development of the Mexican Springs Demonstration Area on the Navajo Indian Reservation and the subsequent creation of the Soil Erosion Service (later Soil Conservation Service) indicated that the way government agencies worked was contrary to Navajo and other tribal land use practices. On the Navajo reservations, soil managers justified their actions, claiming they were saving the Navajo from themselves, which meant the Navajos' past grazing practices with sheep were the cause of their current problems.

Allan Harper defended the program that also requested the removal of "non-productive horses. It is a program which must make its way against a mal-distribution of range rights among the Navajos. It is a program which must take account of 2,500 families that own no sheep." He added, "It is a program that involves the imposition of controls over the individual's livestock operations, from which he has hitherto been wholly exempt."[16]

Once a conservation agency assumed control of reservation resource decisions, that agency was often unresponsive to tribal needs. Twenty years after the New Deal, the Soil and Moisture Conservation Service office was still drafting grazing regulations for range units without tribal land users' input. Others suffered the same fate. Rosebud member Alfred Left Hand Bull in 1965 observed that grazing rules eliminated small Indian operators: "There is hardly any chance for Indians to survive as small operators. . . . Some who have the spark of such a motivation are hampered. . . . When are Indians going to have a say about their own land?"[17]

Officials as well as conservationists, when drawing additional attention to the severity of the erosion problem on the Navajo Reservation, correlated the runoff of sedimentation into reservoirs such as Lake Mead, inundated by the construction of Hoover Dam and related works on the Colorado River, with tribal grazing practices.[18]

Some scholars contended that there was greater concern for the reservoirs and the production of electric power than for the conservation of tribal resources. More than a decade ago, Lynn Fuller revisited the Navajo problem of desertification, noting that even after responsibility for enforcing grazing regulations on the reservation transferred to the Navajo Nation after 1950, "the political unpopularity of range conservation among Navajos led to a laissez-faire approach to grazing controls."[19] Fuller stressed that demographic and economic factors remained strongly responsible for the deterioration of Navajo rangeland. Her study also underscored the century-old tradition in which livestock had come to represent prestige, well-being, and harmonious existence in the world.[20]

The Navajo were not alone in their opposition to New Deal reservation resource conservation programs. Tribal rejection of government-imposed projects or even advice became more general, and thus one can understand the Tohono O'odham reaction to trustee efforts to constrain the use of range lands in a very arid region of the Southwest. Peter Booth demonstrates in his case study that *intra*tribal relationships of families and clans constituted—to the government and many observers—an outdated and perhaps reactionary factor in efforts to bring the tribes into the modern era of conservation. Indians in their own ways had to struggle with these internecine embroilments, and Collier's edict under the IRA to force non-Indian-style governments on many tribes only caused greater tribal entrenchment in traditional ways.

A few tribes sought various means to take the reins of responsibility and seek alternative environmental and institutional ways to deal with resource matters. The complexity of landownership allotment had set in motion turned many tribes to the issue of land consolidation and some means to make better use of allotted parcels heavily divided by heirship. Such is the case of the Rosebud Sioux (South Dakota). For the ten-year period 1943–1953, the Rosebud endorsed the operations of a Tribal Land Enterprise (TLE), which sought to consolidate heirship lands through the issuance of land stock certificates to allottees and their heirs.[21] Once consolidated, the tribe could then reassign larger blocks of land to Indians intent on farming or ranching. The TLE had good intentions—alleviate land heirship. Ultimately, 72,000 acres were entered into the program, but the difficulty of developing viable economic land units crippled the plan. Still, TLE represented an early and unique effort to consolidate heirship lands.

Today a great acreage generally sits idle in complex inheritance and too often is subject to the vagaries of nature and sometimes ranged by unmanaged cattle. This land problem is both environmental and institutional. Tribal governments' attempts to consolidate encumbered parcels have also been stymied by the Supreme Court ruling that the Land Consolidation Act (1982), in part, is unconstitutional, when tribes escheat allotments belonging to heirs.[22]

The conservation movement also encouraged some tribes to take a more active role to protect cultural resources.[23] Generally, tribal involvement followed the long period of litigation and adjudication of Indian land claims that began in the 1950s subsequent to the passage of the Indian Claims Commission Act of 1946.[24] One of the earliest efforts was pursued by the Taos Pueblo as early as the 1920s and reached a positive resolution only forty years later by the transfer of Blue Lake from the Kit Carson National Forest to the Taos.[25]

In fact, one could logically conclude that the quest to protect traditional resources on lands no longer part of reservations had to wait until claims litigation demonstrated that money, not land, would be the compensation for adjudications favorable to tribes. Early on, a few tribes did assume limited management of a range of resources that have possessed cultural meaning—mountains, waterfalls and caves and other natural phenomena; archaeological, sacred, and historic sites, as well as burial grounds and other human features.

For most of the twentieth century, lack of government action and a loosely conceived policy allowed countless cultural resources to deteriorate. Imre Sutton reminds us that important traditional cultural resources continue to exist on and beyond trust lands and that tribes early on had the opportunity to develop preservation programs on reservations, where more positive management would likely have occurred were funds and technical training available to tribal members. True, not until the government embraced the environmental movement in the 1970s did some tribes show much interest in preserving their past. As for traditional resources on public or private lands, tribes began to embrace several laws—for example, the American Indian Freedom Religious Act, the Native American Graves Protection and Reparations Act—in efforts to protect their heritage.

If tribes resisted imposed management policies regarding Indian farming and ranching, they were not encouraged to support similar efforts to regulate aspects of Indian forestry to establish wilderness areas on reservations. Governmental efforts to establish roadless areas as part of the management of Indian timber stands as well as wilderness represented other well-intentioned yet often misplaced goals that tribes came to translate in their own way and much later in time. Several tribes possessing timber stands opposed further restrictions on the exploitation of their forested lands.

As part of the trustee's role, Secretary of the Interior Harold Ickes issued a proclamation in 1936—which tribes could *not* review—creating roadless areas within reservations. This decision prohibited tribesmen from entering roadless areas with motorized vehicles or proceeding with logging projects in designated roadless areas. It was hoped that tribes would embrace this decision, but even

Robert Marshall, the chief forester who developed these areas, sought unsuccessfully to convince some Apaches and other tribes to adopt the roadless area review and evaluation program for wilderness management of forested lands on their reservation. One might argue that few tribes and a paucity of individual Indians grasped the need for conservation, especially of a limited resource, but the real issue behind tribal opposition was that tribes were not consulted and their sovereignty was violated.[26]

Although Marshall partially succeeded, resistance remained strong enough to cause the withdrawal of such designated areas by the time the Wilderness Act was being debated in the early 1960s. Tribes, of course, did not fare well under the Wilderness Act. Such designated wilderness areas lie mostly within federal public lands. But subsequent to the decisions of the Indian Claims Commission, one tribe after another sought an alternative route to land restoration, exclusive occupancy, or joint management. In terms of wilderness, the Yakama Indian Nation, subsequent to land claims adjudication in 1972, successfully gained a limited restoration of Mt. Adams, already a designated wilderness, by executive order.[27] On the other hand, the efforts of the Confederated Salish and Kootenai Tribes of Montana to develop their own wilderness program, recounted here in Diane Krahe's study of the Mission Mountain Tribal Wilderness, demonstrated that tribes could and would initiate wilderness management on their own lands. These and other tribal efforts, despite coming somewhat later in time, demonstrate the logical outcome of efforts to establish self-determination as a policy goal of the last quarter of the twentieth century.

References

1. Kicke Kickingbird and Karen Ducheneaux, *One Hundred Million Acres* (New York: Macmillan, 1973): 67. Government ambivalence in its efforts to assist the tribes occurred when the so-called submarginal lands homesteaders abandoned or lost by bankruptcy were acquired by the Federal Emergency Relief Administration in 1933 and later were distributed to various tribes (much of the acreage had been part of the diminished reservations opened to homesteaders decades earlier).
2. Lewis Meriam et al., *The Problem of Indian Administration, Studies in Administration,* 17 (Baltimore: Brookings Institution for Government Research, 1928).
3. Porter J. Preston and Charles A. Engle, "Irrigation on Indian Reservations," *Survey of Conditions on Indian Reservations in the U.S.,* Hearing before Subcommittee of the Senate Committee on Indian Affairs, 71st Cong., 2d sess. (Washington, DC: Government Printing Office [GPO], 1930): 2211, 2217–22, 2224.
4. Ibid., pp. 540–541.
5. Imre Sutton, "Land Tenure and Changing Occupance on Indian Reservations in Southern California," Ph.D. diss. in geography (Los Angeles: University of California, 1964); Sutton, "Private Property in Land Among Reservation Indians in Southern California," *Yearbook, Association of Pacific Coast Geographers,* 29 (1969): 69–89. One should keep in mind that unlike highly rural parts of Indian Country, reservations in Southern California are never too remote from towns and cities in terms of alternative means of livelihood.

6. Larry A. DiMatteo and Michael J. Meagher, "Broken Promises: The Failure of the 1920s Native American Irrigation and Assimilation Policies," *University of Hawaii Law Review,* 19 (spring 1997): 1–36. They cite other case studies of the failure of irrigation projects—e.g., the Flathead, the Crow, the Shoshone, and others—and also examine the Indian Office's support for the reclamation movement. Cf. observations by Ann Caylor, " 'A Promise Long Deferred': Federal Reclamation on the Colorado River Indian Reservations," *Pacific Historical Review,* 69:2 (May 2000): 193–215. We include a photo (Fig. II.1) of a portable water pump delivering irrigation or cattle water on the Flathead IR, suggesting its limited capacity yet also its flexibility.
7. Lee Muck, Percy E. Melis, and George M. Nyce, "An Economic Survey of the Range Resources and Grazing Activities on Indian Reservations," in U.S. Cong., Senate, Survey of Conditions of the Indians in the United States, Hearings before Subcommittee of the Committee on Indian Affairs, 71st Cong., 2d sess. (Washington, DC: GPO, 1932): part 22, pp. 12248–12303.
8. Allan G. Harper, "The Indian and the Land," *Indians and the Land,* Contributions by the Delegation of the United States, First Inter-American Conference on Indian Life, Patzcuaro, Mexico, April 1940, p. 2.
9. South Dakota State Planning Board, *Indians of South Dakota: A Preliminary Report* (Brookings: South Dakota State Planning Board, 1937): 16.
10. Quoted in Rebekah C. Beatty Davis, *Conservation and Culture: The Soil Conservation Service, Social Science, and Conservation on Tribal Lands in the Southwest,* Historical Notes 6 (Washington, DC: Natural Resources Conservation Service, 1997): 27, 31.
11. Ibid., p. 31. On contemporary agricultural concerns, see Tracy J. Andrews and Castle McLaughlin, eds., "Farming and Ranching in Reservation Economies," *American Indian Culture and Research Journal,* 22:3 (1998): 1–222.
12. Richard White, *The Roots of Dependency: Subsistence, Environment, and Social Change Among the Choctaws, Pawnees, and Navajos* (Lincoln: University of Nebraska Press, 1983): 320. Two other studies report Navajo reaction to and participation in conservation when it first got under way: George A. Boyce, *When Navajos Had Too Many Sheep: The 1940s* (San Francisco: Indian Historian Press, 1974), and Edward T. Hall, *West of the Thirties: Discoveries Among the Navajo and Hopi* (New York: Doubleday, 1994). Hall, an anthropologist, served as a team leader working with Navajos on various conservation projects.
13. F. Cohen, *Handbook of Federal Indian Law,* 2d ed. (Charlottesville, VA: Michie, Bobbs-Merrill, 1982): 32.
14. I. Sutton, in "Land Tenure and Changing Occupance," discovered numerous individual soil conservation contracts between allottees and the SCS in the files for the Southern California Indian office at Riverside. By the 1960s, however, most of the allotments whose Indian owners had embraced soil conservation were not in production or were being farmed by non-Indian lessees.
15. Indian Reorganization Act, 48 *Stat.* part 1: 984–988 (1934).
16. Harper, "The Indian and the Land," p. 10; cf. Hall, *West of the Thirties.*
17. Alfred Left Hand Bull, Rosebud Sioux Tribe, addressing Subcommittee on Indian Affairs, U.S. Congress, House, *Sioux Indian Tribes, North and South Dakota,* Hearings, 84th Cong., 1st sess., pursuant to H. Res. 30 "to authorize . . . investigations into any matter within its jurisdiction" (Washington, DC: GPO, 1956): 139–140.

18. See Leonard S. Fonaroff, "Conservation and Stock Reduction on the Navajo Tribal Range," *Geographical Review,* 53 (April 1963): 200–223. Cf. W. L. Graf, "Fluvial Erosion and Federal Public Policy in the Navajo Nation," *Physical Geography,* 7:2 (1986): 97–115.
19. Lynn Fuller, "Desertification on the Navajo Reservation: A Legal and Historical Analysis," *Stanford Environmental Law Journal,* 8 (1989): 229–291, quote on p. 231.
20. Ibid., p. 233.
21. An earlier study explored the geography of the Rosebud: Donald J. Ballas, "A Cultural Geography of Todd County, South Dakota, and the Rosebud Indian Reservation," Ph.D. diss., Lincoln, University of Nebraska, 1970.
22. 25 *U.S.C.A.* §§ 2201–2211. Mark Fogarty, "The Dawes Act Legacy: Indians Moving Vigorously to Recover Their Lost Land," *American Indian Report,* 15:3 (1999): 8–10. According to Fogarty, although consolidation has a worthy goal, the protection of individual Indian property rights is a strong, although seemingly counterproductive, factor in creating sustainable land use on countless reservations. In 1999 the Indian Land Working Group (ILWG) sought to propose its own legislation to abet consolidation yet protect property rights. The proposed bill would have provided for estate planning, accurate and accessible land records, removal of regulatory barriers impacting real estate transactions, creation of an acquisition fund for tribes and individual Indians, and creation of a federal probate code that would prevent non-Indian inheritance of allotments. The ILWG has been critical of the BIA's legislative answer to the problem, for the agency has proposed removing the trust responsibility to individual allottees by terminating trust status over individually held allotments. Whichever way the current conflict goes, one wonders if consolidation were to prevail how much more vigorous environmental management would actually become. For an earlier historical analysis of heirship and efforts at consolidation, see Michael Lawson, "The Fractionated Estate: The Problem of American Indian Heirship," *South Dakota History,* 21 (spring 1991): 1–42.
23. Cf. Pauline Arrillaga, "Treading on Holy Ground: Indians Fight to Protect Sacred Sites From Compelling Interests," *Missoulian* (July 23, 2000): E1, E9. The article cites a quote by Jerry Flute, executive director, Association of American Indian Affairs: "We need a simple law to protect American Indian cultural properties, particularly where they are known sacred sites that have been used by tribes for millennia." The article reports on the Medicine Wheel and Devil's Tower.
24. See Imre Sutton, "Incident or Event? Land Restoration in the Claims Process," in Sutton, ed., *Irredeemable America: The Indians' Estate and Land Claims* (Albuquerque: University of New Mexico Press, 1985): 211–232.
25. Ibid., pp. 215–216, fig. 9. 1.
26. "Establishment of Roadless and Wild Areas on Indian Reservations, October 25, 1937," *Federal Register,* 3 (March 22, 1938): 709–710. Of all the roadless areas, only one on the Wind River Indian Reservation had remained until 1994.
27. 29 *ICC* 125 (1972); Presidential Executive Order 11679, May 23, 1972; Sutton, *Irredeemable America,* p. 215, fig. 9. 1.

Chapter 5

"If the Cattle Are Going to Die, Let Them Die": Tohono O'odham and New Deal Conservation*

Peter M. Booth

Change often comes about for conservative reasons—when faced with a challenge, a people will alter the world around them to preserve that which is most important to them. The Tohono O'odham's (formerly known as Papago) conservative reaction to federal government conservation efforts during the mid- through the late 1930s caused some of the most dramatic political culture changes ever experienced by these southern Arizona residents. Although designed to help the O'odham out of the Great Depression, these Uto-Aztecan speakers felt threatened by New Deal conservation efforts. Specifically, the federal government through the Office of Indian Affairs (OIA) wanted to restore the Papaguería cattle ranges in an effort to develop the O'odham Reservation's livestock industry through "range management."[1]

Although appearing beneficial at best and harmless at worst, the conservation program endangered the O'odham *Himdag,* the "people's way," a philosophy of life that controlled a person's existence. This outlook taught that disturbing the natural order would cause ill throughout the world. One O'odham leader echoed that fear when he exclaimed that once the range management program began, "the World will end." The O'odham resisted by various means, but the most far-reaching tactic came when some co-opted the OIA's growing colonial-reservation structure to stall, divide, separate, and eventually thwart the conservation agenda. From this arose a new world along with a new entity known as the Papago Tribe, which eventually evolved into the Tohono O'odham Nation.[2]

When the Jesuit missionary Francisco Eusebio Kino first introduced cattle to Papaguería in the 1690s, the O'odham feared the animals would deplete their

*This chapter is based on portions of my dissertation in history, "Creation of a Nation: The Development of the Tohono O'odham Political Culture, 1900–1937," Purdue University, 2000.

water. It became one of the causes of the Spanish-O'odham Conflict in 1695. Over the next 240 years cattle slowly become a part of the O'odham *Himdag*, especially after the development of Arizona's ranching industry in the late nineteenth century when the O'odham inherited cattle abandoned by ranchers who tried and failed in the desert conditions. Most families owned a small number, as the livestock became part of the O'odham's diversified subsistence lifestyle. Horses became an important beast of burden, and cattle raising replaced hunting as game animals dwindled. Cattle served as an insurance against starvation during times of drought when the crops failed.

In addition, livestock fulfilled an important social role. In the community-based society that shunned individual advancement, exchanging gifts and contributing to village celebrations were vital obligations. Having the freedom to utilize the cattle reserve any time of the year and in any way deemed necessary was paramount. Disruption of this way of life endangered not only a system of economic distribution but also the very fabric of the O'odham life cycle and obligations—their *Himdag*.[3]

A few families in the southeast area of the 12,774,450-acre Papago Reservation (Figure 5.1), along the Baboquivari Mountain's west slope, did venture into commercial cattle raising. This shift drastically disrupted the older village-based social system, as seven to eight families established near feudal control over the area. Nevertheless, the leading ranching families had serious obligations to their kinsmen—supplying food, employment, leadership, charity, and loans. The area's new *Himdag* depended on the survival of those families' cattle fortunes.[4]

Soon after the Papago Reservation's establishment in 1916, OIA officials identified cattle raising instead of traditional desert farming as the best economic pursuit for the O'odham in the U.S. economic system. But to enhance this industry the government recognized the need to curtail the overgrazing of O'odham rangelands. One of the main reasons the OIA dug deep wells was to spread the grazing over a larger area and reduce the loss of forage close to the existing water sources, but it only promoted O'odham cattle raising. Despite serious droughts in 1921 and 1924, the number of ranching O'odham jumped dramatically in the 1920s. A lack of resources prevented the OIA from effectively curtailing overgrazing.

Entering the 1930s the conditions of O'odham rangelands and cattle herds were still a primary concern of the OIA. The Papago Reservation's superintendent, Joseph Elliott, agreed that the OIA management plans were needed "so that the range will not deteriorate further through erosion and destroy the wonderful possibilities existing." Starting in 1931, with the promise of an increase in resources, Elliott made a more concerted effort. The range management plan that evolved (and became the framework of the New Deal conservation plan) was to educate O'odham ranchers about raising fewer but higher-quality cattle,

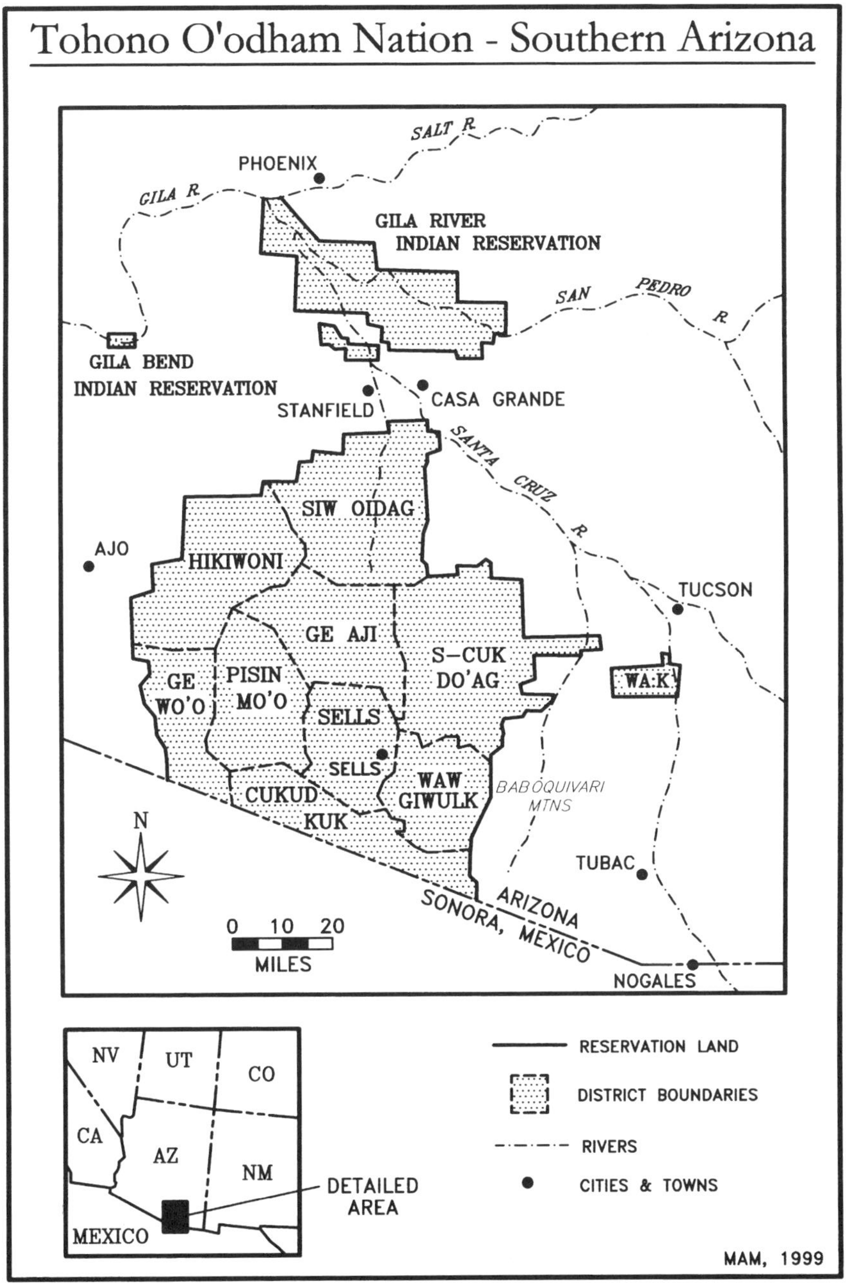

Fig. 5.1 Tohono O'odham Nation (southern Arizona). Formerly named the Papago Indian Reservation, the Tohono O'odham Indian Reservation is located in southern Arizona and along the Mexican border. This map identifies district boundaries, important settlements, and nearby Indian reservations.

divide the reservation into range districts, establish grazing regulations, reduce the size of the herds to the carrying capacity, establish a tribal herd, and improve the range through water development, erosion control, and grass reseeding. Key to maintaining the improvements and enforcing the regulations would be some form of Indian organization such as a cattle association or a tribal government to manage the range.[5]

In addition to bad planning, poor relations with the O'odham doomed Elliott's plans. He succeeded only in kindling ill feelings toward any OIA range conservation efforts. Fundamentally, the O'odham resisted Elliott's efforts because they did not see range management recommendations as in their best interest. The increased OIA-directed control over their cattle herds jeopardized the O'odham *Himdag*. On a practical level, limiting O'odham cattle numbers threatened the emergency food supply. On a cultural level, OIA efforts questioned the entire O'odham system of social obligations, which the livestock made possible. Basically, the OIA viewed the cattle as an economic issue and the O'odham saw them as a subsistence and cultural issue.[6]

The independent O'odham villages also were suspicious of anything that threatened to restrict their freedom. Past OIA efforts, such as trying to eradicate the Saguaro Cactus Wine Rain Ceremony in the 1920s, had not been well received by the O'odham. Even seemingly innocuous ideas such as well drilling engendered opposition because the OIA habitually failed to consult the people affected. Distrust developed toward any government project. With this as a backdrop, range management seemed like another in a series of OIA intrusions on their lives. The O'odham cared less about the cattle than they did about the loss of independence. Peter Blaine, O'odham interpreter for the agency during the New Deal and later tribal chairman, expressed the opinion of many O'odham when he said, "If the cattle are going to die, let them die. But they will die right here on their reservation."[7]

Social divisions among the O'odham also impacted any OIA range management plan. Superintendent Elliott denigrated the split as "progressives" versus "backwards," yet the division had far more complex cultural roots. A united O'odham people had never existed. An individual O'odham gave his or her loyalty to one of eleven "pueblos" or "village complexes," each consisting of a collection of related communities descended from a common parent village. The integrity of the pueblos was maintained through ceremonial, marital, economic, social, and limited political ties. Each village practiced consensus politics presided over by a headman. The settlements within each village complex then gave deference to the original parent village's headman.[8]

Each independent village complex or pueblo had its own territory, which the others recognized and respected. Among the eleven pueblos, no formal political or social ties were shared, and cultural variations further reinforced their independence. Nevertheless, the O'odham recognized that the pueblos fit into six dialectal groups. Elliott's "Progressive" O'dham were the *Ko-lo:di.* He labeled the remaining five dialect groups "backwards." Of these, the most populous dialect group, the *Aji,*[9] were politically the most moderate people to follow the older *Himdag* and practice a traditional folk religion known as Sonoran Catholicism. A more conservative dialect was the *Ko:adk,* distant relatives of the *Aji,* who made the northernmost areas of the reservation their home. Close association with the Akimel O'odham (also known as the Pima) on the Gila River Reservation to the north kept the *Ko:adk* outside most Papaguería political issues. Out west lived the *Gigimai, Hu:uwos,* and *Hu:hu'ula.* Situated on the driest part of the reservation, these extremely conservative followers of the *Himdag* lived in sparsely populated and widely scattered villages[10]* (Figure 5.2).

In accord with the teachings of the older O'odham *Himdag,* these conservative dialect groups followed a diversified economy. Relying on one income source in the desert was risky. Taking advantage of late summer and winter rains allowed them to practice a form of flood irrigation known as *ak cin* farming. In the late fall many Aji and Ko:adk picked cotton around Casa Grande and Phoenix. Other Aji, as well as western O'odham, worked in the mines at Ajo on the reservation. The women also made and sold either bear grass or willow basketry, as well as pots known as *ollas,* and men produced leather or horsehair ropes. Other Aji from both San Xavier and the bigger reservation sold mesquite wood to non-Indians, and a few found other odd jobs in Tucson. Many also had a few cattle that served as protection from starvation whenever the crops failed or they lost employment in the mine for a short time. The average O'odham family owned fewer than ten animals in addition to a few draft horses.[11]

The sixth and last dialect group, the *Ko-lo:di,* lived in the southern extremes of the Papago Reservation. Those from the Cukud Kuk pueblo had drastically changed their *Himdag* after years of contact with Hispanic settlers to the south. They abandoned much of the diversified economy and adopted ranching as their livelihood. Leadership by a strong family patriarch replaced the older village-based political system. Many forsook the older O'odham faith for Presbyterianism. They began to look at the conservative O'odham and the older *Himdag* as hindering the progress of the people. For example, one Presbyterian Ko-lo:di claimed that God had caused the increasingly dry conditions because "old-fashioned" O'odham continued to practice heathen ceremonies such as the wine ceremony. Elliott and other non-Indians viewed Ko-lo:di as the "progressives" of the O'odham.[12]

---

* For this one paragraph we have shown dialects in *italics* so readers can more easily relate text and map (Figure 5.2).

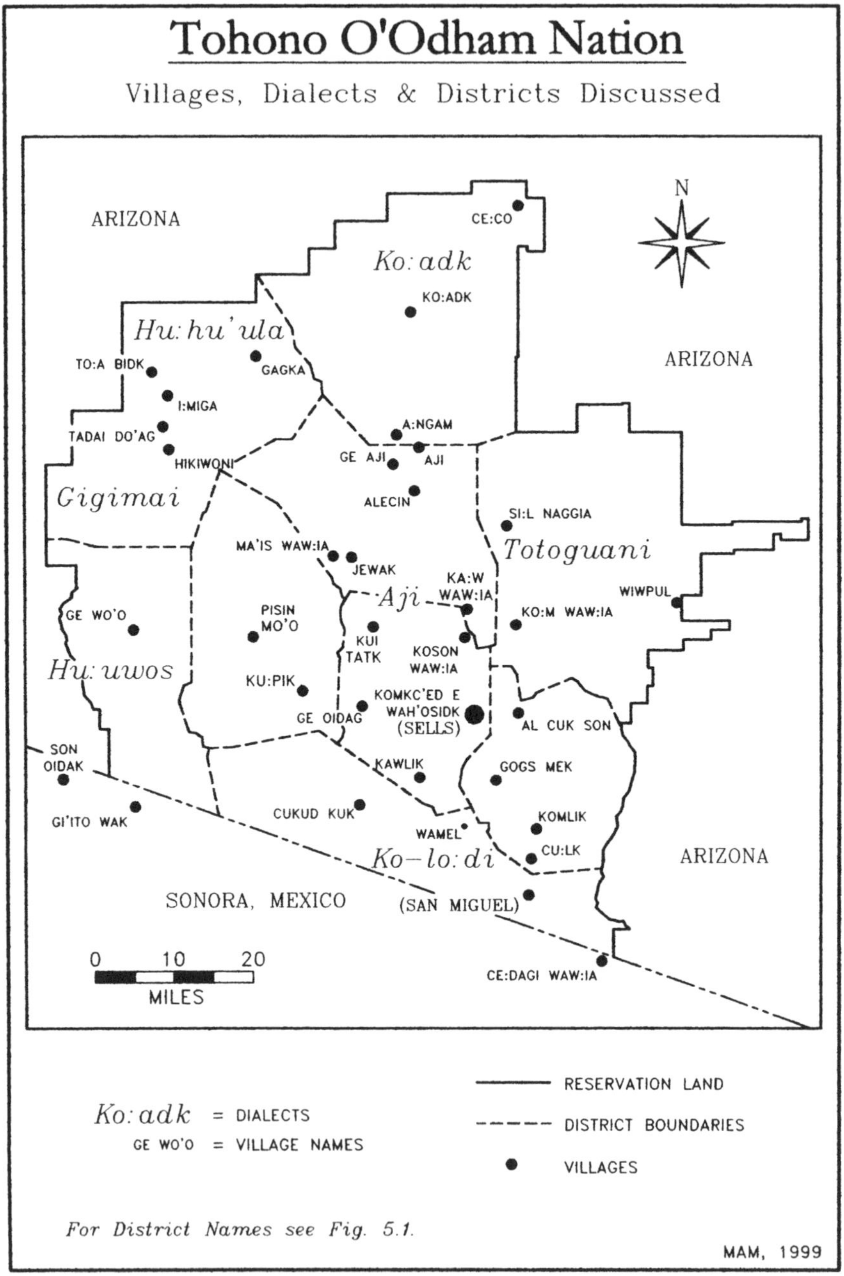

Fig. 5.2 Tohono O'odham Nation: Villages, Dialects, and Districts Discussed. Important villages and language dialects are depicted as an accompaniment to the discussion in the text. The discussion excludes Gila Bend and San Xavier (Wa:k).

Not all within a dialect group, though, followed the same *Himdag.* The Ko-lo:di descending from the defensive village of Ku:pik were far more conservative, following the old ways in contrast to their brethren from the parent village of Cukud Kuk. Likewise, Aji from the Komelik pueblo, located on the west slope of the Baboquivari Mountains, closely associated with and adopted the ways of the Cukud Kuk Ko-lo:di.

To better protect the people's interests as they defined them, certain O'odham from the southeast part of the reservation formed the Executive Committee of the Papago Council (Executive Committee). This body was led by successful ranchers and boarding school graduates such as Cukud Kuk Ko-lo:di Juan Harvey and Richard Hendricks and Komlik Aji Martin Moristo, most of whom were Presbyterian. Besides being the owners of some of the largest herds on the reservation, many of these men were influential with the OIA agency at Sells. For example, leading Executive Committee member Jose X. Pablo, a graduate of the Presbyterian-run Tucson Boarding School and a Cukud Kuk Ko-lo:di who established his ranch northeast of Sells in Aji territory, had worked as the agency stockman since 1917. Men like Pablo made it easy for the Executive Committee to work closely with Superintendent Elliott, whose policies mainly benefited the cattle ranchers in the southeastern part of the reservation. Aji and Ku:pik Ko-lo:di, along with a few Ko:adk, Hu:hu'ula, and Gigimai villages, protested when the Executive Committee and Elliott—against the wishes of local headmen—leased land to white miners, granted trading post licenses, and tried to establish a tribal herd pasture. Most important, these conservative O'odham felt the Executive Committee threatened the autonomy of the pueblos.[13]

This division between the villages served as a backdrop for another concern facing the O'odham—the worsening economic crisis caused by the Great Depression. The economic downhill slide ended most off-reservation jobs, including mining. Even cotton picking disappeared, as Oklahomans and others from the Great Plains fled the Dust Bowl looking for employment. This forced the O'odham back to the reservation. Unfortunately, it also had little to offer, since drought had dried up the O'odham crops and decimated their herds. The drop in the market made selling cattle nearly impossible. One government official stationed at Sells commented that "practically all who had previously been employed away from home were compelled to return to the reservation [where] considerable suffering was felt."[14]

In an effort to provide relief for the entire country, President Franklin D. Roosevelt launched a host of agencies as part of his overall recovery plan—the New Deal. OIA Commissioner John Collier saw the New Deal as more than just a relief effort and as a step toward solid reform of the nation's Indian policies. Collier hoped to strengthen tribal values by abandoning the OIA's assimilation policy in favor of cultural pluralism. To build up the resources available to the Indians, Collier used such New Deal programs as the Civilian

Fig. 5.3 Commissioner John Collier visits the Tohono O'odham. John Collier, commissioner of Indian Affairs, and Peter Blaine, Jr., Tohono O'odham interpreter and later tribal chairman, at the dedication of the Tribal Council building, November 1940. Courtesy of the Arizona Historical Society, Tucson.

Conservation Corps–Indian Division (CCC-ID) to make the reservations self-sufficient. This goal involved curbing the depletion of American Indian resources. Collier planned for the CCC-ID to "produce changed people, living within a changed land"[15] (Fig. 5.3).

To start the CCC-ID projects, Elliott received $400,000, a sizable increase in his budget, which had been around $100,000 in 1932. On June 27, 1933, Elliott began enrolling any male regardless of age in the CCC-ID, but the program had trouble getting started on the Papago Reservation because the O'odham initially balked. Many expressed misgivings about submitting themselves to a medical examination, whereas others felt the work projects would only benefit the southeastern villages. Conservatives such as Ramon, the Gigimai headman of Ge Wo'o, voiced the fear that the CCC-ID threatened the people's self-reliance by making them dependent on the federal government.

Feeling pressure from superiors, Elliott sparked interest among the O'odham by recruiting enrollees in their home villages, allowing them to run their own camps called "family camps," and deemphasizing the need for a medical exam.

Fig. 5.4 Tohono O'odham Indian work crew. Part of the conservation program on the Tohono O'odham Reservation was to encourage tribal members to form Civilian Conservation Corps–Indian Division work crews as represented by this group, circa 1930s. Courtesy of the Arizona Historical Society, Tucson.

The O'odham recruits selected foremen from their own ranks and with very little direction; many of the crews simply started working where they felt a project was needed. Most of these projects focused on those areas of range improvement most O'odlham agreed were necessary, such as building small earthen water reservoirs known as charcos. After these changes the CCC-ID's popularity began to soar[16] (Fig. 5.4).

By late 1933, 891 O'odham men were working all over the reservation. At thirty dollars a month, the CCC-ID positions were the highest-paying jobs many of these men had ever had. Elliott proved a failure at planning, but he did raise CCC-ID acceptance on the reservation. Although the Sells Agency got money from other New Deal work programs, such as the Public Works Administration and the Federal Emergency Relief Administration, the CCC-ID remained the largest New Deal endeavor among the O'odham. Because the O'odham were never a people to take direct aid, the CCC-ID's work-based aid meshed smoothly with O'odham values. Not surprisingly, the CCC-ID became a key tool in the OIA's range management efforts on the reservation.[17]

Whereas the CCC-ID produced a "changed land," Collier's Indian Reorganization Act (IRA) endeavored to create a "changed people." Signed into law on June 18, 1934, this legislation promoted Indian self-rule through the establishment of tribal governments. Despite its lofty intentions, buried in Section 6 of the act was a more dictatorial conservation clause. Collier felt that unless the

Indian land was saved, self-rule was meaningless. The IRA authorized the Department of the Interior, and thus the OIA, to take the necessary steps "to assure the full utilization of the range." This gave Collier the power to force superintendents, and ultimately Indians, to follow the OIA conservation policies.[18]

Unaware of the conservation section, some moderate O'odham identified the IRA's self-rule aspects as a way to protect against the expanding influence of the agency and the ranching families of the southeast. On March 15, 1934, Collier's assistants, A. C. Monahan and Walter Woehlke, hosted a regional congress in Phoenix so Arizona Indians could learn and ask questions about the proposed legislation. Twenty O'odham attended the meeting. Although Sells Agency Stockman Jose X. Pablo felt the O'odham would not accept the proposed plan because of a fear of all government programs, others expressed a belief that economic, political, and environmental pressures were forcing change. Aji headmen Jose Listo of Ge Aji and Jose Joaquin of Gogs Mek (the two largest O'odham villages) argued that the IRA might give them a way to protect their village autonomy amid that change. They asked if an individual pueblo could use the IRA to set up its own government. Although they answered in the affirmative, the OIA representatives acted less than enthusiastic at the prospect.[19]

With the congressional political battle over the IRA's passage behind him, Collier now concentrated on getting Indians to accept the IRA, complete with its conservation section. On the Papago Reservation this translated into a concern about soil erosion caused by overgrazing. Despite his efforts, Elliott had accomplished little except to have the CCC-ID dig more wells and charcos to spread out the grazing. In May 1934 H. S. Bennett, head of the newly established Soil Erosion Service (the next year it became the Soil Conservation Service [SCS]) told Collier that O'odham lands "have become subject to extremely severe, accelerated erosion and increased runoff," which required immediate steps or the reservation would soon be beyond help. He predicted that if something was not done, the O'odham would have to move.[20]

The OIA started forcing its conservation agenda in August 1934, when Elliott received word that his 1934–1935 fiscal year CCC-ID proposals had been rejected for lack of a coordinated range control plan. This loss devastated many O'odham families who depended on the wages. Other problems continued to hinder Elliott. Poorly constructed projects, questions about CCC-ID expenditures, an earlier mining scandal, and open criticism in Congress all damaged Elliott's reputation in the OIA. In addition, Elliott differed with Collier over the development of the reservation's livestock industry. Elliott's demise, though, was most likely linked to his ideological differences with Collier over Indian policy goals; the superintendent favored assimilation, and the commissioner pushed for cultural pluralism. Soon after rejecting his CCC-ID plans, the OIA transferred Elliott to the Fort Peck Agency in Montana, a much less prestigious post than the Papago Reservation.[21]

His replacement, Theodore Hall, arrived at Sells in September 1934. A firm advocate of Collier's ideas, Hall had served briefly as an employee on the Gila River Reservation with the Akimel O'odham and later as superintendent of the Osage Agency in Oklahoma. A young man, Hall overflowed with energy, ethics, idealism, and a touch of socialism. Although he had a unique ability to work with people, Hall's self-assured attitude often caused him to forge ahead before adequately consulting with all the O'odham pueblos.[22]

Hall received an ultimatum from the OIA four days after his arrival. Collier let Hall know that if the O'odham did not agree to a range management plan, all CCC-ID funds would be cut. Already hurting from the rejection of Elliott's proposed projects, the O'odham would be seriously harmed by the ending of the program.[23]

Working in a state of panic, Hall quickly devised a plan after consulting with his staff and O'odham (probably the Executive Committee). To get the O'odham to accept a range management program, Hall realized he needed to link it with the popular CCC-ID and the desire by moderate pueblos to protect their autonomy through the IRA. For assistance with his CCC-IRA-conservation plan, Hall approached Franciscan missionary to the O'odham, Father Bonaventura Oblasser, and J. W. Hoover, a geography professor at Arizona State Teacher's College in Tempe. The three men prepared a map dividing the reservation into grazing districts that roughly matched the territory of the village complexes. Each area would also become its own political entity governed by an elected district council that, among its other responsibilities, would direct the CCC-ID and manage the range in that locality. CCC-ID would eventually be involved in only range improvement projects. A tribal council would then link the districts politically. Hall hoped the popularity of the CCC-ID would enhance the IRA governmental plan and that the district scheme would alleviate O'odham fears that the autonomous nature of their pueblos was endangered. In turn, the district and tribal councils would become intimately involved with the conservation agenda.[24]

When something affected the entire reservation, it was customary to call for a general council. Hall presented his plan at such a meeting in Sells on October 6, 1934. Gathering at 10:00 A.M. were delegates from the largest Aji, Ko-lo:di, and Ko:adk villages, representing a majority of the O'odham population. Nevertheless, except for the moderate Gigimai community of I:miga and the Hu:hu'ula at Gila Bend, no other Hu:uwos, Gigimai, or Hu:hu'ula representatives attended. The turnout, though, still proved significant.[25]

The council became rather contentious as delegates, sitting on old bridge timbers arranged under a crude roof of wagon sheets, debated Hall's proposed CCC-IRA-conservation plan long into the night. At one point Jose Piteroi, Aji headman of Si:l Naggia—long an area of antigovernment sentiment—stood in frustration and angrily told Hall, "You are going too fast, young man, you don't know our country. If you don't slow down, we'll get you out of here." The headman of the oldest Aji village, Louis Piteroi, remembered later that "we thought, 'Now the world will end.'"[26]

Hall called for districts to be fenced, grazing regulated, reductions made, and a cooperative range management plan designed. Hall argued that the range-district plan would protect the autonomy of individual villages and bring in more government aid. Using the OIA threat to his advantage, Hall told the O'odham that unless they accepted the plan, the CCC-ID would be ended. Anytime an O'odham raised a complaint, Hall promised wells, charcos, new schools, better roads, stock driveways, and other projects. In all, Hall committed the OIA to $4 million in public works at that meeting.[27]

At 1:30 in the morning, Hall's promises and threats persuaded a majority of the leaders to approve his plan. An agreement dividing the reservation along his district scheme was signed—pending acceptance of the IRA by a reservation-wide referendum and subsequent drafting of a tribal constitution. The records are unclear whether a "majority" of the attendees meant just over 50 percent—reflecting American political thought—or a consensus of all participants, reflecting O'odham political thought. Nevertheless, the IRA acceptance vote was set for December 15 of that year.[28]

When the election arrived, reports from the polling places indicated that the O'odham approached the polls very seriously. They knew village protection and the continuation of the CCC-ID were at stake. The O'odham accepted the IRA and Hall's district plan 1,443 to 188, with overwhelming Aji, Cukud Kuk Ko-lo:di, and Ko:adk support. This was important, since it represented both the leading ranching villages in the southeast and the most populous and conservative-to-moderate Aji areas around Ge Aji.[29]

Two sources of opposition materialized. In the west, the main Ku:pik Ko-lo:di village of Pisin Mo'o voted the proposal down, whereas other Hu:u:wos, Gigimai, and Hu:hu'ula took the normal O'odham path of showing disfavor by not voting. For example, not trusting the OIA precinct workers, Hu:hu'ula headman Pia Machita of To:a Bidk—possibly the most resistant leader on the reservation—demanded to view each man's vote. When told that was not possible, Pia Machita defiantly took his whole village away without casting a single ballot. The other source of opposition came from a minority of Presbyterians in the Ko-lo:di cattle areas stretching from Sells to San Miguel. Fearing the loss of control they enjoyed over the reservation's bureaucracy, they had approached Hall back in November saying that the proposed IRA would discriminate against them. Although not significant at this point, this opposition became much more strenuous later.[30]

After the election, the lopsided vote gave Hall the mistaken impression he had a mandate to freely pursue his conservation policies, whereas the O'odham mistakenly believed they now had much more control over their reservation.

These two opinions clashed on January 5, 1935, when Hall called for a general council to discuss the writing of an IRA constitution for a tribal government. Before commencing with the business at hand, Hall made the offhand comment that he had appointed two Indian judges for Sells. This sparked an impromptu protest from two important Aji headmen, Juan Joaquin of Gogs Mek and Barnabe Lopez of Wiwpul. Both men had long been at odds with the agency over various OIA actions. Back in 1924, Lopez had led a protest against the OIA's lack of effort to protect O'odham interests on land left outside the reservation, and Joaquin had headed the League of Papago Chiefs that had successfully spearheaded a drive to remove an unpopular superintendent in 1930. They were keenly sensitive to any sign that the OIA planned to continue its paternalistic practices and thus expressed anger that the judges were not elected in the spirit of the IRA's self-rule provisions. The meeting deteriorated from there as O'odham realized Hall had different priorities than they. Coming out of the meeting, Hall commented that the anti-OIA faction was on the ascendancy.[31]

Undeterred, Hall launched into laying the foundations for a range management plan. The first task was to take a census of the livestock on the reservation. This concerned O'odham such as Juan Joaquin and Barnabe Lopez, who felt such a survey would lead to increased regulations, followed invariably by reductions. For this reason many O'odham refused to answer the surveyor's questions.[32]

In the agency's newsletter, the *Aw-o-tahm Ah-pa-tac,* Hall spelled out the details of the range management plan, which confirmed many of the O'odham fears. His editorial clearly showed that Hall linked range management with self-rule. Hall wanted an IRA tribal government to reinforce a reservation-wide livestock association and to help initiate range management and organize cooperative sales. Although a few ranchers from the foothills of the Baboquivari Mountains, such as Henry Throssell and Richard Hendricks, supported the OIA's conservation plans, most O'odham saw an association infringing on the very independence they had hoped the IRA would protect. Hall also mentioned that one of the association's jobs was cattle reduction. Rumors of the controversial Navajo sheep reduction program immediately made the O'odham very concerned about any OIA conservation effort on their own reservation. Hall's proposal became extremely unpopular, turning some permanently against the very word *association.* In addition, Hall called for the construction of district fences. Although some welcomed this as a way to limit cattle from other areas using their resources, others feared it would restrict the movement of livestock between traditional ranges. Finally, in relation to the proposed tribal government, Hall tried to show the democratic nature of his plan, which called for each district to elect representatives to a reservation-wide political body. For a people used to consensus decisions made in open village councils, a representative system seemed like a step away from democracy.[33]

The opposition forces got another boost on February 1, 1935, when Hall fired Jose X. Pablo as the agency stockman, a position he had held for eighteen years. Hall accused him of taking kickbacks from the cattle buyers but never brought charges against him. Pablo immediately went to work for cattle buyers and started campaigning among O'odham livestock owners against a livestock association.[34]

After years of service, Pablo held the respect and trust of many O'odham, and his influence proved damaging to Hall's plans. Pablo's actions fed into a growing concern even among the originally supportive Aji. Events on the reservation made many extremely sensitive to any possible threat of infringement on the people's freedoms and control over their land. An example of the increasing tension occurred when the Arizona Livestock Board insisted on testing a sample of O'odham cattle for tuberculosis in hopes of stemming a possible statewide epidemic. Although the southeastern ranchers cooperated, the central and western villages saw this as a possible attempt to reduce their cattle herds. At a meeting in Ge Wo'o, Hall told O'odham from nearly all the western pueblos that they would be arrested if they interfered with the testing program. The ultraconservative Hu:hu'ula headman Pia Machita laughed at Hall and dared him to send the police. Ten days later the testers, who had rounded up a few head at Ge Wo'o, suddenly found themselves surrounded by armed and mounted O'odham. Threats and insults were made, but after a short while the O'odham dispersed. The testers decided the few cattle in the corral constituted a sufficient sample and quickly left.[35]

Through the summer of 1935, the CCC-ID escaped direct criticism. The rumor that the O'odham would have to pay for the projects never totally disappeared, but the program itself remained popular over much of the reservation. One reason was that the CCC-ID concentrated on relatively noncontroversial water development projects. The all-O'odham work crews cheerfully competed with each other to see which crew could dig a charco fastest. Before that summer the only two potentially contentious range projects pursued had been a very limited horse reduction that amounted only to a few hundred head and a range survey project that went largely unnoticed. The district fencing, which would have caused some trouble, was still in the planning stages. Regardless, the OIA insisted Hall do some efficiency reforms of this popular program, and that did trouble the O'odham. Hall centralized all planning with himself and his agency forester, R. D. Holtz. This meant the O'odham had less say over the projects, resulting in an increase of incidents during which the O'odham complained about where and what the CCC-ID did. Another reform was to replace the popular family camps with a program in which all enrollees lived at home. Hall also reduced the number of enrollees from a high of 875 to 300. Although this was a more realistic number, the move no doubt angered many of the young men who had come to depend on those jobs.[36]

As the summer of 1935 approached, Hall grew impatient waiting for the O'odham to start organizing a tribal government or a livestock association. The only progress was an agreement on a CCC-ID wage tax that would eventually finance a new tribal government when it was established. Back in April, the OIA had recommended Hall write a constitution himself and then get the Indians to accept it. Not wanting to take that approach, Hall tried to break the stalemate by appointing a constitutional committee and naming another for a livestock association. The former was made up entirely of O'odham, but the latter consisted mainly of OIA staff with only a few O'odham such as Hendricks, a strong advocate of range reform. The constitutional committee, feeling uneasy about the link between an association and a new tribal government, waffled and never produced a draft. When Hall returned after a month-long business trip, he was angered that only the cattle association by-laws had been completed, and he wrote a draft constitution himself. His frustration was also evidenced when Hall suggested ending the CCC-ID until the O'odham accepted the constitution and the range management plan.[37]

In August 1935 *Aw-o-tahm Ah-pa-tac* published the proposed cattle association by-laws for discussion. The result, though, was a rise in opposition, as they seemed to confirm much of the criticism Pablo had been expressing to the O'odham. Misunderstandings caused some of the complaints. For example, the draft called on O'odham with more than seventeen head of cattle to pay for grazing privileges, but many thought this meant they were limited to only seventeen cattle. Others thought a clause allowing money advances to prevent premature sales seemed like a trick to get the O'odham into debt and then have their land confiscated. Other, more legitimate complaints argued that the time between organized sales was too long, division fences would restrict range use, ranchers would be tied into a system with other O'odham who did not care about cattle, and the proposed regulations took away the ability to barter cattle for goods. Most of all, they cut back on an individual's freedom of movement on the range and forced successful ranchers on one pueblo to surrender grazing land to villages in other pueblos. One O'odham complained that the association idea treated the tribal members "like a monkey on a stick. He gets just so far and they push him down." In addition, Hall said that the range management plan would be part of the constitution, thus confirming the O'odham fear that an IRA government would be an association in disguise. Instead of protecting their autonomy, the IRA constitution now seemed to threaten it.[38]

Soon after the publication of the proposed association by-laws, the O'odham fear of losing uncontrolled use of the range started to become reality when a trainload of barbed wire and fenceposts arrived in late August 1935. Within days, fencing started in Siw Oidag and Waw Giwulk districts. Fencing became the main focus of the CCC-ID projects on the Papago Reservation in 1935–1936. Wealthy O'odham ranchers from lower desert areas who seasonally grazed their cattle in the Baboquivari foothills bitterly complained that the new fences restricted their operations. In the Ku:pik Ko-lo:di district of Pisin Mo'o, some fence cutting occurred as division lines separated a few O'odham from their fields. Nevertheless, this program received enough support to continue. Drawing the boundaries along existing pueblo territorial lines meant the fences disturbed few O'odham. Indeed, the residents of Gogs Mek and San Miguel saw the boundaries as a way to eliminate "foreign" cattle from their district. By the following summer, 306 miles of district fences had been completed.[39]

Although many acquiesced, fencing operations brought the debate over a combined IRA government and range management program to a critical point. Much of the trouble was aggravated by Hall's approach to the situation. Although many of the range management proposals troubled the O'odham, who automatically suspected any government program, Hall's failure to deal directly with the villages and their concerns had added to the problem. The reclusive western O'odham pueblos, along with the Ku:pik Ko-lo:di and Ko:adk, were almost completely alienated, and Cukud Kuk Ko-lo:di ranchers and Presbyterians saw the association as detrimental. More important, major elements of Aji who had supported the IRA now questioned the proposed tribal government as long as it was linked to range management.

During the fall of 1935, criticism from two sources challenged the idea of combining an IRA government with range management. The first source came from the O'odham themselves. A series of anti-IRA government meetings demonstrated how serious and widespread the resistance had become. On October 26 Hall, in the company of Richard Hendricks, attended a conference of leaders and headmen from different pueblos at the secluded village of Koson Waw:ia. He referred to them as the "usual group of Arrogant irreconisilables [sic]." Nevertheless, they included some very influential O'odham leaders, including the most successful O'odham rancher, Sanford Toro, a Cukud Kuk Ko-lo:di once called the "Papago Rockefeller." Also in attendance was the Ko:adk headman Charlie Anton and Aji leaders Barnabe Lopez of Wiwpul and Jose Piteroi of Si:l Naggia. Anger was expressed at both the fences and the way tribal organization had developed. One week later Hall and Peter Blaine met with a gathering of Hu:hu'ula at Tadai Do'ag, another secluded village. Pia Machita dominated the meeting when he halted Hall in mid-defense of the OIA's actions, telling the superintendent to "sit down young man, you've talked long enough, let me talk awhile." He then drew the seal of Mexico in the sand, telling Hall that he owed his allegiance to that nation and that the OIA representative had no business in Hu:hu'ula country.[40]

The second source of criticism came when the Social-Economic Section of the recently organized Technical Cooperation–Bureau of Indian Affairs (TC-BIA) returned its critiques of Hall's constitution and livestock association by-laws. The TC-BIA's O'odham expert, anthropologist Dr. Ruth Underhill, recommended that Hall start all over, move slower, separate the IRA from range management, have the O'odham organize a tribal government first, and start the discussion at the village level to build an emotional foundation of support for the plan. Underhill had started this process by spending two days with the influential Barnabe Lopez and convincing the Aji leader of the IRA constitution's value. In the end he commented, "We know there are two ways, the Indian way and the white way. We thought we could have only one and so we wanted the Indian way. But now we see we can have our old religion and our old chiefs and have the schools too. We will keep both ways together." After this, Lopez remained a steadfast supporter of Hall and the IRA. Underhill argued Hall could transform other leaders by exploiting one-on-one discussions.[41]

After reading the critiques, Collier did not give Hall a chance to readjust his efforts. The commissioner agreed with Underhill that organization of a tribal government needed to occur before a range management plan was enacted. He authorized the use of IRA organizational funds to send John Holst, supervisor of Indian schools and experienced in preparing other IRA constitutions, to help get the O'odham organization back on track.[42]

On December 4 Holst arrived in Sells and immediately set out to bring in pueblos he felt had not been well represented. He rejected Hall's earlier draft and insisted on a more representative council than the Executive Committee. After an initial general council attended by over 200 O'odham in Sells, a constitutional committee was called for with representatives from throughout the reservation. On December 16 delegates came from the main Aji communities including Ge Aji through Ge Oidag and Gogs Mek to Wiwpul, the mixed Aji and Sobaipuri village of San Xavier, the Cukud Kuk Ko-lo:di areas from Kawlik to San Miguel including Sanford Toro, the mixed Aji and Ko-lo:di community of Sells, Ko:adk from the village of the same name, and some pro-IRA Gigimai from the Hikiwoni pueblo. Not all the pueblos, though, were in attendance, as resistance in the north and west prevented anyone coming from the Ko:adk villages of A:ngam and Ce:co, the Gigimai and Hu:uwos of Ge Wo'o, the Ku:pik Ko-lo:di, and the more hard-line Hu:hu'ula in Gagka and To:a Bidk. Nevertheless, having all the major Aji areas represented accounted for a majority of the O'odham; thus Holst felt justified in proceeding with the constitutional committee.[43]

Ranchers moved to capture control of the constitutional committee by electing the former agency stockman Jose X. Pablo as the chair. Hall stayed out of the proceedings, and Holst turned the meeting over to Pablo. Not knowing how to proceed, Pablo introduced the Pima IRA constitution to use as a model for their own. The first day was spent going over the document article by article. Most of it was lost on many in the meeting, and several people such as Barnabe Lopez were frustrated by the unclear discussion. By that afternoon the more conservative forces took charge after one O'odham exclaimed, "We want to have our old laws and customs." They threw out the Pima constitution, started over, and proceeded to make progress.[44]

By the following January 6, the constitutional committee had completed a draft. Holst commented that it was crude and clearly not pleasing to pro–range reform O'odham such as Hendricks, but it did reflect moderate and conservative Aji views, down to the name of the tribe. Instead of "Papago," Aji leaders called for using the older term *Tho-ho-no O'tam*. In addition, they mandated that the council follow the old laws and customs, that districts manage their own affairs, and that judges be elected by the people. Another important section especially desired by ranchers was the right to remove the district fences if they were found to be "a detriment." Many such as Sanford Toro hoped this would be the end of district fences. Also clearly separating OIA range management from the tribal government was Article 8, which gave individuals the right to act freely in regard to the selling, branding, and pasturing of their cattle. On January 7, 1936, they presented the draft to Hall, and thus it "started on a stormy way."[45]

Hall, along with Hendricks and other members of the older Executive Committee, were not pleased with the new draft constitution. In addition, TC-BIA head Allan Harper, disagreeing with the Social-Economic Section within his own agency, also opposed the O'odham draft because it gave the O'odham individual control over their own herds. He claimed that would destroy all the conservation gains Hall had achieved. Among the O'odham, Executive Committee members and OIA Indian employees feared losing control over the reservation to groups they felt were "backwards" and unable to successfully chart the people's future. Large ranching interests along with Presbyterians and other pro-agency O'odham also feared the possibility of Aji and other western pueblos ruling their lives through a tribal government.[46]

Forces opposing the draft constitution or wanting more time to discuss it gained control when a general council met on January 18, 1936. Scheduled originally only to review and approve the constitution, this became the first in a series of mass meetings that attempted to rewrite the draft. Leading up to the council, Hall gave the pro-agency O'odham an upper hand by sending only Executive Committee members such as Hendricks and OIA O'odham employees such as Peter Blaine around the reservation to "explain" the draft. To further delay O'odham approval so he could reword the constitution, Hall brought in nearly 400 O'odham. The meeting degenerated as people challenged almost every section.

That became the first of seven such meetings, with discussion revolving around nineteen specific points including fences, livestock, ballots, and even the tribal name. After "four months of strife and turmoil and the building up of antagonisms," Pablo finally submitted the draft to Collier on May 4, 1936. Changes in the document included replacing "Tho-ho-no O'tam" with "Papago." Upsetting ranchers like Toro, Article 8, allowing individuals to sell their cattle independently, had also been stricken from the draft. Otherwise, much of what the original constitutional committee wanted remained, such as the option to remove the fences, give districts local control, and follow the "old laws and customs." For many O'odham but not all, this seemed to adequately separate the IRA process from range management.[47]

As the debate continued, Hall went cautiously forward with his conservation goals. He felt it was necessary because there "are still many improvements needed on the range if the best possible use is [to be] made of the range resources which are available." By getting rid of Article 8, Hall still hoped a single O'odham governing body such as the IRA government could be in charge of controlling all the cattle herds on the reservation. Hall realized, though, that he needed to be careful not to give the impression that the tribal government was mainly for range management purposes.[48]

With conservation as his hidden agenda, Hall proposed establishing a temporary tribal government. Hall took Underhill's advice and started the effort at the local level by proposing that the O'odham first form temporary district councils. To give these bodies purpose and to strengthen their legitimacy in the eyes of the O'odham, Hall had the district councils plan the CCC-ID projects for the next fiscal year. By increasing O'odham input, that would improve the program's popularity, which was still meeting western opposition. Hall asked the O'odham "to choose your best men from all the country to make a Council of wise men so that when the Government has any plans to help with your cattle, or anything else, we can ask those men, 'Do you want this and how shall we do it?' " Hall hoped that once the O'odham leaders were in the position of planning projects, they would see the need for conservation. Ultimately, what this did do in the eyes of the O'odham was to change the CCC-ID from an OIA-supervised program to a locally directed "O'odham-CCC."[49]

Recognizing a chance to establish more control over their land and not seeing these temporary districts as part of the OIA's range management designs, many O'odham quickly established temporary district councils. Having the opportunity to design the O'odham-CCC projects gave them considerable incentive, but that was not their only motivation. Many felt these bodies might be able to exert influence over the OIA and protect their freedoms. Showing his support for the temporary councils, Narcho Pablo of Sells expressed this view when he said, "There have been things in the past that the Tribe did not know anything about until later on, then the Tribe goes around trying to find out what it is about—these things that the Government has been doing. I feel that it is safe to start right now so the Tribe will know what is going on."[50]

Not surprisingly, the mixed Aji and Ko-lo:di district of Waw Giwulk, with its heavy pro-agency constituency, became the first district to organize, followed by Barnabe Lopez's district, officially called S-cuk Do'ag. Lopez's backing demonstrated that the Aji supported organization once they felt conservation was no longer an issue. By May, all the districts except Cukud Kuk and Ge Wo'o had organized and sent in their O'odham-CCC requests. In Ge Wo'o the general fear of the government's intentions, reinforced by a recent effort to drill an unwanted well, hampered participation. By June, though, the Gigimai and Hu:uwos in that pueblo had also organized the Ge Wo'o district council by agreeing to a compromise wherein the very conservative headman, Ramon, received the honorary position of "adviser on old Papago customs." Meanwhile, a few significant Ko-lo:di ranchers, namely Toro, stalled organization of Cukud Kuk. Even after that district did establish a district council, it did not send a district CCC-ID plan. Others such as the Hu:hu'ula of the Gagka villages never participated. To cover up this area of nonsupport, the OIA combined it with the more cooperative Gigimai of the Hikiwoni pueblo to form one district of the same name.[51]

Now given a chance to help design the O'odham-CCC plans, the district councils wanted programs ranging from new schools to household plumbing. Many proposals did not fit within the CCC-ID authority and were referred to other programs such as the Public Works Administration. Of the other requests, the O'odham's first priority was water development. This included approximately fifty charcos, more wells, and steel storage tanks. Such projects helped cattle owners without restricting their independence. Not surprisingly, the only fencing requests were for protecting the water projects, not for boundaries. Local planning also allowed O'odham farmers to turn some CCC efforts away from livestock to agriculture. In a request never considered by the OIA, the O'odham-CCC called for projects improving fields by checking erosion. Other O'odham interests turned toward infrastructure, with a request for over 120 miles of road and 127 miles of telephone lines. Only half the projects were funded that fiscal year, but the Indian input firmly redirected the O'odham-CCC, and except for water development, range control was not part of the program.[52]

Not to be thwarted, Hall next placed his hopes on a reservation-wide temporary council he could more easily control. Such a body came into existence on July 10, 1936, with two representatives from each district except Cukud Kuk, which still refused to participate. This gave Hall an O'odham-endorsed legislative body from which he could get reservation-wide initiatives approved. It replaced the Executive Committee, which only a few eastern O'odham supported. Some questioned organizing the council before the constitution was approved, but most at the first meeting agreed with Jose X. Pablo—now pro-IRA—when he supported the move "because work is always going on, government business is always going on, so I thought it was a good thing that we had the temporary council elected by the districts." At that first meeting of the temporary council, many O'odham even began supporting the idea of a united O'odham entity. Jose Ignacio of Sells saw the tribal council as a way to instill a spirit of cooperation among all the O'odham with a "singleness of purpose and thought which was previously undreamed of." In a very surprising statement Barnabe Lopez, who spent his entire career as a headman fighting for the rights of his village, asked the group to look out for the interests of the entire tribe and not just their own pueblos.[53]

Right at this moment of seeming success, Hall made some key mistakes. First, Ko-lo:di rancher opposition led by Sanford Toro had prevented the election of representatives from that district, but Hall insisted on proceeding without Cukud Kuk District's involvement. This further alienated the most successful ranchers. At that first meeting Hall also introduced the OIA's Southwest regional forester, who told the council the OIA was sending two more men to work with them on range improvement and control. Although warmly applauded, the news no doubt caused others to think the OIA would try to use the temporary councils to increase restrictions on O'odham's use of the land. Hall reminded the council that it was their job to protect the district fences, which were still unpopular in some areas. Finally, the temporary council also passed a few questionable ordinances. They decided to sell hunting licenses to pay their own travel expenses. The idea of the council being partially financed by white hunters bothered some O'odham, who had previously had bad experiences with non-Indian hunters shooting stock. A more serious situation resulted when they allowed the El Paso Gas Company to build a line across the northwest, or Hu:hu'ula, portion of the reservation. In separate incidents, villagers from Gagka and To:a Bidk drove the workers off with a show of armed force. Pia Machita allowed the workers to proceed only after it was clearly understood he opposed the gas line.[54]

These acts increased the number of O'odham listening to Toro's argument that the IRA tribal government would lead to range management and the loss of freedoms. In August Hall came across one of Toro's meetings at the Gigimai and Hu:uwos village of Ge Wo'o. Despite the earlier compromise allowing the Ge Wo'o District to organize, the headman Ramon now opposed the IRA. He and his followers joined Ku:pik Ko-lo:di, led by Juan Diego and Jose Lorenzo of Pisin Mo'o along with Toro from the Cukud Kuk pueblo, in their resistance to tribal organization. Except for hard-line Hu:hu'ula, the opposition began to consolidate.[55]

In November 1936 the OIA finally accepted the O'odham draft constitution and called for an election to approve the document. The council and Hall launched a "campaign of explanation" to sell the organization plan. Toro made the proposed constitution the focus of the opposition and worked equally hard against it. In the midst of the campaign, the TC-BIA wanted to start a range survey of the reservation. Realizing that this would jeopardize the constitution's chances of acceptance, Hall persuaded the TC-BIA workers to wait until after the vote.[56]

On December 12 the O'odham went to the polls to decide. As Holst said with a sigh of relief, the intensity of the past year was over. Fifty-eight percent of eligible O'odham voted, as opposed to only 48 percent two years earlier during the IRA vote. Ballot boxes were sent not only all over the reservation but also to Tucson's Indian barrio, the copper mining camp at Ajo, and the Casa Grande and Eloy cotton fields. The final vote was 1,340 in favor of the constitution to 580 against. By non-Indian standards, the constitution had been accepted overwhelmingly. By more traditional O'odham standards, however, the victory was problematic. Not surprisingly, the constitution won by a landslide in most Aji villages as well as in the cotton fields.[57]

Although it won clear approval, opposition did exist in the largest Aji village of Ge Aji and the mixed Aji and Ko-lo:di towns of Gogs Mek and Sells, as well as at San Xavier. Opposition was strongest among southeastern ranchers and western conservatives, as well as in the north. Although the vote was narrowly affirmative, serious opposition did appear in the Gigimai and Hu:uwos villages as well as the Ku:pik Ko-lo:di villages of Pisin Mo'o. The Hu:hu'ula areas had the lowest turnout, with only 14 voting from the Gagka villages. The constitution lost in the Cukud Kuk Ko-lo:di villages, as well as in one Aji village located on the west slope of the Baboquivari Mountains in the middle of ranching country. The northern losses in the Ko:adk villages, including the important community of Ce:co, were unexpected but probably occurred because the pro-organization faction spent very little time campaigning in this area. The constitution also failed in the Ajo mining camp, which was made up largely of O'odham from the Gigimai pueblo. Toro had done wonders to organize the opposition, but enough O'odham remained convinced that the new tribal government would protect their freedoms and remain separate from OIA range management.[58]

Despite the opposition, the O'odham as one people now had a federally recognized constitution and tribal government. By January 1937 the first council had been organized, with Jose Ignacio of Sells as its chairman. As Ignacio argued, the government was slowly "welding the Papagos into a tribe." Although not accepted by all the southern ranchers and western and northern headmen, the idea of a politically unified Papago Tribe had been born.[59]

More than anything else, it would be the O'odham-CCC that breathed life into the new tribal entity. After the government started functioning, the funds raised from the O'odham-CCC wage tax helped finance operations. In addition, the elected district councils continued to plan O'odham-CCC projects, easing Hall and his staff into an advisory role. This tribal government–CCC cooperation helped entrench the new body as well as seriously weaken any range control program by removing O'odham-CCC workers from carrying out the OIA's conservation plans. Enhancing its stature, the council also started the popular Papago Rodeo and the Papago Arts and Craft Association, as well as becoming a source of money through a revolving loan fund.[60]

Contrary to Hall's hope, the tribal government thus successfully stayed separate from the OIA's range management agenda. The O'odham's desire to keep local control in the hands of the district councils effectively rendered the new tribal government useless for the OIA's conservation purposes. In this way the O'odham achieved their goal of protecting the integrity of the pueblos while maintaining the popular O'odham-CCC. Nevertheless, the OIA did try to get the Tribal Council to endorse district-level livestock associations; the idea was officially rejected. The O'odham had unraveled Hall's plan, taken what they wanted, and left the OIA with the dysfunctional rest.[61]

This did not totally end the OIA's range control efforts, though. Instead of the CCC-ID or a tribal association, the main conservation agency on the Papago Reservation now became the TC-BIA. Under its local director, John Pearmain, the agency's work started almost as soon as the polls for voting on the constitution closed. Three days after the election, Hall announced in the December *Aw-o-tahm Ah-pa-tac* that the TC-BIA "is about to descend on us." Starting in January 1937, the cooperative effort between the OIA and the SCS initiated a field survey of the reservation's resources and O'odham land use patterns.[62]

Although the successful efforts of the O'odham to separate the IRA tribal constitution from range control did the most to thwart New Deal conservation efforts, the results of the TC-BIA surveys virtually killed OIA determination for range control. Not surprisingly, the conclusions found that contrary to two decades of OIA opinions, cattle did not offer the best hope for the O'odham. Instead, they would either have to be relocated to another reservation (which was out of the question), or other economic pursuits should be encouraged besides ranching. The surveys also discovered that most O'odham followed a diversified lifestyle that centered around flood farming and not cattle, which only served as an insurance policy against crop failure. In short, most O'odham were not commercial ranchers and did not desire to become such. Only the Presbyterian Ko-lo:di in the southeast had adopted cattle raising as a full-time occupation. This information influenced Harper to turn the TC-BIA's attention away from the Papago Reservation. Likewise, Hall turned his attention elsewhere as he started to stress agricultural programs. Thus ended the OIA's New Deal effort toward a comprehensive range management program on the Papago Reservation.[63]

Going into the New Deal, the O'odham had two concerns—surviving the Depression and protecting their independence. Meanwhile, the OIA desire to help the O'odham adjust to a changed land endangered the very essence of the people's *Himdag*. The rest of the 1930s were dominated by an interplay between these conflicting goals. As the decade came to a close, the OIA's efforts had seriously altered the O'odham world, as the New Deal programs brought the reservation into direct contact with outside society. The O'odham, though, had been active in shaping that change. The OIA had only had one vision and had committed its resources to conservation with self-government to make the O'odham self-sufficient. For the O'odham, the accompanying range management proposals threatened their self-sufficiency. To maintain control over their own lives, the O'odham resistance unraveled the OIA plan, selected what would help them preserve that which was most valuable, and discarded the rest. To best protect their *Himdag,* their way of life, they co-opted aspects of the colonial infrastructure presented by the IRA and the O'odham-CCC in the creation of a new world. In that effort they acquired other challenges, such as working out the problem of being a single tribal entity when one had not existed before, but for now the O'odham had accomplished the goal of defending what was most important to them—their *Himdag*-inspired sovereignty.

References

1. Quoted in Ruth Underhill to Duncan Strong, n.d., 9675-A-1936-Sells-068, Bureau of Indian Affairs, Record Group 75, National Archives, Washington, DC (hereafter cited as RG-75, NA). The idea of *Himdag* is discussed by Bernard Fontana, "The O'odham," in James E. Officer et al., eds., *Pimeria Alta: Missions and More* (Tucson: Southwest Mission Research Society, 1996): 26.
2. For an overview of early O'odham history and culture, see Bernard Fontana, "Papago Indians" (unpublished, 1964; unofficially printed by the Tohono O'odham Nation, housed at the Arizona State Museum—hereafter ASM); Fontana, *Of Earth and Little Rain: The Papago Indians* (Tucson: University of Arizona Press, 1989); Alice Joseph, Rosemond Spicer, and Jane Chesky, *The Desert People: A Study of the Papago Indians* (Chicago: University of Chicago Press, 1949); Ruth Underhill, *Social Organization of the Papago Indians* (New York: Columbia University Press, 1939); Winston Erickson, *Sharing the Desert: The Tohono O'odham in History* (Tucson: University of Arizona Press, 1994).
3. For the 1695 conflict, see Herbert Eugene Bolton, *Rim of Christendom: A Biography of Eusebio Francisco Bolton, Pacific Coast Pioneer* (New York: Russell and Russell, 1960 [1936]): 259, 296–318; Rolf W. Bauer, "Development of a Papago Cattle Industry: History and Case Studies" (unpublished, 1968; housed at ASM): 3–10; Gwyneth Hairington Xavier, "The Cattle Industry of the Southern Papago Districts With Some Information on the Reservation Cattle Industry as a Whole" (1937), published in Indian Claims Commission, Docket no. 345, Defense Exhibit 3, no. 110, in *Papago Indians,* Vol. 1 (New York: Garland, 1974): 1–5, 20–21, 48.
4. For a discussion of the development of the ranching culture in the southeast section of the reservation, see Richard Donald Jones, "An Analysis of Papago Communities, 1900–1920," Ph.D. diss., University of Arizona, 1969.
5. Quote from Joseph Elliott, "Annual Narrative Report, Sells Agency, Arizona, Calendar Year 1931," M-1011, Roll 130, RG-75, National Archives–Pacific Southwest Branch (hereafter cited as NA-PSB), Laguna Nigual, California; William Zeh, "Grazing Report, Papago Indian Reservation," 6192-1932-Sells-310, RG-75, NA.
6. Elliott to Commissioner, April 15, 1932, File 1932, Tohono O'odham History Files, Vinito Garcia Library, Sells (Arizona) (hereafter cited as O'odham history files); Elliott to Commissioner, January 24, 1933, 4113-1933-Sells-301, RG-75, NA; Elliott to Commissioner, March 22, 1933, Box 54, Greenway Collection, Arizona Historical Society, Tucson (Arizona) (hereafter cited as Greenway Collection).

7. Quote from Peter Blaine Sr., with Michael S. Adams, *Papago and Politics* (Tucson: Arizona Historical Society, 1981): 77; see also John Holst, "The Organization of the Papagos," in *Indians at Work* (Washington, DC: OIA, February 1, 1937), housed in the ASM; Blaine, *Papago and Politics,* pp. 87–88; Fontana, "Papago Indians," pp. 193–194.
8. The O'odham divided into three distinct subcultures: the agricultural Akimel O'odham, or River People (Pima), who lived in sedentary villages along perennial streams; the nomadic hunting-and-gathering Hia C-ed O'odham, or the Sand People, in western Papaguería; and the focus of this chapter, the Tohono O'odham, or the desert people, who before the drilling of deep wells migrated between two villages—a mountain spring village in the winter and a flood-farming village in the summer. In historical times Tohono O'odham further divided into the eleven village complexes or pueblos. The first non-Indian to identify the different village complexes or pueblos was Franciscan missionary Bonaventure Oblasser. Oblasser to E .H. Hammond, March 18, 1930, File 1930, O'odham Files; Oblasser, "Papagueria: The Domain of the Papago," *Arizona Historical Review,* 7 (April 1936): 3–9; J. W. Hoover, "Generic Descent of the Papago Villages," *American Anthropologist,* 37 (1935): 257–264; Underhill, *Social Organization,* pp. 13–23, 30, 59–69; Joseph, Spicer, and Chesky, *The Desert People,* pp. 3–28, 60–72; Jones, "An Analysis of Papago Communities," pp. 31–48, 153; A. K. Mark, "Descriptions of and Variables Relating to Ecological Change in the History of the Papago Indian Population," M.A. thesis, University of Arizona, 1960.
9. The O'odham dialect names come from Dean and Lucille Saxton, *Dictionary: Papago and Pima to English to Papago and Pima* (Tucson: University of Arizona Press, 1969); the spellings come from the Albert Alvarez and Kenneth Hale orthographic system, which the Tohono O'odham Nation accepted as its official version in 1974. See Ofelia Zepeda, *A Papago Grammar* (Tucson: University of Arizona Press, 1994). Village names are spelled according to the Alvarez and Hale orthography, even though they may not match most maps, for the same places may have up to three other designations.
10. The pueblos of these O'odham dialectical groups are as follows:
    (1) Aji pueblos include *Aji* (the oldest), *Ge Aji* (the largest; one of its related villages includes *W:ak* near San Xavier), *Akcin, Kui Tatk,* and *Komalik.*
    (2) *Gigimal* pueblos include *Ge Wo'o* and *Hikiwani.*
    (3) *Hu:hu'ula* pueblo is *Gagka.*
    (4) *Ko:adk* pueblos include *A:ngam* and *Ko:adk*; the *Ko:adk* had intermarried and developed close ties with the farming Akimel O'odham (Pima).
    (5) *Hu:uwos* pueblos include *Gi'ito Wak* in Mexico (which includes villages around the Rio Sonoita) and *Ge Wo'o,* which they share with *Gigimal.*

    Hoover, "Generic Descent," pp. 257–264; Underhill, *Social Organization,* pp. 13–23, 59–69; Joseph, Spicer, and Chesky, *The Desert People,* pp. 3–28, 60–72; Oblasser, "Papaqueria," pp. 3–7; William S. King and Delmos J. Jones, "Papago Population Studies," Indian Claims Commission, Docket no. 345, in *Papago Indians,* vol. 2 (New York: Garland, 1974).
11. Underhill, *Social Organization,* pp. 90–112; Zeh, "Grazing Report"; Theodore Hall, "Annual Narrative Report, Sells Agency, Arizona, 1936," Microcopy 1011,

Roll 130, Superintendent's Annual Narrative and Statistical Reports From Field Jurisdictions, Bureau of Indian Affairs, RG-75, NA, Pacific Southwest Branch, Laguna Niguel, California (hereafter cited as M-1011, Roll 130, RG-75, NA-PSB); Allan Harper to Walter Woehlke, March 18, 1938, 37102-37-Sells-021.5, RG-75, NA; Edward F. Castetter and Willis H. Bell *Inter-American Studies,* vol. 1, *Pima and Papago Indian Agriculture* (Albuquerque: University of New Mexico Press, 1942): 42–48, 77–102, 108–121, 203.

12. The Ko-lo:di pueblos include Ku:pik and Cukud Kuk. Other Ko-lo:di had fled from the Rio Altar area in Mexico in the late nineteenth century. See Hoover, "Generic Descent," pp. 257–264; Underhill, *Social Organization,* pp. 13–23, 59–69; Joseph, Spicer, and Chesky, *The Desert People,* pp. 3–28, 60–72; Oblasser, "Papaqueria," pp. 7–9; Jones, "An Analysis of Papago Communities," pp. 31–48, 153; King and Jones, "Population Studies."
13. Elliott to John Collier, March 20, 1931, 6167-1931-Sells-902, RG-75, NA; Elliott to Commissioner, March 22, 1933, Box 54, Greenway Collection; Jose Carlos et al. (164 O'odham) to Collier, June 19, 1933, Box 54, Greenway Collection; Oblasser to Right Reverend William Hughes, February 8, 1932, 10658-1932-Sells-301, RG-75, NA; Elliott to Commissioner, March 8, 1932, File 1932, O'odham Files; Oblasser to Carl Hayden, November 25, 1932, Folder 8, Box 612, Carl Hayden Papers, Arizona State University Library, Tempe, Arizona (hereafter cited as Hayden Papers); Elliott to Commissioner, January 24, 1933, 4113-1933-Sells-301, RG-75, NA.
14. Quote from Hall, "Annual Narrative Report, Sells Agency, Arizona, 1935," M-1011, Roll 130, RG-75, NA-PSB. Also see A. W. Simington, Report to Collier, "Indian Reorganization Act Land Acquisition, Papago Project," n.d., File 1936, O'odham History Files; Fontana, "Papago," pp. 190–192. On statistics see Leonard J. Arrington, "Arizona in the Great Depression," *Arizona Review,* 17 (December 1968): 11–19; Arrington, "The New Deal in the West: A Preliminary Statistical Inquiry," *Pacific Historical Review,* 38 (August 1969): 311–317; Erickson, *Sharing the Desert,* pp. 131–133.
15. Quote from Donald Parman, "The Indians and the Civilian Conservation Corps," *Pacific Historical Review,* 40 (February 1971): 40; *Indians at Work,* August 1 and September 15, 1933; Collier to Hayden, May 20, 1933, Folder 2, Box 618, Hayden Papers; Hayden to Bailey, May 23, 1933, Folder 2, Box 619, Hayden Papers; John Salmond, *The Civilian Conservation Corps, 1933–1943: A New Deal Case Study* (Durham, NC: Duke University Press, 1967); Richard Lowitt, *The New Deal and the West* (Bloomington: Indiana University Press, 1984); Peter MacMillan Booth, "Civilian Conservation Corps in Arizona," M.A. thesis, University of Arizona, 1991; Booth, "Cactizonians: The Civilian Conservation Corps in Pima County, Arizona," *Journal of Arizona History,* 32 (fall 1991): 291–332.
16. Elliott to Commissioner, March 20, 1931, 6167-193 1-Sells-902, RG-75, NA; Elliott to Commissioner, March 22, 1933, Box 54, Greenway Collection; Elliott, "Sells Agency, Monthly Report, Expenditures," October 1933, Box 139, PAO-ECW and CCC-ID BIA, RG-75, NAPSB; Joseph, Spicer, and Chesky, *The Desert People,* p, 26; Blaine, *Papago and Politics,* pp. 67–71.
17. Milton J. Nolan, Report, "Charco Construction Program," June 1935, Box 243, Phoenix Area Office, Emergency Conservation Works and Civilian Conservation Corps–Indian Division, Bureau of Indian Affairs, RG-75, NA-PSB, Laguna Niguel, California (hereafter cited as PAO-ECW and CCC-ID BIA, RG-75, NA-PSB);

Theodore Hall, Diary, November 1, 1934, recorded by Hall for Richard Donald Jones, April 14, 1965 (hereafter cited as Hall's Diary); *Tucson Citizen,* June 27 and July 12, 1933, housed in the AHS; *Arizona (Tucson) Daily Star,* May 1, 1933, housed in the AHS; Holst, "Organization of the Papagos Under the Indian Reorganization Act," n.d., 9675A-1936-Sells-068, RG-75, NA; Nolan, Report, "Charco," June 1935, Box 243, PAO-ECW and CCC-ID BIA, RG-75, NAPSB; Hall, "Annual Report, Sells Agency, 1935"; Cromwell to Collier, July 9, 1934, Box 236, PAO-ECW and CCC-ID BIA, RG-75, NAPSB.

18. Indian Reorganization Act, June 18, 1934; Vine Deloria Jr. and Clifford Lytle, *The Nations Within: The Past and Future of American Indian Sovereignty* (New York: Pantheon, 1984): 55–79.
19. Office of Indian Affairs, "Report of Southern Arizona Indian Conference Held at Phoenix, Arizona, March 15–16, 1934, for the Purpose of Explaining the Howard-Wheeler Bill to the Assembled Indians" (Phoenix: Phoenix Indian School Printing Shop, 1934), in Box 54, Greenway Collection; Oblasser to Collier, July 4, 1934, File 1934, O'odham History Files; Donald Parman, *Indians and the American West in the Twentieth Century* (Bloomington: Indiana University Press, 1994): 94–97; Deloria and Lytle, *The Nations Within,* pp. 101–102, 109–110.
20. Zeh, "Grazing Report"; Collier, "The Papago Mineral Question," May 5, 1934, Folder 8, Box 612, Hayden Collection; H. S. Bennett to Collier, May 31, 1934, Folder 8, Box 612, Hayden Collection; Vivian Juan, "Tohono O'odham Constitution in Transition," M.A. thesis, University of Arizona, 1992, pp. 16–17.
21. Hall to William Zimmerman Jr., March 24, 1936, in Verna Ivey, "Model Tribal Council: Tohono O'odham Nation Student Leadership Day," n.d., housed in Baboquivari High School, Sells, Arizona (hereafter cited as Ivey, "Model"); U.S. Congress, House, Committee on Indian Affairs, Hearing, "Readjustment of Indian Affairs," 73rd Cong., 2d sess., part 5 (March 5, 12, 13, April 9, 1934): 143; Blaine, *Papago and Politics,* pp. 58–61; Hall, "Annual Narrative Report, Sells Agency, Arizona, 1935"; Santa Rosa Ranch Indian Livestock Associations, n.d., 36479-1934-Sells-916, RG-75, NA; Cornwall to Collier, October 4, 1935, Box 245, PAO-ECW and CCC-ID, BIA, RG-75, NA-PSB; W. J. Keays to Commissioner, December 9, 1935, Box 245, PAO-ECW and CCC-ID, BIA, RG-75, NA-PSB. Elliott left sometime in late August or early October, and Hall arrived on September 4. In the interim, J. W. Johnson acted as temporary agent. *Arizona (Tucson) Daily Star,* August 31, 1934.
22. Hall's Diary, September 4, 1934; Underhill to Duncan Strong, n.d., 9675-A-i 936-Sells-068, RG-75, NA; Blaine, *Papago and Politics,* p. 84.
23. Hall, "Annual Narrative Report, Sells Agency, Arizona, 1935"; Hall's Diary, September 1934; Ivey, "Model"; Hall, "One Year," *Aw-o-tahm An-pa-tac,* September 15, 1935, in the Special Collection, University of Arizona, Tucson; Hall, "Report of Referendum Vote," December 1934, File 1934, O'odham History Files.
24. Hall's Diary, September 1934; Hall, "Papago Indian Reservation District Organization Plan," February 13, 1935, File 1935, O'odham Files; Hall, "Report of Referendum Vote"; Hoover, "Generic Descent," pp. 257–264; Oblasser, "Papaqueria," pp. 3–9.
25. Underhill to Strong, n.d., 9675-A-1936-Sells-068, RG-75, NA; *Arizona (Tucson) Daily Star,* October 8 and 31, 1934; Ivey, "Model"; Hall, "Annual Narrative Report, Sells Agency, 1935"; Hall, "Report of Referendum Vote."

26. Quote from Hall's Diary, October 6, 1934.
27. Ibid.
28. Hall's Diary, October 6, 1934.
29. Hall, "Report of Referendum Vote."
30. *Aw-o-tahm Ah-pa-tac,* September 1, 1935; *Ajo (Arizona) Copper,* November 15, 1934, in the AHS; Hall to Indian Traders, Papago Reservation, February 12, 1935, File 1935, O'odham History Files; Hall, "Papago Plan," February 13, 1935, File 1935, O'odham Files; Hall, "Annual Narrative Report, Sells Agency, Arizona, 1935"; Hall's Diary, November 11 and December 15, 1934. For a discussion of O'odham attitudes, see Joseph, Spicer, and Chesky, *The Desert People,* pp. 60–114.
31. Hall's Diary, January 5, 1934.
32. Harper to Woehlke, March 18, 1938, 37102-1937-Sells-021.5, RG-75, NA.
33. Hall to Indian Traders, Papago Reservation, February 20, 1935, 13105-1935-Sells-301, RG-75, NA; *Aw-o-tahm An-pa-tac,* January, February, March, April 1935; Xavier, "The Cattle Industry," pp. 17, 20–21, 33; Bauer, "Development of a Papago Cattle Industry," pp. 6, 8–12.
34. Hall's Dairy, February 1, 1935; John Holst interview with Spicer, February 19, 1943, Subject File 819-823, Box A-485, Spicer Collection; *Aw-o-tahm Ah-ap-tac,* March 1935.
35. Hall's Diary, June 15, July 7, July 13, July 14, July 20, July 22, July 23, 1935; *Aw-o-tahm Ah-pa-tac,* June 1935.
36. Hall, "Annual Narrative Report, Sells Agency, 1935"; *Aw-o-tahm An-pa-tac,* January 1934; Hall, Sells Agency, "Weekly Groups Reports" for 1935, Folder 14, Box 244, BIA, PAO-ECW and CCC-ID, RG-75, NA-PSB; Claude Cornwall to McCarthy, June 1933, Box 230, PAO-ECW and CCC-ID, BIA, RG-75, NA-PSB; Claude Cromwell to Collier, October 31, 1934, Box 245, PAO-ECW and CCC-ID, BIA, RG-75, NA-PSB; Cromwell to Collier, July 9, 1934, Box 236, PAO-ECW and CCC-ID, BIA, RG-75, NA-PSB; Blaine, *Papago and Politics,* pp. 73–76.
37. Hall's Diary, May 4, June 1, August 20, 1935; *Aw-o-tahm Ah-pa-tac,* May 1935; "Stipulation of the Papago Tribe," May 18, 1935, File 1935, O'odham History Files; "Minutes of Tribal Meeting," June 1, 1935, 13105-1935-Sells-301, RG-75, NA; Woehlke to Hall, April 11, 1935, 9734-1936-Sells-066, RG-75, NA; "Papago Livestock Association By-Laws," August 2, 1935, 13105-1935-Sells-301, RG-75, NA; Underhill to Duncan Strong, October 30, 1935, File 1935, O'odham History Files.
38. Quote from Underhill to Strong, n.d., 9675-A-1936-Sells-068, RG-75, NA. See also *Aw-o-tahm Ah-pa-tac,* August 1935; Underhill to Strong, October 30, 1935, File 1935, O'odham History Files.
39. Hall's Diary, August 29, 1935; Underhill to Strong, n.d.; Hall, "Annual Narrative Report, Sells Agency, Arizona, 1936"; *Aw-o-ahm Aw-pa-tac,* August 1936; Manuel Puella, O'odham, interview with Spicer, n.d., Subject File 753, Box A-485, Spicer Collection; Xavier, "The Cattle Industry," pp. 29–33; Blaine, *Papago and Politics,* pp. 79–80.
40. Hall's Diary, October 26 and November 1, 1935.
41. Quote from Underhill to Strong, n.d., 9675-A-1936-Sells-068, RG-75, NA; Underhill to Strong, October 30, 1935, File 1935, O'odham History File; Strong to Collier, October 29, 1935, 9675-A-1936-Sells-068, RG-75, NA. For a discussion

of the Social-Economic Section of the Technical Cooperation–Bureau of Indian Affairs, see Rebekah C. Beatty Davis, *Conservation and Culture: The Soil Service, Social Science and Conservation on Tribal Lands in the Southwest* (Washington, DC: U.S. Department of Agriculture, Natural Resources Conservation Service, Historical Notes no. 6, July 1997): 7–29.

42. Holst interview with Spicer, February 19, 1943, Subject File 819–823, Box A-485, Spicer Collection; Strong to Collier, October 29, 1935, 9675-A-i 936-Sells-068, RG-75, NA.
43. Holst interview with Spicer, February 19, 1943; Holst, *Indians at Work* (Washington, DC: OIA, February 1, 1937); Hall, "Annual Narrative Report, Sells Agency, Arizona, 1936," M-1011, Roll 130, RG-75, NA-PSB; Hall's Diary, December 8, 11, 16, 1935.
44. Quote from Holst interview with Spicer, February 19, 1943. See also Holst to Underhill, January 6, 1936, 9675-A-1936-Sells-068, RO75, NA; Hall, "Annual Narrative Report, Sells Agency, Arizona, 1936"; Hall's Diary, January 7, 1936; Blaine, *Papago and Politics,* pp. 81–82.
45. Quote from Holst, *Indians at Work*. See also "Proposed Constitution and By-Laws of the Tho-ho-no O'tam Tribe," n. 9675-A-1936-Sells-068, RG-75, NA; Underhill to Strong, December 21, 1935, 9675-A-1936-Sells-068, RG-75, NA; Zimmerman to Commissioner, October 31, 1936, 9675-A-1936-Sells-068, RG-75, NA; Kenneth Marmon to Collier, January 9, 1936, 9675-A-1936-Sells-068, RG-75, NA; Hall's Diary, January 7, 1936.
46. Hall to Fred Daiker, January 21, 1936, 9675-A-i 936-Sells-068, RG-75, NA; Felix Cohen, "Memo for Indian Organization," February 19, 1936, 9675-A-1936-Sells-068, RG-75, NA; "Comments on the Proposed Constitution and By Laws of the Tho-ho-no O'tam Tribe," n.d., 9675-A-1936-Sells-068, RG-75, NA; Zimmerman to Commissioner, October 31, 1936, 9675-A-1936-Sells-068, RG-75, NA.
47. Quote from Holst, *Indians at Work.* See also Holst interview with Spicer, February 19, 1943; H. Scudder Mekeel to Jennings, February 18, 1936, 9675-A-1936-Sells-068, RG-75, NA; Ruth Underhill, "Comments on the Constitution," February 24, 1936, 9675-A-1936-Sells-068, RG-75, NA; "Minutes, Tribal Meeting," February 29, 1936, File 1936, O'odham History Files; "Minutes, Papago Council Meeting," April 18, 1936, File 1936, O'odham History Files; Holst, "Data Accompanying Proposed Papago Constitution," May 5, 1936, 9675-A-1936-Sells-068, RG-75, NA; Jose X. Pablo et al. to Harold Ickes, "Revised Draft of Proposed Constitution and By-Laws, Papago Tribe," May 4, 1936, File 1936, O'odham History Files; Hall's Diary, May 1, 6, 1936; Hall, "Annual Narrative Report, Sells Agency, Arizona, 1936"; Blaine, *Papago and Politics,* pp. 82–84.
48. Quote from Hall, "Annual Narrative Report, Sells Agency, Arizona, 1936."
49. Quote from Hall, "Annual Narrative Report, Sells Agency, Arizona, 1936"; *Aw-o-tahm Ah-pa-tac,* March 1936; Hall to Robert Marshall, March 10, 1936, File 1936, O'odham History Files; John Harrick to Hall, May 21, 1936, 16944-1936-Sells-301, RG-75, NA; Hall to Commissioner, March 7, 1940, 16944-1936-Sells-301, RG-75, NA; Hall's Diary, August 29, 1935; Julian Hayden, CCC-ID Foreman, interview with Peter Booth, March 19, 1990, in Oral History Collection, AHS.
50. Quote from "Minutes, Papago Temporary Council Meeting," July 10, 1936, File 1936, O'odham History Files. See also Hall's Diary, July 10, 1936.

51. Ariel Costello et al. to Hall, March 14, 1936, File 1936, O'odham History Files; Hall to Zimmerman, March 24, 1936, File 1936, O'odham History Files; Oblasser to Senator Henry Ashurst, February 28, 1936, File 1936, O'odham History Files; *Aw-o-tahm Ah-pa-tac,* February and June 1936; Hall's Diary, February 11, June 11, 21, 1936; "Minutes, Temporary Papago Council Meeting," July 10, 1936, File 1936, O'odham History Files.
52. *Aw-o-tahm Ah-pa-tac,* September 1936: Hall, "Annual Narrative Report, Sells Agency, 1936."
53. Quotes from "Minutes, Temporary Papago Council Meeting," and *Aw-o-tahm Ah-pa-tac,* June 1938; Hall, "Annual Narrative Report, Sells Agency, Arizona, 1936."
54. "Minutes, Temporary Papago Council Meeting"; *Aw-o-tahm Ah-pa-tac,* August 1936; Hall's Diary, September 28 and 30, October 13, 1936.
55. Hall's Diary, August 30, October 31, 1936.
56. Quote from Holst to Collier, December 8, 1936, 9675-A-1936-Sells-068, RG-75, NA. See also Jose X. Pablo et al. to Harold Ickes, n.d., 9675-A-1936-Sells-068, RG-75, NA; T. A. Walters to Hall, November 12, 1936, 9675-A-1936-Sells-068, RG-75, NA; Zimmerman to Secretary of Interior, October 31, 1936, 9675-A-1936-Sells-068, RG-75, NA; Hall to Commissioner, November 9, 1936, 9675-A-1936-Sells-068, RG-75, NA; Hall's Diary, October 31, November 5, 8, 21, 1936; Woehlke to Harper, November 11, 1936, 9675-A-1936-Sells-068, RG-75, NA; Blaine, *Papago and Politics,* pp. 83–84.
57. Hall, "After Election," in *Indians at Work* (Washington, DC: OIA, February 1, 1937); Hall's Diary, December 12, 1936; *Aw-o-tahm Ah-pa-tac,* December 1936.
58. Hall to Commissioner, December 12, 1936, 9675-A-1936-Sells-068, RG-75, NA; Hall to Ickes, December 24, 1936, 9675-A-1936-Sells-068, RG-75, NA.
59. Quote from *Aw-o-tahm Ah-ap-tac,* June 1938. See also Ickes, "Resolution," January 6, 1937, 9675-A-1936-Sells-068, RG-75, NA; Harper to Hall, January 6, 1937, 9675-A-1936-Sells-068, RG-75, NA; Blaine, *Papago and Politics,* pp. 84–86; Erickson, *Sharing the Desert,* p. 151. The first Papago Council was pictured in *Indians at Work* (Washington, DC: OIA, May 1937).
60. *Aw-o-tahm Ah-pa-tac,* February, June, October 1937; Papago Council Resolution, no. 10, 1937, Box A-435b, Spicer Collection; Papago Council Resolutions, nos. 21, 22, 29, 31, 41, 42, 45, 46, 50, 1938, Box A-435b, Spicer Collection.
61. Oblasser to Hayden, April 20, 1937, 26547-1937-Sells-013, RG-75, NA; Blaine, *Papago and Politics,* pp. 86–87.
62. Quote from *Aw-o-tahm Ah-pa-tac,* December 1936. See also Hall's Diary, January 5, April 22, 1937; Zeh to Collier, January 29, 1937, Folder 12, Box 245, PAO-ECW and CCC-ID, BIA, RG-75, NA-PSB.
63. Davis, *Conservation and Culture,* pp. 14, 27–28; Harper to Woehlke, March 18, 1938, 37102-1937-Sells-021.5, RG-75, NA; Hall, "Annual Narrative Report, Sells Agency, Arizona, 1937," File 1937, O'odham History File; Hall to A. C. Cooley, July 1937, 45355-1937-Sells-900, RG-75, NA; Cooley, Memorandum, March 22, 1939, 41942-1937-Sells-919, RG-75, NA; Henry Dobyns, "Blunders With Bolsas," *Human Organization,* 10 (fall 1951): 25; Dobyns, "Report on Investigation on the Papago Reservation" (unpublished, Cornell University, 1949; copy in ASM): 28–29; Parman, "New Deal Indian Agriculture Policy," pp. 31–32.

Chapter 6

The Rosebud Tribe and the Creation of TLE, 1943–1955: A Case of Tribal Heirship Land Management

Richmond L. Clow

Allotment Begets Heirship and a New Deal Policy

Reservation allotment policy gave small tracts of tribal land to individual Indians in preparation for their eventual citizenship. The objective was to create self-supporting, assimilated farmers. Although citizenship was reached, allotting land in severalty created extensive heirship land fragmentation of the original allotment. As the land was continually partitioned among the heirs, the second and third generations became essentially landless, owning very small, economically unproductive tracts. Reversing this trend by consolidating fragmented heirship land into larger and more productive land units was a prominent Indian Service New Deal objective on Rosebud, as well as other Great Plains reservations, with extensive heirship problems that persist today.[1]

With escalating heirship problems, New Deal resource managers began to stress land consolidation in nonirrigated semiarid regions to ensure maximum productivity. In line with the era's new reservation land planning goal, Indian Service superintendent Claude R. Whitlock initiated a complex land certificate exchange plan in 1943 to combine Indian heirship estates on the Rosebud Sioux Reservation in south-central South Dakota. His goal was to consolidate tribal and individual lands into viable economic units and then reassign those tracts to Indian operators.[2] A decade after implementing his plan, Whitlock realized that reversing the General Allotment Act's results was harder than either he or his supporters had envisioned.

Heirship land emanated from the 1887 General Allotment Act that mandated when an allottee died the allotment would remain in trust but would be divided among the living heirs according to state law.[3] Continual fragmentation of individual allotted lands whose owners died intestate contributed to scattered and absentee ownership. This also made each tribe's and the Indian Service's reservation land management decisions more difficult, destroying opportunities for Indian landowners to accrue meaningful economic gain from these partitioned lands. Congress attempted to correct this problem as early as June 25, 1910, in legislation granting the secretary of the interior authority to determine heirs and to sell the fractionalized property if either he or she could not subdivide the real estate.[4]

The 1910 legislation did not slow land partitioning. In fact, the birth and death of each successive heir compounded the fractionalization of these divided allotted lands. Within a generation many original allotments were partitioned into unproductive units, and they grew smaller with each generation. On the other hand, the Rosebud acreage required for an Indian family to earn a living from the land was larger than the original 160-acre allotment. For example, in 1944, 1,000 to 1,200 acres were required for a rancher living in northwest Rosebud (Mellette County) to run fifty cows, and that was still an inadequate land base and cattle herd for a family to earn a decent living. In reality, after several generations many individual heirs owned only a few acres or less of an original allotment. This also demonstrated that New Deal land reorganization and consolidation efforts could be economically successful for only a few Indians. Despite that realization, land readjustment became a powerful and emotional idea whose followers justified their stand as a way to put tribal members back on the land during the 1930s.[5]

Fractionalized allotments aggravated reservation economic programs, but effective land consolidation plans remained elusive. As early as 1927 Assistant Commissioner of Indian Affairs Joseph Henry Scattergood proposed that Congress should provide "a continuing large appropriation to buy heirship lands and to put them into some new status which could be protected hereafter."[6] The authors of *The Problem of Indian Administration* suggested in 1928 that tribes should assume ownership of heirship lands by purchasing those lands from their heirs with a revolving fund.[7]

The Indian Reorganization Act and Rosebud Heirship Issues

The following year Commissioner of Indian Affairs Charles J. Rhoads recommended that tribes assume control of the heirship lands.[8] Rhoads declared that "the indefinite partitioning of allotments is not practicable. . . . The allotted Indians of the second generation largely become landless. By the time the third generation has arrived, substantially all of the allotted Indian land will have passed into white ownership."[9] Rhoads's solution was simple, organize tribes as corporations, then "allotments might be turned back into the tribal estate in exchange for shares of stock."[10] This became the foundation for Whitlock's plan and all these early consolidation proposals were based on tribes assuming a greater role in reservation land management plans. Such tribal land consolidation ideas required congressional policymakers to reverse past policies of selling heirship lands or dividing them further among even more heirs.

The advent of the Great Depression, the Dust Bowl, and Franklin D. Roosevelt's election brought land tenure and land resource planning to the forefront, and many government agencies began to discuss the ties among land use, land conservation, land ownership, and community stability.[11] An initial Indian Service movement toward land consolidation under tribal management emerged in the Indian Reorganization Act of 1934 (IRA). Section 4 authorized the secretary of the interior to approve voluntary exchanges of individual heirship land with the tribe when the trade benefited the tribe. At the same time Congress provided property protection for the heirs by making these exchanges voluntary and denied Commissioner of Indian Affairs John Collier's request for mandatory tribal assumption of heirship land.[12]

Despite this legislative setback, Collier described the Indian Reorganization Act as "taking the first hesitant step toward the solution of this problem," providing the heirs with an opportunity to "transfer the title to their individual holdings to the tribe or to the tribal corporation."[13] On the other hand, the section of the IRA that prohibited land sales made it nearly impossible for heirs to sell their property to anyone except the tribe. General land sales resumed when Congress amended the Indian Reorganization Act in 1948.[14]

The IRA was enabling legislation and required a reservation vote to either accept or reject the law's provisions. Rosebud residents accepted the act on October 27, 1934. Over a year later, on November 23, 1935, they went to the polls and approved the tribe's Indian Reorganization Act constitution and bylaws. The secretary of the interior approved these documents four weeks later. Next the Rosebud people petitioned for a corporate charter, the last step in reorganization, which was issued to the Rosebud Sioux Tribe on March 16, 1937.[15] Collier stressed tribal incorporation as an important step in unraveling the heirship knot. Ever since the 1927 Klamath incorporation discussions, Collier noted "the suggestion had been made that the allottees be given the choice of receiving patents in fee or delivering title back into the tribe" for compensation.[16]

Rosebud's incorporation as a nonprofit business enterprise qualified the tribe for IRA loans. Since the Rosebud tribe had no money, Superintendent Whitlock and tribal leaders believed such a loan would give the tribe an opportunity to purchase heirship lands. Sadly, Congress did not appropriate adequate monies to fund that provision of the act. Nothing changed, even after Department of the Interior officials informed both congressional appropriation and budget committees of the continual consumption of tax dollars to oversee these unproductive heirship lands. Congressional committee members expressed interest in the plans but refused to fund tribal land consolidation projects.[17]

Fiscal frustrations did not stop land tenure and resource management planning, a common government agency activity of the Roosevelt administration. The Indian Service participated in land planning by sponsoring a Land-Tenure

Adjustment Conference on reservation allotted and heirship lands. In August 1938, at Glacier National Park, superintendents from Rosebud, Pine Ridge, and Blackfeet, as well as other reservation representatives with extensive land tenure problems, met with Collier and Department of Agriculture, Technical Soil Conservation support staff. Important goals for the participants were to develop political plans to circumvent congressional funding apathy while interesting the president in the Indian Service's heirship planning activities.[18]

During conference heirship land discussions, Rosebud Superintendent Whitlock presented a land–stock option scheme for consolidating fragmented heirship lands under tribal control. The tribal population's decision to incorporate their tribe was the foundation of Whitlock's plan. He argued that the tribe's corporate charter authorized the issuance of "corporate property in exchange for restricted lands, the forms of such interests to be approved by the Secretary of the Interior." Whitlock added that this language permitted the tribe "to act as a corporation to accept lands and issue shares against the corporate holdings. Or the tribe under its Constitution might charter a holding company for this purpose."[19]

Whitlock wanted the Rosebud Sioux Tribe to assume responsibility for consolidation and management of the reservation's heirship estate even though neither congressional nor tribal funds were available. Despite Whitlock's enthusiasm, conference participants doubted that Northern Plains Indian people would convey their heirship lands to their tribes without adequate compensation.[20]

Undaunted by skeptics, Whitlock continued to refine his Rosebud land consolidation plan after the Glacier National Park Conference. In July 1941 he prepared a working paper titled "Stock Certificate Plan for Handling Heirship Estates." Again, Whitlock wanted to consolidate heirship land under tribal ownership and then have the tribe reassign larger workable tracts to a few individual tribesmen who would use these readjusted land units for farming and grazing purposes. To accomplish land reorganization, individual heirs would trade their inherited tracts to the tribe in exchange for the "common denominator of stock certifications in a tribal corporation." This was possible, Whitlock argued, because the Rosebud Sioux Tribe's corporate charter authorized the issuance of certificates.[21]

Rules, regulations, and changes were necessary to make the land exchange–consolidation concept work. The Rosebud Sioux Tribe had to create a tribal organization with the power to accept fractionalized trust-allotted land and to issue tribal corporation stock certificates to the heirs in exchange for their land. An immediate concern was certificate transferability. Whitlock initially believed the corporation stock certificates should be nontransferable. Tribal leaders disagreed. They wanted flexible certificates so individuals could use them to repay reimbursable tribal loans or to pay rent securities. As land was consolidated and assignments were made to individuals for their use, those receiving assignments paid rent to the tribal corporation, and the rent income then paid dividends to the individuals who exchanged land for stock.[22] Three years after the Glacier Park Conference, Whitlock's plan was ready for further review.

Since fractionalization was increasing, Commissioner Collier convened a two-day Lakota land tenure field conference on September 1, 1941. Collier had high hopes, claiming "the conference is dedicated to the task of discovering feasible and practical ways and means of simplifying the ownership pattern, of working out a program for each one of the five reservations, of making progressively increasing areas of Indian lands actually available for Indians."[23]

In line with Collier's directive, Whitlock presented his updated land stock certificate plan, as the Rosebud heirship consolidation vehicle, to other Indian Service personnel for comment. The revised Rosebud plan raised several minor queries. James M. Stewart, director of lands, asked if the certificates' inheritability would perpetuate ongoing paper heirship problems. Also, Stewart believed the stock certificates should have expiration dates ending their value. These were minor problems that did not dampen Stewart's support for Rosebud's land heirship consolidation concept. He stressed that the scheme would be improved by eliminating "a good deal of the complex procedure outlined in the draft of Superintendent Whitlock's plan." Stewart added, "I believe it has a fair chance of working out successfully."[24] One reason Stewart advanced for supporting Whitlock's idea was that "it actually does give the Indians something 'tangible' [to the heirs] in return for turning over their fractionated interests."[25] This was important because the IRA had made it difficult for heirs to sell lands, and this plan gave them the potential to gain something from their partitioned unproductive properties.

The conference ended before the participants were able to solve complicated Lakota heirship land problems. Responding to that truth, Collier established a "Sioux land-use adjustment project" in 1941, headquartered in Pierre, South Dakota. Knowledgeable Indian Service staff were assigned to the Pierre office and began determining the extent of ongoing heirship problems, assisting reservation planners, and examining "land-use adjustment" plans for the Cheyenne River, Crow Creek, Lower Brule, Rosebud, and Pine Ridge Reservations.[26]

The Sioux land-use adjustment project staff determined that 2,756 Rosebud allotments had from 1 to 131 heirs per allotment.[27] The Bear Stands Up estate represented a typical heirship tract. Twenty-nine heirs shared unequal interests in this 323-and-a-half-acre allotment valued at $647. The heirs did not share equally in the estate because not all heirs were first-generation kin to Bear Stands Up. Each subsequent generation received a smaller interest than the previous generation. The Sioux Land-Use Adjustment Project staff recommended purchasing the land interests of twenty-one heirs that had a value of less than $25 per tract. The last eight heirs would retain their tracts (Table 6.1).[28]

Table 6.1—Estate of Bear Stands Up

Estate of Bear Stands Up Acreage 323.50
Total Heirs—29

Appraised Value of Tract—323.50 acres @ $2.00 per acre = $647.00
Number of heirs whose interest is less than $1.00—None

Number of heirs whose interest is over $1.00 but does not exceed $5.00—2
Total value of land in this class (3 acres)—$6.00

Number of heirs whose interest is over $5.00 but does not exceed $10.00—7
Total value of land in this class (22.50 acres)—$45.00

Number of heirs whose interest is over $10.00 but does not exceed $25.00—12
Total value of land in this class (109.90 acres)—$219.80

Number of heirs whose interest is over $25.00 but does not exceed $50.00–6
Total value of land in this class (94.40 acres)—$188.80

Number of heirs whose interest is over $50.00 but does not exceed $75.00—1
Total value of land in this class (30.70 acres)—$61.40

Number of heirs whose interest exceeds $100—1
Total value of land in this class (63 acres)—$126.00

To solve the problem, the staff suggested that the smallest fractionalized heirship interests should be purchased because Indian Service land administrative costs were greater than the land's value. As heirship lands were consolidated, rental payments would provide funds to purchase additional heirship lands following a simple rule of "eliminating the greatest number of heirs at the lowest possible cost."[29]

The lack of funds to purchase any heirship lands blocked the simple plan. That actuality convinced Whitlock to push his land certificate exchange program, and Assistant Commissioner of Indian Affairs Walter Woehlke supported Whitlock's decision. A strong selling feature for Woehlke was that Whitlock's plan required minimal funding. Likewise, the Indian Service and the tribal council favored Whitlock's plan, as neither had moneys to spend for land consolidation, and none were forthcoming. Woehlke stressed that no gratuity funds, moneys given "in recognition of the general duty of the government toward the Indians to improve their social, physical, or economic condition,"[30] would be provided.[31]

At the same time, Whitlock's 1941 plan provided financial hope for heirs wanting to rid themselves of unworkable heirship lands while relieving the government of some costly management activities.[32] Even Field Agent A. L. Hook, assigned to the Sioux Land-Use Adjustment Project, accepted that truth and noted "the burden of financing must rest largely with the Rosebud Sioux Tribe from funds which they are to borrow."[33]

Moving Toward the Tribal Land Enterprise

As planners stressed shifting both the heirship land financial and management responsibilities from the United States to the tribe, Director of Lands Stewart praised the tribe's efforts, noting that both "the Superintendent and the tribal council have shown great initiative and enthusiasm in developing the plan to its present state."[34] The Rosebud council supported the land unification plan because land consolidation complimented the council's goals of making Indian lands available for Indian use and increasing tribal family income to levels of white rural neighbors.[35] In addition, the council would be helping heirs sell their lands during this era of no sales. At this point in the planning process, the council wanted to make the land certificate program mandatory, but Stewart recommended that the plan remain voluntary, as stipulated in the Rosebud Sioux Tribal Constitution of 1936, to eliminate the need for special congressional legislation.[36]

After further study, Field Agent Hook's enthusiasm dropped. He asserted the Rosebud stock certificate plan was cumbersome and that using the exchange assignment principle would produce the same results with less complexity. Still, he acknowledged, the Rosebud certificate stock plan would work "not so much on any special merits of the plan itself but rather as a recognition of the enthusiasm and ability of Mr. Whitlock for this idea of land consolidation which he has developed."[37]

The Rosebud land stock certificate plan assumed nearly final form at a Chicago, January 1943, meeting. At that time Rosebud delegates, led by Chairman Dan Hollow Horn Bear and Superintendent Whitlock, met with the Office of Indian Affairs staff to discuss final details. In the end, Commissioner Collier endorsed the tribe's stock certificate plan.[38] To show his support, Collier awarded the Rosebud Sioux Tribe funds for heirship purchases to aid the council in its endeavors.[39]

Following the Chicago meeting, council members prepared to vote on land consolidation, but council sentiment had shifted over the past two years. Now a vocal minority opposed the creation of a subsidiary to manage tribal lands, claiming a new organization might take power from the council and tribe and reduce the tribe's sovereignty. The debate ended in a thirteen-to-eight vote when the Rosebud Sioux Tribal Council passed a resolution on April 6, 1943, creating the Tribal Land Enterprise (TLE). This tribal subsidiary was authorized to issue certificates in exchange for land and then to consolidate fractionated heirship lands and reassign these large units to tribal operators.[40] The TLE had two primary functions: first, "to alleviate the heirship problem and second, to provide a means whereby individuals may acquire economic units of land."[41]

The council had initiated tribal land purchases four months earlier, on October 9, 1942, authorizing the Executive Committee of the council to acquire lands. On the day of the TLE vote, the Executive Committee also authorized the first heirship land procurements, using funds Collier had given council delegates at the Chicago meeting. The Executive Committee approved a fractionalized allotment purchase called Tract No. 1, which was part of allotment 6239, on March 3, 1943, for $186.66. Other heirship land purchases followed.[42] From this start, the tribe began managing some of the reservation heirship lands, moving the Rosebud land tenure adjustment program forward.

These complex land exchanges required formal procedures. To meet these new needs the Rosebud Sioux Tribal Council approved by-laws for the Tribal Land Enterprise on April 6, 1943, to oversee the organization's operation.[43] The by-laws authorized a seven-member board of directors—which included the reservation superintendent, council chairman, and treasurer—to administer TLE activities; the organization was to operate as a corporation, issuing certificates of interest to heirs in exchange for their lands. Then the Tribal Land Enterprise conveyed the lands to the Rosebud Tribe. The TLE would manage the heirship lands that were exchanged for certificates. The main objectives were to acquire and consolidate heirship lands and then assign these properties to tribal ranchers. Through this land consolidation scheme, Tribal Land Enterprise backers hoped the organization would bring fractionalized lands into economic production.[44]

At this juncture the Rosebud Tribe was ready to assume a large part of the trustee's heirship land management obligations. From the beginning, Alfred Bordeaux Sr. provided direction for the TLE, serving as both a member of the board and an officer. Bordeaux influenced the "active cause of TLE in the management of the corporation and conduct of its business throughout its corporate existence from April 13, 1943," until his death in 1951.[45]

Bordeaux began to work after the council approved the by-laws, but the TLE was still inoperative. The 1936 Rosebud constitution required the secretary of the interior to approve the Tribal Land Enterprise. Secretarial approval revealed an irony of the Indian New Deal. Despite returning allotted heirship lands to tribal management under home rule claims, paternalism continued through the secretarial approval provisions found in the tribal Indian Reorganization Act constitutions. Months passed as correspondence traveled between the Indian Service and the secretary's office, as personnel added, changed, and eliminated words and phrases from the tribe's by-laws. At one point the assistant secretary of the interior suggested that tribal residents should vote on the TLE as a constitutional amendment since the council vote on the organization resolution had been so close. Whitlock and tribal officers countered, claiming the TLE's administrative by-laws, with the pending changes, already conformed to the tribal constitution, making a popular reservation referendum vote unnecessary.[46]

The assistant secretary of the interior also wanted affirmation that the heirs' interests would be protected after their lands were assigned to the tribe.

Woehlke responded that the Tribal Land Enterprise was "a tribal operation intended to facilitate management of land of the tribe" and that the certificates of interest protected the heirs' equity from being lost. He added that the by-laws maintained "the separateness of the tribal land enterprise from other tribal activities." This was done to assure those who conveyed lands to the tribe that they would receive revenue from the lands through their certificates, minus "the cost of administering the land." Since the heirs created TLE's assets, they should receive benefits. One way to protect the heirs' interests was to ensure that certificate holders had the right to vote on the Tribal Land Enterprise's operations.[47]

These interoffice discussions ended when the secretary of the interior supported the departmental changes. The most significant amendment to the April 6, 1943, tribal by-laws was the introduction of Class A and Class B land certificates. Class A certificates were issued to tribal members who conveyed land to the Rosebud Sioux Tribe for interests in certificates. Class B certificates were issued to non-Rosebud members who transferred their interests in their heirship property to the TLE. Holders of Class B certificate were denied voting rights in the Tribal Land Enterprise but were entitled to dividends, whereas Class A certificate holders received both dividends and voting privileges.[48]

Another Department of the Interior revision established a certificate base price tying the document's worth to local real estate values. The face value of a land certificate was assigned at a dollar per share, and land appraisal price was based on the 1943 Bureau of Agricultural Economics Real Estate Market price index for South Dakota.[49] The land certificates were issued in a bloc to the individual who conveyed land to the TLE and ultimately the tribe. For example, if a tribal member conveyed a tract of land to the tribe appraised at $450, the TLE would issue that applicant a 450-unit or bloc of Class A land certificates. With these changes in place and assurances that the TLE would work, the secretary of the interior approved the revised by-laws on December 15, 1943.[50]

Secretarial approval encouraged some tribal members to apply for certificates of interest. By mid-April 1944, 199 individuals had made applications to exchange their heirship lands for certificates of interest. One week in early April 1944, 24 persons from Blackpipe requested land certificate trades. The Blackpipe community's actions were unusual and did not reflect the general reservation population's views.

Tribal Members Disagree on Merits of TLE

Only a handful of tribesmen defended the council's land consolidation efforts, believing the land unification advocates were sincere in their efforts "to help them clear up their land ownership and land holding situations."[51] Others who endorsed the Tribal Land Enterprise did so because the TLE gave them an avenue to sell partitioned land. Land exchanges were nearly impossible in 1943, since the Indian Reorganization Act prohibited Indian land sales except by a private act of Congress. The Tribal Land Enterprise "circumvented this statute to some extent in that an individual Indian could convey his land to the tribe and receive in return certificates of interest in TLE which he then could convert to cash." In short, the TLE's operating "procedure relieved some of the pressure from individuals seeking to sell their land."[52]

A substantial group of tribal members viewed the TLE "with suspicion and openly declared they will have nothing to do with it." Many were "loud in their denunciation and advice to others to avoid TLE." Superintendent Whitlock countered this condemnation, claiming the critics "will be convinced only by the progressive success of the enterprise."[53] Reasons for the distrust varied, ranging from dislike of the existing structure of tribal government to fear of losing control of what little real estate they still possessed.

Like the members of the tribe, the council's disillusion increased over time. The tribal council's frustration with the TLE surfaced when debates began over tribal management of submarginal lands. On April 5, 1944, tribal council approved the Department of the Interior assignment of submarginal lands to the tribe with a "revocable permit" for a period of ten years. These were former reservation lands that had been ceded and sold to homesteaders decades ago who subsequently left them during the dust years. The lands were not unproductive but were simply not in production. The federal government acquired the abandoned lands from farmers and ranchers under authority of the Emergency Relief Appropriation Act of April 8, 1935, the National Industrial Recovery Act of June 16, 1933, and the Bankhead-Jones Farm Tenant Act of July 22, 1937.[54] The federal submarginal land programs conveyed nearly 28,000 acres to the tribe, which initiated the council management debate.[55]

Some councilmen were reluctant to turn the submarginal lands over to the TLE, claiming the organization failed to practice low-cost management.[56] The critics lost another close vote, and the tribal council authorized the Tribal Land Enterprise to assign the lands to tribal members.[57] Illustrative of the weak support for the TLE, the tribal council unanimously agreed that officers of the tribal government had to oversee the tribe's land interests. As early as 1942 the council members decided to "empower the Executive Committee to act on all lands deeded to the tribe for an exchange assignment on tribal lands of equal value."[58] The council implemented the tribe's land consolidation program following the submarginal vote, but success proved illusive. To make matters more difficult, the same officers sitting on the council executive committee also sat on TLE's board of directors, setting the stage for a future conflict of interest.

After operating for a decade, the Tribal Land Enterprise had achieved little success. A large minority of the council continued to proclaim "that this system deprives" the Rosebud government of "just income from the leasing and use of tribal land." Council criticism was partially justified because the tribe was to receive a dividend based on the number of certificates held. After transacting land exchanges, consolidations, and rentals for ten years, "the tribe received no dividends" because TLE was unable to raise money to pay all shareholders, and the TLE board decided individuals came before the tribe.[59] Jake Kills In Sight, TLE board chairman, countered council charges in 1955, claiming that during the first ten years the council agreed to forgo dividends from TLE.[60]

The dividend dispute extended to individual TLE certificate holders who also suffered financially during the first ten years. A TLE selling point to potential shareholders was that the certificates of interest would appreciate in value as the land the certificates represented appreciated in value. An additional incentive was that TLE had a goal to pay an annual 4 percent dividend to individuals holding these certificates. Even though the TLE was designed as a self-funding operation, the organization was not able to finance a small dividend. Since the Indian Service was unable to assist the certificate holders financially, the Rosebud Sioux Tribe assumed that obligation. To maintain even a small dividend to individuals, the tribe authorized income from other tribal lands to be applied to the cost of Tribal Land Enterprise operations.[61]

TLE's inability to pay dividends stemmed in part from the fact that substantial acres assigned to TLE management remained idle. During the first ten years of operation, individuals conveyed nearly 72,000 acres to the TLE for certificates. Many of these small individual conveyances represented detached, isolated heirship tracts that could not be consolidated in a single land assignment because of their scattered locations. Likewise, only half of the 28,000 acres of submarginal lands were placed in assignments, for similar reasons.[62] When the tribe's ten-year term for managing submarginal lands ended, the Bureau of Land Management received authorization to contract these tracts to the Rosebud Sioux Tribe. This arrangement ended TLE's use of submarginal lands, further reducing income potential.[63]

Without funds for dividends, abandoned submarginal lands and leased heirship land restoration projects also suffered from a shortage of funds. Before the 1930s drought, local farmers planted crops and grazed cattle, and then the wind eroded the land. Another goal of land consolidation was to fund land and soil classification projects, as well as to create sliding grazing scales that corresponded to a tract's carrying capacity. After a decade of operation, only a few acres had been reseeded because moneys had to be diverted from rents for other purposes. As long as some lands remained idle during the duration of a reseeding project, the revenues these lands had the potential to generate were further reduced, prohibiting large-scale restoration projects.[64] Despite funding shortages for land improvement projects, TLE cooperated "with the Soil and Moisture Conservation Service [and] has re-seeded some of the best tracts with Crested Wheat Grass, from which seed has been harvested and used to re-seed the poorer or barren tracts. To accomplish this, it has been necessary to forgo current lease revenue."[65]

The passage of time brought more criticism, as TLE participants even became disenchanted. After operating for ten years, some individuals who had exchanged heirship land for certificates charged "that they did not understand the full situation when they conveyed their land to the tribe under TLE [regulations], and they have also complained bitterly that they were misled when they received TLE assignments." The very few who received a productive land unit were upset to learn that "TLE assignments carry only a use right with certain rights to reassign on the death of the assignee." Elderly Rosebud residents resentfully grumbled "that TLE has been for the sole benefit of a few highly aggressive mixed bloods and that a few mixed bloods are acquiring control of the reservation by the purchase of TLE certificates and the receiving of TLE assignment of land." Although only partially true, that view became "the general opinion of a great many members of the tribe."[66]

Land certificate transferability made TLE attractive, allowing heirs to circumvent Indian Reorganization Act land sales restrictions, but certificate exchange created deep problems. From the beginning, tribal leaders supported share trades. Whitlock also conceded that certificate exchange was necessary to consolidate lands and to make the consolidated tracts beneficial to at least a few Indians. Transferability ideally would permit an individual with ownership in different tracts at different places to exchange certificates to consolidate lands in one location on the reservation. Whitlock contended that one great advantage to the individual Indian is that through this plan he can consolidate his interests independently from any other heir through certificate liquidity. The ends justified the means because "this process leads directly to the liquidation of the bothersome heirship interests."[67] The reality was that heirs used this feature to rid themselves of fractionalized lands because they lacked either sufficient capital or number of acres required to ranch. Then the land stood idle if TLE could not place it quickly in an assignment for leasing or if it could not become part of a restoration project. That truth stood in stark contrast to Whitlock's optimism regarding land consolidation and tribal utilization.

Certificate transfers extended beyond the land rhetoric of consolidation; certificate holders used shares as money. Whitlock noted, "The Indians find the use of these certificates of interest a flexible commodity which may be used among themselves in the matter of exchange." He described a situation where if "an individual holds a block of interests and desired to buy a team from another member of the tribe, it is possible for him to use these interests in payment of the team by conveying to the vendor sufficient number of interests to make payment."[68]

The TLE board of directors often approved certificate sales between tribal members without secretary approval to ease financial suffering because many certificate holders faced economic hardships. For example, Minnie Star Boy sold certificates to get $30 to repair her well pump and water well even though the house was on tribal property. Given the great social need and economic hardship, Whitlock argued the TLE board was justified in making these transactions.[69] Kills In Sight also defended the practice, noting that TLE had purchased certificates in 1955 for $2.43 a share so Indians "could send their kids to school or repair their house[s]."[70]

Other Indian Service staff did not share Kills In Sight's and Whitlock's enthusiasm for certificate liquidity when the shares were used as legal tender. Hook reported, "There has been presented to the Office from the Rosebud Agency a number of cases involving negotiations of TLE certificates among Indians." He added that "the consideration in some cases is cash and other cases it is to be paid in kind; all transactions are presented to the Office for the approval of the Secretary of the Interior." He continued, "Whitlock considers this procedure as a part of the Tribal Land Enterprise program authorized under the approved by-laws." Hook cautiously urged, "The Office should give these matters careful consideration as to their legality and the advisability of such a program as a matter of policy."[71]

Hook's concern was justified because some Rosebud certificate holders were exchanging shares, which represented trust lands, in questionable transactions. During the 1950s Rosebud Chairman Robert Burnette angrily described unauthorized deals involving Indians, whites, Indian Service officials, and members of the TLE board of directors.[72] Certificate liquidity encouraged shady transactions. On a negative note, these transactions hurt the shareholders, who suffered from a "general misunderstanding of the true value and marketability of these shares, [which] resulted in many of the original shareholders selling or trading their shares" and lands at a fraction of both the land's and the certificate's value.[73]

Liability concerns were real because of the trust status the certificates represented, and that fact forced the secretary of the interior to revise the by-laws in 1947. The new amendment required an individual trading shares to do so "in the presence of two witnesses of his choice" and with the approval of the commissioner of Indian Affairs.[74] Tighter restrictions did not stop people in need from selling certificates. One year after implementing the new rule on certificate sales, Paul L. Fickinger, regional director, Billings Office, observed "that TLE certificates are in some instances used as a common medium of exchange, much like legal tender, and to the extent that the work of keeping account of them might become greater than would be justified by the benefit from such a practice."[75] Regardless of the reason for transferring or selling certificates, 841 heirs of the 1,821 individuals originally issued Tribal Land Enterprise shares had no ownership claims by 1952.[76] As a result, many certificate holders received only a fraction of the certificates' face value when they disposed of their paper.

Two fundamental problems underscored the shareholders' fiscal losses. Since the shareholders received fixed value paper instead of proportional value shares, the certificates did not appreciate (or decline) as the value of TLE's assets escalated. At the same time, the initial land appraisals were too low, which then resulted in underappraising the certificates. Undervalued certificates were tied to a fundamental problem of establishing too low an original value for each certificate of interest.

In 1943 the planners authorized a too "conservative valuation . . . upon the assets of the enterprise and upon the shares of the enterprise." No one was at fault "because the valuation used in 1943 was pretty much in line with the concept of the 1935–1939 pre-war years of the 'normal' investment value of ranch real estate." Western South Dakota land values escalated after 1943 and by March 1952 had risen 243 percent above the 1935–1939 prewar values and 140 percent over the 1943 valuations. In short, "Most of this rise in the dollar value of western ranch and range land has occurred since the year 1943, when the Tribal Land Enterprise was organized." In the end, holders of certificates of interest had exchanged their heirship land for paper shares of TLE that were of less value than the land they had conveyed. Certificate undervaluation forced "many hundreds of the tribal people to lose their equity in reservation lands."[77]

The appraisal process designed to protect individuals broke under the weight of rising land prices. Reservation real estate increased quickly in value, making it difficult to produce accurate appraisals. To offset rapidly rising land prices, the TLE board increased lease rates to cover escalating increasing land values. The board hoped to preserve the 4 percent dividend to individual shareholders.[78]

TLE and the Future of the Rosebud

At the administrative level, the Tribal Land Enterprise added another tribal agency instead of reducing reservation management. Nor did creating the TLE reduce Indian Service administrative costs. TLE transactions required trained personnel to negotiate deeds, appraise land, and plan future decisions. The ongoing complex heirship land transactions prevented the Indian Service and the tribe from eliminating Indian Service personnel's review of land records.[79] One TLE land transaction included "the sale of Indian lands; the reinvestment of the funds received therefrom in other land or land interests; the granting of exchange assignments to such lands or land interests or TLE certificates to the Indian grantors, constituting a simultaneous transaction."[80] Consequently, staff time increased. Land consolidation was designed to reduce the time staff devoted to title and record work, but TLE made the process too complicated.[81]

After ten years of operation the Tribal Land Enterprise reached a crossroads. The view from one direction showed promise. By 1955 the TLE had issued 857,536 certificates of interest, of which 126,000 certificates were held by the Rosebud Tribe for scattered lands turned over to the TLE to manage. In the process of exchanging certificates for land, "the tribe has acquired undivided interest in 800 allotments."[82] The board gave lease preference to tribal members, and leases were as great as 5,000 acres; but non-Indian ranchers then bid

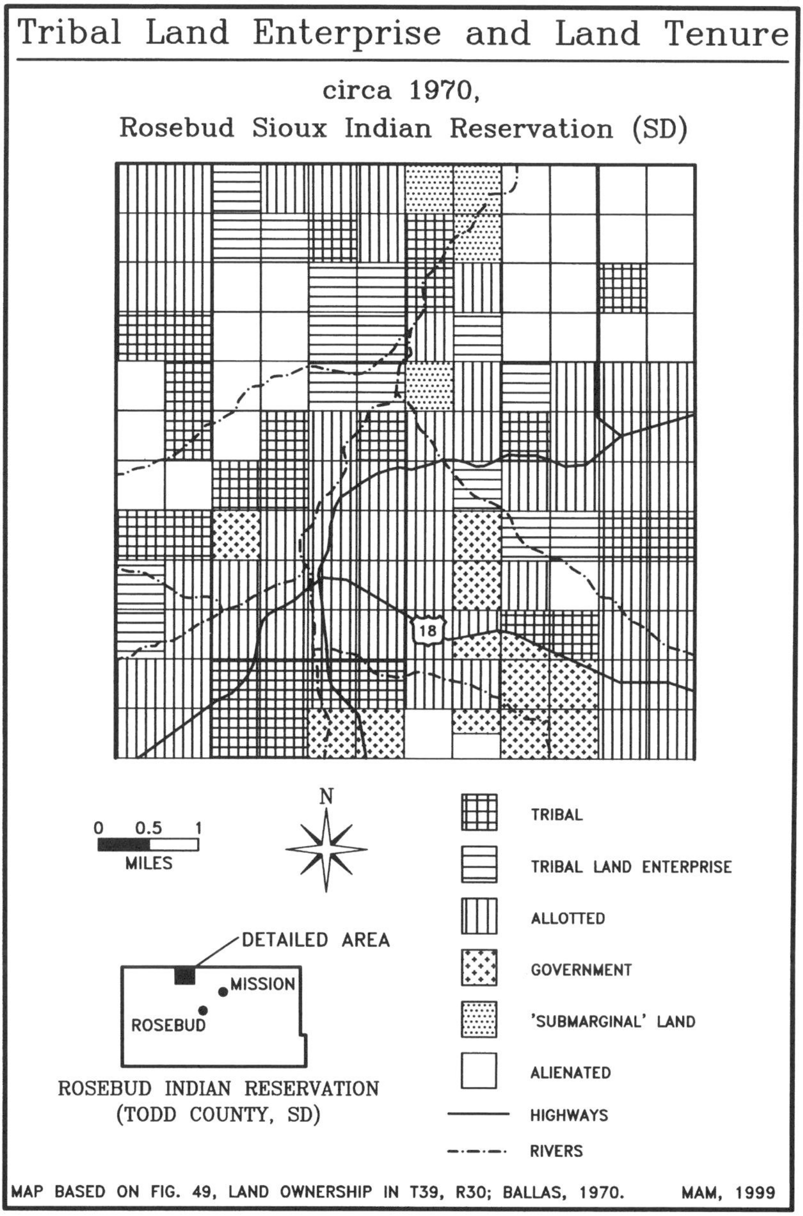

Fig. 6.1 Tribal Land Enterprise (TLE) and Land Tenure, circa 1970, Rosebud Sioux Indian Reservation (South Dakota). Whereas text discussion focuses on the period of the late 1940s–mid 1950s, the best extant maps depicting the Tribal Land Enterprise were prepared in 1970 by Donald Ballas for a doctoral dissertation in geography ("A Cultural Geography of Todd County, South Dakota, and the Rosebud Sioux Indian Reservation," Ph.D. diss. in geography, University of Nebraska, Lincoln, 1970). The original map has been modified to accent the TLE in this sampling.

for leases if no tribesmen made offers, which was frequent. As a result, ranch numbers dropped as ranch size grew and operating expenses increased. In line with this trend, the TLE did not support new ranchers but provided additional lands to assist 203 existing ranchers in running an average of seventy-two head of cattle, a small operation.[83] Shareholders, tribal leaders, and the remaining tribal membership did not consider these marginal individual gains beneficial. Many argued, "Too many people have been hurt in the process of the Tribal Land Enterprise"[84] (Figure 6.1[85]).

The last straw for the Rosebud council officers was that the seven-member TLE board and 700 certificate holders controlled 7,500 members' tribal lands, except for the tribal timber reserve and isolated tracts.[86] As a result, the council passed Resolution No. 54-R-10 on July 22, 1954, to revoke TLE's charter, wanting to liquidate its assets and return the lands to council control. In accordance with the Rosebud constitution, article 4, section 2, Superintendent Will J. Pitner disapproved the resolution, thereby preserving the trustee's past managerial transfers of heirship lands to the TLE. The council passed another resolution the following year to terminate the Tribal Land Enterprise, claiming the TLE was inconsistent with the tribal constitution, but the trustee ignored the council's request. Pitner's intervention protected the TLE, enabling the land subsidiary to continue operation.[87]

The council's resolution reflected a decade of frustration with the TLE, but on a philosophical level no one disputed the need to improve heirship land use by increasing tribal control over reservation lands. Both tribal and Indian Service officials supported the logic behind the TLE: tribal management over consolidated reservation properties would, it was hoped, improve land use and restoration practices. In the end, similar problems that had prohibited other governmental and private landowners from achieving land development and management plans also affected the Rosebud land consolidation program. TLE's complex operation, fiscal shortages, and community politics all contributed to the high cost of Rosebud's heirship land tenure and consolidation program. The difficulties of the plan reveal that direct tribal purchases of heirship lands would be less volatile, and even that approach would only place a very limited number of Indian operators to use the land productivity.

Although the TLE failed to achieve its organizer's dream, the Tribal Land Enterprise continues operating to the present despite the council's 1954 resolutions to terminate this unique tribal subsidiary. Ending the TLE was much harder than starting the program, especially after the secretary of the interior approved all the land contractual exchanges between heirs and the tribe. Therefore, the TLE endures amid charges of misuse and even the lack of "sufficient records to reconstruct the financial relationship between the Tribe and TLE."[88] Continual by-law adjustments and the ongoing operational discussions made the TLE a common reservation topic of discussion and reminded the Rosebud people of just how illusive postwar land consolidation and management programs remained.

References

1. National Resources Board, Department of the Interior, *Indian Land Tenure, Economic Status and Population Trends, Part X of the Supplementary Report of the Land Planning Committee to the National Resources Board* (Washington, DC: Government Printing Office (GPO), 1935): 8–9.
2. Claude R. Whitlock, "Stock Certificate Plan for Handling Heirship Estates," July 14, 1941, TLE, Realty Records, Bureau of Indian Affairs (BIA), Aberdeen Area Office.
3. 24 *Stat.,* 388 (1887).
4. 36 *Stat.,* 855 (1910); see also Michael L. Lawson, "The Fractionated Estate: The Problem of American Indian Heirship," *South Dakota History,* 21 (spring 1991): 1–42, quote on pp. 15–16.
5. "Resume of Proceedings, Conference on Indian Allotted and Heirship-Land Problem," August 14–17, 1938, Glacier Park, Montana, Department of the Interior Library, Washington, DC, p. 19; Claude R. Whitlock to Commissioner of Indian Affairs, March 10, 1944, TLE, 060, Realty Records, BIA, Aberdeen Area Office.
6. "Resume of Proceedings," p. 4.
7. Lewis Meriam et al., *The Problem of Indian Administration* (Baltimore: The Johns Hopkins University Press, 1928): 40–41.
8. *Congressional Record,* 72, 71st Cong., 2d sess., December 21, 1929, pp. 1051–1053.
9. Ibid., p. 1052.
10. Ibid.
11. For example, see National Resources Board, *Indian Land Tenure,* pp. 8–9.
12. 48 *Stat.,* 984–988 (1934).
13. *Annual Report of the Secretary of the Interior* (Washington, DC: GPO, 1934): 81.
14. 62 *Stat.,* part 1, 236 (1948).
15. Richmond L. Clow, "The Rosebud Sioux: The Federal Government and the Reservation Years, 1878–1940," Ph.D. diss. in history, University of New Mexico, Albuquerque, 1977, pp. 238–244.
16. "Resume of Proceedings," p. 4.
17. Ibid., pp. 4–5.
18. Ibid., pp. 4–7.
19. Ibid., pp. 19–20.
20. Ibid., p. 46.
21. Claude R. Whitlock, "Stock Certificate Plan for Handling Heirship Estates," July 14, 1941, Realty Records, BIA, Aberdeen Area Office.
22. Ibid.
23. John Collier to James M. Stewart, September 9, 1941, Realty Records, BIA, Aberdeen Area Office.
24. James M. Stewart to Ward Shepard, Memorandum, November 26, 1941, TLE, 060, Realty Records, BIA, Aberdeen Area Office.
25. Ibid.
26. John Collier to James M. Stewart, September 9, 1941, Realty Records, BIA, Aberdeen Area Office.

27. Land Division Staff, Pierre, South Dakota, "Information Relative to the Heirship Problem on Selected Sioux Reservations of South Dakota," Realty Records, BIA, Aberdeen Area Office, pp. 7, 15.
28. Ibid., p. 21.
29. Ibid., p. 15.
30. Laurence F. Schmeckebier, *The Office of Indian Affairs: Its History, Activities and Organization* (Baltimore: The Johns Hopkins University Press, 1927): 510.
31. Walter V. Woehlke to A. L. Hook, June 15, 1942, TLE, 060, Realty Records, BIA, Aberdeen Area Office.
32. Ibid.
33. A. L. Hook to Commissioner of Indian Affairs, February 5, 1944, TLE, 060, Realty Records, BIA, Aberdeen Area Office.
34. James M. Stewart and Ward Shepard to Commissioner of Indian Affairs, Memorandum, February 6, 1942, TLE, O60, Realty Records, BIA, Aberdeen Area Office.
35. H. D. McCullough, Economic Program, Rosebud Indian Reservation, Missouri River Basin Investigations Unit, Office of Indian Affairs, Billings, Montana, 1945–1946, p. 9.
36. Ibid.
37. A. L. Hook to Allan G. Harper, January 1, 1943, TLE, 060, Realty Records, BIA, Aberdeen Area Office.
38. *Indians at Work,* 10: 2–6 (winter 1943): 31–33.
39. Clyde W. Flinn to Allan G. Harper, April 9, 1943, TLE, 060, Realty Records, BIA, Aberdeen Area Office; Flinn to Harper, April 13, 1943, TLE, 060, Realty Records, BIA, Aberdeen Area Office.
40. Clyde Flinn, Claude R. Whitlock, telegram to A. L. Hook, April 6, 1943, TLE, 060, Realty Records, BIA, Aberdeen Area Office.
41. "Preliminary Report Concerning Rosebud TLE, Yankton and Cheyenne River," September 2, 1955, TLE, RG 75, Federal Records Center, Suitland (Maryland).
42. Clyde W. Flinn to Allan G. Harper, April 9, 1943, TLE, 060, Realty Records, BIA, Aberdeen Area Office.
43. Clyde W. Flinn to Allan G. Harper, April 17, 1943, TLE, 060, Realty Records, BIA, Aberdeen Area Office.
44. By-Laws, Tribal Land Enterprise, approved April 6, 1943, Rosebud Indian Reservation (South Dakota), TLE, 060, Realty Records, BIA, Aberdeen Area Office, pp. 4, 9–10; Schmucker, Paul, Nohr, and Associates, and Francis-Meador-Gellhaus, Inc., "A Water Resource Inventory, Prepared for the Rosebud Sioux Tribe and U.S. Department of the Interior, Bureau of Indian Affairs, Phase 2, Present and Future Water Requirements," 1974, p. 28. In 1962 the board was reconstructed and the superintendent was dropped, the tribal secretary was added, and four tribal members filled the remaining seats.
45. Minutes, Annual Meeting of Holders of Interest in the Tribal Land Enterprise, Rosebud Indian Agency, Rosebud (South Dakota), May 23, 1951, File Folder 1, Document Box 140, Record Group I, Karl E. Mundt Papers, Karl E. Mundt Archives, Dakota State College, Madison (South Dakota).
46. Walter V. Woehlke to Assistant Secretary, Memorandum, September 22, 1943, TLE, 060, Realty Records, BIA, Aberdeen Area Office.

47. Ibid.
48. By-Laws, Tribal Land Enterprise, Rosebud Indian Reservation, adopted by the Rosebud Sioux Tribal Council, April 6, 1943, Realty Records, BIA, Aberdeen Area Office; By-Laws, TLE, Rosebud Indian Reservation, Rosebud (South Dakota), approved December 15, 1943, p. 9.
49. Ibid., p. 10.
50. Ibid., p. 15; Oscar Chapman to Commissioner of Indian Affairs, Memorandum, June 28, 1944; Clyde W. Flinn to Commissioner of Indian Affairs, January 17, 1944, TLE, 060, Realty Records, BIA, Aberdeen Area Office.
51. Claude R. Whitlock to Commissioner of Indian Affairs, April 10, 1944, TLE, 060, Realty Records, BIA, Aberdeen Area Office.
52. "Preliminary Report Concerning Rosebud TLE, Yankton and Cheyenne River," September 2, 1955, TLE, RG 75, Federal Records Center, Suitland (Maryland).
53. Claude R. Whitlock to Commissioner of Indian Affairs, April 10, 1944, TLE, 060, Realty Records, BIA, Aberdeen Area Office.
54. Ibid.; Resolution 53-10, Rosebud Sioux Tribal Council, November 5, 1953, Indian Files, 82nd Congress, 1951–1952, Rosebud Indian Agency, Francis Case Papers, Dakota Wesleyan University, Mitchell (South Dakota).
55. "Preliminary Report Concerning Rosebud TLE, Yankton and Cheyenne River," September 2, 1955, TLE, RG 75, Federal Records Center, Suitland (Maryland). For a general overview of submarginal lands, see Kicke Kickingbird and Karen Ducheneaux, *One Hundred Million Acres* (New York: Macmillan, 1973): chapter 5, "Submarginal Lands Are Alive and . . . Well?"
56. Claude R. Whitlock to Commissioner of Indian Affairs, April 10, 1944, TLE, 060, Realty Records, BIA, Aberdeen Area Office.
57. Resolution 53-10, Rosebud Sioux Tribal Council.
58. Claude R. Whitlock to A. L. Hook, August 7, 1944, TLE, 060, Realty Records, BIA, Aberdeen Area Office.
59. "Preliminary Report Concerning Rosebud TLE, Yankton and Cheyenne River," September 2, 1955, TLE, RG 75, Federal Records Center, Suitland (Maryland); *Argus Leader* (Sioux Falls, South Dakota), "Prosecutor Helps Tribe Close Tax Bite on Ranchers," pp. 1, 13, June 19, 1957.
60. U.S. Congress, House, Committee on Interior and Insular Affairs, *Sioux Indian Tribes, North and South Dakota,* Hearings before a subcommittee on H. Res. 30, 84th Cong., lst sess., 1956, p. 129.
61. Claude R. Whitlock to Commissioner of Indian Affairs, April 10, 1944, TLE, 060, Realty Records, BIA, Aberdeen Area Office.
62. Montgomery H. Saunderson, "A Report on a Study of the Organization and Operation of the Tribal Lands Enterprise of the Rosebud Sioux Tribe," 1953, TLE, 060, Realty Records, BIA, Aberdeen Area Office, p. 2.
63. Donald J. Ballas, "A Cultural Geography of Todd County, South Dakota, and the Rosebud Sioux Indian Reservation," Ph.D. diss. in geography, University of Nebraska, Lincoln, 1970, p. 112.
64. Saunderson, "A Report on a Study of the Organization," pp. 2–3.
65. Resolution 53-10, Rosebud Sioux Tribal Council.
66. "Preliminary Report Concerning Rosebud TLE, Yankton and Cheyenne River," September 2, 1955, TLE, RG 75, Federal Records Center, Suitland (Maryland).

67. Claude R. Whitlock to Firman H. Brown, September 13, 1946, TLE, 060, Realty Records, BIA, Aberdeen Area Office.
68. Ibid.
69. Claude R. Whitlock to Commissioner of Indian Affairs, July 30, 1946, TLE, 060, Realty Records, BIA, Aberdeen Area Office.
70. U.S. Congress, House, *Sioux Indians,* p. 129.
71. A. L. Hook to Commissioner of Indian Affairs, May 8, 1946, TLE, 060, Realty Records, BIA, Aberdeen Area Office.
72. Robert Burnette, *The Tortured Americans* (Englewood Cliffs, NJ: Prentice-Hall, 1971): 35–39, 43, 52–53, 99–100, 107, 120–121.
73. Saunderson, "A Report on a Study of the Organization," p. 2.
74. By-Laws, TLE, Rosebud Sioux Tribe, Rosebud (South Dakota), p. 7.
75. Paul L. Fickinger to Claude R. Whitlock, March 10, 1948, TLE, 060, Realty Records, BIA, Aberdeen Area Office.
76. Saunderson, "A Report on a Study of the Organization," p. 2.
77. Ibid., pp. 1–3.
78. Claude R. Whitlock to Commissioner of Indian Affairs, August 17, 1944, TLE, 060, Realty Records, BIA, Aberdeen Area Office.
79. A. L. Hook to Commissioner of Indian Affairs, February 5, 1944, TLE, 060, Realty Records, BIA, Aberdeen Area Office.
80. A. L. Hook to Commissioner of Indian Affairs, March 7, 1944, TLE, 060, Realty Records, BIA, Aberdeen Area Office.
81. A. L. Hook to Clyde W. Flinn, April 10, 1946, TLE, 060, Realty Records, BIA, Aberdeen Area Office.
82. U.S. Congress, House, *Sioux Indians,* p. 124.
83. Schmucker, Paul, Nohr, and Associates and Francis-Meador-Gellhaus, Inc., "A Water Resource Inventory of the Rosebud Indian Reservation, Prepared for the Rosebud Sioux Tribe and U.S. Department of the Interior, Bureau of Indian Affairs, Phase 2, Present and Future Water Requirements," 1974, p. 28.
84. Saunderson, "A Report on a Study of the Organization," p. 5.
85. Figure 6.1 displays one township of 36 sections (640 acres± each), which equals 23,040 acres; each section is one square mile divided into 160- or 320-acre units. TLE lands represent 2,560 acres, or just over 11% of the township.
86. U.S. Congress, House, *Sioux Indians,* pp. 116, 119–120.
87. Ibid., p. 126.
88. Carl Wahn, "A Fresh Look at TLE," *Todd County Tribune,* Mission (South Dakota), December 29, 1982.

CHAPTER 7

Indian Cultural, Historical, and Sacred Resources: How Tribes, Trustees, and the Citizenry Have Invoked Conservation*

IMRE SUTTON

> Every part of this soil is sacred . . . every hillside, every valley, every plain and grove, has been hallowed by some sad and happy event in days long vanished.[1]

Cultures differ in multiple ways. Among significant differences are those that reflect place—specific environments identified with ethnic memories, heroes, events, and spiritual or religious interaction with that environment.[2] For countless Indians such interaction between the spiritual and natural worlds has encompassed a holistic perception of the environment—a perception that encompasses larger geographic areas and multiple resources rather than just specific sites. Moreover, Native American territoriality has not as commonly been delimited in geopolitical terms as has Western culture; rather, territoriality continues to be culturally and spiritually based. Tribe after tribe that lost much or all of its territory virtually lost much or all of its environmentally based culture.

Native Americans continue to be concerned, angry, often alarmed, even militant over the disturbance and desecration of burial grounds and graves, campsites, and caves that are all too frequently uncovered and either destroyed or severely modified during resource exploitation or construction on former Indian lands. These concerns focus not only on protection and preservation but also on access, restoration, or repatriation of cultural resources. Within and beyond Indian Country tribes have viewed access to and exclusive utilization of sacred places as their right, yet time and again tribes have been frustrated in efforts to gain support from law and environmental management. Attempts to reestablish sacred ground as part of trust land have proven even less successful.

---

*Many thanks to Professor Stephen Jett of the geography faculty at the University of California, Davis, for his review of an earlier draft of this chapter.

(EPA) and other federal agencies have successfully invoked various laws—especially AIRFA, NHPA, and NAGPRA, as well as the Archaeological Resources Protection Act (ARPA). Compliance regulations by public land agencies have existed for decades, and AIRFA has indirectly abetted access to and exclusive utilization of a few Indian sites, yet conflict has arisen where sites are on either private or public property (e.g., national forestlands).[7]

For Indian cultural resources found on private lands, not only are constitutional issues of property rights invoked, but vested interests in resource exploitation such as mining resist the protection and setting aside of sites such as ceremonial grounds or cemeteries. As part of state monitoring of Native American cultural resources, it has become the obligation of cities and counties—often through their planning agencies—to oversee the protection of such resources as private developers seek to modify former Indian environments. Most states comply under NHPA by creating a state historic preservation officer (SHPO) who oversees compliance.[8] Laws require a survey of such cultural resources in given jurisdictions, and several states mandate that an Indian must be present at any excavation site, and so on. Conservation is often the better approach to the management of such resources than is preservation, which may no longer be possible because of environmental modifications and ownership by other than Indians.[9] In the instance of conservation of cultural resources on non-Indian lands, careful excavation and removal to an Indian site or a museum may be the only alternative.

Frequently, Indians are forcibly removed from former tribal lands, where they have chosen to squat as a protest against their original loss and in the expectation that some restoration might occur (e.g., Indians of northern California within Six Rivers National Forest; Wabenaki and other Indians at Mt. Katahdin, Maine.)[10] But very little historic or sacred ground is restored to tribes, although Indians may be granted exclusive access and utilization of the latter but at the option of those holding and managing such land. Despite laws to create appropriate oversight and management of Indian cultural resources, success is piecemeal; thereby Indians are less than satisfied. What confounds many tribes today is that neither Congress nor the justice system consistently sustains tribal jurisdiction over various environmental issues even as the nation embraces a policy of self-determination for Native Americans.[11] Although tribal jurisdiction seems well in place on trust lands—as in the development of resource management programs, preservation institutions, and the like—tribes must act cautiously and judiciously in terms of non-Indian holdings.

Loci of Cultural Resources

Land tenure and jurisdiction play variable roles in how the conservation and preservation of Indian cultural resources can be accomplished. Within Indian Country one encounters three broad tenures—trust, public, and private—as well as every level of government—tribal, federal, state, and local (see

Figure 7.1[12]). Land tenure configurations reveal many admixtures—for example, trust includes tribal, tenancy in common, and allotment—but reservations may well contain both trust and fee simple holdings, the latter significantly owned by non-Indians. Beyond Indian Country private property prevails across the nation, although in the western states public lands represent nearly 50 percent of total acreage. Conflicts over the protection and restoration of Indian cultural resources may and do occur in nearly all states, including parallel complaints by Native Hawaiians in Hawaii.[13] Moreover, land claims litigation, which adjudicated original Indian title lands, drew additional attention to cultural resources no longer within tribal proprietorship or jurisdiction over much of irredeemable America.

Trust Lands: Focus on Tribal Management

Protection and management of a variety of cultural resources on trust lands depend on the willing involvement of tribal government and assistance—both technical and financial—of federal and state agencies. Although tribal authority to enforce regulations governing cultural resource preservation on lands now owned by non-Indians has diminished,[14] NAGPRA embraces much more than the limited definition of tribal land and somewhat ambiguously includes privately owned lands within reservation boundaries but only under the protection of the Fifth Amendment for compensation.[15] Tribes may indeed have more clout to manage historical and cultural resources on fee lands within reservations. Only a small number of tribes have established departments or offices that deal specifically with cultural heritage or archaeology; most do not even articulate specific concerns.[16] We have examples of sites such as Wounded Knee, which the Pine Ridge Sioux commemorate but have poorly managed up to now; the idea of creating a tribal monument or one under the supervision of the National Park Service (NPS) has been suggested from time to time. The Crow once sought jurisdiction over the Custer Battlefield in eastern Montana, but because the NPS renamed it the Little Bighorn National Battlefield Monument and has presented a positive interpretation of Indians in its exhibits, perhaps the Indians are somewhat appeased.[17]

In the 1992 amendments to NHPA the authority to develop and run historic preservation programs resides with the tribes. The amended law directs the NPS to assist the tribes in preserving and managing such resources and provides for grant monies through the Historic Preservation Fund. This program authorizes tribes to assume all or certain functions of an SHPO, and as of summer 1996 around a dozen tribes were also approved to assume a role equivalent to that of a state government.[18] Tribes, of course, must submit appropriate plans to the NPS, and that agency must consult with SHPOs and other tribes whose trust or aboriginal lands might be affected by such plans. These provisions suggest that Congress continues to encourage tribes to take charge of their homeland and thus manage cultural resources.[19]

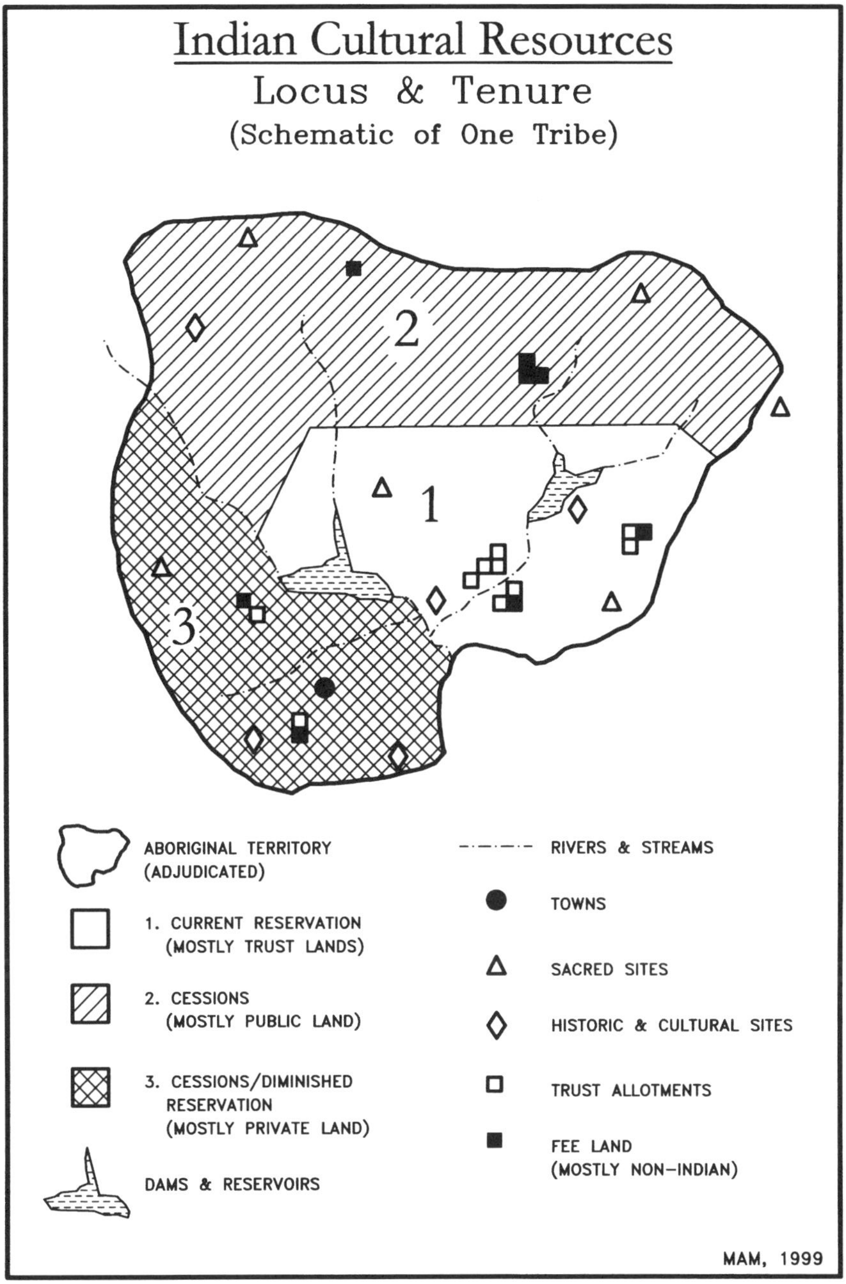

Fig. 7.1 Indian Cultural Resources, Locus and Tenure. This three-part diagram suggests where various cultural resources would be found on trust, public, and private lands; the text parallels this scheme. The greater controversy and hence litigation are associated with areas 2 and 3.

Fig. 7.2 Navajo Farmstead in Canyon de Chelly. Unlike Monument Valley, Canyon de Chelly National Monument is administered jointly by the Navajo Nation and the National Park Service (NPS). Mostly older Navajos continue to live in the canyon but must obtain land-use permits from the NPS. "The canyon may present an extreme example of how development . . . is disrupting Navajo customary uses of the land. . . . The canyon . . . forms one sacred landscape with a high density of places of special power, among which Navajos live, farm, and keep livestock" (Klara B. Kelly and Harris Francis, *Navajo Sacred Places* [Bloomington: Indiana University Press, 1994]: 163–164). Photo by Imre Sutton.

There is some concern, however, as to what Indian lands may be included in this preservation program. The statutory definition of Indian Country presents no problem, but lands not formally set aside as reservations may preclude some acreage from the program. It is perhaps much too soon to determine how successful tribal preservation programs will be under the NPS-assisted guidelines. Not all sites represent sacred places; many have historic meaning such as Wounded Knee and certain National Historic Trails such as the "Trail of Tears"—which retraces the forced removal of Cherokee, Chickasaw, Choctaw, Creek, and Seminole—and the Nez Perce National Park, which collectively designates battle and other sites.[20] Others may be singled out for multiple reasons, including unique scenic value deserving of special protection (e.g., Monument Valley on the Navajo Indian Reservation compared with Canyon de Chelley National Monument) (Figure 7.2).

Although many more tribes today have taken important steps toward protecting and even developing both historic and scenic places and have created historic commissions and natural resource branches that include management of these tribal resources, few tribes have also established museums. In mid-1998 the Mashantucket Pequot at Ledyard, Connecticut, opened a tribal museum on the site of its well-known Foxwoods casino and resort. Moreover, the tribe has chosen to finance archaeological research for tribal history with profits from gaming.[21]

In general, the Bureau of Indian Affairs (BIA) has developed a cultural resource program as part of its compliance under the National Environmental Policy Act (NEPA); however, this does not represent a high priority. Tribes, of course, may opt to create their own cultural resource conservation programs. Until recently, tribes were largely excluded from national historic preservation programs because NHPA made no reference to tribes. But the 1980 amended law includes them and authorizes grants to tribes for preservation of historic sites and cultural resources. Not only do tribes assume the role of the SHPO, but they may enter into agreements with the National Advisory Council on Historic Preservation under Section 106 of that law. Any federal undertaking today requires consent of tribes, but state officers may be essential when sacred places lie outside reservations. For non-Indian lands within reservations, tribes must allow the SHPO to participate.[22]

Environmental law has expanded the responsibilities of other federal agencies to the tribes. Such responsibilities not only relate to the maintenance of clean water, clean air, and other environmental concerns but also to historic sites, burial grounds, and the like. For example, the Army Corps of Engineers has engaged in government-to-government relations with tribes to spell out Corps functions under NAGPRA.[23] It is reported that many tribes have been distressed about unclear agency processes regarding that act. Many tribal-agency interrelations have grown out of the government-to-government policy. Although not many tribes have organized for cultural resource management, review of a few programs will be instructive.

The Navajo Nation's efforts at historic and sacred preservation—among the earliest by the tribes—began in part with the Cultural Resources Protection Act (1988), giving the tribe more clout in such management. The Navajo had to overcome the bureaucratic bias that gave the BIA virtually unilateral decisionmaking power over any tribal program to protect sacred sites and environments. Once amendments to NHPA went into effect, the tribe began to assume management of its own cultural resource program. The Nation had already established an archaeological program, and then, under the impetus of Indian claims litigation, it established not only archaeological but ethnographic investigations to determine irredeemable lands for which the Nation sought compensation. At the local level, site stewardships exist where local people watch over landmarks and archaeological sites, report vandalism, and the like.

The Navajo Nation zones natural landmarks and sensitive areas and has a historic preservation department, which requires that developers must document the concerns of local land users, chapters, medicine people, and the like. Since the Navajos conceptualize a holistic landscape approach to what is sacred in an environment, that view goes counter to many developments that would otherwise disturb not only immediate sites but also much larger territory. The tribe criticizes the triage concept as piecemeal, for it asks people to choose more important sites and sacrifice others. Mining is one example of development that destroys important places as well as disrupts customary activities on the landscape. Black Mesa comes to mind because of the Peabody Coal Company's practices; mining has made significant inroads on sacred landscapes.[24]

The Navajo Nation has assumed responsibility for archeological surveys NHPA requires before each timber sale in the Navajo forest. Navajos contend that lumbering is too excessive and should be stopped to allow for forest regeneration, whereas foresters contend that overgrazing by Navajos prevents reforestation.[25] Ultimately, however, "by accepting federal funding . . . HPD [Historic Preservation Department] has forfeited to a large degree the Navajo Nation's controls over its own preservation agenda." It is contended that the program tends to fulfill federal mandates, and the limitations placed on Navajo efforts strongly suggest some of the weaknesses or pitfalls inherent in the 1992 amendments to NHPA and NAGPRA.[26] Navajos somewhat forestall their own efforts because they are reluctant to disclose the secret locations of sacred places for planning purposes. Professor Stephen Jett, who has worked with the tribe to identify sacred landmarks and the reasons for their sanctity, acknowledges concern for restricting certain information; nonetheless, he suggests there is considerable gain by providing for public interpretation of sacred places—for example, others would become more aware and sensitive to Navajo culture, and visitors would gain an "enhanced experience of interactive participation" in an environment generally unavailable to most of the populace.[27]

In recent years Zunis operating under the Zuni Land Conservation Act (1990) have been reviewing the effect of roads on nearly 2,000 archaeological sites where graves have been unearthed, ancient villages plowed up, and cultural heritage despoiled by construction practices. The law provides $25 million for a sustainable development plan by the tribe. The act embraces both on-reservation and off-reservation sites, and in response the tribe has created a historical-cultural code and established an office for historic management.[28]

Intertribal conflicts over sacred sites rarely occur. Yet since the early 1980s the Hopi have protested the intrusion by neighboring Navajos on their sacred sites that lie within Navajo territory, especially as a result of the resettlement program.[29] As mandated by the 1992 amendments to NHPA, these sites were to be protected. Besides problems over sites on private lands, the Hopi had to contend with alleged Navajo vandalism at Ki'iswu (Cliff Springs)—lands awarded to the Navajo (*Healing v. Jones*), although Hopis have access rights under the law. Navajos there have prevented Hopis from placing their prayer sticks (*pahos*) or otherwise have thrown them about. Ironically, the NHPA affords protection of sites of historic but not *spiritual* significance. Conversely, Navajos have opposed range conservation programs proposed for Hopi lands, where by law Navajos may still utilize sacred sites no longer within their territory. Hopis have also proposed more coal mining and power plant construction on former Navajo lands.[30] It is argued that the BIA and the courts have failed to acknowledge that American Indian religious freedom requires preserving not only access but also natural conditions at sites and surrounding landscape.

Thus far the emphasis has been on cultural, sacred, and archaeological resources on trust lands. A recent case—*Black Hills Institute of Geological Research v. South Dakota School of Mines and Technology*—reveals why we must broaden the tribal commitment to on-reservation environmental management.[31] In *Black Hills* the courts argued that a Tyrannosaurus rex fossil excavated on the Cheyenne River Sioux Indian Reservation belonged to the Indians. The Black Hills Institute apparently had paid an Indian rancher for the right to excavate and remove the fossil from his allotment. It is also reported that the Institute did not secure approval from either the secretary of the interior or the tribal government. In reaching the decision that the tribal government held ownership to the fossil, the courts had relied on the federal statutory definition of trust lands and the state of South Dakota's definition of land. "Absent from this analysis was consideration of the traditional Native American understanding of the nature of land and the fossils and other materials that compose it."[32]

This case may well establish a precedent that asserts the role of the federal government, not tribal sovereignty, as the basis for jurisdiction over such resources, even on trust lands. Also, the courts' "opinion failed to recognize that the excavation and removal of the fossil are simply the most recent example of paleontologists' historical failure to respect tribal sovereignty."[33] In *Black Hills* the government successfully argued that the fossil, through time, became part of the land, and like trust land itself, the fossil could not be alienated without consent of Congress. Even South Dakota's definition of land confirmed the concept that the fossil in a sense became land and therefore was subject to federal approval.

Although Congress has favorably endorsed the protection and management of cultural and archaeological resources, it has not addressed the need to regulate or manage paleontological resources. Recall that ARPA only embraces paleontological resources when they are found in an archaeological context. If tribes continue to see their sovereignty diminished by decisions in environmental cases, the necessary regulatory authority could be forthcoming through ARPA and NAGPRA, which now provide for tribal jurisdiction over archaeological resources on reservations. Reliance on NAGPRA as a model for the protection of paleontological resources is useful because that law defines tribal lands to include "all lands within the exterior boundaries of any Indian reservation" and thus implies the inclusion of non-Indian holdings of former trust lands. NAGPRA "does not specifically exclude paleontological resources from coverage, and it is conceivable that a particular fossil might fit the definition of a 'sacred object' or an object of 'cultural patrimony.' "[34] I agree that Native American rights have long been disregarded and subordinated to the interests of paleontologists; obviously, law already exists that provides models for the enactment of appropriate legislation to give tribes comprehensive jurisdiction on reservation of the paleontological past.

Public Lands: Conflicts Among Uses

Public land agencies by law must promote some protection and management of Indian cultural, historical, and religious resources, although coverage is uneven.[35] For federal lands the agencies must consult the appropriate tribe under ARPA, and under NAGPRA it is possible to determine which tribe must be consulted on the basis of adjudication of the land in question by the Indian Claims Commission.[36] Despite regulations in place, case law indicates that Indian cultural resources and sacred places located on public lands are not so readily protected. In fact, some critics identify the federal government as an antagonist in tribal efforts to regain ownership or sustain exclusive use of culturally significant sites no longer part of tribal territory.

Several cases suggest that most tribes, despite their perception of the force of AIRFA, will continue to have difficulty in securing more than a modicum of access, and few tribes will ever regain appropriate land. It took more than forty years for the Taos to regain sacred Blue Lake (New Mexico)—then not contiguous to the pueblo itself; Congress did transfer a contiguous portion of Kit Carson National Forest.[37] Conversely, when Congress restored Kolhu/wala:wa to the Zuni, their two-day pilgrimage to the shrine has continued to necessitate crossing noncontiguous public and private lands. In some instances Indians still hold access rights by agreement with the National Park Service, as in the instance of Yosemite National Park, even though the government years ago effectively "forced" the local Indians to relocate outside park boundaries.[38]

Relative to private lands, one might presume that it is easier to restore (transfer) ownership of culturally significant places from public lands to the tribes; nothing in national policy directly furthers such transfer. Each tribe must marshal support and labor for years without the expectation of a successful transfer.

For many tribes sacred landscapes convey the most spiritually, and of those, mountains are the most ubiquitous—for example, Mt. Adams and the Yakama

(Yakima); the San Francisco Peaks, Bill Williams Mountain, and the Navajo, Hopi, Havasupai, and Southern Paiute; the four sacred mountains of the Navajo, and others.[39] Lakes and rivers also assume sacred importance, as do geomorphic features such as rock formations and caves. Caves take on additional cultural meaning when they become the home of spirits or folk heroes, serve as burial grounds, are utilized for pictographic or other artistic expressions, and are established as ethnoastronomical sites. In 1996 President Bill Clinton promulgated an executive order that, although charging public land agencies with the responsibility to accommodate Indian access and ceremonial use of sacred places and to avoid adverse physical impact, also declared that

> Nothing in this order shall be construed to require a taking of vested property interests. Nor shall this order be construed to impair enforceable rights to use of Federal lands that have been granted to third parties through final agency action. The order does oblige federal agencies to facilitate consultation with appropriate Indian tribes . . . but, while intending to improve management, does not create any right, benefit, or trust responsibility . . . enforceable at law or equity . . . against the United States.[40]

Frankly, as a gesture in good faith, this order is doublespeak in terms of effective national policy. It leaves open-ended the protection of sacred sites and other cultural resources, despite provisions for Indian access. Concern and conflict continue to exist with respect to many sites because Indians are not granted exclusive use of the location.

For example, in early 1998 the Quechan Indians of southeast California invoked this executive order, contending that mining on adjacent public lands (administered by the Bureau of Land Management [BLM]) was sacrilegious. Quechans consider that adjacent area sacred, and although mining laws do permit the development of a 1,600-acre pit for gold mining, it would despoil sacred lands. One tribal member spoke to the issue: "You can mitigate for the loss of natural resources. But you can't mitigate the loss of religious resources. This land is our entry to the other world. If it is gone, so are we."[41]

Differences between Indian and government perceptions of and values toward cultural resources cause frustration and conflict to occur over certain types of development.[42] Tourism, for example, is a constant frustration for many tribes—for example, in the Black Hills (South Dakota) and in the San Francisco Peaks area (Arizona), where the U.S. Forest Service has openly promoted non-Indian interests in skiing in the Arizona Snow Bowl. Although a few successful examples of government protection of Indian cultural resources and about as many transfers of sacred sites to the tribes exist, many more sites remain unprotected or poorly protected and generally lie out of the reach of Indians.

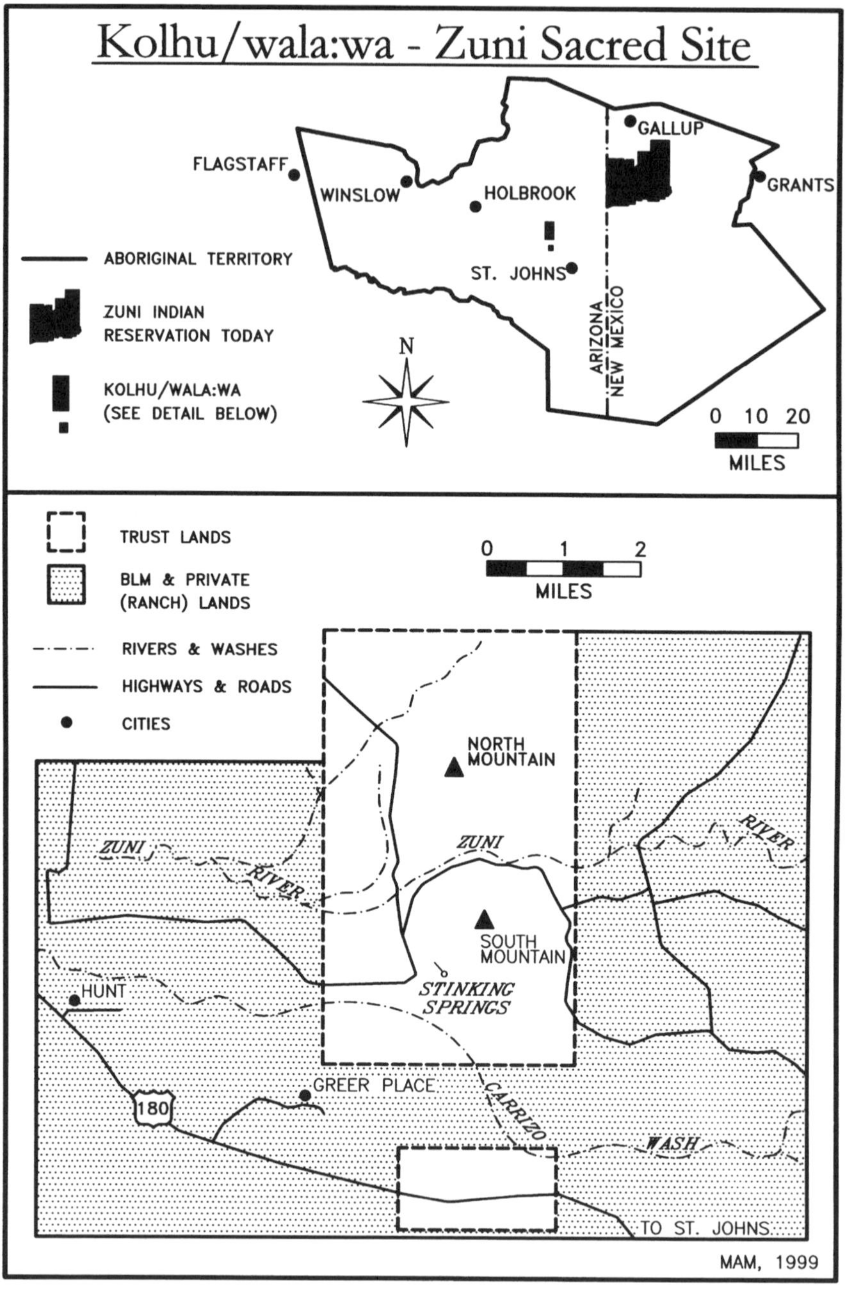

Fig. 7.3 Kolhu/wala:wa-Zuni Sacred Site. Zuni Heaven or Kolhu/wala:wa, located in Arizona, is one of the most recent restorations of sacred lands to the tribes. Note importantly that the site is *not contiguous* to the Zuni Indian Reservation in New Mexico. Reprinted from *American Indian Culture and Research Journal,* 24:1 (2000) by permission of the American Indian Studies Center, UCLA, © Regents of the University of California.

Sometimes the government listens and then acts contrary to or disregards what the tribes say. The Bighorn Medicine Wheel (Wyoming) represents a government effort to accommodate Indians; the site is designated a National Historic Landmark. The Forest Service at one time wanted to construct a visitor center and viewing platform near Medicine Wheel but was convinced to scrap the plan, prohibit motorized vehicles, and grant twelve days of the year for exclusive Indian use of the site. In 1985 the forest managers established a 264,000-acre management site for logging within Bighorn National Forest and then later amended the plan to create an "area of consultation" that favored the various tribes that frequented the Medicine Wheel. Among arguments against this special area was the constitutional provision for separation of state and church, but tribes invoked the American Indian Religious Freedom Act.[43]

Conversely, at Mount Graham (Arizona), sacred to western Apaches, the Indians have had to contend with bulldozing and blasting on top of the mountain to make way for an astronomical complex under the aegis of the University of Arizona—a development approved by Congress. As for Mt. Adams, located on the western edge of the Yakama Indian Reservation (Washington), it had been designated a wilderness to be administered under the Wilderness Act, but the tribe eventually gained limited restoration—at least on paper—when a small part of the mountain was reconfigured within tribal boundaries.[44]

As of this writing, the most recent example has been Kolhu/wala:wa, the Zuni sacred site, which has never been contiguous to the Zuni Indian Reservation (New Mexico). Tribal members pilgrimage to the site by traversing traditional routes to the west of the reservation and into Arizona (Figure 7.3). Located within public lands administered by the BLM, the site is surrounded by private ranchlands and BLM grazing allotments. After considerable negotiations and litigation, the government restored the sacred site to the Zuni. The transfer guaranteed that tribal members would freely access intervening public lands and, by an easement formalized by a court order and an agreement with one rancher, would be able to traverse private ranchlands. Nonetheless, the physical separation of the reservation in New Mexico from Kolhu/wala:wa in eastern Arizona frustrates the tribe.[45]

Some federal land agencies openly reject or oppose tribal efforts to protect or preserve cultural, historical, or sacred sites or to pursue land restoration or exclusive access and use of sites on former tribal lands. For example, the Navajo expressed their fears to the Bureau of Reclamation about the flooding of Rainbow Bridge by Lake Powell (impounded by Glen Canyon Dam), but no one seemed to be listening; and the court did not prevent the construction of Tellico Dam on the Little Tennessee River (part of the Tennessee Valley Authority), which flooded Cherokee cherished ground (*Sequoyah v. TVA*).[46] Both the Black Hills of South Dakota—sacred to all the western Sioux tribes—and the San Francisco Peaks in northern Arizona—sacred to Piute, Hopi, Navajo, and Havasupai—have remained beyond tribal reach.

Even though Sioux tribes won a significant financial reward in the courts, pursuant to major land claims, for the loss of the Black Hills in 1877—*Sioux Nation of Indians v. the United States*—to date litigant tribes have refused more than $100 million and continue to campaign for restoration of some of the upland. A bill was introduced unsuccessfully in Congress to reaffirm boundaries that would have conveyed lands within the Black Hills to the Sioux. Only federal lands—approximately 1.3 million acres—would have been restored. Many politicians and others did ask whether the hills had been sacred in the past and, if so, what evidence sustains that view. Environmental historian Donald Worster suggested that tribal leaders more than a century ago did not deem the hills sacred but were more concerned to secure valuable lands at lower elevations. Even Black Elk, a revered religious leader, did not "explicitly refer to the Black Hills as the sacred land of the Lakota." Ultimately, Worster insisted that the best evidence suggests that the hills "were a place of legend and importance but . . . [signified] nothing really about sacredness." He also suggested that "what is going on among the Lakota is not so much the presentation of a legal case for sacredness as it is the awakening of a new or revitalized religion. If the Black Hills have not been certifiably sacred in the historical past . . . they are becoming so in the present."[47]

As for the San Francisco Peaks, the courts rejected Indian claims to sacred religious sites but offered nominal tribal exclusive access (*Wilson v. Block*). In *Wilson* the Arizona SHPO concurred with the U.S. Forest Service that the San Francisco Peaks were ineligible for the National Register, which contradicted the positions taken by the Navajo and Hopi. The Forest Service proceeded to develop the Arizona Snow Bowl, which brings in thousands of skiers and tourists yearly.[48]

A further example of the opposing posture of the U.S. Forest Service occurred in northern California. In *Lyng v. Northwest Indian Cemetery Protective Assn* (1988), Yurok and Karok Indians sought to occupy and preserve sacred burial grounds within Six Rivers National Forest, where the Forest Service intended to construct a road. The Indians argued that the construction would violate First Amendment rights under AIRFA, but the U.S. Supreme Court did not concur with that interpretation, noting an important difference between prohibiting Indian religious use of the site versus their incidental use. It boiled down to the fact that the Forest Service could not be restricted in carrying out its normal functions as a steward of the public lands. Ironically, the site in Six Rivers National Forest was listed on the National Register of historic places, but that does not of itself protect historic property. *Lyng* does not prevent a federal agency from managing federal lands; the majority opinion of the U.S. Supreme Court acknowledged the site-specific nature of religion and the fact that Indians could claim access under the First Amendment, but the court held that the Indians could not prevent the federal government from utilizing public lands in their charge. Because the opinion rejected the theory and practice that only for a compelling reason—which the Indians demonstrated—could the government reject Indian religious reasons for exclusive access, one has to believe justice is blind even to the meaning of the First Amendment.[49]

The court's rejection of the plaintiff's position in *Lyng* implies that there may no longer be an opportunity for tribes to seek exclusive access under the First Amendment. Yet destruction of the isolation and sacredness of Chimney Rock prevents the exercise of the world renewal ceremony of the Yurok; elimination of the site further precludes Native practices central to their religion. Congress and federal agencies should give proper regard to the sacred character of such places; however, although AIRFA invokes a policy to protect and preserve freedom to believe in, express, and exercise religion, the act lacks the capacity to protect sacred places.[50]

A new and different issue has arisen over the interpretation of the First Amendment vis-à-vis the preservation of Indian cultural, historical, or sacred places: Must efforts to accommodate Indian religious practices on federal lands go forward in the face of violating the Establishment Clause? In *Bear Lodge Multiple Use Ass'n v. Babbitt* the National Park Service did attempt such an accommodation at Devil's Tower National Monument, perceived as a sacred site by Dakota, Lakota, and Nakota Sioux. But the tower is also generally acknowledged to be a popular rock-climbing natural feature. The NPS did deny permits for commercially guided climbs during June and asked the public to voluntarily refrain from climbing at that time. June is the month when Indians revere the tower. Although the court found the voluntary closure permissible, the ban against commercial use was declared unconstitutional.

At issue is the comparative right of (native) religion versus rock climbing. Vine Deloria Jr. and David E. Wilkins have asked, "Why . . . is recreational rock climbing considered a constitutionally protected First Amendment right, while having access to sacred land in the peace and quiet required to practice living spiritual traditions . . . is not?"[51] For the claimant Indians, exclusive access was to be protected by AIRFA, but the court did not contend that the Establishment Clause denied them a separate religious right. Instead, the court sustained the argument that rock climbers had an equal right to exercise their outdoor activity. This is just one of several cases in which the Free Exercise Clause rather than the Establishment Clause has been the point of law that has defeated tribes who have invoked AIRFA.

In sum, since 1980 Indian efforts to secure exclusive rights and access to unimpaired sacred sites have been denied on the grounds that the construction of dams (e.g., Tellico Dam and Glen Canyon Dam) did not violate the Free Exercise Clause, nor did expansion of an existing ski facility (San Francisco Peaks) or the development of timber harvesting (Six Rivers National Forest) in a sacred area. "Not surprisingly, attempts to protect sacred lands by asserting a violation of the Free Exercise Clause have not been successful after *Lyng*."[52] The

Forest Service did decide to redirect development of the Santa Fe Ski Area (New Mexico) because of potential adverse impact on Pueblo religious beliefs: "Congressional authority to protect sacred lands and provide for Indian religious practices is quite broad and potentially powerful, *but Congress has used the authority only sparingly.*"[53]

To date, Congress has not enacted any comprehensive sacred lands protection statute, although specific legislation authorizes the temporary closure of sensitive areas to the public at large—as in El Malpais National Monument and Conservation Area and in the California Desert Protection Area. Citing the Bald and Golden Eagle Protection Act, which prohibits possession of eagles or eagle parts yet provides for a specific exemption allowing Indians to possess eagles and eagle parts for religious purposes, Lydia Grimm suggests that Congress could enact a general sacred lands statute providing for temporary closures of sacred sites in the interest of Indian religious practices. But "federal land managers cannot cite the federal-tribal relationship to protect sacred lands . . . unless Congress has first granted that authority."[54]

Finally, Indian historic and sacred places may be eligible for listing on the National Register of Historic Places and can be entered as traditional cultural properties (TCPs) under the NHPA. Because of these provisions, government agencies must consult with Indian tribes (as well as Native Hawaiians) before developing plans for areas that embrace special sites. Several places have already been declared and listed—for example, Kootenai Falls as a vision questing site by the Kootenai Tribe. And under the National Forest Management Act, the Forest Service must also coordinate with Indian tribes on future management plans. Some forest plans already identify sacred lands, even in the Six Rivers National Forest, the locale of the dispute in *Lyng.*

State and local government agencies have responded in various ways to tribal claims to historic and sacred places. Sioux and Cheyenne opposed the South Dakota Game, Fish, and Parks Department's road programs that were designed to improve access for development, but the court contended that such development did not harm Indian religious areas (*Crow v. Gullet*).[55] A site on the campus of California State University, Long Beach, was placed on the National Register of Historic Places because some authorities and descendant Indians claimed it was that of the village of Puvungna, home to the god Chinichnich who was much venerated among the Gabrielino Indians of Los Angeles County and the surrounding area. A contract archaeologist's report deemed the site only that of postcontact farming. But when the university sought to develop a mini-mall on the site, Gabrielino and Juaneño Indians approached California's Native American Heritage Commission (NAHC), which ruled that the university's plans would "result in severe and irreparable damage, and bar Native Americans from the land."[56] As of mid-2001 the university has continued to leave the site as a garden.[57]

Although most tribal claims to sacred places occur in the West, a number involve other parts of the nation. Since the mid-1970s the Wabenaki have sought restoration of or exclusive access to Mt. Katahdin—a 5,267-foot mountain in the northern Appalachians of Maine—where members of the Maliseet, Micmac, Passamaquoddy, and Penobscot had confronted the state government by trespassing and encamping in Baxter State Park. The Indians gained permission to use the wilderness park for spiritual practices, but some hoped to return to traditional hunting, trapping, and related activities, which park officials rejected. They also failed to gain a grant of land on Chesuncook Lake, part of the sacred area.[58]

Private Lands: Tribes, Citizens, and State and Local Governments

Private ownership of land dominates the American scene. In plowed fields we have found artifacts; along the right-of-way for a highway we have discovered human remains. The construction of dams is normally preceded by a careful survey of the reservoir site because in so many instances archaeologists have found encampments, burial sites, and significant artifacts. Burial sites are common in nearly all states, as are encampments; so are caves, some of which represent the sites of hunting caches, but several take on greater significance as ethnoastronomical sites. Indian cultural resources on private lands may or may not be discovered, perhaps because they were destroyed long ago in the occupation of the land or landowners have chosen not to disclose any Indian presence on their property. In other instances artifacts such as tools and art pieces may have been pillaged from sites long known to be of significant cultural heritage. Many locales and sites were transferred under homestead and other public laws without regard for preservation or knowledge of the existence of Indian settlements or artifacts. Even without surviving artifacts or other evidence on the ground, countless sites continue to have cultural meaning to given tribes.

In addition to applicable federal laws identified earlier, most states have enacted appropriate legislation for the protection of Indian remains and recovery of artifacts, yet few have enacted parallel legislation governing repatriation.[59] On occasion, Indians and private parties enter into agreements to set aside limited sites and otherwise provide some modicum of protection for cultural resources on former tribal lands. Generally, statutes assign responsibility to a state agency such as a historic commission, Indian commission, or museum and require that landowners immediately report the uncovering of potential Native American remains and artifacts. As a rule, these laws encourage Native American input into the ultimate disposition of remains. California, for example, established the Native American Heritage Commission, and Arizona has placed responsibility with the State Museum. Several states permit scientific study of Indian remains for a limited time before their final disposition under the guidance of appropriate tribes. A few states specifically indicate in the wording of law that remains "shall be transferred to appropriate Indian tribes . . . for reburial."[60] Of course, private landowners are protected from "uncompensated takings" by the restrictions of the 5th and 14th Amendments to the Constitution. A few examples will demonstrate how law and society have responded to the Indians' collective concerns.

In northwestern Kentucky in 1987, authorities discovered that considerable digging under lease led to the exploitation of a major village site of possible Shawnee heritage.[61] Perpetrators were stopped and charged with "desecration of a venerated object" under Kentucky law. About 450 holes had been dug by the looters, who uncovered some 650 graves and made off with a rich haul of artifacts, later sold commercially. This desecration of Indian ruins at Slack Farm, privately owned acreage overlooking the Ohio River near the center of both the Woodland culture (500 B.C.–A.D. 800) and the Mississippian (A.D. 800–1650), so rankled Kentucky legislators that they rewrote the governing statute so such a crime would become a felony. As a misdemeanor the fine was small, and none of the looters who escaped across the state line could be extradited.

At issue here and elsewhere in the nation is the conflict between state regulation of archaeological excavations and the rights of landowners to utilize their property as they see fit. In the Kentucky case, only if local law had been violated would the federal Archaeological Resources Protection Act (1979) lead to the entry of federal authorities. Cheryl Ann Munson, a senior archaeologist at Indiana University, was reported to comment:

> The really sad thing is that we'll never know what's been taken or how it relates to what remains in the ground. Everything has been scrambled. This field [Slack Farm] is one of the prime Mississippian sites of the Ohio River Valley from the time of European contact. Now much of what we could have known is lost forever.[62]

Fortunately, in 1858 an amateur archaeologist who had excavated and mapped mound sites at Slack Farm forwarded artifacts to the Smithsonian Institution. Interpreters have concluded that this was a flourishing village site during A.D. 1450—1650. The mound culture, for example, relates to other well-known sites such as Cahokia in Illinois and others in Indiana and Alabama. As Pamela D'Innocenzo remarked regarding this disastrous example of commercial exploitation, "legal exploitation does not, in fact, make it ethically permissible to blatantly disregard the rights of the descendants of the dead or the rights of future generations to know, and perhaps even possess access to, their heritage."[63] As she further noted, the protection of archaeological sites is essential to preserve the past record of various cultural groups that may seek to establish an aboriginal or treaty homeland.[64]

Unlike Kentucky's recent legal efforts to amend laws to regulate exploitation of Indian cultural sites, the state of Texas boldly asserts the property rights of its citizens. In Texas the few repatriations have been of human remains. Steve

Russell, a retired judge and member of the Cherokee Nation of Oklahoma, noted that "the additional proof NAGPRA requires to identify sacred objects and cultural patrimony could be daunting given the political atmosphere in Texas—where 'property rights' reign supreme."[65] Working against or limiting preservation and repatriation is the fact that so many rightful (indigenous) claimant Indians reside out of state. Indians direct their protests to both the amateur and the scientist, whose "imperial archaeology" (Russell citing Pawnee historian James Riding In) creates a catch-22 for those who are concerned with reconstruction of Native American culture and thus assert the need to excavate and remove artifacts and human remains. This argument is not isolated to Texas. Russell reports that around 66,000 Indians are living in Texas, but the three reservations (Alabama-Coushatta, Kickapoo, and Tigua) are occupied by nonindigenous Indians.

Grave robbing in Texas is not new. Caddo exploitation, for example, resulted from the fact that their burial practices were lavish—disinterment has revealed ceramics, bone tools, pipes, jewelry, and similar objects—and their pottery artistry has had such a fine reputation that both amateur and professional pot hunters make "every Caddoan grave a potential bonanza."[66] The Wichita Indians—who migrated to Texas and later were relocated to Oklahoma—also buried tribal members with considerable funerary artifacts, putting their gravesites in great danger of desecration, as contemporary members of the tribe are well aware.

The problem with Texas and all other states is that NAGPRA limits the right of repatriation to Indians indigenous to the claimed territory in which a sacred or funereal site is found. Because none of the tribes in Texas has aboriginal lands within the state and the indigenous groups reside out of state, it is next to impossible to enforce the law. Moreover, tribes that had been expelled from Texas have no way to be informed that their sacred grounds have been excavated and artifacts confiscated. Consequently, the major indigenous tribes—the Caddo, Wichita, Tonkawa, and Comanche—assert their rights through the American Indian Resource and Education Coalition, an intertribal agency that has acted as a proxy only for Indian tribes formerly residing in Texas. The group is also the trustee for the Comanche National Cemetery, which occupies donated federal land and serves as a resting place for remains repatriated under NAGPRA.

Thus without a state's willing participation in and effective administration of appropriate law, Indian cultural resources at best receive only limited protection. This is especially critical if other organizations in a state respond in the negative, as did the Texas Historical Commission, which has not been supportive of nonresident Indian tribes. In fact, "The absence of Texas Indians from their aboriginal lands . . . has left the SHPO, by default, the only source of information and advice concerning compliance with NAGPRA."[67]

Perhaps because California has the most Indians of any U.S. state—more than 200,000, according to the 1990 census—it has been officially sensitive to Native American issues and concerns. About half of the Indian numbers are indigenous Californians, but only a fragment reside on trust lands. Most California Indians live in rural areas, often adjacent to reservations, or reside in urban areas, where there are concentrations of Indians in the major metropolitan areas (Los Angeles, San Diego, and the San Francisco Bay Area).[68] Although a selective number of conflicts over human remains and artifacts occur in rural areas, far more have surfaced in urban settings and relate closely to home and commercial developments and highway construction. In fact, more than thirty years ago State Archaeologist Francis A. Riddell reported that around 25 percent of heavily damaged or destroyed archaeological sites had been damaged by land leveling, another 21 percent by urban development, 17 percent by reservoir construction and related flood projects, another 17 percent by vandalism, and 10 percent by highway or road construction.[69] California passed appropriate legislation and thereby also endorsed parallel federal statutes to ameliorate negative impact on archaeological as well as other cultural resources. But most local governments have long focused emphasis on historic preservation and urban design rather than on preservation of archaeological or other sites of cultural heritage. The need in this state and elsewhere—to establish professional standards and practices in regard to such cultural resource research and protection—led to the creation of the Society of Professional Archaeologists in 1976. Also, a new branch of archaeology came about: cultural resource management.[70]

Almost all states have enacted legislation governing the protection of antiquities. Whereas most states acted only by the 1970s, California's efforts to protect and manage cultural resources began in the late 1930s and cut across the statutes—for example, the Health and Safety Code establishes a felony for mutilation, disturbance, or disinterment of human remains disturbed in the course of pot hunting;[71] the Penal Code establishes a misdemeanor for injuring or destroying objects of historic or archaeologic value on either public or private lands, but apparently the landowner is exempt from these provisions; the Public Resource Code requires that state agencies must inventory and protect state-owned historic and other resources, or otherwise the State Historical Preservation Office must be notified. California's Environmental Quality Act of 1970 offers the strongest provisions that affect the development of private land resources. This environmental legislation plays a large role in mitigating harm and loss to Indian cultural resources. The requirement in general is modeled after NEPA—an environmental impact report (EIR) must be filed whenever a project would adversely affect such resources. California also requires under its planning law that local jurisdictions, when preparing and maintaining general plans, must address land use, housing, transportation, *conservation,* open space, and the like; cultural resources are normally addressed in the conservation elements of most local as well as regional general plans.[72]

In addition to the SHPO, the Native American Heritage Commission responds to NAGPRA, which is responsible for the "preservation and protection of Native American human remains and associated grave goods." The commission is the best outlet through which Indians in the state can make known their concerns regarding the need for sensitive treatment and disposition of burials and items associated with burials. The commission serves as an advisory agency and does not acquire any land in terms of sacred or similar sites. In 1988 the state legislature amended the Public Resources Code to make it a felony for anyone to obtain or possess Native American human remains or artifacts from a grave or cairn except as otherwise provided by law.[73] In other instances the SHPO may step in or be called on to intervene with respect to Indian cultural resources.

California is also a good testing ground for the indigenous rights of native Californians who are not among the acknowledged or recognized groups. Although Indian tribes, as cultural groups, may exist without federal recognition, they must be acknowledged to take advantage of provisions, for example, in NAGPRA. Professor Carole Goldberg of the UCLA Law School disparages the limitations of NAGPRA but notes that native Californians can approach the University of California and the Native American Heritage Commission and invoke the California Environmental Quality Act in pursuit of legal support to protect indigenous cultural resources. But she concludes that new legislation is needed here and elsewhere to expand the rights of unacknowledged Indian groups.[74]

Several factors argue for legislative resolution of the complaints of unacknowledged Indian communities. For example, Indians who possess trust lands hold a stronger position in laying claim to cultural, historical, and sacred sites and materials than do their "brethren" who lack such lands. An example is the Santa Ynez Indian Reservation in Santa Barbara County, which represents only a fraction of the Chumash people, yet these acknowledged Indians assert more jurisdiction over sites and materials than other Chumash communities who live closer to the sites and can readily demonstrate their continuity with such resources. Diane Wilson, an anthropologist, encourages unrecognized Indian communities to join with the recognized tribes and use their legal status to secure repatriation of cultural resources. She notes that two interrelated definitions of recognition encumber many Indian groups. Federal recognition by the BIA, which opens the door to federal services and may lead to the establishment of trust lands, also entitles tribes and groups to the benefits of NAGPRA; unrecognized communities are characterized as "nonplayers."[75] Ethnographic recognition relates to cultural affiliation—that is, the continuity that links present-day Indians to their ancestors; NAGPRA requires proof of this continuity before repatriation becomes an acknowledged right. Wilson succinctly sums up the position of countless Indian communities: "The bottom line is that ancestral remains and memorial offerings are connected to their original context: the land itself."[76] As much as they want their ancestors' bones back, Native Americans want respect for that land, respect for the cultural resources of the land, and the recognition that both people (tribes) and their lands are still living entities today. To deny that recognition in the repatriation process is neither empirical nor ethical.[77]

Some Closing Thoughts

Native Americans have not fared nearly as well as one would hope in their quest for the protection, preservation, and repatriation of cultural resources and sacred places. A modicum of benign gestures on behalf of specific tribal communities does not represent good faith or ethnic justice on the part of federal or state agencies or the general citizenry, especially property owners. Because tribes have greater clout in developing appropriate cultural resource management within their own jurisdictions, Dean Suagee suggests that "tribal governments should perform the lead role in carrying out federal cultural resources management laws within reservation boundaries."[78] It is hoped that individual Indians and families will feel strongly enough about their own heritage that they will support the protection of such resources when discovered on allotted lands. It is unclear whether tribes can really impose restrictions on land use for those former trust lands lying within reservations borders. Surely tribes should note the negative impact of cases that denied tribal jurisdiction over so-called open areas and modify their planning objectives to embrace the protection of cultural resources no longer within trust lands yet still a part of Indian Country.

As for public lands, we have seen that few land restorations have taken place and that Indians have unsuccessfully brought suit against federal agencies in their pursuit of having lands set aside or transferred or of gaining exclusive access for religious purposes. If it has not been easy to ameliorate the impact on native cultural resources and sacred places on the public domain and been problematic in terms of fee lands within reservations, one should not expect Indians to applaud the society at large in its meager and infrequent gestures to protect and repatriate native heritage and land within the private sector. Some progress has been made, and it is hoped more progress will occur as the general populace and public officials become better informed about and more sensitive to the importance of cultural diversity to this nation.

References

1. Chief Sealth [Seattle], speech, 1851 [Washington State Historical Society], quoted in Jana Stone, ed., *Every Part of This Earth Is Sacred: Native American Voices in Praise of Nature* (New York: HarperSan Francisco, 1993): 83.

2. See Christopher Vecsey, ed., *Handbook of American Indian Religious Freedom* (New York: Crossroad, 1991); Belden C. Lane, *Landscapes of the Sacred: Geography and Narrative in American Spirituality,* chapter 2, "Seeking a Sacred Center: Places and Themes in Native American Spirituality" (New York:. Paulist, 1988): 45–65; Christopher Vecsey and Robert W. Venables, eds., *American Indian Environments: Ecological Issues in Native American History* (Syracuse: Syracuse University Press, 1980). A recent study is Andrew Gulliford, *Sacred Objects and Sacred Places: Preserving Tribal Traditions* (Boulder: University Press of Colorado, 2000).
3. Richard W. Stoffle and Michael J. Evans, "Holistic Conservation and Cultural Triage: American Indian Perspectives on Cultural Resources," *Human Organization,* 49:2 (1990): 91–99; Klara B. Kelly and Harris Francis, *Navajo Sacred Places* (Bloomington: Indiana University Press, 1994): 91–104.
4. Dean B. Suagee and Karen J. Funk, "Cultural Resources Conservation in Indian Country," special issue of *Natural Resources and Environment,* 7:4 (1993): 30–33, 61–63; "The Native American Graves Protection and Repatriation Act [NAGPRA]," symposium, *Arizona Law Journal,* 24:1 (1992); Devon A. Mihesuah, ed., "Repatriation: An Interdisciplinary Dialogue," *American Indian Quarterly,* 20:2 (1996): 153–307.
5. Jhon Goes in Center and Bryan Marozas, cochairs, "The Relevance of Tribal Aboriginal Territories in the Interpretation, Protection, and Restoration of Cultural Resources," proposed session for the meeting of the 1999 American Association for State and Local History, Baltimore, Maryland, October 1999. Copy of prepared talk sent to me by Bryan Marozas, July 1999. Goes in Center is president of Innovative GIS [Geographic Information Systems] Solutions, Inc. (Fort Collins, Colorado), and Marozas is GIS coordinator, BIA (Albuquerque, New Mexico); see also Goes in Center and Marozas, "The Role of Spatial Information in the Assessment of Cultural Affiliation," in "Native American Graves Protection and Repatriation Act," *Hearings . . . on PL 101-601,* U.S. Senate, Committee on Indian Affairs, 106th Cong., 1st sess. (Washington, DC: Government Printing Office (GPO), 1999).
6. Patrick T. Noonan, "Mining Desecration and the Protection of Indian Sacred Sites: A Lesson in First Amendment Hurdling," *University of Pittsburgh Law Review,* 50 (1990): 89ff; Robert C. Ward, "The Spirit Will Leave: Preventing the Desecration and Destruction of Native American Sacred Sites on Federal Lands," *Ecology Law Quarterly,* 19 (1992): 795–846.
7. Suagee and Funk, "Cultural Resources Conservation"; Pamela D'Innocenzo, " 'Not in My Backyard': Protecting Archaeological Sites on Private Lands," *American Indian Law Review,* 21:1 (1997): 131–155; Dean B. Suagee, "Tribal Voices in Historic Preservation: Sacred Landscapes, Cross-Cultural Bridges, and Common Ground," *Vermont Law Review,* 21 (1996): 145–224; Lydia T. Grimm, "Sacred Lands and the Establishment Clause: Indian Religious Practices on Federal Lands," *Natural Resources and Environment,* 12:1 (1997): 19–24, 78.
8. NHPA does not provide directly for Native Hawaiians comparable to provisions for Indian tribes (Native Alaskans are treated as tribes), but 1992 amendments obliged the SHPO of Hawaii to consult with Native Hawaiians. See Suagee, "Tribal Voices," p. 186. As an example at the local level, the planning department of the City of Paso Robles (California) affirmed the setting aside of a sacred site of the Chumash in the EIR for the development of a shopping center that includes a Wal-Mart. See Richard

C. Paddock, "A Clash of Cultures and Property Values," *Los Angeles Times,* June 13, 1993, A1, 14; planner Mary Oien, Paso Robles Planning Department, telephone interview, June 6, 1998.

9. Dean B. Suagee and Karen J. Funk utilize *cultural resources conservation* rather than *management* because it "reflects that the people are conserving cultural resources as well as using them in their daily lives, while management connotes detachment." "Cultural Resources Conservation in Indian Country," in Richard J. Fink, ed., *Natural Resources Law Manual* (1995): 458–459 (cited in note 345 in Suagee, "Tribal Voices," p. 211).
10. M. Annette Jaimes [Guerrero], "The Pit River Indian Claim Dispute in Northern California," *Journal of Ethnic Studies,* 14:4 (1987): 47–74; Suagee, "Tribal Voices," pp. 172–173; P. Austin, "Taking Back Katahdin: Wabenaki Claim Their Right to Worship a Big Mountain Spirit," *AMC Outdoors,* 59:9 (1993): 30–33.
11. N. Bruce Duthu, "Implicit Divestiture of Tribal Powers: Locating Legitimate Sources of Authority in Indian Country," *American Indian Law Review,* 19:2 (1994): 353–403; symposium, "Developing Resources on American Indian Lands," *Natural Resources and Environment,* 7:4 (1993).
12. Figure 7.1 attempts a schematic view of typical tribal territory as based on both original and recognized title; see Imre Sutton, "Configurations of Land Claims: Toward a Model," in Sutton, ed., *Irredeemable America: The Indians' Estate and Land Claims* (Albuquerque: University of New Mexico Press, 1985): 111–132.
13. This book does not embrace Hawaiian land issues; see Jerry Mander, *In the Absence of the Sacred: The Failure of Technology and the Survival of the Indian Nations,* chapter 18, "Desecration of Sacred Lands" (San Francisco: Sierra Club, 1991): 319–340.
14. The consensus seems to be that non-Indian holdings within reservation boundaries are not generally subject to tribal jurisdiction, but states may not intervene in just any environmental management. See Chapter 9.
15. Suagee, "Tribal Voices," pp. 205–206. On the constitution and the tribes, see John R. Wunder, *"Retained by the People": A History of American Indians and the Bill of Rights* (New York: Oxford University Press, 1994).
16. See U.S. Environmental Protection Agency, *Survey of American Indian Environmental Protection Needs on Reservation Lands: 1986* (Washington, DC: EPA, 1986); Alan S. Downer and Alexandra Roberts, "The Navajo Experience With the Federal Historic Preservation Program," *Natural Resources and Environment,* 10:3 (1996): 39–44, 78; Suagee, "Tribal Voices," p. 211.
17. The National Parks and Conservation Association emphasizes that "Wounded Knee is a site of true national significance to the American people. It should be protected and preserved for future generations." Mario Gonzalez and Elizabeth Cook-Lynn, *The Politics of Hallowed Ground: Wounded Knee and the Struggle for Indian Sovereignty* (Urbana: University of Illinois Press, 1999): 227. In 1997 a controversy arose over the construction of a monument commemorating the Indians who fought and died at the Little Bighorn Battlefield Monument. *New York Times,* August 24, 1997: I18:1, August 28, 1997: A31:1.
18. Suagee, "Tribal Voices," note 167, p. 181, lists the twelve: Hualapai (AZ), Navajo (AZ, NM, UT), Yurok (CA), Leech Lake Band of Chippewa (MN), Mille Lacs Band of Ojibwe (MN), Confederated Salish and Kootenai of the Flathead Nation (MT), Standing Rock Sioux (ND, SD), Confederated Tribes of Umatilla (OR), Confeder-

ated Tribes of Warm Springs (OR), Confederated Tribes of Colville (WA), Spokane (WA), and Lac Du Flambeau of Lake Superior Chippewa (WI). No doubt, other tribes have joined since that date.

19. Ibid., note 173, p. 182, cites the Safe Drinking Water Act; the Comprehensive Environmental Response, Compensation, and Liability Act; Clean Water Act; Clean Air Act. John S. Harbison, "The Downstream People: Treating Indian Tribes as States Under the Clean Water Act," *North Dakota Law Review,* 71 (1995): 473–495.
20. Steven Elkinton and Donald C. Maglinenti, "Preserving America's Historic Trails," *Historic Preservation Foundation,* July-August 1994, cited in Suagee, "Tribal Voices."
21. Personal phone interview with Dr. Jack Campisi, anthropologist, technical adviser to the Mashantucket Pequot, spring 1997; Suagee, "Tribal Voices," pp. 212–213; Anne-Marie d'Hauteserre, "Foxwoods Casino Resort: An Unusual Experiment in Economic Development," *Economic Geography,* extra issue (1998): 112–121. On archaeological research, see *New York Times,* September 1, 1997: A1:2.
22. Walter E. Stern and Lynn H. Slade, "Effects of Historic and Cultural Resources and Indian Religious Freedom on Public Lands Development: A Practical Primer," *Natural Resources Journal,* 35 (1995): 133–183; Suagee and Funk, "Cultural Resources Conservation."
23. Native American Intergovernmental Relations Task Force, *Assessment of Corps/Tribal Intergovernmental Relations,* Interim Report, IWR 96-R-6 (Washington, DC: U.S. Army Corps of Engineers, 1996).
24. Kelley and Francis, *Navajo Sacred Places,* p. 151; Stoffle and Evans, "Holistic Conservation"; Downer and Roberts, "The Navajo Experience"; Stephen C. Jett, "Navajo Sacred Places: Management and Interpretation of Mythic History," *Public Historian,* 17:2 (1995): 39–47.
25. Stoffle and Evans, "Holistic Conservation," p. 158.
26. Quoted in Downer and Roberts, "The Navajo Experience," p. 78.
27. Jett, "Navajo Sacred Places," pp. 45, 47.
28. E. Richard Hart, ed., *Zuni and the Courts: A Struggle for Sovereign Land Rights* (Lawrence: University Press of Kansas, 1995); telephone interview with Dr. Hart, June 21, 1995; T. J. Ferguson and Cal A. Seciwa, "Zuni," in M. Davis, ed., *Native America in the Twentieth Century: An Encyclopedia* (New York: Garland, 1991): 723–727.
29. Kurt E. Dongoske, Leigh Jenkins, and T. J. Ferguson, "Issues Relating to the Use and Preservation of Hopi Sacred Sites," *Historic Preservation Forum,* 8:2 (1994): 12–14.
30. Kelley and Francis, *Navajo Sacred Places,* pp. 152–153.
31. 12 F. 3d 737 (8th Cir. 1993, *cert. denied,* 115 S. Ct. 61 (1994). See Allison M. Dussias, "Science, Sovereignty, and the Sacred Text: Paleontological Resources and Native American Rights," *Maryland Law Review,* 55 (1996): 84–159.
32. Dussias, "Science, Sovereignty," p. 88.
33. Ibid., p. 125 (note 290). According to Dussias, "Archaeologists have demonstrated similar attitudes toward Native American rights and tribal interests" [quoting James Riding In, "Without Ethics and Morality: A Historical Overview of Imperial Archaeology and American Indians," *Arizona State Law Journal,* 24 (1992): 11]. This fossil was auctioned by Sotheby's in New York for a winning bid of $7.6 million, and the fossil was to be housed at Chicago's Field Museum of Natural History. The Indian on whose allotment the fossil was found is the beneficiary of the sale. David Roberts, "Digging for Dinosaur Gold," *Smithsonian,* 28:12 (1998): 40–53.

34. Dussias, "Science, Sovereignty," p. 123 (note 286).
35. The ensuing discussion does not include questions of Indians' killing of wildlife for religious purposes, although wildlife plays an important role in Indian traditional lifeways. See Tina S. Boradianisky, "Conflicting Values: The Religious Killing of Federally Protected Wildlife," *Natural Resources Journal,* 30 (1990): 729–732.
36. Suagee, "Tribal Voices," pp. 207–208.
37. For a general discussion of land restorations and sacred sites, including Blue Lake and Mt. Adams, see Imre Sutton, "Incident or Event? Land Restoration in the Claims Process," in *Irredeemable America,* pp. 211–232. In recent years the Taos Pueblo has administered the Blue Lake Wilderness as a religious sanctuary and has developed forest management plans for lands once part of Kit Carson National Forest. Veronica E. Velarde Tiller, ed., *Tiller's Guide to Indian Country: Economic Profiles of American Indian Reservations* (Albuquerque: BowArrow, 1996): 466.
38. Mark Spence, "Dispossessing the Wilderness: Yosemite Indians and the National Park Ideal, 1864–1930," *Pacific Historical Review,* 65 (February 1996): 27–59; also Bruce J. Noble Jr., "A Legacy of Distrust: The Ute Mountain Utes and the Boundaries of Mesa Verde National Park," *Colorado Heritage* [journal of the Colorado Historical Society] (summer 1995): 32–42. For a current controversy, see Stephen Crum, "A Tripartite State of Affairs: The Timbisha Shoshone Tribe, the National Park Service, and the Bureau of Indian Affairs, 1933–1994," *American Indian Culture and Research Journal,* 22:1 (1998): 117–136; Steven Haberfeld, "Government-to-Government Negotiations: How the Timbisha Shoshone Got Its Land Back," *American Indian Culture and Research Journal,* 24:4 (2000): 127–165.
39. Besides Austin, "Taking Back Katahdin"; D'Innocenzo, "Not in My Backyard," p. 153; Stern and Slade, "Effects of Historic and Cultural Resources"; Sutton, "Incident or Event," see Ann M. Hooker, "American Indian Sacred Sites on Federal Public Lands: Resolving Conflicts Between Religious Use and Multiple Use at El Malpais National Monument," *American Indian Law Review,* 19:1 (1994): 133–158; Edward Lazarus, *Black Hills, White Justice: The Sioux Nation Versus the United States, 1775 to the Present* (New York: HarperCollins, 1991); George Lubick, "Sacred Mountains, *Kachinas,* and Skiers: The Controversy Over the San Francisco Peaks," in R. Lora, ed., *The American West: Essays in Honor of W. Eugene Hollon* (Toledo: University of Toledo Press, 1980): 133–153; Daniel McCool, "Federal Indian Policy and the Sacred Mountains of the Papago Indians," *Journal of Ethnic Studies,* 9:3 (1981): 57–69.
40. President William J. Clinton, "Executive Order 13007—Indian Sacred Places," May 24, 1996, *Weekly Compilation of Presidential Documents,* 32 (May 27, 1996): 942–943; Grimm, "Sacred Lands," pp. 24, 78.
41. Tony Perry, "Rights and Rites Clash in Mine Plan," *Los Angeles Times,* February 9, 1998: A3, A21–22.
42. See a special issue of *Cultural Survival Quarterly,* winter 1996; also Suagee, "Tribal Voices," pp. 163–167.
43. Pauline Arrillaga, "Treading on Holy Ground: Indians Fight to Protect Sacred Sites From Competing Interests," *Missoulian,* July 23, 2000: E1, E9. See also Chapter 11 and the discussion of Hopi shrines on the Kaibab National Forest.
44. Suagee, "Tribal Voices," cites the views of a Professor Robert Williams, who notes that the lack of success in preventing desecration of the sacred site resulted from the presentation by university scientists who were talking about fundamental questions

of the universe. Apaches talked about the *Gaans,* which helps them imagine their relationship to Mt. Graham, to which Williams commented, "Our environmental law is simply incapable of reflecting the types of connection that the story of the Gaans on Mt. Graham can teach us" (p. 167). Suagee takes exception: environmental law is not incapable, for "NHPA provides a framework in which tribal voices can explain why a sacred mountain . . . matters. . . . It can do this by bringing our stories into the processes through which federal officials and others make decisions that affect places which hold religious or cultural importance for tribes. . . . In my view, using NHPA to protect such places is more likely to prove successful if we keep in mind the need to share at least some of our stories with the larger American society, and if we never lose sight of the power that our stories hold." Ibid. With respect to Mt. Adams, see Sutton, "Incident or Event," p. 216, figure 9. 1, which shows the reconfigured wilderness to enclose part of it within the Yakama Indian Reservation. Discussion is on p. 215.

45. Hart, *Zuni and the Courts,* esp. chapters 19 and 20. The sacred site became a formal part, albeit noncontiguous, of the Zuni Indian Reservation, held in trust. Figure 7.3 is based on maps provided by the Bureau of Land Management, Tucson, Arizona, and the interpolation of map data in both Hart, *Zuni and the Courts,* and Ferguson and Seciwa, "Zuni."
46. Ward, "The Spirit Will Leave," pp. 803, 806; 620 F.2d 1159 (6th Cir. 1980), *cert. denied,* 449 U.S. 953 (1980).
47. Donald Worster, *Under Western Skies: Nature and History in the American West,* chapter 8, "The Black Hills: Sacred or Profane?" (New York: Oxford University Press, 1992): 106–153, quotes on pp. 145, 147, 150. *Sioux Nation of Indians v. United States,* 862 F.2d 275 (Fed. Cir. 1988).
48. Cf. Kimla McDonald, "Sacred Land in Environmental Planning," *Environmental Professional,* 9 (1987): 27–32; *Wilson v. Block,* 708 F.2d 735 (D.C. Cir. 1983), *cert. denied,* 464 U.S. 1056 (1984).
49. *Lyng v. Northwest Indian Cemetery Protective Assn.,* 485 U.S. 439 (1988); Stoffle and Evans, "Holistic Conservation." One group, the Pit River Indians, still rejects the monetary award of land claims litigation and has sought to regain traditional lands within the Six Rivers National Forest. See Jaimes, "The Pit River." See also David H. Getches, Charles F. Wilkinson, and Robert A. Williams Jr., *Cases and Materials on Federal Indian Law,* 4th ed. (St. Paul: West, 1998): 754–768.
50. Ward, "The Spirit Will Leave," pp. 310–315; Suagee, "Tribal Voices," pp. 218–219, notes the contrary positions taken by SHPOs, wherein the California SHPO supported Indians in Six Rivers National Forest, yet the Arizona SHPO opposed tribal contentions for the San Francisco Peaks.
51. Vine Deloria Jr. and David E. Wilkins, *Tribes, Treaties, and Constitutional Tribulations* (Austin: University of Texas Press, 1999), quote on p. 120; *Bear Lodge Multiple Use Ass'n. v. Babbitt,* 96 CV-063 (D. Wyo 1996), 175 Fed 3d 814 (10th Cir. 1999); Grimm, "Sacred Lands." See also Joel Brady, " 'Land Is Itself a Sacred, Living Being': Native American Sacred Site Protection on Federal Public Lands Amidst the Shadows of *Bear Lodge,*" *American Indian Law Review,* 24:1 (1999–2000): 153–189. Brady identifies several other sacred sites that are in contention: the "Great Kiva" at Chaco Canyon National Historic Park, "Lions' Shrine" in Bandelier National Monument, and others. Quote on p. 181.

52. Grimm, "Sacred Lands," p. 20, cites *Havasupai Tribe v. Robertson,* 943 F. 2d 32 (9th Cir. 1991), *cert. denied,* 503 U.S. 959 (1992), in which development of a uranium mine on the Kaibab National Forest in an area sacred to the Havasupai was not deemed an unconstitutional burden.
53. Grimm, "Sacred Lands," p. 22 (emphasis added).
54. Ibid., p. 24. For more discussion of the Bald and Golden Eagle Protection Act, see the Prologue in this book, p. 12.
55. *Crow v. Gullet,* 541 F. Supp. 785 (D.S.D. 1982), *cert. denied,* 464 U.S. 977 (1983); Ward, "The Spirit Will Leave," p. 802.
56. Michael Flagg, "Differing Reports Often Are Bone of Contention," *Los Angeles Times,* September 27, 1993, A20–21, quote attributed to Keith Polakoff, associate vice president, California State University, Long Beach (CSULB), p. A21.
57. Jill Gottesman, "Plans to Build on Indian Site Blocked," *Los Angeles Times,* August 15, 1993, A24–25; phone interview with Assistant Vice President Toni Beron, CSULB, February 5, 1997. In 1994 the State Court of Appeals upheld a lower court decision to prevent any further archaeological survey of the disputed site. The suit was filed by the American Civil Liberties Union and the NAHC. As of spring 2001, no policy change has been reported by the university administration.
58. Austin, "Taking Back Katahdin."
59. Catherine B. Yalung and Laurel I. Wala, "A Survey of State Repatriation and Burial Protection Statutes," *Arizona State Law Journal,* 24:1 (1992): 419–433. This issue offers a symposium on NAGPRA. With reference to archaeology D'Innocenzo observes that "cultural protective statutes address only those cultural treasures located on federal or Indian land—virtually no meaningful protection is extended over those artifacts unfortunate enough to be located on privately owned property." "Not in My Backyard," p. 133. Herein she discusses the conservation easement of South Dakota, which other states such as Idaho, Maryland, and Rhode Island have introduced, noting that operating as a negative easement the holder can enforce its terms against landowners to protect cultural or historic sites. Wunder, *Retained by the People,* reports that Nebraska passed the most comprehensive act, under which the Pawnee successfully reinterred more than 400 ancestors (p. 209); see also Mihesuah, "Repatriation."
60. Yalung and Wala, "A State Survey of Repatriation." As an example, tribal representatives and federal officials reburied remains dating back to the eleventh century that were excavated during a construction project near Cincinnati, Ohio. Around twenty-five Indians and various tribes participated. *New York Times,* May 27, 1997, p. D12.
61. This section is freely adapted from Harvey Arden, "Who Owns the Past?" *National Geographic,* 175:3 (1989): 376–393; for maps and text of Mississippian culture, see Michael Coe, Dean Snow, and Elizabeth Benson, *Atlas of Ancient America* (New York: Facts on File, 1986): 51, 54. The locale is part of the Crab Orchard Hopewellian and Middle Mississippian.
62. Quoted in Arden, "Who Owns the Past," p. 383. Cf. Yalung and Wala, "A Survey of State Repatriation." Also see *United States v. Gerber,* 999 F 2d 1112 (7th Cir. 1993), *cert. denied,* 510 U.S. 1071 (1994).
63. D'Innocenzo, "Not in My Backyard," p. 139.
64. Many tribes made considerable legal use of archaeological evidence in an effort to delimit original territory as part of their land claim before the Indian Claims Commission; Sutton, *Irredeemable America.*

65. Steve Russell, "The Legacy of Ethnic Cleansing: Implementation of NAGPRA in Texas," *American Indian Culture and Research Journal,* 19:4 (1995): 193–211, quote on p. 194; cf. Yalung and Wala, "The Survey of State Repatriation," pp. 419–433; D'Innocenzo, "Not in My Backyard."
66. Russell, "The Legacy," p. 197.
67. Ibid., p. 204.
68. A good general overview is provided by Dolan H. Eargle Jr., *California Indian Country: The Land and the People* (San Francisco: Trees Company, 1992).
69. Francis A. Riddell, "The State Administered Archaeological Program in California," in F. Curtis, ed., *Symposium on Central California Archaeology: Problems, Programs, and Interdisciplinary Approaches* (Sacramento: Sacramento Anthropological Society and Central California Archaeology Foundation, 1965): 1–4.
70. Leslie Mouriquand Blodgett, "Planning for Community Archaeology: Its Applications to the Eastern Coachella Valley," Masters thesis in anthropology, California State University, Fullerton, 1991, pp. 4–5; on earlier efforts see Imre Sutton, "Geographical Aspects of Construction Planning: *Hoover Dam Revisited,*" *Journal of the West,* 7:3 (1968): 301–344.
71. *California Statutes 1939*: 60: 672; see also *California Public Resources Code,* § 5097.9 (St. Paul: West, 1984).
72. Blodgett, "Planning for Community Archaeology," pp. 27–33; Yalung and Wala, "The Survey of State Repatriation," pp. 421–423. Where public and private lands intermingle, see Bureau of Land Management, *The California Desert Conservation Area Plan, 1980* (Riverside: BLM, 1980): pp. 22–29.
73. From "A Professional Guide" [brochure] (Sacramento: Native American Heritage Commission, 1994); telephone interview with Gail McNulty, NAHC, Sacramento, September 21, 1995. See supplement to *California Public Resources Code,* § 5097.9 (1988). Cf. Yalung and Wala, "The Survey of State Repatriation."
74. The role of law vis-à-vis Native California rights is discussed in Carole Goldberg, "Acknowledging the Repatriation Claims of Unacknowledged California Tribes," *American Indian Culture and Research Journal,* 21:3 (1997): 183–190.
75. Diane D. Wilson, "California Indian Participation in Repatriation: Working Toward Recognition," *American Indian Culture and Research Journal,* 21:3 (1997): 191–209, esp. pp. 202–206.
76. Wilson, "California Indian Participation," p. 195.
77. Ibid., p. 206.
78. Suagee, "Tribal Voices," p. 224.

Chapter 8

A Sovereign Prescription for Preservation: The Mission Mountains Tribal Wilderness*

Diane L. Krahe

Unfettered by foothills, the Mission Mountains' western front appears to pull upward from the Mission Valley like a great line of surf, frozen just before it crests and crashes. Dark arms of forest buttress the Missions' bald, angular mountaintops, white capped year-round with snowfields and a few receding glaciers. Among a dozen 9,000-foot peaks congregated toward its southern end, the range's tallest mountain, McDonald Peak, at nearly 10,000 feet, looms a full mile and a third over the Mission Valley. The divide of this narrow string of mountains in northwestern Montana marks the eastern edge of the 1.3 million-acre Flathead Reservation, home to the Kootenai, lower Pend d'Oreille, and Salish Tribes (Figure 8.1).

As a 1990 study of tribal politics on the seven Montana reservations recaps, "Native American life generally . . . has been a story of attempted recovery from savage assaults of various kinds, and in this respect the Indians of the Flathead reservation are typical."[1] But the story of the Confederated Salish and Kootenai Tribes generally has been a bit brighter than most, in part because they have adjusted well to change, given their openness to it. Their "native disposition to borrow and adapt, marked by progressive admixture and assimilation," as the study describes the tribes,[2] has known few religious, political, or economic boundaries.

As a result, the Confederated Salish and Kootenai Tribes are represented by one of the most efficient, autonomous Indian governments in the United States and are sustained by a healthy coffer of funds, largely because of their savvy

*This chapter is based mostly on Diane L. Krahe, "A Confluence of Sovereignty and Conformity: The Mission Mountains Tribal Wilderness," M.S. thesis in environmental studies, University of Montana, Missoula, 1995.

Fig. 8.1 Mission Mountains Tribal Wilderness (Montana). Looking east from the Mission Valley into the middle portion of the tribal wilderness, with Mount Calowahcan most prominent. Photo taken by Diane L. Krahe, 1994.

management of the reservation's bountiful and renewable water and timber resources. As well as procuring profits, the tribes' extensive natural resource program also attests to the environmental progression. In 1980, for example, the Flathead Reservation was only the second in the nation to be granted Class I air status by the federal government, which allows for no degradation in air quality, keeping nearly all industry at bay. And in 1984 the tribes declared their reservation a nuclear-free zone, the first reservation to do so.[3]

But above this regulated modern world, high in the Mission Mountains, Eagle still soars and cunning Coyote still saunters between mountain peaks named for a diverse cast, including the Virgin Mary; Angus McDonald, a Scotsman who opened the valley's first trading post in the 1840s; and Kakashe, a respected tribal judge in the early 1900s. Certainly by name, the Mission Mountains have not altogether escaped the inroads white society has made on the nearby valleys and on the valleys' Native people. Yet the inhospitable, rugged terrain of the Mission Mountains has deterred much of the technological affront, in terms of farming and logging, that has transformed the rest of the reservation's landscape. To the Confederated Salish and Kootenai Tribes, the towering mountains stand as a timeless backdrop to contemporary tribal life. According to a statement of policy issued by the tribal government in the early 1980s, the Mission Range harbors "the essence of traditional Indian religion and has served the Indian people of these Tribes as a place to hunt, as a place to gather medicinal herbs and roots, as a vision-seeking ground, as a sanctuary, and in countless other ways for thousands of years."[4]

In 1982 the Tribal Council of the Confederated Salish and Kootenai Tribes passed an ordinance that withdrew nearly 90,000 acres of the Mission Mountains' western front from logging and other development and consecrated it the Mission Mountains Tribal Wilderness.[5] This area—tribally designated and tribally managed—offers an innovative model for preserving the natural integrity of Indian lands on Indian terms, although the model is closely aligned with the ultimate level of landscape protection prescribed for federal lands, in the name of Wilderness (Fig. 8.2).

The Mission Mountains Tribal Wilderness itself is only a tiny accession to the 103 million acres of land within the United States that have received this highest protection status outlined by Congress in the Wilderness Act of 1964. Most of this acreage is within national forests and parks and on national wildlife refuges.[6] After centuries of general contemplation concerning the goodness or wickedness of "wildness" in our surroundings and after eight years of intense national deliberation, the passage of the 1964 act lent a legal definition to *federal* wilderness. A concept that had long spanned the spectrum of Euro-American feeling, from loathed barrier of progress to precious sanctum, wilderness at last won its legitimate place in American culture. The legislation sketched a blueprint for saving those *public* lands valued for their

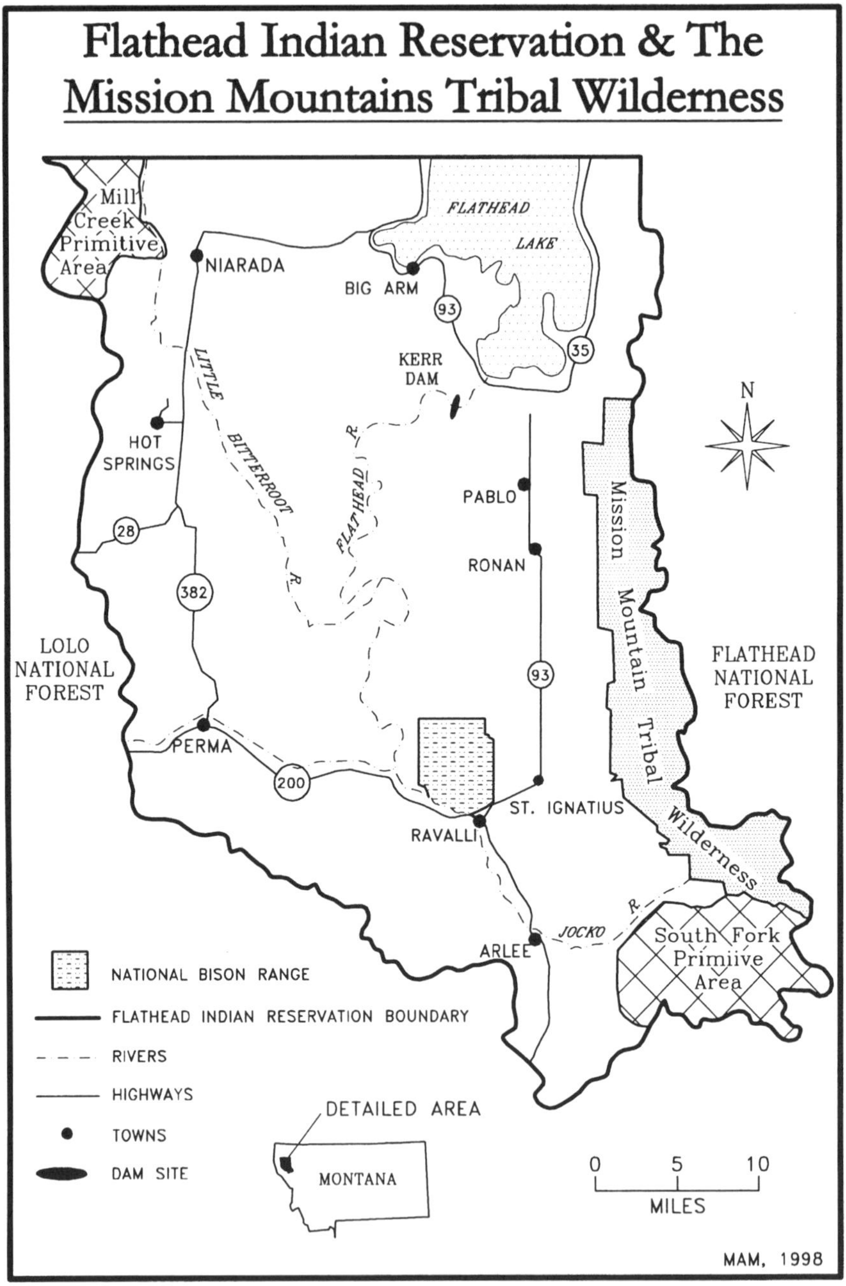

Fig. 8.2 Flathead Indian Reservation and the Mission Mountains Tribal Wilderness (Montana). Special land designations on the Flathead Indian Reservation include the Mission Mountains Tribal Wilderness, the South Fork and Mill Creek Primitive Areas (open to tribal members only), and the National Bison Range, a popular tourist destination.

undeveloped and scenic character from "expanding settlement and growing mechanization."[7]

This elevated status of wilderness came about when precious little American soil was left untouched by agricultural, industrial, and residential advances and when the nation could afford to forgo any potential economic benefit of those lands, however minor. Only then did our collective conscience finally cast a wary eye to the questionable future our technological ambitions impose on us. Reduce this national scenario to the microcosm of a single Indian reservation, and the motivation behind the *creation of the* Mission Mountains Tribal Wilderness does not wander far from the legacy of the federally owned remnants of the former "wilderness continent," although the designation of this unique tribal wilderness in the early 1980s was a sovereign choice of the Confederated Salish and Kootenai Tribes.

Typical of the heritage of the Confederated Salish and Kootenai, the tribes borrowed significantly from the federal wilderness model in creating their own tribal wilderness management plan for the Mission Mountains. This borrowing is most obvious in the tribes' statement defining wilderness, which is nearly identical to the Wilderness Act's wording, and their use of federal procedures to monitor and mitigate recreational use. But the tribes chose selectively, incorporating only those federal principles and tools that serve the explicit needs of their tribal wilderness and their culturally specific wilderness values.

Original management policies, further minimizing human interference in the natural processes of the Missions' west side, round out the management plan. For example, a 10,000-acre cross-section of the tribal wilderness, which surrounds McDonald Peak and includes some of the range's most spectacular backcountry, is off-limits to all recreational use every year from July to October so the grizzly bears can have to themselves this haven the tribes have designated the Grizzly Bear Conservation Zone. The other perennial wilderness closure is a ban on saddle and pack animals from the entire area from March 1 to June 30 for erosion control. A comparison of the tribal wilderness with the federal Mission Mountains Wilderness Area on the east side of the range, part of the Flathead National Forest, reveals two related but notably different management approaches presiding over these opposite slopes of the same mountain ecosystem.

The vast majority of the tribes' designated wilderness, like most mountain wilderness areas, is basically an economic wasteland: too high, too inaccessible, and too rocky for logging, grazing, and other multiple uses common to many public lands. This "rocks and ice" characterization of many wilderness areas accounts for their marginal value as wildlife habitat as well. Animal presence atop these alpine showcases dwindles after the short summer season, when many species must descend to wintering grounds in lower, more hospitable territory. To date, scenic and recreational values have prompted most of the wilderness designations across the country, priorities advocates of biological diversity scorn.[8] To protect a wider range of wildlife habitat and for aesthetic reasons, the tribes included some commercially productive timberlands in their wilderness and undoubtedly forfeited some financial gain by doing so. But the bulk of the tribal wilderness, by sheer topographical intimidation alone, was already relatively safe from human exploitation.

The Mission Mountains Tribal Wilderness fits the basic profile of classic American wilderness, yet there is no denying the uniqueness of this wilderness, both in its tribally ordained inception and in its pliable, autonomous management, dictated by the tribes' view and value of their mountains, of their home. The Salish, Pend d'Oreille, and Kootenai peoples have a long history here and a much more personal stake in their tribal wilderness than the American public at large has in the National Wilderness Preservation System. "We realize the importance of these mountains to our elders, to ourselves, and for the perpetuation of our Indian culture because of [our] stories," the Flathead Culture Committee summarized in its 1978 statement supporting the proposed wilderness. The statement continued:

> [The Mission Mountains] are lands where our people walked and lived. Lands and landmarks carved through the minds of our ancestors through Coyote stories and actual experiences. Lands, landmarks, trees, mountain tops, crevices that we should look up to with respect. . . . They have become for us, the descendants of Indians, sacred ground.[9]

Today, most of these descendants are content to look up to the vertical sacred ground of the Missions' west face from the valley below instead of venturing into its harsh terrain themselves. Therefore tribal members value most the scenic beauty of the Missions (as experienced from the valley below) and the intrinsic worth of the range's wildlife, trees, and water. It is fitting, then, that the tribes choose to sanctify their mountains in the name of wilderness—defined by federal law as a sublime landscape unspoiled by human presence, where humans do not belong except for brief visits. Yet this American ideal has little traditional grounding for an indigenous people whose ancestors did not separate themselves from the land, for the good of the land or for the good of the people.

The Confederated Salish and Kootenai Tribes have encased their contemporary cultural and spiritual values of the Mission Mountains within the protective construct of Wilderness, a symbol borrowed from the mainstream Western mentality. But the circumstances leading to the Confederated Salish and Kootenai's sovereign decision to protect their mountains in the name of wilderness reveal that the Mission Mountains Tribal Wilderness also embodies the ambitious pragmatism of tribal politics and economics. Although logging threats to the most scenic Mission slopes in the 1970s prompted the tribes to create their own wilderness, this story actually begins several decades earlier in the Washington, D.C., headquarters of the Indian Office, where wilderness advocates aspired to include Indian lands in their scheme for a national wilderness system.

The National Wilderness Movement and Reservation Lands

The American Wilderness Movement, which took definitive shape in the mid-twentieth century, was just beginning to be nailed down to the new science of ecology and governmental management in the 1930s. In 1929 the U.S. Forest Service created its first system of protected lands, although local district foresters still made their own decisions about specific restrictions on logging, grazing, and road construction within these remote areas labeled either "primitive" or "wild." In 1931, 67,000 acres of the east slope of the Mission Range, on national forestland, gained official recognition as the Mission Mountains Primitive Area. U.S. Forester Aldo Leopold, a primary force behind this first step toward a national policy for wilderness preservation, advocated "protecting wild country . . . [as] a matter of scientific necessity as well as sentiment,"[10] referring to the growing appreciation of "unspoiled" landscapes first popularized by Romantic writers and Transcendentalists of the nineteenth century.

An uncanny concentration of Leopold's peers, the nation's most vocal and influential champions of wilderness, held the highest positions in the Department of the Interior's Indian Office in the 1930s. Among these wilderness cronies were John Collier, the progressive new commissioner of Indian Affairs; Collier's assistant commissioner, William Zimmerman Jr.; and Bob Marshall, chief forester of the Indian Office. While implementing the Indian Reorganization Act (IRA) of 1934—designed to foster political and economic autonomy, as well as cultural revitalization, on reservations—these men made the most of their powerful posts by promoting the wilderness cause on Indian reservations.

In October 1937 Secretary of the Interior Harold Ickes approved an administrative order from the Indian Office that established twelve "roadless" areas, each over 100,000 acres, and four smaller "wild" areas on undeveloped reservation lands. Marshall, the leading wilderness advocate in the United States, drafted the policy, which was easily seconded by the like-minded Collier, Zimmerman, and Ickes. It affected a dozen reservations and encompassed 4.8 million acres of Indian land.[11]

Among the new designations was the 125,000-acre Mission Range Roadless Area (Figure 8.3a), which encompassed the Flathead Reservation's western slope of the Mission Mountains and comprised about 10 percent of the reservation's total area. The largest of all the roadless designations was the Navajo's Rainbow Bridge Roadless Area, covering 1.6 million acres of desert in both Arizona and Utah. At the other end of the acreage spectrum was the Cape Flattery Wild Area, a 6,000-acre section of the Makah Reservation jutting into the Pacific Ocean from the northwest corner of the Olympic Peninsula in Washington.

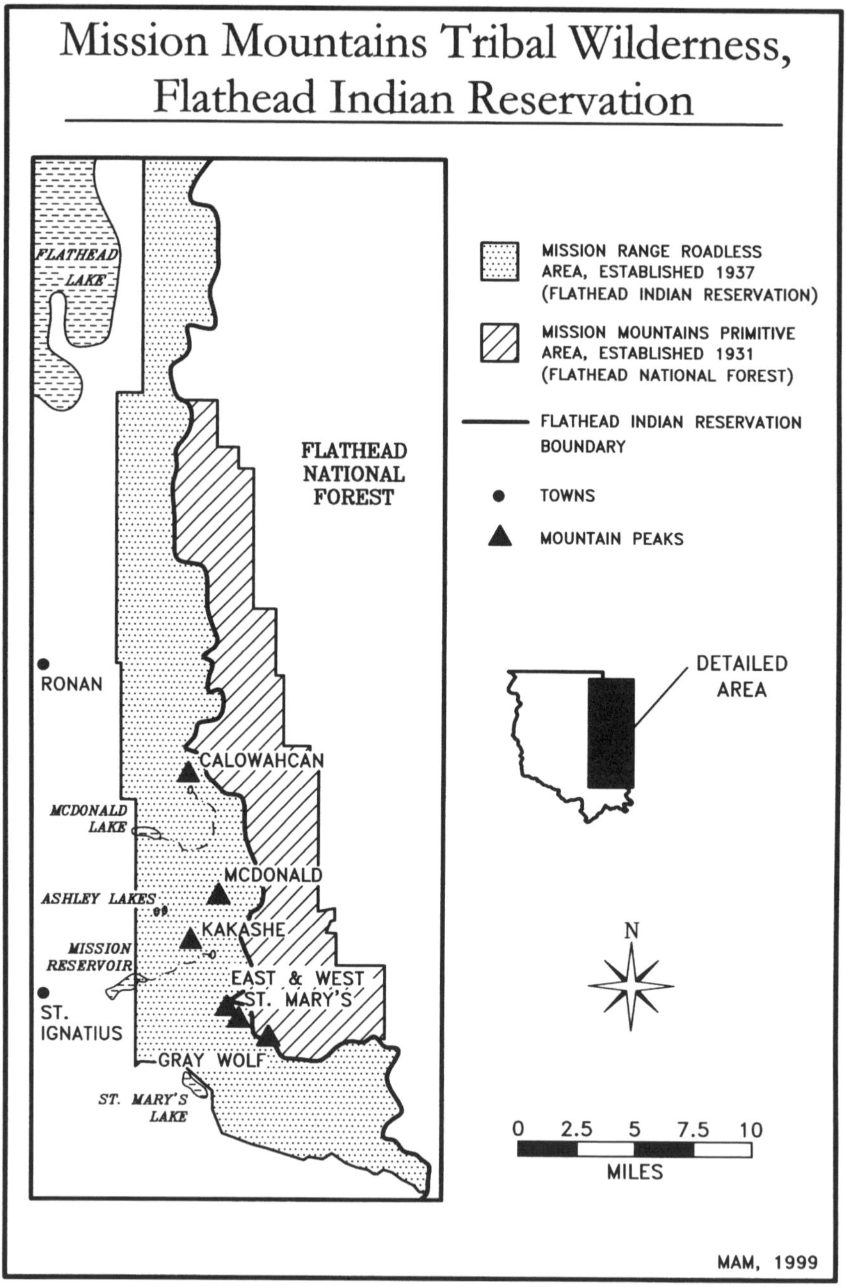

Fig. 8.3a Mission Mountains Tribal Wilderness, Flathead Indian Reservation. By the end of the 1930s, the federal government had assigned protective status to both sides of the Mission Range: the eastern slope was designated as a federal "primitive area" and the western slope as an Indian "roadless area."

The energetic, flamboyant Marshall had found time to survey all these Indian areas over the preceding few summers while touring reservations to carry out his more official duties as the Indian Office's chief forester. In these Indian lands of "almost unbelievable scenery," Marshall wrote, he exercised his famous zeal for wilderness excursions, sometimes squeezing 30-mile day hikes into his touring schedule.[12]

On the side, Marshall had been actively lobbying Secretary of the Interior Ickes to appoint a wilderness planning board to study federal lands and recommend certain areas for Congress to set aside legislatively as wilderness, just like national parks. In addition to public lands, this larger wilderness scheme included undeveloped trust lands on Indian reservations: the newly established roadless and wild areas. "Since Indian cultures had evolved in wilderness, it seemed to him very consistent with the Indian New Deal to deem some reservation lands roadless," wrote Marshall's biographer, James Glover.[13] Indeed, this roadless policy was in line with the Collier administration's goals. The Indian commissioner's unshakable conviction to revive "traditional" Indian culture, which he believed included the preservation of wilderness, justified all paternalistic means to make it happen. And in terms of the new Indian roadless areas, the larger American public could benefit as well.

Marshall's roadless order for Indian lands spoke passionately on behalf of the "millions" of Americans who "cannot believe . . . it is necessary to make every nook and corner of the country a part of the machine world and to wipe out all sizable traces of the primitive." About a third of the way into the document outlining the policy, "the standpoint of the Indian" was addressed:

> Almost everywhere they go the Indians encounter the competition and disturbances of the white race. Most of them desire some place which is all their own. If, on reservations where the Indians desire privacy, sizable areas are uninvaded by roads, then it will be possible for the Indians of these tribes to maintain a retreat where they may escape from constant contact with white men.[14]

Although the roadless areas were to serve as a reprieve from the white world for Indians, Marshall believed these areas could also generate tribal income by drawing non-Indian visitors into the backcountry. His order touted the new employment opportunities the roadless areas would present for tribal members willing to act as guides for non-Indians wishing to explore these dramatic, remote landscapes. "It is obvious that no one is going to require a guide to travel down a road," the order read, reiterating the need to keep the areas "in a wild enough condition so that some one visiting them might conceivably need a guide."[15]

The Indian Office, not the Indian tribes, would maintain these "retreats" for both tribal members and the larger American public by the following means:

> Existing areas without road or settlement on Indian reservations should be preserved in such a condition, unless the requirement of fire protection, commercial use for the Indians' benefit, or actual need of the Indians clearly demand otherwise. . . . It will be the policy of the Interior Department to refuse consent to the construction or establishment of any route passable to motor transportation [within these areas].[16]

Shortly after this announcement in late 1937, letters of gratitude from representatives of those "millions" of advocates of "the primitive" crossed the desks of Collier and Ickes. From the far corners of the United States, conservation groups praised Collier for his gutsy move to preserve "wilderness, wherever found," as Robert Sterling Yard, president of the (new) Wilderness Society, put it.[17]

But on the reservations, reviews of the new roadless and wild areas were not so glowing. The primary source of Indians' discontent? Tribal members, including tribal leaders, were never asked if they desired privacy, if their contemporary cultural values of these landscapes were in agreement with Collier administration policy, or if they wanted the economic limitations that accompanied these road-building moratoriums.

Before Ickes unveiled the roadless order, the Department of the Interior's Solicitor's Office and the Indian Office had debated the legality of making these designations without consent of the tribes. The IRA had guaranteed every tribal council the right to advise and consult the Department of the Interior on all matters affecting their reservations. Would this order be skirting the tribes' right to participate? Acting Solicitor Frederic Kirgis requested that the order's wording concerning "absolutely no roads" be softened. The Indian Office complied. With the reminder that the Indian Office would allow development within these areas if tribes demonstrated sufficient need and the reassurance that the proposed order was "simply an announcement of policy guiding departmental action," Kirgis let slide the legal technicalities concerning tribal consent.[18] Ultimately, the Indian tribes would not tolerate this dismissal.

The Confederated Salish and Kootenai Tribes first formally protested "the setting aside of a Wilderness and Roadless Area [their Mission Range Roadless Area] without the approval of the Tribal Council" in 1939. Tribal Resolution No. 157 reminded Collier that a few years earlier, the Confederated Salish and Kootenai had requested that the Mission Range be preserved as a recreational park, given "that the Tribe should have exclusive control at all times." (This request had drawn no response from the Indian Office.) In contrast, the Tribal Council saw the designation of the Mission Range Roadless Area by the federal government as an "action . . . contrary to the Constitution and By-laws of the Tribe," which the Confederated Salish and Kootenai had devised only a few years before as the first tribal nation to accept the IRA guidelines for self-government.[19] As had the tribes' proposal to make a park of their mountains, this early protest against the Mission Range Roadless Area fell on deaf ears in Washington. For the next twenty years all tribes with roadless designations had to appeal case by case to the national Indian Office concerning any development within their roadless areas, and Interior granted very few requests for even minor improvements.[20]

Even as the economic potential of portions of the Indian lands increased after World War II, tribal frustration over the roadless restrictions found no substantial voice until the late 1950s, when early versions of what would become the Wilderness Act of 1964 proposed that the Indian roadless areas be part of a national system of wilderness protected by law in perpetuity. At this point all but one of the tribes encumbered with a roadless designation protested loudly and convincingly. The tribes' resentment over inclusion of their tribal lands in national wilderness legislation proved powerful enough to reverse Marshall and Collier's twenty-year-old policy to preserve Indian wilderness.

The first wilderness bill introduced to the U.S. Congress in 1956 included the existing Indian roadless areas if the respective Indian governments "consented," but the final bill that became law eight years later made no mention of Indian lands. Congress considered a total of sixty-five wilderness bills before it passed the Wilderness Act of 1964, which served as the ordination of the National Wilderness Preservation System. Lands included in the system would be off-limits to most development indefinitely or until the unlikely passage of a law rescinding the protective status of an area. The Wilderness Act had survived the battery of its numerous opponents—industry, the Forest Service, the National Park Service, and Indian tribes among them—but not without compromise. It deviated significantly from what wilderness purists had proposed with the first wilderness bill. Among the concessions was the exclusion of the 5 million acres of Indian roadless areas—8 percent of the original 65 million acres proposed for wilderness status back in 1956.[21] At the end of this long legislative saga, Indian reservation lands were no longer part of the national blueprint "to secure for the American people of present and future generations the benefits of an enduring resource of wilderness."[22]

Many Indians saw this exclusion as a victory, an escape from "the mysterious and evil interests reach[ing] out to grab Indian lands, once again," as Navajo Chairman Paul Jones testified at an early congressional hearing in 1958.[23] Making Indian land wilderness under federal rules was as good as surrendering it, he thought. Many Indians found simply illogical and unacceptable the fact that the government would attempt, in this perpetual contract, to lump their tribal holdings (communally owned by tribal members, although still held in trust by the federal government) together with federal lands (which belong to all Americans). By the time the Wilderness Act finally passed in 1964, all but one of the Indian roadless areas had become defunct anyway. Indians' protests against the earlier wilderness bills, which included Indian lands, precipitated the demise of nearly all Indian roadless areas within a very short time.

Bob Marshall created the Indian roadless areas back in the 1930s with the romantic and noble intent of providing "a retreat where [Indians] may escape from constant contact with white men."[24] During the wilderness debates in the late 1950s, an unnamed Tribal Council member from the Warm Springs Reservation in Oregon was quoted as saying "from the testimony here today, it appears that [it is] the white man [who] wants to get away from other white men."[25]

Most of the tribes already saddled with roadless designations wanted no part of this even more binding law that would preside over their lands forever, and they voiced their ardent opposition at various congressional hearings on the wilderness bill in 1957, 1958, and 1959. Most Indian representatives at these hearings prefaced their testimony with either neutral or supportive statements concerning national wilderness legislation that steered clear of Indian lands. Their opposition ranged from demands that tribal consent to wilderness designations be secured beforehand to insistence that tribal lands be dropped from the bill altogether.[26]

Among the most vehement Indian protesters against the wilderness bill was the Confederated Salish and Kootenai's probusiness chairman, Walter McDonald, who sought bold new timber options for his people now that "the cream of our crop of timber is gone."[27] In an intertribal memo to rally his fellow bill bashers he wrote: "If this bill becomes law the Indians will have lost their prestige and dignity, along with their natural resources as well as their existing culture. . . . Today we have all joined hands in encouraging industrial development on all reservations, and certainly we do not want any obstacles in the way."[28]

Other Northwest tribes earning income from timber and subject to existing roadless designations expressed opposition to the wilderness bill for many of the same reasons. The Indians of the Warm Springs, Yakama, and Colville Reservations had also been affected for two decades by the Interior Department's rarely bending roadless rules. Demands for declassification of their roadless areas, based on the need for commercial development, accompanied many individual tribes' protests against the wilderness bill. As the larger wilderness debate raged on, Secretary of the Interior Fred Seaton lifted the roadless restrictions for all tribes that made the request.[29]

A few years before, in 1956, the Makah Indians had asked that the Cape Flattery Wild Area be abolished because of damage from the construction of military installations during World War II.[30] The Indians of the Warm Springs Reservation were the first to have a larger roadless designation—their 105,000 acres surrounding Mt. Jefferson in the Oregon Cascades—officially removed from the federal list of Indian roadless areas in August 1958. The next month the Hualapai Indians in Arizona quickly followed suit with their 530,000 acres of the Grand Canyon.

On the last day of 1958, the Confederated Salish and Kootenai Tribal Council requested that the secretary of the interior "withdraw and revoke" the Mission Range from the Indian Office's roadless order: there was no beating around the bush as to why: "A large supply of merchantable timber is presently available within the existing 'Roadless and Wild Area,' and . . . the Tribes are desirous of cutting and marketing this timber, now." Tribal Resolution No. 1003 claimed the Indian Office's Department of Roads was constructing 8 miles of new road within the area anyway, and logging roads would be necessary for the tribes "to cut and market their merchantable timber in accordance with the [IRA's] sustained yield program."[31]

The following year the Confederated Salish and Kootenai Tribes, together with the Indians of the Colville and Grand Portage Reservations, comprised "the respective tribes [that] requested the elimination of these areas to facilitate economic development" in one joint amendment to the dwindling roadless order. Upon publication of this announcement in the October 10, 1959, *Federal Register,* the Mission Range Roadless Area ceased to be.[32] By 1962 only the Wind River Roadless Area on the Wind River Indian Reservation in Wyoming remained intact, since the Shoshone and Arapahoe Tribes did not request its elimination. (Today, the Bureau of Indian Affairs and the Shoshone and Arapahoe Tribes still manage this southwest corner of the Wind River Reservation as a roadless area.)

Once the inventory of roadless designations had shrunk to only a few, the days of Indian lands remaining part of the wilderness bill were numbered. The last version of the bill that included Indian lands, S. 1123, strengthened the "consent" language, stating that inclusion of reservation areas would occur "upon the recommendation of or with the consent of the tribes."[33] Despite this improvement, another round of hearings produced more negative testimony from Indians. In February 1961 the S. 174 version of the wilderness bill was introduced, altogether devoid of Section 2(d), which had discussed Indian lands. From that point on, all wilderness bills introduced in Congress made no reference to Indian lands.

Just as the Department of the Interior did not resist relinquishing the roadless areas, it did not resist removing Indian lands from the wilderness bill. Interior was a leading opponent of many of the bill's provisions, especially those that stood in direct conflict with "Mission 66," a ten-year building program initiated in 1956 to ready the nation's parks for the increasing volume and demands of visitors. By all appearances the Department of the Interior was relieved to let the Indian lands go; at least the territory managed by its Indian Office (now referred to as the Bureau of Indian Affairs [BIA]) would be free of wilderness considerations.[34] The overwhelming protests of tribes with roadless designations indicated that the consent of the respective tribes required for each of these areas to join the national wilderness system was highly unlikely anyway.

Moreover, the era of great wilderness advocates running the BIA had passed. By the late 1950s the major problem confronting the BIA was "too many people and not enough land," Don Foster, Portland area director of the BIA, reported at the Sierra Club's Fifth Biennial Wilderness Conference in 1957. The agency's policy of the day emphasized the modernization of health and educational facilities and pushed for economic development on reservations to foster the Indians' self-sufficiency. Termination of reservations, which meant the dissolution of reservations as trust entities and the end of federal assistance to Indians, was the ultimate goal of the BIA in the 1950s.[35] The tide of Indian policy had turned, and the ideals of BIA leadership had shifted once again.

"Is wilderness un-democratic?" the retired John Collier asked himself just prior to passage of the Wilderness Act. While constructing an argument that no, it was not, in an essay entitled "Wilderness and Modern Man," Collier reflected on the fall of the Indian roadless areas. Bob Marshall's order was "meant, in part, as a commencement of the Wilderness policy broadly conceived," Collier conceded. "In the hindsight of the whole Wilderness struggle, it would have been better if we had done what we did not do."[36] Collier admitted that not consulting the tribes concerning the Indian roadless areas was a big mistake, one that proved shortsighted and, in the long run, counterproductive to the larger wilderness-saving mission.

Weighing Wilderness and Timber Values on the Flathead Reservation

As the ink dried on the nation's new Wilderness Act, the Flathead's BIA foresters pondered the new frontiers to be explored given the power of "intensive" logging technologies, including state-of-the-art equipment that allowed logging operations to climb into formerly inaccessible higher-elevation forests. The northern end of the bygone Mission Range Roadless Area sat front and center on their drawing board. Between 1966 and 1976 loggers removed 131 million board feet of timber from these less spectacular, gentler slopes of the Mission Range (Figure 8.3b). Combined, these cuts in the northern Missions poured $5.6 million into the tribal treasury.[37] To entice loggers to tackle the greater challenge and higher cost of constructing roads into high, rugged country (only to extract the lower-value alpine species), the reservation's forestry office prescribed clear-cutting as a primary harvesting method for the area.[38]

The visual consequences of the first clear-cuts on the west face of the Mission Mountains upset some valley residents, including David Rorvik, a non-Indian who lived just north of the reservation. Rorvik wrote to reservation forestry officials and his congressmen in 1971, condemning the clear-cuts on "the steep, clearly visible" mountainsides that had degraded the natural beauty of the Missions. "The devastation . . . has been appalling," he wrote. "Here, where scenic values should count for so much, there has been absolutely no regard for the environment."[39] Rorvik's complaints initiated public debate on the question,

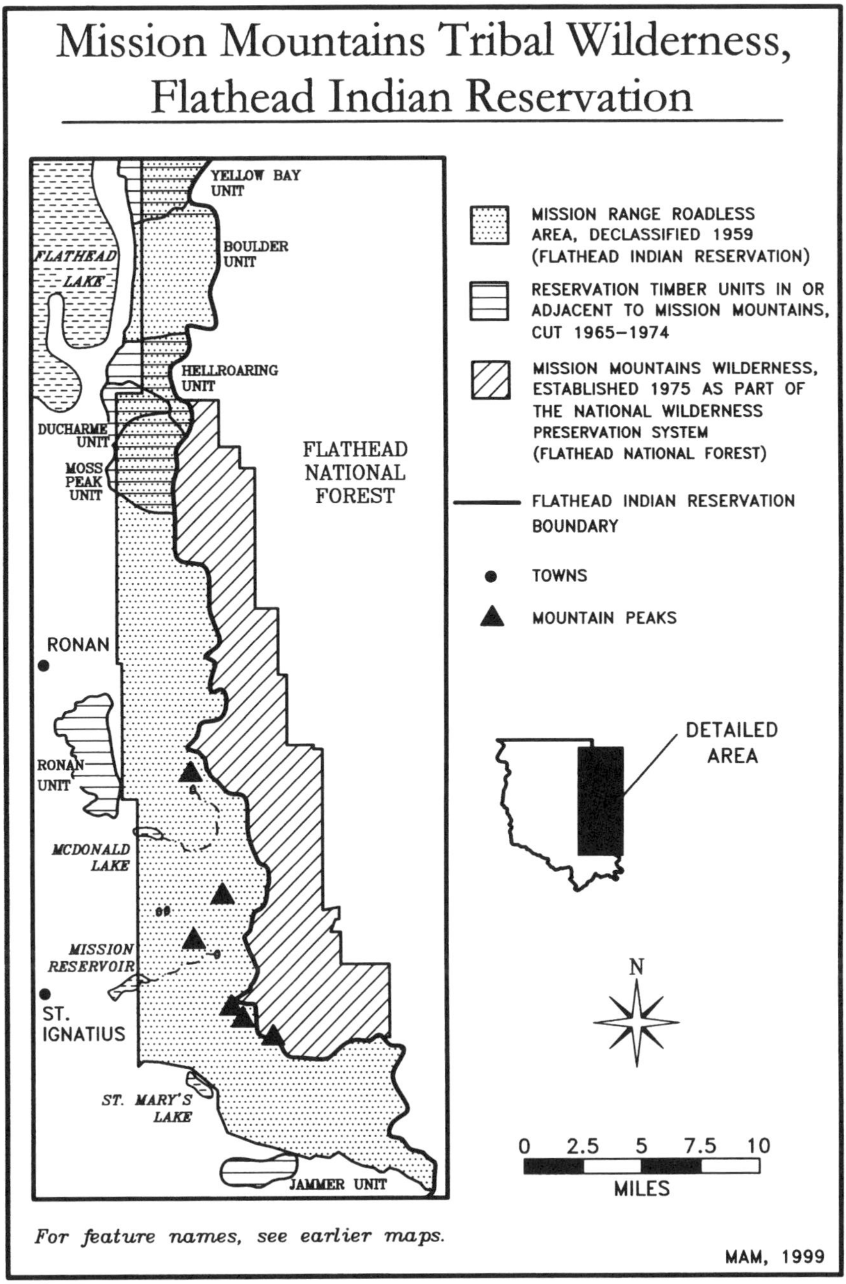

Fig. 8.3b Mission Mountains Tribal Wilderness, Flathead Indian Reservation. Following the declassification of the Mission Range Roadless Area, the Confederated Salish and Kootenai Tribes approved a number of timber sales in the northern Missions and several at the base of the southern Missions as well.

would the BIA and the Tribal Council continue to allow logging operations to scale the scenic slopes of the Missions? The answer: for a time, yes, but ultimately, no.

Even more ambitious plans were in the works for the remainder of the Mission Range. Foresters slated eight timber units for selected "valley-facing" mountainsides, with an estimated total harvest of 223 million board feet to be completed by the early 1980s. The first proposed sale was the 2,200-acre Ashley Lakes Unit, a narrow 7-mile strip along the base slopes of McDonald and Kakashe Peaks (Fig.8.3b). For this unit the BIA allocated the removal of 40 percent of the area's trees and between-tree spacing up to 20 feet. This project alone would require 30 miles of new roads.[40]

Some tribal members were already scrutinizing the overzealous management methods of the reservation's timber program, especially its clear-cuts, thinning practices, excessive roads, and the sale of such large timber units. The BIA's announcement of the conspicuous Mission sales, which threatened the venerable face of the Missions, elevated the scrutiny to blatant protest.

Some Indians wanted no logging of any kind along the Mission Front. These tribal members believed "the Mission forests [were] worth far more in cultural and recreational value than in stumpage," an article on the Ashley sale reported in spring of 1974.[41] From overseas, serviceman Kenneth Orr wrote the *Char-Koosta News* about the ominous predicament the Mission sales precipitated. He painted the scene of a bleak futuristic homecoming, his return to the reservation to view the desecrated, defeated Mission Range with a crisscross of roads etched across the lower slopes and small stands of pines huddled on otherwise naked, ravaged hillsides: "Instantly I feel a great loss in my soul. It is as though some madman had come into my home and literally tore up the living room. . . . The Indian has little left of the old ways and world; is he ready now to give [the Missions] up also?"[42] Tribal member Clarence Woodcock, for one, affirmed that he was not. Above and beyond a logging site, the Mission Range was a place of greater meaning and more uses, "a place to gather a lot of the herbs and berries and plants and, in addition, a place that the Indian people link with home and with Indianness."[43]

But Mission logging had supporters on the reservation, too. Some Indians endorsed timber harvest along the Mission Front, only with special precautions to minimize environmental and aesthetic damage. Others favored the industry's business-as-usual methods and the addition of the Mission units to the current timber schedule, largely responsible for the tribes' continued financial success. In 1972 annual tribal income from timber approached $5 million, and per capita checks to all tribal members grew fatter.[44]

Thurman Trosper, a Salish retiree and former supervisor of the Bitterroot National Forest, editorialized in the March 15, 1974, edition of the *Char-Koosta News* just how detrimental business as usual on the Mission Front could be:

> The management of timber on the reservation has reached a point of crisis. . . . Sales are too large and poorly supervised. Stands are being overcut. Too many roads are being built. . . . It can be safely assumed that, unless corrective measures are taken, this area will be logged in the conventional manner. Should this occur, the beautiful Missions will be defaced beyond redemption. We cannot, in all conscience, leave to our children and to all future generations a legacy of a defaced and scarred Mission face.[45]

The proposed Mission sales had swiftly become a political hot potato on the reservation. The Tribal Council election in December 1973 focused largely on logging, especially logging in the Missions, with many candidates favoring the exclusion of the Mission Mountains from the forestry schedule and the reform of those timber practices criticized as too intensive. Following the election, the Tribal Council hired faculty from the University of Montana's Forestry School to conduct studies of the reservation's timber operations. The new council members also agreed to look again at a proposal Trosper had first introduced to their unresponsive predecessors a few years before.[46]

In 1970 Trosper had propositioned tribal leaders with the idea of preserving most of the Mission Range as wilderness, a concept with which he was quite familiar given his career with the Forest Service and the Park Service and his longtime involvement with the Wilderness Society. He proposed that the upper two-thirds of the Mission Range be protected from all development and extractive use, leaving the forests of the lower slopes as commercial timberlands. Tribal Chairman Walter McDonald, who fought adamantly to eliminate Indian lands from the Wilderness Act of 1964, was not impressed. Trosper could not appease the Tribal Council's fear that any wilderness designation would mean surrendering some control to the federal government. His argument for a tribal wilderness, governed by tribal policies and as easily dissolved as created by tribal resolution, did not motivate the council to take any action, and the issue was dropped.[47]

As the new council contemplated plans and awaited studies concerning the Mission forests, the BIA placed a moratorium on all Mission logging in March 1974. Acting Flathead Agency Forestry Manager Fred Malroy explained that he had halted all preparations for the sales because he was "getting the message" that tribal members were unhappy with the BIA and "that we are over cutting the timber supply on the reservation. That the allowable annual cut is too high and is unreliable."[48]

Seizing the opportunity in this official delay of the Mission sales, Trosper recommended that the Tribal Council commission another independent study by the University of Montana's Forestry School: an analysis of the reservation's timber growth and annual harvest. This new inventory would allow the tribes to set their own, more sustainable quotas and guidelines for the BIA managers to follow. The reservation's forests, especially the Mission forests, Trosper argued, were too valuable not to pursue this role reversal: "We do not need to follow in the footsteps of traditional bureaucratic forest practices or be beholden to BIA on how the timber on the Missions should be managed. . . . We have the capability and foresight to manage this area in a manner that will leave intact the scenic, wildlife, and watershed values."[49]

Councilman Tom "Bearhead" Swaney shared Trosper's mistrust of the BIA's trust responsibilities to the tribes, arguing that the Mission Front was not the place to parade the agency's incompetence: "How can we turn you [BIA Forestry] loose on a more important, delicate and complicated project [like the Mission timber sales] when you have shown us that you can't even control the easy projects you already have?"[50]

Nevertheless, in July 1974 the Tribal Council voted five to three to prematurely lift the yearlong logging ban in the Missions and proceed with the Ashley sale. After months of capricious decisionmaking by the council on this emotional issue, this latest flip-flop in policy fanned the flame of opposition. Surprised by the sudden approval of the Ashley sale, opponents of Mission logging claimed they had been deceived by the council's flimsy commitment to postponement. A petition calling for a permanent ban on all logging in the Mission Mountains—shelved in the spring when the council voted to suspend the Ashley sale—circulated once more.

A small but potent team of angry tribal members confronted the Tribal Council at its August meeting. In hindsight, many consider the persuasive words of three of the protesters to be the pivotal testimony in the tribal discourse on wilderness preservation for the Mission Mountains. Christine Woodcock, Louise McDonald, and Annie Pierre, each wearing her long gray hair bound behind her head in a bun and gazing steadily through spectacles, stood before the Tribal Council to give the members a stern reprimand. These respected elders were known as *yayas,* Salish grandmothers to the whole tribe, not just to their blood kin. They spoke on behalf of the Flathead Culture Committee when they told the council to abandon the logging plans for the Mission Mountains for good.[51] Later that evening the council voted six to two to reverse its decision one last time, reinstating an experimental clean logging project on less conspicuous forests elsewhere on the reservation and postponing the Ashley sale.[52] From this point a failing timber market began to erode the practicality of logging the higher, more visible Missions forests and contributed significantly to the defeat of the most controversial Mission sales.

When the three Salish *yayas* convinced the Tribal Council to hold off on the Ashley timber sale in the summer of 1974, they in effect drew a line in the sand, a line tribal leadership dared not cross again. As a faltering timber economy lessened the appeal of the Mission sales and more Indians (council members included) came to envision a nonlogging future for the range, Trosper lobbied hard for the ultimate protection for the Missions behind that ethical line the *yayas* had set. A man of the white conservation movement, Trosper was well versed in contemporary wilderness philosophy and practice. Following his high-ranking career with the Forest Service and the Park Service, he retired to the reservation in 1973 and immediately accepted a three-year term as president of the Wilderness Society.[53] While steering the nation's premier wilderness advocacy organization, at home Trosper kept steady pressure on the Tribal Council to choose wilderness protection for the Mission Mountains.

In 1977 he persuaded the council to commission the University of Montana once again, this time to conduct a wilderness study of the Missions' west slope. One year later the university's Wilderness Institute presented the tribes with a management proposal for a "Mission Mountains Tribal Wilderness." The document outlined a boundary for the wilderness area, summarized current recreational use and the status of wilderness resources, and formulated both a general management directive for the entire area and short-term management recommendations for each of the area's twelve "wildland units."[54]

When the Wilderness Institute study was just getting started in spring of 1977, a newly formed group of tribal members offered another approach to protecting the Missions' scenic west face. The Save the Mission Mountains Committee unveiled a new petition that called for a tribal referendum creating a tribal primitive area of the Mission Range. The proposed Mission Mountains Primitive Area would "be managed strictly for the Cultural, Recreational, and Aesthetic use of the Confederated Salish and Kootenai Tribes," the petition read, to the exclusion of nontribal members.[55]

Although this referendum was never realized, the Tribal Council remained receptive to the wilderness idea proposed by Trosper and researched by the Wilderness Institute. Upon receipt of the institute's extensive study, the Council chose to proceed with plans to establish the Mission Mountains Tribal Wilderness, which would be accessible to both tribal members and non-Indians alike (Fig. 8.3c).

In November 1979 the Tribal Council approved a BIA-amended set of wilderness boundaries for the Missions that differed only slightly from the institute's original recommendations. Downhill from the wilderness area's western edge, varying in elevation from 3,500 to 4,500 feet, logging would continue. But within the boundaries timber harvest was banned, along with nearly all other development. (The most significant exception to the antidevelopment rule was the secured potential for small hydroelectric installations in the northern section of the tribal wilderness.)[56]

Ken Dupuis, BIA forestry supervisor for the Flathead Reservation, reported that the wilderness designation reduced the annual allowable cut in the Mission Mountains forestry area by one-third, from 9 million board feet to 6 million board feet, only a 5 percent loss to the reservation's total annual yield of 54.6

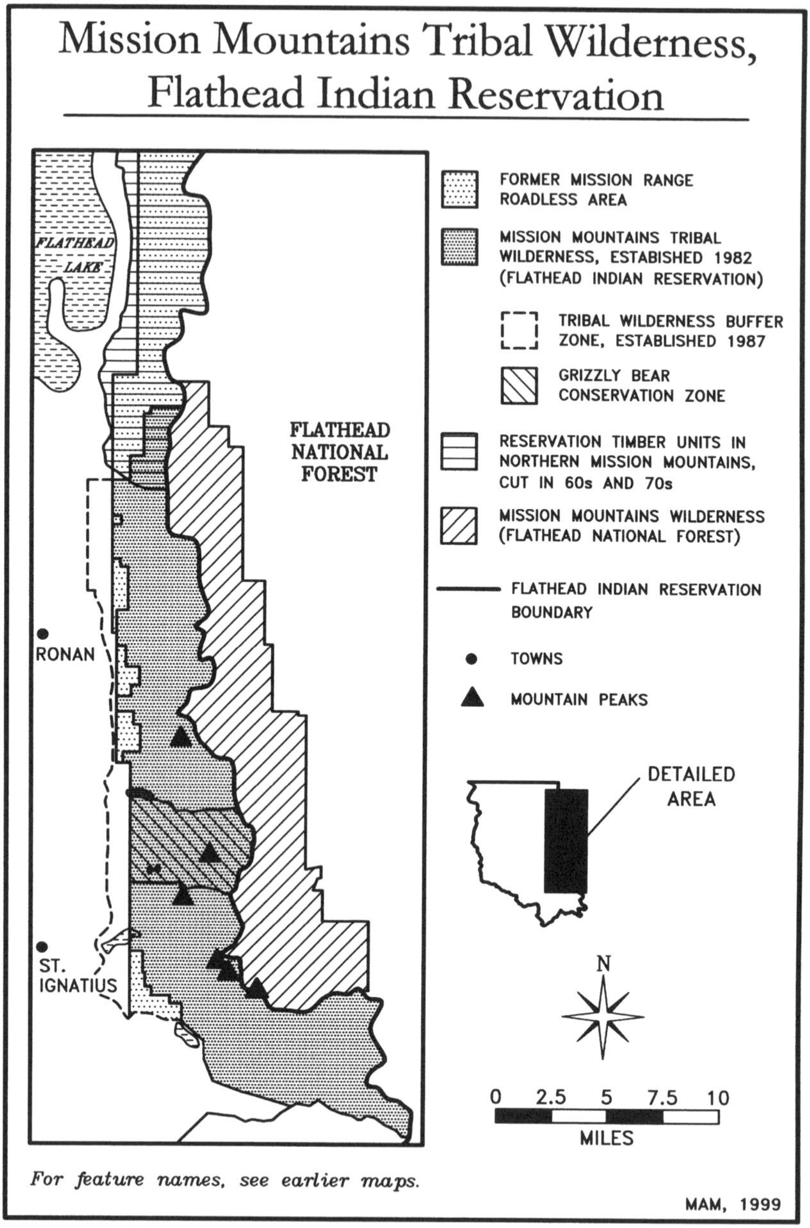

Fig. 8.3c Mission Mountains Tribal Wilderness, Flathead Indian Reservation. Confederal Salish and Kootenai Tribes chose to preserve the southern two-thirds of the former Mission Range Roadless Area as a tribal wilderness in 1982. Unique management features of the Mission Mountains Tribal Wilderness include its Grizzly Bear Conservation Zone, off limits to all recreational use from July to October each year, and its Tribal Wilderness Buffer Zone, which extends the protected area westward a mile or more toward the Mission Valley.

million board feet. Dupuis said special logging procedures would be developed for cuts along the base of the mountains for "the maintenance of wildlife and aesthetic resources."[57]

The most concrete result of the council's 1979 resolution to approve the tribal wilderness and its boundaries was the final removal of the Missions' higher-elevation forests from the forestry schedule. The notorious Ashley Lakes sale and the other Mission timber units within the new wilderness boundaries at last were stricken from the schedule. These long-delayed sales had remained on the books as long as possible so the BIA could better justify its sustained-yield quotas, reflected Joe McDonald, who served on the Tribal Council at the time. Once the projected footage to be harvested from the Missions each year was gone from the timber schedule, foresters picked up the pace of logging elsewhere on the reservation to make up for the loss.[58] (Although the BIA was, and still is, entrenched in many workings of the Tribe's Natural Resources Department, its influence began to dissipate as provisions of the Indian Self-Determination Act of 1975—designed to encourage tribal autonomy—gradually took a substantive hold. Today, federal money flows directly to the tribal government of the Flathead Reservation, funding tribally run programs that are phasing out BIA operations.)

Although the lines were drawn and the logging was halted, the 1979 wilderness resolution otherwise only held the designation in a tentative holding pattern while the tribes developed a management plan for the tribal wilderness. The bulk of this task fell to David Rockwell, primary author of the Wilderness Institute's tribal wilderness proposal. Over the next three years Rockwell honed the institute's management recommendations to the tribes' liking. Alterations to the recommendations better reflected the tribes' culturally specific wilderness values, which weigh heavily on aesthetics, intrinsic appreciation, and wildlife habitat. Recreation was pushed down the management priority list, and ultimately all commercial recreation—namely, outfitting—was prohibited from the tribal wilderness altogether. The tribes chose for their wilderness a no-frills management style with diminished concessions for visitors because recreation figures only marginally in the tribal value of the Mission Mountains. The 1982 management plan for the tribal wilderness states: "The needs and values of tribal members take precedence over those of nontribal members. A common thread through all management considerations is the tribes' own cultural and spiritual ties to wilderness."[59]

After a dozen years of contemplation and preparation, the Tribal Council of the Confederated Salish and Kootenai Tribes declared their side of the Mission Range a protected wilderness on June 15, 1982.[60] The motion to approve the official proclamation of the Mission Mountains Tribal Wilderness—Ordinance 79A—carried seven to one. At this point Rockwell passed his duties on to his assistant, Herschel Mays, a tribal member. Thereafter the tribes' Wildland Recreation Program, created specifically to oversee the tribal wilderness, would be led by Indian directors. Currently, that position is held by Tom McDonald, whose grandfather Edward participated in the tribal park campaign for the Mission Range in the 1930s and whose great-uncle Walter was the ardent antiwilderness chairman of the Tribal Council in the 1950s and 1960s. "I guess we're all indicators of our times," Tom mused on the roles he and his family members have played in the evolution of the tribal wilderness, an evolution he unequivocally regards as "all economically driven."[61]

Economic and Philosophical Perspectives on "Indian Wilderness"

"The American people in general can afford much more easily than Indians to set aside wilderness," wrote Bob Marshall's biographer James Glover in light of the declassification of Marshall's roadless and wild designations on Indian reservations in the 1950s.[62] Preserving wilderness may preserve culture as well but likely also sacrifices some degree of economic opportunity that could ease the acute poverty Indians on many reservations endure. The relative economic stability of the Confederated Salish and Kootenai has afforded them the choice of leaving productive forests on the Mission slopes uncut and protected as wilderness. The likelihood of having to open the Mission Mountains to logging once again because of lulls in the tribal economy decreases as the reservation's monetary might shifts from timber profits to the tribes' ultimate ownership of Kerr Dam in 2015. Currently, the tribes collect an annual rental fee of $12.4 million from the Montana Power Company's hydroelectric facility, located on the reservation. After the tribes' scheduled acquisition of Kerr Dam, they should receive about $50 million a year from its operation.[63]

Quite fittingly this Indian wilderness, frequented most often by non-Indians, is supported almost entirely by white dollars. The largest sources of income that currently sustain the tribal wilderness—BIA funds, conservation permit fees required of non-Indian users of the wilderness, timber revenue, and the Kerr Dam rental—come from nontribal pocketbooks.[64] The monetary tie between the Mission Mountains Tribal Wilderness and the larger American society is undeniable, as are the philosophical and managerial links between this singular wilderness and the national norm.

Unlike federal wilderness areas that belong to us all, the Mission Mountains Tribal Wilderness carries the anomalous distinction of being a wilderness retained by one distinct Native community. The nearly 92,000 acres within the tribal wilderness boundaries are all trust land, owned collectively by the Tribes. Whereas federal wilderness officials are supposed to answer to the concerns and needs of the American public, the Mission Mountains Tribal Wilderness has a much smaller constituency: the 6,800 enrolled members of the Confederated Salish and Kootenai Tribes.[65]

According to the traditional stories of these Indian peoples, the notion of wilderness as a place separate from themselves—the notion of wilderness period—was at one time alien. Obviously, it is no longer. Today, the tribes accentuate the ideal of human absence from wilderness with management policies that either prohibit or discourage the presence of recreationists in the tribal wilderness. The overall tribal contentment with revering the tribal wilderness without setting foot within it further elevates this ideal. This contentment could also support the argument that the Confederated Salish and Kootenai have come to separate themselves from wilderness, from nature, to a degree greater than mainstream America, now accused of loving federal parks and wildernesses to death with overuse. Or perhaps the Indians' departure can be viewed more accurately in terms of a lower level of consumption—in this case recreational consumption—of nature.

Yet the option to rethink or even undo the Mission Mountains Tribal Wilderness remains in the flexible, reversible legislation that declares, outlines, and details its existence. A pragmatic Tribal Council in 1982 created the tribal wilderness with an ordinance rather than a more binding referendum, knowing future circumstances might shift tribal priorities concerning the Mission Range and its timber resources yet again. The initial prudence surrounding the designation of the tribal wilderness remains, since no referendum calling for perpetual protection of the Missions has been put before the tribal membership.

So far all revisions to the original tribal wilderness ordinance have only strengthened its protective measures regarding the Mission Mountains. In the late 1980s the Tribal Council approved the designation of a transitional management zone along the base of the wilderness area (Figure 8.3c). In this 23,000-acre buffer zone, the tribes keep a tight rein on activities that "may encroach into and compromise the integrity of the Wilderness," including grazing, timber harvesting, and home building.[66] In recent years, the tribes have considered closing certain portions of the tribal wilderness to non-Indian recreationalists year-round, expanding the wilderness northward as areas logged in the 1960s recover, and creating a new wilderness area on the west side of the reservation along the Nine Mile Divide.[67]

The Mission Mountains Tribal Wilderness represents much more than the environmental progressivism of the Confederated Salish and Kootenai Tribes, although that in itself is exemplary. The tribal wilderness typifies the shrewd workings of tribal politics and tribal economics, as well as the tribes' renewed dedication to their cultural heritage. The Missions' west face, protected in the name of Wilderness, symbolizes a borrowed devotion and a sovereign sanctity at the same time. Here the once unlikely pair of wilderness ideology and tribal autonomy have wed.

References

1. James J. Lopach, Margery Hunter Brown, and Richmond L. Clow, *Tribal Government Today: Politics on Montana Indian Reservations* (Boulder: Westview, 1990): 153.

2. Ibid.
3. William L. Bryan Jr., *Montana's Indians, Yesterday and Today* (Helena: Montana Magazine, 1985): 125.
4. Confederated Salish and Kootenai Tribes, Ordinance 79A, "An Ordinance Establishing the Mission Mountains Tribal Wilderness and Outlining Broad Guidelines and Policies for Its Management," June 15, 1982, Records Office, Tribal Complex, Pablo, Montana.
5. Ibid.
6. U.S. wilderness in 1990 totaled 92 million acres, cited in John C. Hendee, George H. Stankey, and Robert C. Lucas, *Wilderness Management* (Golden, CO: North American Press, 1990): 530. Since then new wilderness acts for the states of California, Colorado, and Nevada have been passed, bringing the national total to approximately 103 million acres, according to Dennis Daly, Wilderness Watch, personal interview, November 10, 1995, Missoula, Montana. Notes in possession of author.
7. The Wilderness Act of 1964, Public Law 88-577, 88th Cong., S. 4, September 3, 1964, in Hendee, Stankey, and Lucas, *Wilderness Management,* appendix G.
8. From Reed F. Noss and Allen Y. Cooperrider, *Saving Nature's Legacy: Protecting and Restoring Biodiversity* (Washington, DC: Island Press, 1994): 23–25, 172–174: "Conservation history in the United States is largely a series of responses to urgent threats against popular species and scenic wonders. . . . Designated wilderness areas do a poor job of representing ecosystem diversity. Many are truly rocks and ice."
9. David B. Rockwell and others, *Mission Mountains Tribal Wilderness Management Proposal* (Missoula: Wilderness Institute, School of Forestry, University of Montana, 1978), quote on p. 2.
10. Roderick Nash, *Wilderness and the American Mind,* 3d ed. (New Haven: Yale University Press, 1982): 182.
11. Office of Indian Affairs, Order No. 486, "Establishment of Roadless and Wild Areas on Indian Reservations," F.R. Doc. 38-807, *Federal Register,* 3:56 (March 22, 1938): 708–709.
12. James M. Glover, *A Wilderness Original: The Life of Bob Marshall* (Seattle: Mountaineers, 1986), quote on p. 159.
13. Ibid., p. 186.
14. Office of Indian Affairs, Order No. 486, p. 708.
15. Ibid.
16. Ibid., pp. 708–709.
17. Robert Sterling Yard to John Collier, July 26, 1938, File 40999-1937-308, General Service 1907–1939, Record Group-75, National Archives (hereafter RG-75, NA).
18. Frederic Kirgis to the Acting Commissioner of Indian Affairs, July 21, 1937, File 40999-1937-308, General Service 1907–1939, RG-75, NA.
19. Confederated Salish and Kootenai Tribes, Tribal Resolution No. 157, March 2, 1939, Records Office, Tribal Complex, Pablo, Montana.
20. The clear intent of the Indian Office's Order No. 486 was to discourage all development within the designated roadless areas, although exceptions could be made if tribes could argue convincingly for "fire protection, commercial use for the Indians' benefit, or actual need." Within the Mission Range Roadless Area the Indian Office ruled that a timber sale preceding the establishment of the roadless area could

continue, but construction of a 12-mile truck trail (already surveyed) in the northern Missions was not approved. See Krahe, "A Confluence of Sovereignty," pp. 44–46.

21. Background on the legislative history of the Wilderness Act obtained from Hendee, Stankey, and Lucas, *Wilderness Management,* pp. 104–106.
22. "Statement of Policy," the Wilderness Act of 1964, in ibid., appendix A.
23. Statement of Paul Jones, chairman, Navajo Tribal Council, in U.S. Congress, Senate, Committee on Interior and Insular Affairs, *National Wilderness Preservation Act, S. 4028: Hearings Before the Committee on Interior and Insular Affairs,* 85th Cong., 2d sess., November 14, 1958, in Albuquerque, New Mexico (Washington, DC: Government Printing Office (GPO), 1959): 936.
24. Office of Indian Affairs, Order No. 486, p. 708.
25. Statement of Q. N. Fanner, attorney, Confederated Tribes of the Warm Springs Indian Reservation, in U.S. Congress, Senate, Committee on Interior and Insular Affairs, *National Wilderness Preservation Act, S. 4028: Hearings Before the Committee on Interior and Insular Affairs,* 85th Cong., 2d sess., November 7, 1958, in Bend, Oregon (Washington, DC: GPO, 1959): 348.
26. Testimony by Indians urging Congress to exclude Indian lands from the wilderness bill can be found throughout the following: *National Wilderness Preservation Act, S. 1176: Hearings Before the Committee on Interior and Insular Affairs,* 85th Cong., 1st sess. (Washington, DC: GPO, 1957); *National Wilderness Preservation Act, S. 1123: Hearings Before the Committee on Interior and Insular Affairs,* 86th Cong., 1st sess. (Washington, DC: GPO, 1959); and *National Wilderness Preservation Act, S. 4028: Hearings Before the Committee on Interior and Insular Affairs,* 85th Cong., 2d sess. (Washington, DC: GPO, 1959).
27. Walter McDonald to Mrs. Dorothy Van de Mark, July 25, 1958, in records of the Wildland Recreation Program, Confederated Salish and Kootenai Tribes, Pablo, Montana.
28. Walter McDonald to "Indian leaders, tribal members, and interested non-Indian citizens," October 30, 1958, in records of the Wildland Recreation Program, Confederated Salish and Kootenai Tribes, Pablo, Montana.
29. Amendments to the Office of Indian Affairs' roadless order, which withdrew individual areas from the list of roadless and wild areas on Indian reservations, cite the need for economic development as the reason tribes requested declassification. These amendments appear in *Federal Register,* 23:165 (August 22, 1958): 6495; 24:7 (January 10, 1959): 251; 24:64 (April 2, 1959): 2559–2560; 24:97 (May 19, 1959): 4030; 24:199 (October 10, 1959): 8257; 25:183 (September 20, 1960): 9002–9003.
30. Statement of William Zimmerman Jr., in *National Wilderness Preservation Act, S. 1176: Hearings Before the Committee on Interior and Insular Affairs,* p. 407.
31. Confederated Salish and Kootenai Tribes, Tribal Resolution No. 1003, December 31, 1958, Records Office, Tribal Complex, Pablo, Montana.
32. Office of Indian Affairs, "Elimination of Certain Areas," amendment to "Establishment of Roadless and Wild Areas on Indian Reservations," F.R. Doc. 59-8544, *Federal Register,* 24:199 (October 10, 1959): 8257.
33. U.S. Congress, Senate, National Wilderness Preservation Act, 86th Cong., 1st sess., S. 1123, as it prefaces *National Wilderness Preservation Act, S. 1123: Hearings Before*

the Committee on Interior and Insular Affairs, April 2, 1959, in Phoenix, Arizona (Washington, DC: GPO, 1959): 4.

34. Jack M. Hession, "The Legislative History of the Wilderness Act," M.A. thesis in history, San Diego State College [University], San Diego, 1967, p. 47.
35. Summaries of proceedings from the Fifth Biennial Wilderness Conference, March 15–16, 1957, in David Brower, ed., *Wildlands in Our Civilization* (San Francisco: Sierra Club, 1964): 170.
36. John Collier, "Wilderness and Modern Man," in ibid., pp. 119–120.
37. Historical Research Associates, *Timber, Tribes, and Trust: A History of Forest Management on the Flathead Indian Reservation, Montana 1855–1975* (Dixon, MT: Confederated Salish and Kootenai Tribes, 1977): 407–409, 411.
38. Ibid., p. 173.
39. David Rorvik to Forestry Department, October 4, 1971, "Yellow Bay Logging Unit, Contract and Bond" file, BIA Branch of Forestry, Ronan, Montana.
40. "64-Million Board Feet of Mission Timber to Be Sold This Fall," *Char-Koosta News,* February 1, 1974: 1, 16; "Mission Unit Logging Will Be Delayed," *Char-Koosta News,* May 1, 1974: 1–2, 10.
41. "Mission Unit Logging," p. 2.
42. Kenneth J. Orr, "Indian Serviceman Thinks Logging the Missions Would Destroy Our Tribal Home," *Char-Koosta News,* April 15, 1974: 4.
43. "Mission Unit Logging," p. 10.
44. Ibid., p. 2.
45. Thurman Trosper, "Tribe Should Bequest Missions to the Future," *Char-Koosta News,* March 15, 1974: 4.
46. "64-Million Board Feet," pp. 1, 16.
47. Thurman Trosper, tribal member, retired U.S. Forest Service and National Park Service official, personal interview, February 23, 1994, Ronan, Montana. Notes in possession of author.
48. "Moratorium on Mission Mountains Logging Projects," *Char-Koosta News,* March 15, 1974: 1.
49. Trosper, "Tribe Should Bequest Mission to the Future," p. 4.
50. "Moratorium on Mission Mountains Logging Projects," p. 11.
51. "Tribal Wilderness: 10 Years Later," *Char-Koosta News,* August 21, 1992: 7.
52. Confederated Salish and Kootenai Tribes, Tribal Council Minutes, August 2, 1974, Records Office, Tribal Complex, Pablo, Montana.
53. Trosper, interview.
54. Rockwell and others, *Mission Mountains Tribal Wilderness Management Proposal.*
55. "Save the Mission Mountains Petition," *Char-Koosta News,* March 15, 1977: 2.
56. CS&KT Wildland Recreation Department, *Mission Mountains Tribal Wilderness Management Plan* (Pablo, MT: Confederated Salish and Kootenai Tribes, 1982): 58–60.
57. Richard Eggert, "Tribes OK Mission Wilderness," *Missoulian,* November 14, 1979: 1, 3.
58. Joe McDonald, former Tribal Council member, president of Salish Kootenai College, personal interview, October 9, 1995, Pablo, Montana. Transcript in possession of author.
59. CS&KT Wildland Recreation Department, *Mission Mountains,* p. 15.

60. Confederated Salish and Kootenai Tribes, Tribal Council Minutes, June 15, 1982, Records Office, Tribal Complex, Pablo, Montana.
61. Tom McDonald, director, Wildland Recreation Program, Confederated Salish and Kootenai Tribes, personal interview, February 22, 1994, Pablo, Montana. Notes in possession of author.
62. Glover, *A Wilderness Original,* p. 212.
63. Tribal Revenue Report, Tribal Treasurer's Office, in Patti M. Sessions, "Timber Sales Still Lag, But the Tribe Isn't Broke," *Char-Koosta News,* August 4, 1995: 3; Roy Big Crane and Thompson Smith, "The Place of the Falling Waters" (Pablo, MT: Native Voices Public Television Workshop and Salish Kootenai College, 1991), film.
64. Tom McDonald, personal interview, October 9, 1995, Pablo, Montana. Notes in possession of author.
65. Tribal enrollment figure obtained from the Montana-Wyoming Tribal Leaders Council (http://tlc.wtp.net), May 10, 2001.
66. Confederated Salish and Kootenai Tribes, Tribal Resolution No. 93-227 approving the 1993 Wilderness Buffer Zone Management Plan, August 27, 1993, Records Office, Tribal Complex, Pablo, Montana.
67. Tom McDonald, personal interview, January 10, 1997, Pablo, Montana. Notes in possession of author.

III

SELF-DETERMINATION

Pursuing Indigenous and Multiagency Management

Introduction

The implementation of tribal self-determination has encouraged tribes to assume control over many resource decisions. If some tribes have shown reluctance to embrace self-determination, it may be because of a lack of sufficient expertise or experience in resource management.[1] Even as some tribes have embraced environmental management and planning, recent case law—for example, *Devils Lake Sioux Tribe v. North Dakota Public Service Commission*—has undermined tribal autonomy with respect to regulation of non-Indian land utilization on former trust lands inside and outside reservation borders.[2] As the shift away from trustee-supervised planning continues, tribal self-determination will depend more on court decisions. As an extension of the meaning of self-determination, numerous tribes have asserted their historical traditions on lands no longer part of reservations.

Reservation land use and resource management constitute foundational concerns for all tribes. Beginning in the 1960s, tribes began to rethink their options to plan and manage reservation resources and oversee development of environmental quality standards. Trained Indian personnel and non-Indian specialists have given many Indian communities the ability to manage conservation programs and archaeological and historic preservation projects. Gaming revenues and claims award monies, and special congressional appropriations have provided some funds to take advantage of newer technology, such as Geographic Information Systems (GIS).[3]

It is important to recognize that the Indian Self-Determination and Education Assistance Act of 1975 did not empower the tribes in the very real sense of turning over total authority to them to run their own affairs without government intervention. As George S. Esber Jr. emphasizes, the wording of the law addresses "orderly transition" to "meaningful participation." He continues, "Inclusion or 'meaningful participation' is not control but at best a limited exercise of power, which must be translated as 'relative powerlessness' given the legal definition of the federal-Indian relationship."[4] He expresses the logical corollary to this idea: "Indian peoples have never had control over the policies that affect them, nor can they expect to, given the asymmetrical relationship that has been defined by the federal government."[5] He contends that "self-determination cannot be equated with participation, but rather must come to mean liberation from domination."[6] It is not our goal to undertake a separation evaluation of self-determination but rather to utilize it as a setting for the discussion of recent events and efforts to implement the spirit, if not the wording, of the 1975 act.

Very real progress has taken place, although it is still selective. For example, the Menominee of Wisconsin in 1997 began to develop, implement, and maintain a reservation and county-wide multipurpose land information system. More recently the tribe has been developing an advanced computer lab utilizing digitized maps that will enhance local capabilities and also provide on-reservation training. These efforts are part of a larger program of the tribal Sustainable Development Institute.[7] It is hoped that self-determination and government-to-government policies will not prove to be simply more examples of official rhetoric but will enable tribes to evolve appropriate and effective land use planning and environmental codes.

With self-determination, some tribes have refused to develop solid waste disposal facilities on their lands; others permit environmental degradation in the pursuit of income from solid waste or mining operations. An appropriate mining example involves the Blackfeet of Montana, who have pursued the development of a vast oil and gas field. The National Park Service (NPS) has expressed concern because the Blackfeet oil field lies just east of Glacier National Park and is valued as a seasonal haven for bears, wolves, elk, and eagles. A lease the tribe approved with a Canadian oil company has caused a rift within the tribe and between government agencies. Unfortunately, the Blackfeet suffer high unemployment and have few alternative opportunities on the land. The Environmental Protection Agency (EPA) has warned that the mining project could cause "significant impacts on important tribal resources, wetlands, endangered species and Glacier National Park."[8] The Bureau of Indian Affairs (BIA), of course, supports self-determination, but the NPS and EPA have criticized the project.

Indian environmental perception, as well as polity and land tenure, can and do interfere with or obstruct sound planning as much as they can abet conservation goals. The dichotomous nature of tenure on numerous reservations that separates the tribe as a corporate entity from individuals and families who hold allotments is both a blessing and a curse. On the other hand, tribes as governments and communities provide the continuity essential to on-reservation resource management. Tribal governments—mostly products of provisions of the Indian Reorganization Act (IRA) (1934), in which in general nonresident

Indian members may participate but non-Indian residents cannot—normally assume responsibility for a range of environmental affairs.

These are the overarching issues—air and water pollution, waste management, degradation from mining and lumbering—but tourism and potential gaming exhibit increasing negative environmental effects such as noise, traffic congestion, and land use conflicts. Many reservations have developed tribal agriculture (e.g., the Colorado River Indian Reservation; see Figure I.1), or they may lease acreage to tribal members or to non-Indians; and they have organized into grazing associations, which may be composed of extended families or outfits (as for the Navajo) or constitute geographic areas of a reservation and operate within designated commons or grazing districts. Tribes normally run irrigation systems, and although non-Indians who utilize trust or fee lands within reservation borders are entitled to a share of water, it is regulated by the tribe, and non-Indians generally have little or no voice in water management.

To be sure, numerous tribes have ultimately become adroit business as well as land managers, effective politicians, and astute lobbyists. But contradictory decisions are not uncommon in Indian Country. For example, Navajo parks are administered by a Navajo who had been an NPS superintendent. The Agua Caliente Indians in California have declared Palm Canyon both a sacred and a scenic area (Figure III.1). Unfortunately, negotiations have not finally led to the enactment into law of the proposed Wounded Knee National Tribal Park, which would otherwise involve joint management by the Cheyenne River Sioux, the Oglala (Pine Ridge Sioux), and the NPS.[9] On the other hand, the Mescalero Apache of New Mexico demonstrate that ambivalent decisionmaking can lead to environmentally sensitive settlement plans that have increased population density in established communities by consolidating housing and yet sustaining reservation open space and wilderness. Self-determination has encouraged the Mescalero to decide to construct a nuclear waste fuel storage facility.[10]

Thus other factors also contribute to difficulties in tribal management of trust lands. Jannette Wolfley, an attorney and member of the Shoshone-Bannock of Fort Hall Indian Reservation in Idaho, notes that "tribes are significantly absent from ecological risk assessments and risk management."[11] Too often, she observes, environmental assessments neglect to identify the effects public or private developments will have on trust lands or, for that matter, on former Indian lands where treaty-right hunting or fishing may still persist. Wolfley argues that most federal agencies disregard policies that mandate government-to-government interaction with the tribes. The necessary tools of the planning process have been enhanced in recent years; tribes have available to them not only GIS but also Integrated Resource Management Plans (IRMP) that can be specially designed to accommodate tribal expectations and resource options.[12]

Fig. III.1 Palm Canyon, Agua Caliente Indian Reservation (California). Hidden at the southern end of a checkerboard reservation, Palm Canyon remains the only significant scenic resource on these trust lands in the desert and mountains of the Coachella Valley. It is a protected area that at one time interested the National Park Service. Photo by Imre Sutton.

The success or failure of tribal efforts to administer their own environmental needs has depended not just on money and know-how but also on tribal politics. Tribes earning considerable revenue from natural resources tend to have greater success in dealing with business enterprises and the government. Whether a reservation has been allotted may also make the difference, since tribal councils on unallotted reservations have less difficulty establishing resource management than those on allotted reservations where many landowners are non-Indians.[13] This also may explain why numerous tribes have turned to gaming as a lucrative source of income.[14] Land under lease to non-Indians also helps tribes raise money. Tribes anticipate lease income for a block of years, and environmental management may take on new dimensions. To a degree, the longer the lease permit, the greater the possibilities for conservation. Larger blocks of land are free from intruding enclaves of ownership, and thus more comprehensive development can be achieved. Still, consolidation of individual Indian and non-Indian holdings is an ideal working only selectively for the betterment of resource management.

In an effort to become more autonomous in resource management, many tribes have pursued the consolidation of fragmented landholdings within their borders. Thus it is with mixed consequences that a 1995 Supreme Court decision knocked down the authority of tribes to acquire certain idle and encumbered allotments under the Land Consolidation Act because of alleged violation of Fifth Amendment rights of individual Indians and families.[15]

Nonetheless, continued purchase of such lands will assist tribal resource management in the long term. To be sure, fragmentation of reservation lands by the allotment process, exacerbated by the problems of heirship, makes it difficult to consolidate adjacent holdings into a working farm or other enterprise. It is also regrettable that the courts have swung to the extreme in deciding that non-Indian-owned lands within the borders of reservations are not subject to tribal jurisdiction and that, in fact, such determinable areas may no longer constitute part of the reservation. Subsequently, in 1998 the Supreme Court in *South Dakota v. Yankton Sioux Tribe et al.* ruled that the tribe could not regulate a landfill site on former trust lands outside the reservation.[16]

Once again the courts, by continuing to erode the geographic extent of tribal jurisdiction over the environment, significantly nullify or constrain tribal long-term efforts at environmental management. Some observers hope Congress will step in and reaffirm its primary jurisdiction over Indian affairs by returning the nation to "settled tenets of Indian law" focusing on "statutory language."[17] Meantime, the political geography of Indian Country remains fluid, subject to contradictory political and legal events that work for or against the tribes.

Self-determination must overcome the countless contradictions and conflicts created by tripartite governmental institutions in Indian Country—federal, tribal, and state or local civil divisions.[18] Imre Sutton explains the importance of understanding that in Indian Country, reservations are both political entity and real property, that they are of a complex order within and without. In the absence of congressional authorization to states and their civil divisions and whenever the federal government does not preempt jurisdiction, tribes may flourish as autonomous communities within their borders. Under self-determination, autonomy has been linked to increased tribal environmental management initiated either by Indians or by dint of federal legislation giving tribes more say over their trust lands.

Self-determination also urges tribes to pursue grants and assistance from agencies other than the BIA and to approach Congress independent of the trustee. Sutton observes that a quantum of environmental situations frustrates various tribes because states have sought to intervene by edict and by litigation to supervise environmental management on reservations in the quest (guise?) to make environmental management whole within a state. The issues are often seen as twofold: (1) states want to embrace the entire reservation as part of state environmental policy, or (2) states presume jurisdiction over non-Indian resource utilization within the borders of reservations. The development of models for government-to-government relations by the Northwest Renewable Resource Center in Seattle suggests that cooperation between tribes and local governments is attainable.[19]

Water as a commodity and as part of flowing rivers and watersheds represents a vital resource to the tribes. Indian reservations lie within the drainages of rivers that emanate elsewhere through lands held publicly and privately. The relationship between water rights and the conservation of water on behalf of tribal needs on reservations involves us in an excursion through customary practices, statutes, case law, and conflict resolution by settlement. Tribes did secure what has been until now a firm hold on water rights to Western rivers and streams—this is the *Winters Doctrine,* dating from the U.S. Supreme Court decision of 1908. But the courts have not sustained tribal water rights as hoped for, and tribes must negotiate to protect what was presumed to be res judicata—judicially protected rights in perpetuity.

Laura Kirwan and Daniel McCool emphasize the role of negotiation in their study of Indian water rights in several Western watersheds.[20] As they state: "The struggle over Indian water is an old one, but the relationship between Indians and environmentalists concerning water has become increasingly complex in the past fifteen years." They report that environmental groups have become increasingly influential with respect to water policy and that their views have had major impacts on water issues critical to Indian tribes. The authors examine four issues in Indian water settlements that have brought environmentalists into the negotiation process: water development, the Endangered Species Act, instream flow, and water marketing; they conclude with a discussion of the relationship between environmental policy and tribal self-determination.

Tribes are concerned about more than the protection of existing water rights. Other concerns relate to on-reservation water uses versus off-reservation transport of water as a means to gain additional revenues. In addition, tribes are concerned about the loss of aquifer sources and by declines in water quality, thus increasingly speaking out in protest. On occasion tribal members may be pitted against their own tribe. For example, a concerned group of Navajo have protested to the Southern California Edison Company over the draining of local groundwater on the reservation that is utilized in the transport of coal off reservation to a power plant near Laughlin, Nevada. The Peabody Western Coal Company holds a long-term lease to mine coal on the reservation and then to transport it as slurry for power operations elsewhere. Despite the fact that the power company pays royalties to both the Navajo and Hopi Nations and employs some Indians, this dissident group contends that aquifers are shrinking and affecting the economy and lifeways in the Black Mesa area.[21]

Tribal dependence on flowing streams is an old issue that does not go away. Such is the case for the Washoe of Nevada and the Hoopa and Yurok of California. The Washoe Indians have complained over sulfuric acid discharge into the Carson River by the Leviathan Mine, owned by the state of California. Since the river drains into Nevada, the pollution, according to the Indians, has been killing fish and turning an upstream mountain refuge held sacred into a scarred no-man's land. In theory, the state has intended to clean up the mine, and the EPA was expected to place the mine on its Superfund list in 1999. In July 2000 the EPA and California's Lahontan Regional Water Quality Control Board agreed on a cleanup plan. Treatment began on five ponds that store acidic waste, and this was considered "an effective stopgap measure."[22]

The Hoopa and Yurok Tribes occupy adjacent reservations within the drainage of the Trinity and Klamath Rivers in California's northwest. The tribes hope to see the restoration of fish life, especially Coho salmon, and Bruce Babbitt, former secretary of the interior, offered a plan that would return waters that now cross the coastal divide. As part of an extended reclamation project in 1962, waters destined to flow to the Pacific Ocean were turned around and today serve irrigation and urban needs in California's Sacramento Valley. The Indians are entitled by law to half of the Trinity and Klamath's harvestable fish, and stream enhancement would augment both subsistent and commercial fishing for the tribes. Restoring the flow of the Trinity is also important to environmentalists, who stress instream water conservation, and to those who run tourist businesses such as river rafting. But an additional roadblock to change was the power demand in summer of 2000 that exceeded available electric production in California and other Western states.[23] Thus tribal concerns over water extend far beyond trust lands to include off-reservation environments.

Since enactment of the Indian Self-Determination and Educational Assistance Act in 1975, a number of tribes have changed their perspective on several federal agencies. Tribes have consulted and worked with the Forest Service and the National Park Service to revise their policies regarding tribal rights on public lands. To be sure, executive orders and congressional legislation have contributed importantly to this turn of events. For example, in recent years the NPS has been supportive of Cheyenne and Arapaho efforts to establish a national monument or park on the site of the Sandy Creek Massacre (1864).[24]

Tribes continue to assert that *comanagement* of public lands and common property resources is a reserved right inferred in the wording of countless treaties. Even as some agencies have entered into partnerships with tribes, it is not yet law that federal public land agencies must make tribes comanagers of certain off-reservation resources. The real issue today is the role of states in the enforcement of environmental regulations that encompass ceded lands, waters, and wildlife. States continue to resist the argument that tribes continue to have treaty rights beyond reservation boundaries.

Although states are reluctant to share management of common property resources, the federal government has been urged in that direction. For example, in *Minnesota v. Mille Lacs Band of Chippewa Indians,* the court reaffirmed tribal usufructuary treaty rights to off-reservation hunting and fishing. The litigation stemmed from Minnesota's assertion of sovereignty over regulation of hunting and fishing, arguing that tribes lost their so-called reserved rights to hunt or fish off-reservation when a state entered the union. Part of the problem also stems from the fact that the federal government does not become more active in the protection of tribal reserved rights and thus in the resolution of conflicts involving the states.[25] It is contended that by virtue of inherent tribal sovereignty, there is a tribal right to comanage off-reservation resources tribes depend on for their livelihood. Although we have not included a separate chapter on comanagement and treaty rights, some discussion ensues in the chapters that follow.[26]

Although not every interaction between a tribe and a federal agency leads to satisfactory results for the tribe, the account of Lawrence Lesko and Renée Thakali, current and past staff members, respectively, of the Kaibab National Forest, reveals how agencies besides the BIA effectively work with the tribes, developing so-called partnerships. Traditional knowledge and indigenous ways of perceiving the management of the environment prevail in Hopi efforts to assume a partnership role.[27]

Because tribes no longer possess direct authority over lands formerly part of their aboriginal territory—according to the Hopi, most of the Kaibab was aboriginal territory—they must enter into joint ventures of mutual value. Several statutes as well as executive orders have mandated that many agencies, especially public land bureaus such as the Forest Service and the National Park Service, consult with tribes and help establish joint ventures on former ancestral lands now administered as part of the public lands.

For the Hopi to achieve their goals regarding former ancestral territory, they created a Cultural Preservation Office that interacts with state and federal agencies as a means to influence the stewardship of sacred and historic resources on national forestlands. The authors characterize this effort as "enriching multicultural land management." In 1987 the tribe established the *Hopi-Tunat'ya/Hopi Comprehensive Plan,* stating that "the Hopi way is a living tradition that shapes every aspect of the lives of the Hopi people." In addition to preserving the Hopi way of life, the tribe seeks to protect sacred places and subsistence gathering areas.[28] Note that the Hopi refer to locations as shrines but do not identify them as boundaries. Only a select number of sacred sites are known to non-Indians—those working on behalf of the tribe.[29]

The laws that oblige public land agencies to develop accords and partnerships with the tribes provide Indian communities with the opportunity to influence management to include adjudicated lands no longer part of the reservation. Hopi ancestral lands on the Kaibab and Coconino National Forests include vast territory—part of *Hopitutskwa*—the Indian Claims Commission did not adjudicate in favor of the tribe. Hopi account for the historic abandonment of settlements in the Little Colorado River Valley and west of present-day Williams, Arizona. Their ancestral territory reached west of the San Francisco Peaks and north of the Grand Canyon, but the U.S. government did not acknowledge such a vast territory as Hopi, mainly on the grounds that those areas had been abandoned.

Although they are not occupied in so many words, Hopi clan members visit various shrines "to pay homage to a greater domain of stewardship and all of *Hopitutskwa*."[30] The current policy of the Forest Service suggests that the agency has accepted its responsibilities to acknowledge the tribal claim despite the history of litigation. Hopi also have interacted with the Coconino National Forest, which is adjacent to the Kaibab.[31]

The Hopi case study is instructive, for it demonstrates the possibilities of greater accord between land or conservation agencies—federal, state, and local—and Indian communities. If one considers that all of the national territory not part of reservations (elsewhere characterized as *Irredeemable America*[32]) represents in the aggregate Indian ancestral lands, then tribe after tribe should assert a right to participate in the planning and management of those lands. In this way, perhaps, Indian environmental perception and resource management approaches will extend beyond reservation borders and, in reality, bring former ancestral lands within the geographic meaning of Indian Country.

Although Hopi–Forest Service relationships demonstrate how cooperation between a tribe and a public land agency can be effective for both parties, near the Kaibab National Forest lies the Wupatki National Monument, administered by the National Park Service. In 1999 park authorities stopped the Hopi practice of gathering fledgling golden eagles as part of their indigenous religion, contending that the law does not exempt Indians from provisions of the Endangered Species Act. The U.S. Fish and Wildlife Service, however, issued permits to the Hopi to gather golden eaglets for religious ceremonies, which essentially exempts them from the 1962 law that protects eagles. The golden eagle is not on the endangered or threatened list at this time, however. The U.S. Forest Service also allows the Hopi to gather these birds. As of spring 2001, the situation remains under review.[33]

If tribes could expect an indefinite era of good faith so they can expand upon their own goals through careful planning and management of their present and past lands, then Indian communities can look to a better future. *Indigenous* planning, which predicates Indian thinking and doing, is not just fashionable today: it is ethnically rational and environmentally logical. Tribes will make mistakes, but so has the federal government. Among the rationales for indigenous planning, of course, is that events take place at the locus of tribal life—the reservation—not in the nation's capital. For too long decisions governing the tribes took place far from Indian Country. Academicians and other observers of Indian affairs point to the successes, however modest and few in number, that have emerged from the perspective of indigenous planning. Self-determination predicates that tribes will continue to assume the primary role of planner and developer of reservation resources.

To correct that imbalance, we asked Ted Jojola, a member of the Isleta Pueblo and a professor of planning, not only to discuss indigenous planning, in which he participates as an instructor, but also to serve as the book's rapporteur. In obliging us, he has pulled together ideas and facts from our collective enterprise and related them to the indigenous planning theme. Readers will note that with this concluding chapter we have progressed from indigenous utilization (hunting) of the environment against the obstacles of a colonial mind-set; through a series of studies that have attempted to reveal the conflicts, failures, and successes in upholding trust responsibilities to manage tribal resources; to indigenous planning increasingly encouraged by the same government more than 150 years later.

References

1. On the preparation of Indians for environmental work, see Richard R. Harris and Randi Cox, "Curriculum on Ecology and Natural Resource Management for Indian Natural Resource Workers," *American Indian Culture and Research Journal,* 21:3 (1997): 33–48.
2. Cf. David J. Wishart and Oliver Froehling, "Land Ownership, Population, and Jurisdiction: The Case of the *Devils Lake Sioux Tribe v. North Dakota Public Service Commission,"* *American Indian Culture and Research Journal,* 20:2 (1996): 33–58; see also Janis Searles, "*South Dakota v. Bourland*: Another Supreme Court Moves Away From Recognition of Tribal Sovereignty," *Environmental Law,* 25:1 (1995): pp. 209–237.
3. The now defunct Branch of Natural Resources, BIA, in Albuquerque, New Mexico, strongly endorsed GIS; one of its staff was Bryan Marozas (Chippewa), whose study

["The Role of Geographic Information Systems in American Land and Water Rights Litigation," *American Indian Culture and Resource Journal,* 15:3 (1991): 77–93] has proved most useful in Indian land management. Marozas addressed the quintessential issue. "Enhancing Tribal Integrated Resource Management Plans by Integrating Traditional Knowledge With Geographic Information System Technology," paper presented at the Society for Applied Anthropology symposium "Anthropological Perspectives on Ecosystem Approaches to Managing Resources: Theory, Practice, and Bureaucracy," Albuquerque, March 31, 1995. See also on GIS issues an exchange of letters between Marozas, the GIS specialist with the BIA, Albuquerque, and Dennis Gebhardt, the GIS specialist for the Washoe Tribe, Nevada, in *Geo Info Systems,* January 1994, pp. 12, 14.

4. Indian Self-Determination and Education Assistance Act, 88 *Stat.* 2203–04 (1975); George S. Esber Jr., "Shortcomings of the Indian Self-Determination Policy,' in George P. Castile and Robert L. Bee, eds., *State and Reservation: New Perspectives on Federal Indian Policy* (Tucson: University of Arizona Press, 1992): 212–223; quote on p. 213.
5. Ibid., p. 214.
6. Ibid., p. 222.
7. A good example of an enlightened tribe developing appropriate on-reservation training is the Menominee Nation, which has established a college and within it a Sustainable Development Institute that offers courses in timber harvest and related environmental matters. Menominee Nation, *Sustainable Nations,* 1:1 (September–December 1999); Menominee Nation, *Sustainable Development Institute, Annual Report FY 99* and "Multipurpose Land Information System—A Collaborative Effort," *Sustainable Nations,* 1:1 (September–December 1999): 4. Courtesy Dr. Holly Youngbear-Tibbetts, dean and director, Keshena, Wisconsin.
8. Frank Clifford, "Oil Field on Reservation Fuels Dispute," *Los Angeles Times,* June 28, 1999: A1, 6.
9. Cf. Robert H. Keller and Michael F. Turek, *American Indians and National Parks* (Tucson: University of Arizona Press, 1998): 193, also xiii; Mario Gonzalez and Elizabeth Cook-Lynn, *The Politics of Hallowed Ground: Wounded Knee and the Struggle for Indian Sovereignty* (Urbana: University of Illinois Press, 1999).
10. Louis G. Leonard III, "Sovereignty, Self-Determination and Environmental Justice in the Mescalero Apache Decision to Store Nuclear Waste," *Boston College Environmental Affairs Law Review,* 24:3 (1997): 651–693.
11. Jannette Wolfley, "Ecological Risk Assessment and Management: Their Failure to Value Indigenous Traditional Ecological Knowledge and Protect Tribal Homelands," *American Indian Culture and Research Journal,* 22:2 (1998): 151–169, quote on p. 157.
12. Marozas, "Enhancing Tribal Integrated Resource Management Plans by Integrating Traditional Knowledge With Geographic Information System Technology," paper presented at Society for Applied Anthropology, Albuquerque, New Mexico, March 31, 1995. Marozas (Ojibway) is a staff member of the BIA in Albuquerque. See also Marozas, "The Role of Geographic Information Systems in American Indian Land and Water Rights Litigation," *American Indian Culture and Research Journal,* 15:3 (1991): 77–93.
13. Donald L. Parman, *Indians and the American West in the Twentieth Century* (Bloomington: Indiana University Press, 1994): 174.

14. Mary H. Cooper, "Native Americans' Future: Do U.S. Policies Block Opportunities for Progress," *CQ Researcher,* 6:26 (July 12, 1996): 601–624; "The Growth of Indian Gaming," *Newsletter,* National Coalition for Indian Education (Albuquerque, New Mexico), 9:2 (1996): 3; Imre Sutton, "Recognition and Casinos Are Separate Issues," *Los Angeles Times,* August 8, 1997: B7. See also Joseph G. Jorgensen, "Gaming and Recent American Indian Economic Development," *American Indian Culture and Research Journal,* 22:3 (1998): 157–172. See a more recent study, W. Dale Mason, *Indian Gaming: Tribal Sovereignty and American Politics* (Norman: University of Oklahoma Press, 2000).
15. See *Youpee v. Babbitt,* 67 F. 3d 194 (9th Cir. 1995), *aff'd sub nom Babbitt v. Youpee,* 117 S. Ct. 727 (1997).
16. No. 96-1581, 118 S. Ct. 789 (1998).
17. A. J. Taylor, "A Lack of Trust: *South Dakota v. Yankton Sioux Tribe* and the Abandonment of the Trust Doctrine in Reservation Diminishment Cases," *Washington Law Review,* 73(4) (1998): 1163; David H. Getches, "Conquering the Cultural Frontier: The New Subjectivism of the Supreme Court in Indian Law," *California Law Review,* 84 (1996): 1573–1655.
18. Cf. Imre Sutton, ed., "The Political Geography of Indian Country," *American Indian Culture and Research Journal,* 15:2 (1991): 1–169.
19. Shirley Solomon, "Tribal-County Intergovernmental Coordination: Towards a New Regionalism," *Western Planner,* 11 (1990): 18–20; Solomon, "Tribal and County Planners Discuss Coordination," *Western Planner,* 13 (1992): 14.
20. Cf. Lloyd Burton, *American Indian Water Rights and the Limits of Law* (Lawrence: University Press of Kansas, 1991); L. H. Storey, "Leasing Indian Water off the Reservation: A Use Consistent With the Reservation's Purpose," *California Law Review,* 76:1 (1988): 179–220.
21. Bobby Cuza, "Navajo Faction Urges Edison to Shut Down Power Plant," *Los Angeles Times,* April 21, 2000: A3, 32.
22. John M. Glionna, "Poisoned River Threatens Tribal Heritage," *Los Angeles Times,* April 22, 2000: A1, 28–29; Anon., "EPA Reaches Cleanup Agreement for Abandoned Sierra Sulfur Mine," *Los Angeles Times,* July 21, 2000: A27.
23. Julie Tamaki, "Farmers, Tribes Have Stake in River Ruling," *Los Angeles Times,* August 9, 2000: A3, 19.
24. "Question Hinders Tribute to Indian Massacre," *Los Angeles Times,* February 27, 1999: A20; "Indians Recall 1864 Colorado Massacre," *Los Angeles Times,* November 30, 1999: A20.
25. *Minnesota v. Mille Lacs Band of Chippewa Indians,* 526 U.S. 172 (1999); Kari Krogseng, "*Minnesota v. Mille Lacs Band of Chippewa Indians,*" *Ecology Law Quarterly,* 27:3 (2000): 771–797.
26. Ed Goodman, "Protecting Habitat for Off-Reservation Tribal Hunting and Fishing Rights: Tribal Comanagement as a Reserved Right," *Environmental Law,* 30:2 (2000): 279–361. Krogseng, "*Minnesota v. Mille Lacs,*" and this study say virtually nothing about the protection of tribal rights on private lands.
27. Various studies examine Native American environmental knowledge and perspectives; see Richard White, ed., "American Indian Environmental History," *Environmental Review,* 9:2 (1985); Christopher Vecsey and Robert W. Venables, eds., *American Indian Environments: Ecological Issues in Native American History* (Syracuse: Syracuse

University Press, 1980). On traditional management of forests by use of fire, see Robert Boyd, ed., *Indians, Fire, and the Land in the Pacific Northwest* (Corvallis: Oregon State University Press, 2000).

28. Louis A. Hieb, "Hopi," in Mary B. Davis, ed., *Native America in the Twentieth Century: An Encyclopedia* (New York: Garland, 1994): 240–243, quote on p. 241.
29. Note, in contrast, that at the time of pursuing a land claim the Zuni Tribe underwrote the publication of T. J. Ferguson and E. Richard Hart, *A Zuni Atlas* (Norman: University of Oklahoma Press, 1985), identifying sacred places "to demonstrate land occupancy beyond present boundaries." The maps were drawn at a scale too small to scrutinize in detail, but "the sites were revealed for litigation purposes, but still kept safe from unwanted visitors." See Robert Rundstrom, Douglas Deur, Kate Berry, and Dick Winchell, "Recent Geographical Research on Indians and Inuit in the United States and Canada," *American Indian Culture and Research Journal,* 24:2 (2000): 85–110, quote on p. 96.
30. T. J. Ferguson, *Öngtupqa niqw Pisisvayu* [Salt Canyon and the Colorado River]: *The Hopi People and the Grand Canyon,* Final Ethnohistoric Report for the Hopi Glen Canyon Environmental Studies Project (Third Mesa: Hopi Cultural Preservation Office, 1998): 60.
31. On Hopi land claims, see 39 *Indian Claims Commission,* 204, 223 (1976); see also "Commission Findings on the Hopi Indians," in *Hopi Indians,* American Indian Ethnohistory, Indians of the Southwest Series (New York: Garland, 1974): 396–397, 402–407; Florence Hawley Ellis, "The Hopi: Their History and Use of Lands," in *Hopi Indians,* pp. 225–277; J. O. Brew, "Hopi Prehistory and History to 1850," in Alfonso Ortiz, ed., *Southwest,* vol. 9 of *Handbook of North American Indians* (Washington, DC: Smithsonian Institution Press, 1979): 514–533; Richard O. Clemmer, "Hopi History, 1940–1974," ibid., pp. 533ff.
32. Cf. Imre Sutton, ed., *Irredeemable America: The Indians' Estate and Land Claims* (Albuquerque: University of New Mexico Press, 1985); Sutton, ed., "The Continuing Saga of Indian Land Claims" (symposium), *American Indian Culture and Research Journal,* 24:1 (2000): 129–198.
33. Matt Kelley, "Hopi Eagle-Taking Creates Conflict," *Missoulian,* July 22, 2000: C4.

The environmental community favors marketing for another reason as well. Many environmentalists feel current policy gives undue priority to development and other activities that have an inimical impact on the environment. They view water marketing as an integral part of a comprehensive water policy reform that stresses improved efficiency and innovative management.

Attempts to include unrestricted water marketing in Indian water settlements have met with resistance. When an early version of the Colorado Ute settlement proposed out-of-basin marketing, it received a hostile reception. Several congressmen from California stopped the bill because they "strongly oppose[d] the off-reservation, out-of-state water sale or lease provisions in the settlement. . . . It would upset the present legal stability [and] . . . open up a Pandora's Box."[38] Senator James A. McClure of Idaho argued that any attempt to fundamentally alter the law of the river was "unconscionable."[39] Part of the reason tribal water marketing is so strongly resisted is because downstream users essentially receive the water for free under existing law. If a tribe is awarded a substantial quantification of water but cannot divert it, then it remains in the watercourse and flows downstream to other water users regardless of whether they have paid for it.[40]

But the larger issue is whether tribal water marketing will indeed open up that "Pandora's box" and initiate a fundamental reordering of water priorities. Many environmental groups have lobbied for such a reform, but current water users fiercely resist any significant changes in the allocation regime. Clearly, the protectors of the water status quo are worried that Indian water marketing could threaten the policy that protects many water users from competition and the open market.

Nevertheless, local water marketing has played a role in most—but not all—settlements. For example, the Southern Arizona Water Rights Settlement Act[41] and subsequent technical revisions[42] permit local water marketing. As a result of conflicts over water rights within the tribe, the Tohono O'odham Nation has not been able to utilize its water from the settlement. So in lieu of on-reservation usage, the tribe has temporarily leased 30,000 acre-feet of water to the city of Tucson.[43] The Fort Hall settlement permits the tribes to rent water from the Shoshone-Bannock Water Bank, which consists of stored water in two reservoirs.[44] The Salt River Pima-Maricopa settlement permits the tribe to negotiate ninety-nine-year water leases with local municipalities if the lessees agree to pay all operation and maintenance costs.[45] The Fort McDowell and Jicarilla Apache settlements have somewhat similar provisions.[46]

It is important to remember that all of these marketing provisions contain restrictions—some of which were demanded by environmentalists, others by non-Indian water users. For example, the Jicarilla Apache settlement stipulates that tribal water transfers must comply with the Endangered Species Act, the National Environmental Policy Act, and other environmental laws. And nearly

CHAPTER 9

Tribes and States: A Political Geography of Indian Environmental Jurisdiction*

IMRE SUTTON

Tripartite Government in Indian Country

In the geography of Indian affairs, few legal, political, and environmental concerns reflect conventional wisdom. Although the general populace may perceive Indian reservations as autonomous areas beyond the reach of local and state jurisdiction, these trust lands are neither states nor civil divisions of government, in spite of recent legislative efforts to characterize them as similar to municipalities or equivalent to states.[1] The reality is that despite the wording *inherent sovereignty* and the existence of a certain autonomy thanks to their federal trust status, tribes do not represent constitutionally based political entities. Land boundaries may define *Indian Country,* but Indian dependent communities and reservations do lie within the borders of states, counties, even municipalities,[2] and this in recent decades has made all the difference in Indian efforts to manage their own affairs.[3]

If Indian Country once meant an extraterritorial area beyond non-Indian settlement and thus buffered from Euro-American cultural influences, that interpretation passed with the opening of reservations subsequent to the land allotment policy enacted more than a century ago.[4] Perhaps it is fair to say that policymakers then had little idea that they opened a Pandora's box when they encouraged non-Indians to homestead so-called surplus lands within reservation borders. These altruistic proponents pushed a policy of fragmenting

---

*Special thanks to Dr. Martin Glassner, Professor Emeritus of geography, Southern Connecticut State University, New Haven, for a careful reading of this chapter and several suggestions that I have incorporated into the final manuscript. Professor Glassner included discussion of my study of the political geography of Indian Country in his text, *Political Geography,* 2d ed. (New York: John Wiley and Sons, 1996), chapter 17, pp. 223–227.

tribal tenancy in common by creating individual trust property as a means to "separate" tribal members from the tribe, and by doing so they hoped to turn Indians into farmers and abiding citizens. They successfully sought the commingling of Indians and non-Indians through changes in land tenure as a measure of enculturation.[5] Over the ensuing decades of interaction on the land and in nearby towns, Indians began to partake of non-Indian culture, but something else was evolving: a jurisdictional conflict involving not two governments—tribal and local—but several—federal as trustee for the tribes; tribal; and state, represented by itself and its several civil divisions, that is, counties and municipalities. Thus whereas Indian reservations, other trust lands, and dependent Indian communities legally constitute Indian Country, geographically they represent only part of an extralegal milieu of tripartite government.[6]

This variable geographic interpretation of Indian Country identifies a political reality in which, at more or less the same time, tribes have been struggling toward greater autonomy and states have been pursuing broader jurisdiction[7] (Figure 9.1[8]). To be sure, tripartite government in one form or another has long existed in Indian Country; only since around 1980 has it assumed a far greater negative force. Statutes and case law have sought to clarify and assign responsibilities to each government—federal, tribal, and state; yet too often they have only created more conflict with confusing statutory provisions and judicial decisions over whose authority shall govern and regulate aspects of land use and environmental management on trust lands. Indeed, too, a number of states even earlier provided sufficient indication that they did not or would not totally honor tribal autonomy.[9]

From Tribalism to Indian Self-Determination

Indian people have undergone environmental and institutional changes from indigenous lifeways to modern governments. In precontact times tribes managed their own affairs, utilizing resources and occupying territory. Territoriality reflected an ecology determined in part by the technology of these first Americans on the continent and by the natural endowment at their disposal.[10] In addition, native mobility in search of subsistence and secure settlement was delimited by competition for resources among neighboring bands and tribes. With the coming of Euro-Americans, conquest and treaties of land cession diminished native territoriality, confined Indians to smaller and smaller geographic areas, and vitally reduced their options to subsist and hence survive as a people. The demographic account is all too well-known: tribes were decimated one way or another—by military aggression and starvation. The relocation of numerous tribes, notably the Five Civilized Tribes of the South but also many smaller groups from the Lake States and within the Great Plains, also diminished native opportunity to flourish as a people.

With the establishment of the reservation system and very shortly thereafter the imposition of land allotment on so many tribes, Indians were obliged—

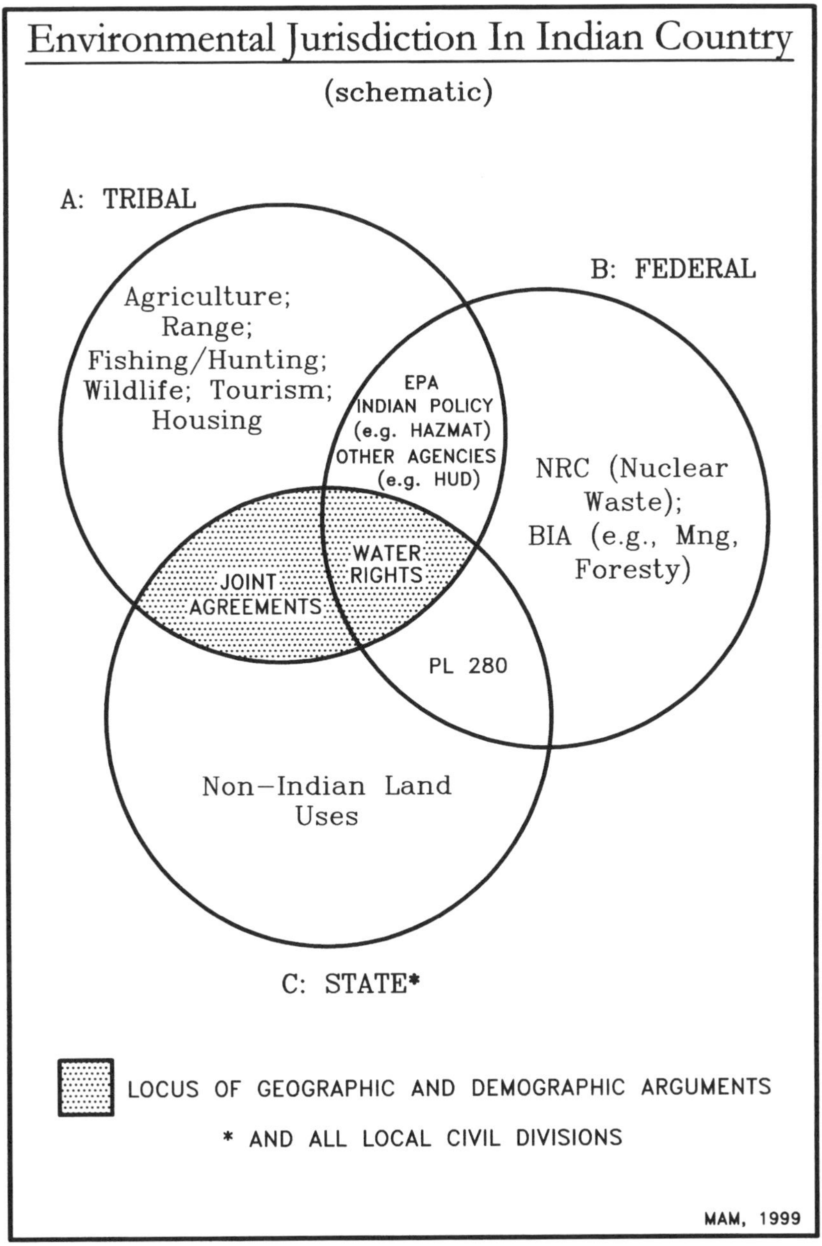

Fig. 9.1 [schematic diagram] Environmental Jurisdiction in Indian Country. Environmental jurisdiction is highly complex in Indian Country. This venn diagram attempts to depict the three major players—tribes and federal and state governments. Considerable overlap characterizes many functions. A good deal of the litigation in recent years has sought to challenge Environmental Protection Agency oversight of tribal operations, and states have won many cases in connection with non-Indian lands within reservation borders.

often by the presence of a garrison—to remain within the bounds of the reservation and were compelled to engage in farming regardless of whether they had any indigenous preparation or inclination toward the activity. The new land tenure structure (ultimately including allotment programs) that introduced farming too quickly became time-warped in that acreage sizes and configurations virtually stood still despite the fact that the expansion of farm acreage became an essential survival factor of American agriculture. Non-Indian farming over the decades aggressively moved into larger and larger acreage configurations. Not only did the allotment system lock Indians into an unwanted occupation, but it came with a price: acreage was much too small for economies of scale, and through leasing laws, Indians could secure only modest and inadequate incomes from non-Indians. Moreover, allotments became mired down in complex heirship, frustrating future land use and leading to much land abandonment. Land allotment on numerous reservations—for example, the Sioux group in the northern Plains, the Crow in Montana, the Yakama in Washington, and others—have yet to recover from the effects of heirship despite efforts by tribes to consolidate some lands into tribal holdings (see Figure P.1).

For more than a century, federal authority virtually dominated most aspects of tribal life. In effect, the federal government was the chief manager of Indian resources. From the 1930s, under the New Deal of Franklin D. Roosevelt, tribes were urged to assume more responsibility for their own governance, land management, and economic development. This policy change received impetus through the enactment of the Indian Reorganization Act (IRA) of 1934.[11] The government intended to pursue a more proactive environmental management policy, as its good intentions suggest in section 6 of the IRA:

> The secretary of the interior is directed to make rules and regulations for the operation and management of Indian forestry units on the principle of sustained-yield management, to restrict the number of livestock grazed on Indian range units to the estimated carrying capacity of such ranges, and to promulgate such other rules and regulations as may be necessary to protect the range from deterioration, to prevent soil erosion, to assure full utilization of the range, and like purposes.[12]

In the ensuing years this section of the law would impose a much greater environmental management role for the Bureau of Indian Affairs, although the agency had already been involved selectively with some farmlands, range, and forests on Indian reservations. Throughout the first century and more of the administration of Indian lands and resources, the *federal* government as the trustee prevailed in whatever management took place on most reservations. For example, Indians were organized in conservation teams on numerous reservations; anthropologist Edward Hall recalls his involvement in soil conservation on the Navajo Indian Reservation in the 1930s.[13] Selectively, tribes did make internal decisions about land use, but allotment set individual Indians off from the tribe, leading to variable land use decisions—including leasing, selling, or abandoning land, often then left idle or vacant and subject to the ravages of nature. From the 1930s forward we see more tribal involvement enabled by law and regulation but with the government still in the supervisory role. Despite allotment, tribal governments have successfully extended land use planning and zoning policies to allotted lands.

In the past several decades other forces have been at work creating new challenges for tribes, as the federal government has "emancipated" tribes from some but not all of the bureaucratic overburden. The IRA perhaps should be credited in part with stimulating change by getting more tribes involved. Other laws have played significant roles in tribal land use decisionmaking, including efforts both to consolidate allotments encumbered by heirship through the Land Consolidation Act of 1983 and to purchase abandoned non-Indian holdings within reservations.[14]

By the 1960s several tribes had taken the reins of reservation management, and thereafter, under the self-determination policy, more and more tribes began asserting nearly ultimate authority to manage their environments, even to the extent of requesting and securing grants from other federal agencies such as Housing and Urban Development (HUD). Tribes were establishing not only agricultural enterprises but tourist attractions including visitor centers and resorts. Only since the mid-1980s have tribes also established casinos. The important point is that tribes have embraced the new responsibilities by creating the appropriate offices of management and planning and by enacting environmental codes. Since the 1960s other federal agencies, as well as a number of state and local public agencies, have assisted many tribes in various pursuits. At the federal level HUD has played a major role in tribal housing programs, and the Environmental Protection Agency (EPA) has advised tribes on matters of environmental management and regulation (Table 9.1). A number of states have set up offices of Indian affairs or the equivalent.

The State as an Entity in Indian Country

Unfortunately, not all state and local government involvement with tribal resource management has been benign or beneficial to the tribes. Some states have argued that they have plenary authority over *all* territory within their borders despite constitutional stipulations that assign responsibility for the tribes to the federal government. But as noted in *EPA v. Washington Dept. of Ecology*,[15] a state may argue that for the sake of holistic conservation, it should assume jurisdiction within reservations. To the extent that some tribes are less skilled or undermotivated to apply high environmental standards to air and water management or to the operation of hazardous waste sites on their lands, states can make a good case. In general, however, such interventions continue to threaten

Table 9.1—Selective Chronology of Laws and Cases in Indian Environmental Affairs*

1953	P.L. 280† [the Civil and Criminal Jurisdiction Act]	Transferred civil and criminal jurisdiction† to named states; permitted others to assume jurisdiction; states intruded on tribal authority over planning, zoning, and taxation.
1950s	Termination† policy	A number of tribes were terminated from trust status, leading to management problems, loss of land. Some restorations occurred later.
1968	[Indian] Civil Rights Act	Among its provisions, tribes could retrocede from P.L. 280.
1970	National Environmental Policy Act	Created Environmental Protection Agency, which in recent years has preempted states in tribal environmental affairs.
1975	Indian Self-Determination† and Education Act	Gives tribes broad autonomy to run their own affairs, including resource management.
1970s–1980s	Various environmental laws.	Clean Air Act; Clean Water Act; as amended, declared tribes to be equivalent to states, hence autonomy to manage own lands.
1981	*Montana v. United States*	State may regulate hunting and fishing on Bighorn River flowing through Crow Indian Reservation.
1982	Land Consolidation† Act	Gave tribes authority to purchase fragmented allotments; helped tribes develop holistic environmental management.
1985	*Wash. Dept. of Ecology v. EPA*	EPA preempted environmental jurisdiction over state.
1989	*Brendale v. Confederated Tribes and Bands of Yakima Indians*	Yakama lost jurisdiction over areas they designated as "open" (as opposed to "closed," the former being essentially non-Indian).†
1990	Native American Graves Protection and Repatriation Act†	Tribes have invoked this act to secure and access and exclusive use of burial grounds and sacred sites on public lands.
1992	Indian Environmental General Assistance Act	Provides for grants to tribes and intertribal consortia to develop capacity to administer environmental regulatory programs.
1993	*Devils Lake Sioux Tribe v. N.D. Public Service Comm.*	Indian and non-Indian occupancy-ownership areas denied tribal jurisdiction over non-Indians.
1993	*South Dakota v. Bourland*	Cheyenne River Sioux lost sovereignty to regulate fishing on waters created by dam.
1997	Secretarial Order on Tribal Rights	Departments of Interior and Commerce. Requires tribes to participate in habitat protection for endangered species; provides some exceptions.

*See various footnotes in text for citations to laws and cases.

†See glossary for terms.

not only tribal autonomy but also the very environmental efforts tribes have already undertaken, especially with the assistance of the EPA.

For recognized tribes the federal government is and has been the trustee, represented by the Bureau of Indian Affairs (BIA). Normally, when the federal government does not enact legislation or promulgate policy to the contrary, tribal governments assume authority and jurisdiction within the bounds of their reservations. The silence of Congress or the chief executive does not mean states can fill any assumed legal void, for there is none. Tribes today have not only demonstrated governmental skills to govern themselves, but they have even successfully regulated certain non-Indian land uses within their borders. This federal-state relationship is long-standing, although its critics have given it mixed reviews. Yet the relationship has essentially worked as long as the executive branch of the government has upheld its obligations and kept faith with the tribes. In matters of criminal affairs, statutes and case law essentially have sorted out tribal versus state jurisdiction over individuals and crimes; generally, tribes have no jurisdiction over non-Indians. As for civil matters—including land use planning, environmental regulation, and the like—case law tends to dominate, and decisions have led to shifts in the destinies of the tribes for reasons that perhaps should not have existed.

In 1953 Congress enacted P.L. 280—the Civil and Criminal Jurisdiction Act of 1953[16]—legislation that came during the era of tribal terminations, when the federal government sought to transfer civil and criminal jurisdiction of tribes to the states in which they are located. The parameters of civil and criminal jurisdiction under the law remained unclear, and thus the law undermined tribal institutions by establishing a measure of state jurisdiction that, in turn, has led to confusion and misstated authority on the part of states and their local political divisions. Whether through P.L. 280 or other laws or by dint of case law, states have been assuming certain authority to intrude on reservation activities, including various forms of land use—for example, waste disposal, casinos, wildlife management, and the like.[17]

Jurisdictional controversy arose quickly, for P.L. 280 opened the door to increased state and local government intervention in tribal land and sovereignty matters. The law granted sweeping authority for states to assume jurisdiction over civil and criminal affairs on reservations but came to be misconstrued to apply also to matters of taxation, zoning, and planning. Although tribes have the means—thanks to the American Indian Civil Rights Act[18]—to retrocede from the application of P.L. 280, the whole issue of jurisdiction in Indian Country has continued to be controversial long after the introduction of the law, in part because Congress created the Indian Self-Determination and Education Assistance Act,[19] which has sought to demote the authority of the Bureau of Indian Affairs by augmenting that of the tribes over their own affairs. Tribes tend to translate this "largess" of freedom as widening the latitude of their sovereignty, which increasingly encounters state and local government resistance.

In any debate over jurisdiction, several factors must be considered. David Getches and Charles Wilkinson have identified those most germane to our discussion: the *geographic area* encompassed by tribal and federal jurisdiction; the *persons, Indian and non-Indian,* over whom state or tribal jurisdiction extends in Indian Country; and the *subject matter* over which state or tribal jurisdiction extends in Indian Country.[20] The external boundaries of various reservations have been diminished by statute or case law, and thus the extent of tribal jurisdiction will vary within Indian Country. For example, in *United States v. Parkinson* (1975),[21] Bennett County, South Dakota, became part of the public domain by being severed from the Pine Ridge Indian Reservation; two years later, in *Rosebud Sioux Tribe v. Kneip,*[22] the U.S. Supreme Court declared that acts of 1904, 1907, and 1910 disestablished certain parts of the Rosebud Indian Reservation. If so, one must presume that here and elsewhere, when statutes or case law disestablishes parts of reservations, Indians occupying land in the designated counties reside outside their reservation (yet are protected by trust status), and non-Indians living on land within the reservation are potentially subject to tribal jurisdiction. Law professor Frank Pommersheim suggests that diminishment really causes us to ask whether the process of acquiring so-called surplus lands for non-Indian homesteading resulted in reducing the external boundaries of reservations. He concludes that "the fact of diminishment makes geography a pertinent factor in ascertaining tribal court jurisdiction and is a salutary reminder that jurisdictional concerns do not automatically end at a diminished reservation's boundaries."[23]

Recently, the court ruled that a land purchase and subsequent development for tribal members—for example, a housing project—did not necessarily constitute Indian Country because trust status had not then been granted by the federal government. The Narragansett Indians of Rhode Island, who had purchased land adjacent to the reservation, could not thus claim the housing area part of a dependent Indian community as interpreted in case law. Brent Eckersley notes that "the obvious effect of *Narragansett* will be to put tribes on notice that lands they purchase, and subsequently establish communities on, may not be dependent Indian communities. Consequently, these lands are not Indian country and may not be presumptively excluded from state laws."[24]

Because of these historical facts and legal interpretations, questions of jurisdiction over land use planning and zoning and management of hunting, fishing, water, and other on-reservation resources continue to aggravate relations between tribes and non-Indian landowners-users and communities within and adjacent to reservations. In general, we can identify two broad sets of factors that contribute to a state's perception that it has jurisdiction on reservations—*geographic,* for example, trust lands lie within the borders of states as well as within watersheds shared by either upstream or downstream non-Indian people; and *demographic,* for example, a significant number, often greater than a majority, of residents living on reservation lands are non-Indians. The latter has more recently dominated case law that has rejected total or partial tribal jurisdiction over non-Indian land and environmental management (Figure 9.1a–c).

Reservations as Extraterritorial Places

When tribes have consummate jurisdiction to manage their own affairs, reservations can be said to be extraterritorial yet lie within state boundaries.[25] The federal government is ever present in some context, as in the supervision of forest management and in mining activities on trust lands.[26] Even so, reservations for these and other purposes lie out of reach of state and local jurisdictions (Fig. 9.1a). This does not mean those jurisdictions have not confronted tribes and caused considerable litigation. Until the 1990s, case law seemed to sustain the position that tribal sovereignty ruled within reservation borders as long as the federal government did not proscribe otherwise, as in treaties, statutes, or case law. Since the 1960s many tribes—for example, the Warm Springs (Oregon), Wind River (Wyoming), Acoma (New Mexico)—have established tourist attractions and resorts under their own auspices[27] (Figure 9.2). On the other hand, hazardous waste management comes to mind when we think of broad federal powers to regulate and supervise waste sites. It is also true, however, that the federal Resource Conservation and Recovery Act (RCRA), which in the past has encouraged states to assume jurisdiction over hazardous waste management, does encourage states to instigate their "superior" jurisdiction within Indian Country.[28]

The state of Washington had sought to establish a uniform program of hazardous waste management within its borders, arguing that the spread of contaminants through groundwater draining some reservations warranted uniform practices under state guidance. In *Washington Dept. of Ecology v. EPA,*[29] the court upheld the EPA's jurisdiction over Indian lands. Many environmentalists, including myself, contend that holistic environmental management is ecologically sensible. Yet as a protagonist of Indian rights, I also subscribe to the view that such state intervention represents one more (and perhaps a greater) threat to tribal sovereignty, pitting tribes against states (Fig. 9.1a-b).

When the state of Washington sought a uniform program of hazardous waste management, it attempted to extend its regulations over the twenty-two reservations within state borders. The state apparently responded to the provisions of the RCRA, but in fact the law does not embrace Indian lands. (Although the Clean Air and Clean Water Acts were amended to identify tribes as the equivalent of states, RCRA was not so amended). In *Washington Dept. of Ecology* and other cases, courts have tended to rule that when the EPA or other federal agencies are charged to administer to tribal lands, states cannot intervene. Indeed, tribes have also invoked the holistic management argument to preserve the

Fig. 9.2 Lodge at Warm Springs Indian Reservation (Oregon). Many tribal tourist facilities such as this lodge and a number of visitors' centers were developed earlier than enactment of self-determination legislation. The Warm Springs tribes are among the most enterprising today. Photograph by Imre Sutton.

geographic integrity of a reservation. Many reservations, because of considerable, almost uninterrupted trust acreage, sustain tribal arguments for holistic management even though non-Indian parcels lie within the external boundaries of trust lands. Note, too, that tribal environmental regulations may indeed equal or exceed those of the state, thus nullifying the logic of state intervention.

A further example of the potential strength of tribal authority relative to state powers has to do with the efforts of the Mescalero Apache to establish a Monitored Retrievable Storage (MRS) facility on tribal lands in New Mexico. The tribe submitted a proposal to the U.S. Nuclear Waste Negotiator (NWN) in 1991 and followed it up with requests for funding into 1993. Subsequently, the state of New Mexico opposed the siting of the facility on the Indian reservation. Moreover, environmental groups reacted negatively to the Apache effort. The Apaches pursued their goal by negotiating with private companies, many of which were interested in storing waste on the Mescalero Indian Reservation. To be sure, the jurisdictional issue discouraged a number of companies from following through. Louis Leonard provides readers with a general road map of federal, tribal, and state jurisdictions that leaves open-ended any long-term questions about tribal autonomy.[30] (See Fig. 9.1b.)

As with other environmental situations, tribes assert sovereignty as the key factor—often supported by the wording of treaties—in the assertion of supremacy to act independently. Leonard notes that "broad constitutional power granted to the IRA-created tribal governments provides the necessary legal authority for the tribe to develop the MRS project within its borders" (subject to federal and state powers).[31] Self-determination has abetted tribes' autonomy over their environment, but in the same instance the EPA's Indian policy and the BIA's charge under trusteeship suggest that federal jurisdiction persists.[32] The implication is that state jurisdiction is measurably preempted.

Generally, states have little or no authority over Indians in Indian Country. Reinforcing this fact is another: New Mexico did not embrace the criminal-civil authority transferred to many states by P.L. 280 (1953). Increasingly, however, reservation lands do not always include by definition lands owned by non-Indians, potentially allowing for state jurisdiction. Despite not accepting the transfer of authority under P.L. 280, the state sought jurisdiction over fish and wildlife management in *New Mexico v. Mescalero Apache Tribe,* but the court ruled that state law is preempted if "it interferes or is incompatible with federal and tribal interests." It is also true that states are generally denied power over trust lands when tribes demonstrate a "willingness to regulate" certain activities.[33] With nuclear matters, there seems little question about federal jurisdiction in Indian Country.

Leonard, as well as many other observers, notes that despite the tug-of-war between opposing views—tribal self-determination and environmental protection—tribes are capable of managing sensitive environmental concerns and indeed are the only entity of the tripartite government in Indian Country to enter into negotiations to operate an MRS. Not only does Leonard develop an argument about racism and environmental justice, but he supports the view that "knowing that tribes are in this desperate economic situation, the federal government is now using the concept of tribal sovereignty as an excuse for allowing nuclear waste to gravitate toward tribal reservations."[34] Congress has apparently been trying to establish greater regulatory measures, but critics say the measures fall short of the essential oversight that parallels what EPA does with solid waste disposal.[35] Ultimately, the Mescalero will likely be allowed to establish an MRS on their land. Time and again it is noted that when tribes follow federal laws in establishing regulations, rarely can states intrude where the federal government has preemptory authority to protect tribes from intervention in their affairs. But other facets of geography do enter into the calculus of state jurisdiction.

Reservations as Sometime Parts of States

In more than one context, Indian Country may be subordinated in part to state jurisdiction over the environment. At a minimum we can point to joint efforts or concurrent jurisdiction of tribes and states. For example, the Indian Gaming Regulatory Act of 1988 provides that tribes and states must negotiate agreements compatible with state gaming regulations. This law gives states considerable clout—for example, in California gaming tribes ultimately had to finance a ballot measure to overcome constitutional limitations on the kinds of gambling allowed statewide. In spring 2000 the Indians overcame the limitations by gaining voter support for a new ballot initiative that changed the state constitutional rules but only for tribal casinos. In similar ways, states and tribes must enter into environmental agreements. However, legitimate environmental issues exist and persist; traffic congestion and potentially troublesome construction sites are factors. Also, a few Indian communities have attempted to establish a casino on land to be purchased outside of traditional territory. Casino income, of course, can lead to fuller employment and development of a number of environmental programs by tribes.[36]

Geography and Holistic Environmental Management

Although a tribe may assert supremacy, albeit under the protective wing of the federal government, because of confusing jurisdictions it is sometimes better to negotiate joint agreements. This is one outcome of *County of San Diego v. Babbitt,*[37] which dealt with a solid waste project on the Campo Indian Reservation (California). The band (legally a tribe but much smaller in number) had in mind a municipal solid waste landfill (MSWLF) and recycling and composting facilities, none of which represented a hazardous waste operation. The band created the Campo Environmental Protection Agency (Campo-EPA), giving it authority to negotiate with both public and private agencies. It also adopted an appropriate Solid Waste Code, and in 1995 the EPA approved the application pursuant to RCRA. Although the EPA recognized that the law does not specify that tribes are states, it "reasoned that the Band is the only government that has the authority to establish a MSWLF permit program under RCRA."[38]

The band also gained the approval of the Indian Bureau by preparing an appropriate environmental impact statement (EIS). San Diego County filed suit contending that the EIS did not meet NEPA requirements. Although the county appealed, the Ninth Circuit sustained the lower court's argument that the EIS met all NEPA regulations. Kevin Gover and James Cooney note that the band continued to assert that state law was preempted but at the same time sought a means to assuage state concerns and yet not forfeit its own jurisdiction. Ultimately, the band succeeded in enlisting the support of the state legislature, which enacted a law that authorized the California Environmental Protection Agency to enter into cooperative agreements with tribes in matters of solid waste facilities[39] (Fig. 9.1a-c).

In this situation and perhaps others, joint agreements between tribes and states may be a good corollary approach. Accordingly, neither the Campo Indians nor Cal-EPA conceded any jurisdiction, and tribal law continues to govern the operation of the landfill. Campo agreed to keep the state informed, and Cal-EPA can intervene only if there is indication of a violation or threat of one in terms of environmental regulations: "The effect is that the state steps in only if Campo-EPA fails to act."[40]

Because tribes share common physical geography with their non-Indian neighbors, it is important to understand that as residents of reservations Indians cannot separate themselves from related, adjacent resource uses and varying legal squabbles and litigation over given resources such as air, water, wildlife, scenery, and the like. At the same time, this common physical geography does not make anyone immune from the environmental disasters created outside the legal boundaries of Indian Country. For example, the explosion of Terra Industry's fertilizer plant in Sioux City, Iowa, created an ammonia cloud that drifted over the Winnebago and Omaha Reservations in northeastern Nebraska, forcing the evacuation of the town of Winnebago and the closure of the tribal offices at Macy.[41] Numerous forest fires, past or present, have threatened or have actually swept into Indian reservations.

For resource management that transcends tribal borders and involves public and even private lands, tribes and federal agencies have not always concurred on environmental priorities. In the case of wildlife, many tribes assert that they are doing a good job of managing critical habitats for birds, mammals, fish, and other wildlife. But pursuant to a Secretarial Order, issued jointly by the Departments of Commerce and the Interior addressing the responsibilities of the National Marine Fisheries Service* and the Fish and Wildlife Service (FWS), respectively, trust lands fall within the domain of the Endangered Species Act (ESA).[42] Tribes understand that the ESA seeks to preserve species and their habitats, but they oppose having their lands designated as critical habitats because this severely curtails economic development. In effect, tribes feel they have been singled out.

Wildlife managers contend that reservations are only part of the larger habitat that requires special management and that the tribes bear no disproportionate burden for the conservation of endangered species. The tribal response is that the designation of a critical habitat on a reservation is tantamount to federal (de facto) zoning, which overrides tribal autonomy.

The experience of the White Mountain Apache points out this conflict of interest in which both conservation and development sustain good arguments. The FWS sought to designate critical habitat on the reservation for the Mexican spotted owl. Tribal Chairman Ronnie Lupe contended that the designation would "undermine the tribe's 'entire wildlife and land-management philosophy' and paralyze tribal resource development activities, including sawmill, cattle

---

*For a discussion of marine resources and the Makah Indians of coastal Washington, see the Introduction to part I (text and note 8), pp. 4–5.

industry, and ski area." Because the tribe adopted appropriate conservation plans, the FWS excluded the reservation from the critical habitat designation. Ultimately, many reservations have been excluded from such a designation, whether it relates to habitats for steelhead (Nez Perce, Yakama, Warm Springs), Coho salmon (Siletz, Coos/Lower Umpqua/Siuslaw, Hoopa), pygmy owl (Tohono O'odham), or other species.[43]

Watersheds as Shared Geography

Like the air, watersheds are also shared (see Figure 9.1a-c). Because Indian reservations lie within the watersheds of rivers shared with non-Indian neighbors, both parties must not only protect their vested water rights to a common water source, but they must be vigilant in environmental management—especially in terms of floods, water supply, and water quality. Tribes may be upstream or downstream members of a watershed. Their geographic position has as much to do with the maintenance of water quality as it does with the distribution of water. One vital question posed by observers is whether tribes should possess regulatory authority under the Clean Water Act.[44] John Harbison, for one, contends that "empowering tribes to establish their own water quality standards and unilaterally enforce them upstream will lead us further away from integrated watershed management."[45] He also contends that "Clean Water Act federalism" is inefficient and that there is an optimal economic level of degradation that will likely not be achieved when more than one entity has jurisdiction in a watershed. Furthermore, he suggests that "by vesting [regulatory authority] in individual states as opposed to a collective association of all affected parties . . . the Clean Water Act inevitably begets conflicts."[46]

The amended Clean Water Act, by treating tribes as states, permits them to establish their own water quality standards. Under this proviso Isleta Pueblo (New Mexico) was the first to establish guidelines as applied to waters within the reservation.[47] The EPA informed upstream dischargers that they must comply. Isleta lies astride the Rio Grande, and upstream is New Mexico's largest city—Albuquerque. The city almost immediately sought a preliminary injunction to stop enforcement because it was getting ready to meet a new and tougher state standard on the discharge of ammonia, but Isleta's standard exceeded that of the state. Apparently, the city's wastewater discharge, upstream of the pueblo, contained ten times more ammonia than the tribal allowance.

Harbison notes that the pueblo's water quality standards relate to the ceremonial use of the river's waters. Interestingly, the city argued that the EPA's approval violated the Constitution's Establishment Clause related to religion. Although the pueblo admitted to its religious concerns, the EPA sustained its approval on the grounds of secular goals of the Clean Water Act. The city additionally argued that the EPA misinterpreted the act by approving tribal water quality at standards higher than EPA minimums and by imposing such standards on upstream dischargers. Says Harbison, "The crux of these arguments was that tribes were not really supposed to be treated like states in all respects."[48]

Ultimately, the court found that both the pueblo and the EPA met all requirements of the Clean Water Act. Apparently, the timing of the decision in *Arkansas v. Oklahoma* gave greater clout to the position taken by Isleta Pueblo—in effect, the Supreme Court said the EPA can enforce downstream water quality standards against upstream users, even with more stringent standards.[49] Gover and Cooney point out that "it is in everyone's interest to resolve these matters in a practical manner, without having to 'give away' anything"[50]—which of course is how both the Isleta water case and the Campo solid waste case worked out. Ultimately, Harbison provides some good advice: "Tribes ought to seek regulatory authority under the Clean Water Act simply to assure that their voices will be heard in the arena of watershed policy."[51]

Although the Isleta Pueblo surmounted legal difficulties to enforce higher water quality standards that sustained their autonomy as an equal voice in a watershed, the example of the Stillaguamish and Tulalip Tribes in Washington state represents one in which the Indians joined forces, as it were, with the state Department of Ecology to form a watershed task force to deal with pollutants entering the Stillaguamish watershed from livestock, farming, logging, development, and wastewater. As reported by Harbison, the resultant Watershed Management Committee comprises members of the tribes and of county, city, environmental, business, and citizens' groups. Such an arrangement suggests again that tribes and states can work cooperatively.[52]

Are Airsheds a Comparable Entity?

In 1990 Congress amended the Clean Air Act (CAA) to delegate power to tribes so they might administer and enforce CAA regulations within reservations. In essence, Congress elevated tribes to states, as had been done in similar legislation.[53] The amendments in effect permitted tribes to upgrade air quality standards to the most stringent classification, permitting almost no deterioration of pristine air quality. Moreover, the amendments were intended to give tribes an equal opportunity to assume primary planning, implementation, and enforcement responsibilities under CAA programs.[54] It was then that the EPA implemented its policy to assist tribal environmental management. Of course, the amended act required that tribes be recognized by the government and possess a governing body with the capacity to carry out air resource protection and management within reservation bounds according to CAA regulations. Tribes had to demonstrate the economic and technical ability to administer air quality programs. And although they had the capacity to enforce regulations on their own membership, there was and still is uncertainty as to whether they can extend air pollution regulations to non-Indians within their borders.[55]

States often contend that they have the apparatus to provide comprehensive ambient air quality management so they can regulate all emissions regardless of location within state borders. States seek to avoid patchwork management and want to sustain consistently high levels of regulation. Julie Reding points out that "states might fear that there would be an incentive for polluters to locate on reservations if they could avoid a state's more stringent standards."[56] She and others note again and again that native perception of environment is holistic, and it is in the best interests of tribes to develop environmental regulations of their own. Perhaps in the long run we have another example of why concurrent jurisdiction might be preferred. Yet self-determination urges tribes to seek their own solutions, for, as Reding comments, "Native Americans view environmental degradation as another form of destruction on the already dwindling tribal land base."[57]

When reviewing *Montana v. United States,* many scholars note that tribes can regulate nonmembers (non-Indians) if they live on trust lands, if they enter into consensual relations with the tribe (as in commercial ventures), and if their activity "threatens or has some direct effect on the political integrity, economic security, or the health or welfare of the tribe." *Montana* also limits the extent of tribal powers to lands on which a tribe exercises "undisturbed use and occupation," and it does not apply to lands subsequently alienated and held in fee by non-Indians pursuant to allotment acts.[58] Other decisions have also diminished tribal authority over non-Indians as well as Indians, and *Brendale v. Confederated Tribes and Bands of Yakima Nation,* for example, seems to be leading to inconsistent and some incompatible zoning policies, which would have a chilling effect on tribal self-government.[59]

Most of these cases reflect the geographic argument that states and local governments, by dint of the fact that trust lands lie within civil division boundaries, may appropriately pursue the issue of jurisdiction over Indian Country. And it is apparent that statutes and case law have been opening up options to the states that threaten to lead to expanded state jurisdiction in matters tribes alone or in conjunction with federal powers have authority to manage. Perhaps for these and other reasons, some tribes have chosen to seek a more cooperative relationship with state and local authorities.

The Case for or Against Demography

More recently, however, the more compelling argument for state and local intervention in tribal environmental affairs is a demographic one: the presence of non-Indians owning and utilizing land and otherwise residing in Indian Country (Figure 9.1a-c). What makes the demographic argument so vital to the states and the courts is the great prevalence of non-Indians on so many reservations. For example, in the state of Washington barely 20 percent of reservation residents are Indian; for the Puyallup the figure is only 3.4 percent. In California, Indian residents represent just 30 percent of those on reservations. In states such as Montana and the Dakotas, at least 50 percent are Indian residents.[60] Of course, the government in many ways intended for something of this sort to happen; land allotment "created" the surplus acreage that was made available under the homestead laws and thus encouraged Indian–non-Indian adjacency, deemed a desirable effect of separating individual Indians from their tribes.

In a way, this demographic argument predicates that a certain geography must exist—adjacency, proximity, density, and the like. Several cases have suggested to legal scholars that the courts are moving toward giving states and local civil divisions more authority over non-Indians and their land uses on lands held in fee, which are defined as "outside" the reservation, but also over trust lands under lease or utilized by non-Indian members of Indian families. Currently, it is the general practice that the federal government directly or indirectly supervises the leasing of tribal land, but a percentage of allottees and their heirs work through the Indian office for lease arrangements. I'll examine a few cases that although perhaps short of landmark, emphasize the direction the courts are taking in support of selective state jurisdiction.

The most frequently cited case is *Montana,* in which the Crow Tribe had sought to regulate hunting and fishing by nonmembers of the tribe, but ultimately the court ruled against the tribe. The tribe had argued that the ownership of the bed of the Bighorn River had been transferred to it by treaty and hence gave it jurisdiction. The court contended that the historic allotment acts and subsequent diminishment of the external boundaries of the reservation precluded any jurisdiction over alienated trust acreage. Moreover, the riverbed, because it was federally owned, transferred to the state. Consequently, the tribe could not regulate non-Indian fishing or hunting on the Bighorn River.[61]

In *Brendale* the issue turned on whether the Yakima (Yakama) Nation or Yakima County (Washington) had the authority to zone fee lands owned by non-Indians within reservation boundaries. The tribe had established a zoning policy that created closed and open areas (designations created by the BIA as part of environmental management), and the court recognized such tribal authority over tribal and individual Indian-owned lands everywhere on the reservation and over any non-Indian lands within the closed area. Although the court rendered a mixed, three-way decision, we can conclude that the court denied the tribe the authority to zone non-Indian lands within the open areas.[62]

In such instances tenurial patterns often nearly match demographics—fee lands signal the fact of identifiable areas of non-Indians, but such discrete distributions of Indian and non-Indian numbers do not always occur on reservations; dispersed patterns are more often the norm. There is a certain rationale in court decisions that separate land and environmental activities of Indian-trust lands from non-Indian-fee lands. Moreover, tribes should probably expect to encounter more and more decisions that make such distinctions, even though the articulated policy of the federal government supports and encourages increased tribal self-determination, which logically enough depends on tribal sovereignty.

In still another case, *South Dakota v. Bourland,* the high court bypassed Congress and abrogated treaty rights that sustained sovereignty. In *Bourland,* when the government negotiated the sale of tribal bottomlands to make way for a dam and reservoir (Oahe on the Missouri), the Cheyenne River Sioux tribe (South Dakota) apparently then "lost" any jurisdiction over these severed lands. Although the treaty establishing the reservation did not explicitly sustain or deny such jurisdiction, the court was clear on the issue. The tribe had tried to regulate non-Indian hunting and fishing on said lands but found the courts reluctant to sustain tribal jurisdiction when the tribe could not sufficiently demonstrate that any loss of jurisdiction impeded tribal government and resource management. *Bourland* did invoke interpretations from *Montana* and *Brendale,* but this suggests to some observers that the Supreme Court has once again moved significantly away from protecting tribal sovereignty.[63]

In their geographic interpretation of *Devils Lake Sioux Tribe v. North Dakota Public Services Commission,*[64] David Wishart and Oliver Froehling's study more closely examines the demographic argument utilized by the court. They analyzed spatial patterns of land ownership and population on the Fort Totten (Devils Lake Sioux) Reservation in North Dakota, noting that as Indian numbers declined from 1870 to 1930, non-Indian numbers increased, but that subsequent to World War II the reverse situation began to transpire.[65] Today the Indian population has seen a revival, whereas non-Indians resident on the reservation have declined in number commensurate with a general decline in rural farm populations in the Northern Plains. These demographic changes play a major role in the tribe's efforts to demonstrate that the Fort Totten IR has retained its Indian character despite the fact that a vast amount of trust acreage had been lost to the tribe through a law that opened the reservation to homesteaders and to individual allottees through alienation.

The critical issue in *Devils Lake* was a threat to tribal sovereignty by a state (North Dakota), for which the tribe sought redress to protect its autonomy against any state intrusion to regulate electric power services on the reservation. The question of whether the reservation retained Indian character entered into the court's argument that non-Indian landownership had rendered the reservation no longer an Indian place, and thus state jurisdiction was applicable. The experts sought to demonstrate, however, that despite the geographic division of Indian and non-Indian residence reflected in landownership, the tribe revered sacred places scattered throughout the reservation. Also, the state had never attempted to assert taxing authority on the reservation. Wishart and Froehling revealed a very high density of Indian population at the core of the reservation, less so at the peripheries where non-Indians, much fewer in number, held increasingly larger farms. Unfortunately, the court decided that "tribal sovereignty is present where its exercise affects mainly tribal members and not present where its impact falls mainly on nontribal members." As the authors note, "The judge left the contentious question of tribal sovereignty over non-Indian-owned lands on the reservation unanswered."[66] They, as well as myself, contend that this reflects the direction of court decisions beginning with *Brendale* where, as it were, tribal sovereignty has been moved inward from its external boundaries to those lands most heavily occupied and owned by Indians.[67]

Autonomy and Compromise in Indian Country: A Summation

We have observed that despite a history of federal preemption of jurisdiction over tribes and trust lands, states and local governments persist in efforts to intervene and regulate various environmental affairs on reservations. States correctly recognize that Indian County is composed of tripartite government and that because of the long-term effects of land allotment and the sale of Indian lands, non-Indians have become a political force within a great many reservations. We have seen how tribes have sought to consolidate fragmented and encumbered allotments to develop holistic environmental management, but the Supreme Court has prohibited tribes from "taking"—for example, by escheat or its equivalent—inherited parcels that sit essentially idle. Many tribes since the 1960s and especially subsequent to the promulgation of the self-determination policy have established offices for agriculture, archaeology, preservation, and the like and thus continue to demonstrate a capacity to manage their own lands.

Unfortunately, case law in recent years has worked to undermine tribal autonomy within its own borders. Such cases as *Bourland, Brendale, Devil's Lake,* and *Montana* point to the shifting position of the courts in favor of excluding non-Indians—a demographic factor—from tribal planning and environmental management. To be sure, some tribes have seen success, especially with the support of the EPA, in managing solid waste and establishing their own air quality standards under the Clean Air Act. Tribes see the need to reach out from reservation borders because of vested interests in watersheds and airsheds and in treaty rights to hunt and fish off reservation.

Perhaps it is incumbent on tribes that to assume and sustain tribal autonomy in environmental matters they must develop strong and effective environmental codes—codes that meet and defeat the challenge of state disapproval or rejection. Dean Suagee and Patrick Parenteau suggest that tribal sovereignty provides the medium in which to write comprehensive environmental review processes and that the National Environmental Policy Act may indeed be the best guideline.[68] Tribes can perhaps also overcome the uncertainties of jurisdiction by mandating that developers on Indian lands meet tribal zoning and other regulations. Walter Stern observes that "state authority . . . does not foreclose tribal authority, and vice versa."[69] Hence the need for greater clarification of jurisdiction and the desirability of cooperative agreements as long as neither side concedes jurisdiction.

It is clear that as self-determination prevails as a government-to-government relationship between tribes and all levels of government—federal, state, and local—more problems over jurisdiction and sovereignty and hence more litigation will occur. Tribes as environmental managers take on new legal meaning as they pursue planning and development of waste disposal facilities, casinos, and other enterprises state and local governments reject or seek control over. Moreover, tribal efforts to zone non-Indian lands as part of holistic environmental management within reservation borders also frustrate non-Indian landholders and have led to litigation, raising issues over the proper assertion of tribal sovereignty. In general, however, tribes may regulate non-Indians on trust lands and may even be able to extend that authority over fee lands, pursuant to *Montana,* when tribes feel threatened by a direct effect on their political integrity, economic security, or the health and welfare of tribal members.[70]

Overall, it appears that tribes must develop stronger environmental planning that rationally encompasses non-Indian land use on fee or trust lands so the current thrust of the demographic argument will be diminished. And most assuredly, tribes must be ever alert to shifting policy at the executive and congressional levels, as well as continue to litigate as a means to sustain gains made over the decades and to overturn efforts that would expand the powers of states in tribal affairs, environmental and otherwise.

References

1. Certain environmental laws, as amended, characterize tribes as states; that is, treat as a state (TAS): the Surface Mining Control and Reclamation Act, 1977, 30 U.S.C., § 1235(k) (1988); the Federal Water Pollution Control Act, 33 U.S.C. § 1377(e) (1994) (otherwise known as the Clean Water Act); the Clean Air Act, 42 U.S.C. § 7601(d)(1) (1994); the Comprehensive Environmental Response, Compensation, and Liability Act of 1980, 42 U.S.C. § 9607 (1994); and the Oil Pollution Act of 1990, 33 U.S.C. § 2706(a) (1994). According to Kevin K. Washburn ["Recent Developments—1. Environmental Law," *American Indian Law Review,* 11 (1997): 183–188], "The existence of congressional authorization has not insulated the EPA from litigation involving approval of tribal programs," p. 184. For a general review of tribal-state cooperation, see Tim De Young and William C. Scott, "Environmental Protection in Indian Country," *American Indian Law Review,* 15:1 (summer 2000): 20–23, 63–64. The authors expand the discussion of TAS and, noting that the Supreme Court has not resolved the question of extent of tribal jurisdiction in environmental matters, state that "certain tribal, state, and federal agencies apparently continue to believe that establishing or maintaining jurisdiction is more important than achieving the objectives of environmental protection" (p. 64).
2. Palm Springs, California, and the Agua Caliente IR represent examples where because of a railroad land grant, the city and the tribe "occupy" alternate sections (1 square mile, or approximately 640 acres) of land—a true checkerboard. In the 1990s Salamanca, New York, negotiated a new lease with the Allegany Seneca.
3. See Francis P. Prucha, *The Great Father: The United States Government and the American Indians* (Lincoln: University of Nebraska Press, 1984); Charles F. Wilkinson, *American Indians, Time, and the Law: Native Societies in a Modern Constitutional Democracy* (New Haven: Yale University Press, 1987); Imre Sutton, "Sovereign States

and the Changing Definition of an Indian Reservation," *Geographical Review,* 66:3 (1976): 281–295.

4. The General Allotment Act (Dawes) of 1887 (24 *Stat.* 388) was preceded by several acts and treaties that set in motion the division of reservations into units equivalent to homesteads. See J. P. Kinney, *A Continent Lost—A Civilization Won: Indian Land Tenure in America* (Baltimore: Johns Hopkins University Press, 1937): 81–161.
5. There are numerous studies of land allotment: cf. Leonard A. Carlson, *Indians, Bureaucrats, and Land: The Dawes Act and the Decline of Indian Farming* (Westport, CT: Greenwood, 1981); Janet A. McDonnell, *The Dispossession of the American Indian, 1887–1934* (Bloomington: Indiana University Press, 1991).
6. The codified definition of Indian Country is stated as follows: "(a) all land within the limits of any reservation under the jurisdiction of the United States government, notwithstanding the issuance of any patent and including rights-of-way running through the reservation, (b) all dependent Indian communities within the borders of the United States whether within the original or subsequently acquired territory thereof, and whether within or without the limits of a state, and (c) all Indian allotments, the Indian titles to which have not been extinguished, including rights-of-way running through the same." 63 *Stat.* 94, 18 U.S.C. § 1511. Cf. for other definitions, Vine Deloria Jr. and Clifford M. Lytle, *American Indians, American Justice* (Austin: University of Texas Press, 1983): 58–79; Charles F. Wilkinson, *American Indians, Time and the Law* (New Haven: Yale University Press, 1987): 90; David Getches, Charles F. Wilkinson, and Robert A. Williams Jr., *Federal Indian Law,* 4th ed. (St. Paul: West, 1993): 438–469; Imre Sutton, "Preface to Indian Country: Geography and Law," *American Indian Culture and Research Journal,* 15:2 (1991): 3–36.
7. David Rich Lewis, "Native Americans and the Environment: A Survey of Twentieth-Century Issues," *American Indian Quarterly,* 19 (1995): 423–450; N. Bruce Duthu, ed., "Symposium: Stewards of the Land: Indian Tribes, the Environment, and the Law," *Vermont Law Review,* 21:1 (1996): 353–403; Getches, Wilkinson, and Williams, *Federal Indian Law,* chapters 10, 12, 13.
8. Figure 9.1, "Environmental Jurisdiction in Indian Country," is a schematic attempt to identify tripartite government patterns in terms of some but not all environmental management concerns of all three government entities as each relates to Indian Country. The venn diagram is based on much of the literature cited in this chapter.
9. Official state perception of tribal autonomy is apparent whenever official state maps leave out reservations or otherwise exclude certain reservation counties dominated by non-Indian residents, as in South Dakota. See Sutton, "Sovereign States." Cf. Glenn A. Phelps, "Mr. Gerry Goes to Arizona: Electoral Geography and Voting Rights in Navajo Country," *American Indian Culture and Research Journal,* 15:2 (1991): 63–92.
10. A good collection of studies that suggest the breadth of indigenous lifeways is Thomas C. Blackburn and Kat Anderson, comps. and eds., *Before the Wilderness: Environmental Management by Native Californians* (Menlo Park, CA: Ballena, 1993).
11. 48 *Stat.* 984 (1934); also called the Wheeler-Howard Act.
12. In addition to the IRA, see Lewis Meriam et al., *The Problem of Indian Administration,* vol. 17 of *Studies in Administration* (Baltimore: Brookings Institution for Government Research, 1928), and William Brophy and Sophie Aberle, *The Indian: America's Unfinished Business* (Norman: University of Oklahoma Press, 1966).

13. Edward T. Hall, *West of the Thirties: Discoveries Among the Navajo and Hopi* (New York: Doubleday, 1994).
14. Land Consolidation Act, 1983—P.L. 97-459, 96 *Stat.* 2517; see *Hodel v. Irving,* 481 U.S. 704 (1987), and *Babbitt v. Youpee,* 67 F. 3d 194 (9th Cir. 1995).
15. 752 F. 2d 1465 (1985). See Getches, Wilkinson, and Williams, *Cases and Materials on Federal Indian Law,* pp. 727–736.
16. 67 *Stat.* 588 (1953).
17. P.L. 250. See Carole Goldberg-Ambrose, *Planting Tail Feathers: Tribal Survival and Public Law 280* (Los Angeles: UCLA–American Indian Studies Center, 1997).
18. 82 *Stat.* 77 (1968).
19. 88 *Stat.* 2203 (1975).
20. David H. Getches and Charles Wilkinson, *Cases and Materials on Federal Indian Law,* 2d ed. (St. Paul: West, 1986): 338–339.
21. 525 Fed. 120 (1975).
22. 430 U.S. 584 (1977). For both cases, see my discussion in "Sovereign States."
23. Frank Pommersheim, "The Reservation as Place: A South Dakota Essay," *South Dakota Law Review,* 34:2 (1989): 252; Sutton, "Preface to Indian Country."
24. Brent Eckersley, "*Narragansett Indian Tribe of Rhode Island v. Narragansett Electric Company*: When Dependent Indian Communities Fall Within Indian Country," *American Indian Law Review,* 21:1 (1997): 193–204, quote on p. 204; 89 F.3d 908 (1st Cir. 1996).
25. In the nineteenth century tribal lands "lay beyond or without the limits of a territory or particular jurisdiction." That is, tribes were said to occupy areas or places *extraterritorial* to the newly formed territories or states. See Sutton, "Sovereign States," quote on p. 286.
26. See West, "Natural Resources Development," pp. 91–92.
27. See Jack Hunt, "Land Tenure and Economic Development on the Warm Springs Indian Reservation," *Journal of the West,* 9:1 (1970): 93–109. I visited such developments already operative in 1984 on the Wind River IR (WY), at Acoma Pueblo, Yakama IR, somewhat later at Gila Bend IR (AZ), and elsewhere in the West.
28. 42 U.S.C. 6901–6987 (1982 and Supp. 3, 1985). A leading case deals with Campo IR near the Mexico border in California.
29. 752 F. 2d 1465 (1985); Leslie Allen, "Who Should Control Hazardous Waste on Native American Lands? Looking Beyond *Washington Dept. of Ecology v. EPA,*" *Ecology Law Quarterly,* 14 (1987): 69–116.
30. This discussion relies heavily on Louis G. Leonard III, "Sovereignty, Self-Determination, and Environmental Justice in the Mescalero Apache's Decision to Store Nuclear Waste," *Environmental Affairs,* 24 (1997): 651–693.
31. Ibid., p. 669. James W. Kuntz ["Nuclear Incidents on Indian Reservations: Who Has Jurisdiction? Tribal Court Exhaustion Versus the Price-Anderson Act," *American Indian Law Review,* 21:1 (1997): 103–129] raises questions about the ultimate authority—federal or tribal—in the case of a nuclear incident; the options seem to preclude any state jurisdiction.
32. The Indian Environmental General Assistance Program Act of 1992 [42 U.S.C. § 4368(b) (1994)], according to Leonard ["Sovereignty, Self-Determination," p. 672], provides funding so that tribes might ascertain their environmental needs.
33. 462 U.S. 324 (1983); Leonard, "Sovereignty, Self-Determination," quotes on pp. 677–678.

34. Ibid., p. 689.
35. Tribes may assert authority to establish solid waste sites, but the federal government determines policy dealing with nuclear wastes; see Nuclear Waste Policy Act Amendments of 1987, 42 U.S.C. §§ 10,101—10,226 (1988).
36. 25 U.S.C.A. §§ 2701—2721 (1988); Cf. Daryl Kelley, "Oxnard Says No Dice to Casino Bid," *L. A. Times,* B1, 10, May 10, 2001. This deals with a Maidu community seeking to establish a casino several hundred miles south of traditional territory. If land were purchased and the federal government placed it in trust for the Maidu, then the Indians would have negotiated with the state for a joint agreement. However, Oxnard city council rejected the casino idea. Elsewhere, other Indian groups want to do much the same at a distance from home ground.
37. No. 94-55548 (9th Cir., July 27, 1995). See Kevin Gover and James B. Cooney, "Cooperation Between Tribes and States in Protecting the Environment," *Natural Resources and Environment,* 10 (winter 1996): 35–38, 77–78; see also *Backcountry Against Dumps v. Environmental Protection Agency,* 100 F.3d 147 (1996), and Getches, Wilkinson, and Williams, *Federal Indian Law,* pp. 628–633.
38. Gover and Cooney, "Cooperation Between Tribes and States," p. 37.
39. Ibid., p. 38.
40. Ibid.
41. "Toxic Blast Forces Winnebago Evacuations," *Indian Country Today,* December 22, 1994: B1.
42. No. 3206, June 5, 1997; ESA can be found at 16 U.S.C. §§ 1531–1544.
43. [Statement before] U.S. Cong., Senate Committee on Environment and Public Works, Subcommittee on Drinking Water, Fisheries, and Wildlife, 104th Cong., 1995: 732, quoted in Getches, Wilkinson, and Williams, *Federal Indian Law,* p. 731. This wildlife discussion is based mostly on Sandi B. Zellmer, "Conserving Ecosystems Through the Secretarial Order on Tribal Rights," *Natural Resources and Environment,* 14:3 (winter 2000): 162–165, 211–214.
44. 33 U.S.C. § 1377 (1988).
45. Much of the discussion in this section relies on John S. Harbison, "The Downstream People: Treating Indian Tribes as States Under the Clean Water Act," *North Dakota Law Review,* 71 (1995): 473–495, quote on p. 473. See also Gover and Cooney, "Cooperation Between Tribes and States." A recent study points out the conflicts between tribes and states: Steven E. Silvern, "Reclaiming the Reservation: The Geopolitics of Wisconsin Anishinaabe Resource Rights," *American Indian Culture and Research Journal,* 24:3 (2000): 131–153.
46. Harbison, "The Downstream People," p. 481.
47. Both ibid. and Gover and Cooney, "Cooperation Between Tribes and States," discuss events at Isleta and *City of Albuquerque v. Browner,* No. CIV-93-82-M (D.N.M., October 21, 1993); 97 F.3d 415 (10th Cir. 1996), *cert. denied,* 118 S. Ct. 410 (1997).
48. Harbison, "The Downstream People," p. 483.
49. Gover and Cooney, "Cooperation Between Tribes and States," pp. 77–78; also 53 U.S. 91 (1992).
50. Gover and Cooney, "Cooperation Between Tribes and States," p. 78.
51. Harbison, "The Downstream People," p. 495.
52. Ibid., p. 492.

53. 42 U.S.C. §§ 7401–7671q (Supp. 2, 1990). This and three other laws are administered by the EPA: Surface Mining Control and Reclamation Act, 1977; Federal Water Pollution Control Act (Clean Water Act); and the Comprehensive Environmental Response, Compensation, and Liability Act, 1980. See note 1 in this chapter.
54. See Julie M. Reding, "Controlling Blue Skies in Indian Country: Who Is the Air Quality Posse—Tribes or States? The Applicability of the Clean Air Act in Indian Country and on Oklahoma Tribal Lands," *American Indian Law Review,* 18 (1993): 161–190. This section relies heavily on Reding.
55. Ibid., p. 175. Earlier discussion noted the passage of P.L. 280 and its essential nullification by the Indian Civil Rights Act of 1968. Under these laws, states can assume concurrent jurisdiction over reservations only with tribal consent.
56. Ibid., p. 183.
57. Ibid., p. 190.
58. *Montana v. United States,* 450 U.S. 544 (1981), 565–566; see Reding, "Controlling Blue Skies," pp. 177–183.
59. *Brendale v. Confederated Tribes and Bands of Yakima Indian Nation,* 492 U.S. 408 (1989); cf. Getches, Wilkinson, and Williams, *Federal Indian Law,* pp. 603–608; see also *White Earth Band of Chippewa Indians v. Alexander* [683 F. 2d 1129 (8th Cir.), *cert. denied,* 459 U.S. 1070 (1982)] permits the state to enforce fish and game laws against tribal members on the Spokane Indian Reservation, and *U.S. v. Anderson* [736 F. 2d 1358 (9th Cir. 1984)] holds that the state may regulate surplus water use by non-Indians on the reservation.
60. Francis Paul Prucha, *Atlas of American Indian Affairs* (Lincoln: University of Nebraska Press, 1990), part 4, "Maps by Geographical Areas," pp. 43–52, and tables, pp. 151–156.
61. 450 U.S. 544 (1981); see Imre Sutton, "Indian Country and the Law: Land Tenure, Tribal Sovereignty, and the States," in Gordon M. Bakken, ed., *Law in the Western United States* (Norman: University of Oklahoma Press, 2000): 251–266, discussion on p. 263.
62. 109 S. Ct. 2994 (1989); ibid.
63. 113 S. Ct. 2309 (1993). See Janis Searles, "*South Dakota v. Bourland*: Another Supreme Court Move Away From Recognition of Tribal Sovereignty," *Environmental Law,* 25:1 (1995): 209–237.
64. U.S. District Court, Dist. of N.D.—Southwestern Div., February 3, 1993, case no. A1-90-179.
65. David J. Wishart and Oliver Froehling, "Land Ownership, Population, and Jurisdiction: The Case of the *Devils Lake Sioux Tribe v. North Dakota Public Service Commission,*" *American Indian Culture and Research Journal,* 20:2 (1996): 33–58.
66. Ibid., p. 54.
67. Cf. Allison M. Dussias, "Geographically Based and Membership-Based Views of Tribal Sovereignty: The Supreme Court's Changing Vision," *University of Pittsburgh Law Review,* 55:1 (1993): 1–97.
68. Dean B. Suagee and Patrick A. Parenteau, "Fashioning a Comprehensive Environmental Review Code for Tribal Governments: Institutions and Processes," *American Indian Law Review,* 21:2 (1997): 297–328.
69. Cf. Walter E. Stern, "Environmental Compliance Considerations for Developers of Indian Lands," *Land and Water Law Review,* 28:1 (1993): 77–113, quote on p.

103. Stern reminds us that "despite express language that tribal lands remain 'under the absolute jurisdiction . . . of the United States,' disclaimer clauses do not preclude exercise of state jurisdictional authority over reservation lands or tribal activities"; p. 105 and note 155.

70. Douglas B.L. Endreson, "A Review of the 1990s and a Look at What's Ahead," *American Indian Law Review,* 22:2 (1998): 611–622, quote on p. 620; Carl G. Hakansson, "Indian Land-Use Zoning Jurisdiction: An Argument in Favor of Tribal Jurisdiction Over Non-Member Fee Lands Within Reservation Boundaries," *North Dakota Law Review,* 73:4 (1977): 721–740. Hakansson cites Justice Blackmun's dissent in *Montana* wherein Blackmun argued that tribes retain exclusive zoning authority whenever a tribe enacts a comprehensive zoning code and that local government should only have authority to step in when the tribe fails to exercise its authority (p. 736). He also reports earlier cases in which lower courts have upheld tribal zoning enforcement against non-Indians on fee lands, citing *Knight v. Shoshone* (the Wind River IR) [670 F. 2d 900 (10th Cir. 1982)] and *Confederated Salish and Kootenai Tribes v. Namen* [665 F. 2d 951 (9th Cir. 1982)] (p. 739).

CHAPTER 10

Negotiated Water Settlements: Environmentalists and American Indians

LAURA KIRWAN AND DANIEL MCCOOL

In recent years there has been a trend in some policymaking arenas to eschew traditional judicial remedies in favor of negotiated settlements. There are numerous variations to this approach, many of which fall under the rubric of alternative dispute resolution. Environmental policy and Indian water rights are two substantive policy areas in which this approach has been utilized successfully. In regard to environmental policy, a number of highly conflictual issues have been resolved using alternative dispute resolution.[1] In regard to Indian water rights, the federal government officially adopted a policy of negotiating rather than litigating Indian water rights in the early 1980s. Since that time fourteen settlements have been signed, and thirty-two more are in negotiation.[2]

It is clear that some difficult natural resource conflicts can be resolved through a process of bargaining and negotiation outside the narrow confines of a lawsuit. The negotiation process becomes considerably more complicated, however, when both environmental policy and Indian water policy are affected by the same negotiation.

A complex relationship exists among American Indians, environmentalists, and water. The struggle over Indian water is an old one, but the relationship between Indians and environmentalists concerning water has become increasingly complex since the mid-1980s, for two reasons. First, environmental organizations' influence over policy has increased dramatically. In the past, their influence was felt only on specific issues and under certain conditions. But today they have a major impact on water issues of critical importance to Indian tribes. Indeed a host of issues bring environmentalists and Indian tribes into contact.[3]

Second, the U.S. government's policy of negotiating rather than litigating Indian water rights cases has involved numerous interest groups, including environmental organizations. Indian tribes have been litigating their water rights since the landmark case of *Winters v. U.S.* in 1908, which created the concept of reserved water rights.[4] This doctrine holds that when Indian reservations were created, an implied water right was also created to permit tribes to take sufficient water to meet the purposes of the reservation. For seventy years tribes fought for their reserved rights in court but with limited success.[5] In the early 1980s the federal government changed strategies and instituted a new policy of negotiating settlements between tribes and other parties rather than litigating Indian claims in court.[6] In these settlements tribes have often agreed to quantify their claims to reserved water rights in exchange for water development funding and other benefits. In this overtly political process, environmentalists often play a role in the negotiations; sometimes they have sided with Indian tribes, but in some cases they have opposed the tribes.

This chapter explores the role environmentalists and their allies in government have played in the negotiation and implementation of Indian water settlements. It examines both conflict and cooperation between tribes and environmentalists in negotiating settlements of water claims on Indian reservations.

The interface between environmentalists and Indian tribes can be viewed from two perspectives. The first we call the *natural allies* perspective. This assumes that the philosophical orientation of Native Americans creates a natural alliance between tribes and environmental organizations. It is well-known that American Indians regard the land as sacred; their metaphysical foundation focuses on the harmony and unity of humans and nature. The natural allies perspective assumes that this can be transcribed into a political orientation that favors environmental protection over development. Thus environmental groups and Indian tribes will work together for common goals.

A very different interpretation is the *last refuge* perspective. In this view environmentalists see Indian reservations not as tribal homelands but as biological preserves—the last refuge of wilderness and open space, wildlife and native flora, and clean air and water. This is the case because Indian reservations have experienced less economic development than non-Indian lands and therefore present an opportunity to preserve remaining islands of ecological integrity. As a result, Indian tribes may bear a disproportionate burden from environmental laws that limit or proscribe the development of natural resources on undeveloped lands. In this perspective, tribes and environmentalists are in conflict over how to use tribal lands and waters.

This chapter examines four issues in Indian water settlements that have brought environmentalists into the negotiation process: water development, especially the construction of dams; the Endangered Species Act; instream flow; and water marketing. The conclusion discusses the relationship between environmental policy and tribal self-determination.

Four Issues

WATER DEVELOPMENT

It is often said that the era of dam building is over. The rigid political alliance that used to push dam authorizations through Congress with ease can no longer overcome objections from environmentalists and cost-conscious urbanites. The end of the dam-building era was recognized in the Bureau of Reclamation's 1992 mission statement.[7] This change in policy has had serious repercussions for Indian tribes. Only now, through the settlement process, are tribes able to generate public funding for water development on reservations. Thus just when tribes develop the capacity to participate in the water development era, that era comes to an end, leaving many reservations without substantial storage capacity (Figure 10.1).

The policy against dam building has made it extremely difficult for tribes to incorporate new storage facilities into their water settlements. Tribes have had to carefully construct settlements within the confines of this new water policy. Settlements that rely on new construction have experienced problems. The Colorado Ute settlement relies on the Animas–La Plata Project, which includes construction of Ridges Basin Dam and other structures. But the current political climate is so hostile to major new structural development that this project may never be built. The greatest legal impediment to the project so far has been the Endangered Species Act (see the following section), but much of the opposition to Animas–La Plata is based on the fact that the project requires building major structural features with a significant environmental impact.[8] A proponent of the project claims environmentalists have ignored the value of the settlement agreement with the Colorado Ute tribes because "it complicates their standard arguments in opposing water conservation through water storage."[9] In 1997, a scaled-down version of the project, dubbed Animas–La Plata Light, was proposed in an effort to appease project opponents.[10]

Other tribes have avoided the contentious issue of dams by purposefully designing their settlements around the issue. Many settlements signed to date rely on storage facilities already in place.[11] The Northern Cheyenne settlement authorized the repair and enlargement of the Tongue River Dam, but it was not an issue with environmentalists because the refurbished dam has little impact beyond that of the original dam.[12] The San Luis Rey settlement was designed from the ground up to rely on increased water efficiency rather than new dams.

Some settlements, however, are inextricably tied to dams. The Northern Ute settlement has been affected by dams in two ways. First, the tribe's settlement is part of an act that authorizes the completion of the Central Utah Project (CUP). Upper Stillwater Dam, which is part of that project, diverts stored water away from the reservation. The dam was built before the settlement was negotiated, but the settlement and an adjoining compact stipulate the payment and diversion schedules for that water.[13] Another part of the CUP is called the

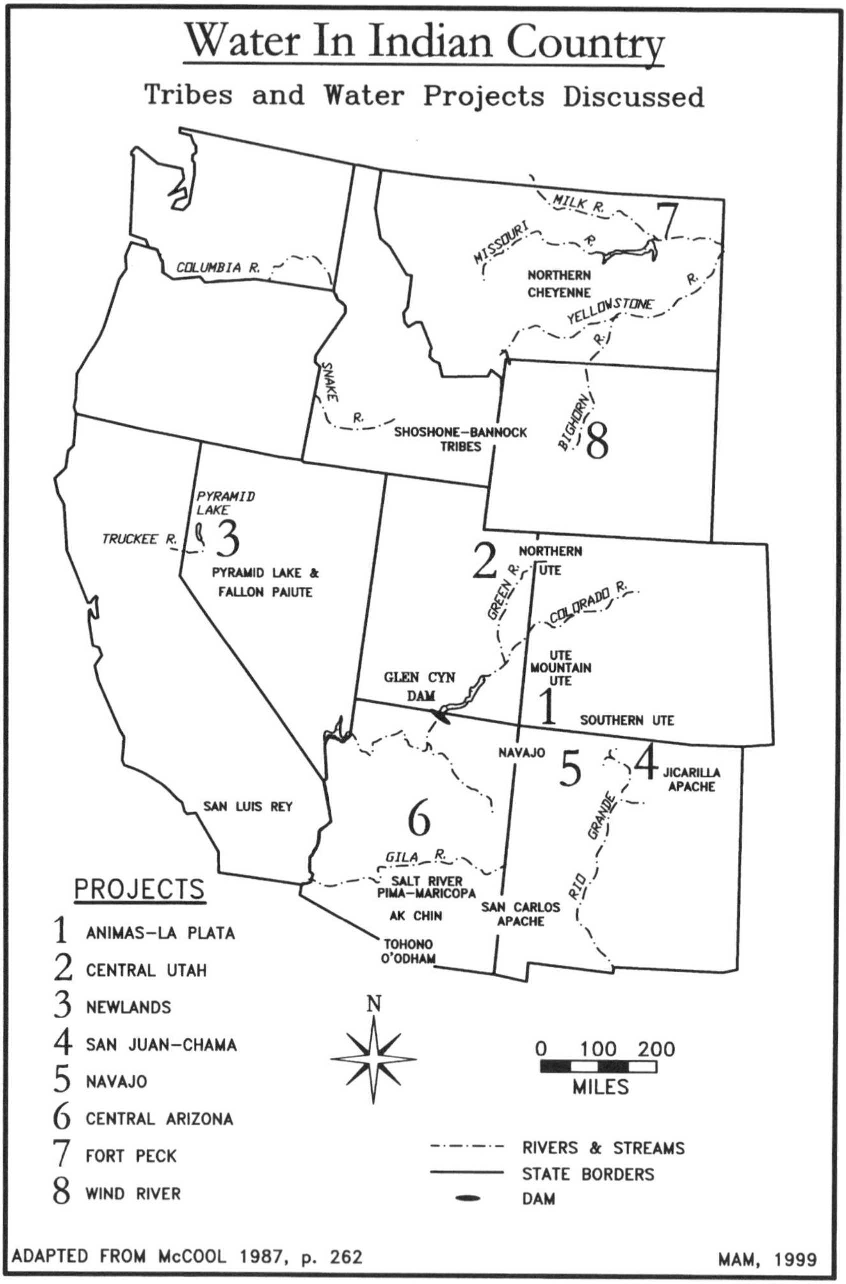

Fig. 10.1 Water in Indian Country, Tribes and Water Projects Discussed. Tribes in all of the western states retain water rights, and many continue to farm by irrigation. Only those projects discussed in the text appear on this map.

Uintah Basin Replacement Project; its objective is to increase storage within the basin for both Indians and non-Indians, but the parties have yet to agree on how that will be accomplished. It is not an option to build a large, traditional storage dam, however, because of environmental opposition.

The most direct impact water development policy has on Indian water settlements concerns the public and private water diversion structures that operate upstream from reservations and divert water to non-Indian uses. In Indian water settlements, negotiators have tried diligently to avoid imposing water losses on non-Indians. In most negotiations little if any unallocated water is left in the watershed. This creates a severe set of constraints; settlements must establish new sources of water or purchase existing water rights, both of which are problematic in an era of tight budgets and environmental scrutiny.

In the future, settlements that are based on conservation and increased efficiency stand the best chance of drawing the support of environmental groups. And the Bureau of Reclamation, as part of its new mission, now recognizes American Indians as an integral part of its constituency: "The water resource needs of Native Americans will be an important new program area for Reclamation. This will include: undertaking water resource management and development activities, working to improve the technical expertise of tribes, and continuing our assistance to the Secretary [of the Interior] in resolving Indian water rights disputes."[14] Thus if funding can be secured, the bureau may be able to help tribes implement water conservation and management programs that benefit reservation water users. It is, however, extremely unlikely that the bureau will construct large new dams for American Indians.

The Endangered Species Act

The Endangered Species Act has played an important role in many settlements, particularly the Colorado Ute, Pyramid Lake Paiute and Fallon Paiute, and Jicarilla Apache settlements. The act is also affecting the Navajo Nation's efforts to settle its water claims on the Little Colorado River. In each of these cases, the tribes' water settlements have been profoundly impacted by the discovery of threatened or endangered fish and plant species in the rivers and watersheds that are subject to tribal water claims.

Environmentalists have discovered that the Endangered Species Act (ESA) is one of the most powerful tools at their disposal. In passing the ESA in 1973, "Congress intended endangered species to be afforded the highest of priorities."[15] When the U.S Fish and Wildlife Service (FWS), the lead agency for administering the act, determines that a species is threatened or endangered, it can halt all activities deemed harmful. The ESA bans the "taking" of a protected species. It also bans activity that indirectly harms species by destroying or altering habitat on which the species relies.

As Indian tribes seek to develop water rights quantified in negotiated settlements, many are impacted by the ESA. Although some tribes are aided in their settlement efforts by the ESA,[16] other tribes may bear a disproportionate share of the ESA's burden.[17] The Pyramid Lake Paiutes' settlement was aided by the presence of endangered species in the tribe's water source. Other tribes such as the Ute Mountain Utes and Southern Utes, the Jicarilla Apaches, and the Navajo Nation have run afoul of the ESA in negotiating or implementing settlements.

The ESA gave the Pyramid Lake Paiutes the legal and political clout they needed to restore their fisheries in the Truckee River and in Pyramid Lake. Without the threat of the ESA's protection, surrounding non-Indian water users, such as the thirsty and rapidly growing Reno-Sparks metropolitan area, might have overwhelmed the tribe's efforts to settle their water claims. The existence of the endangered cui-ui and the Lahontan cutthroat trout in the disputed waters, however, tipped the conflict in favor of the tribe's fishery restoration efforts.[18]

The ESA has had a much different effect on the tribes of the San Juan Basin of the Colorado Plateau. Discovery of endangered fish species—the Colorado squawfish, humpback chub, and razorback sucker—in the waters of the San Juan, a tributary of the Colorado River, has effectively halted the implementation of the Colorado Utes' water settlement, which relies on the completion of the Animas–La Plata Project. The Jicarilla Apaches are not permitted to use most of the water they obtained in their water settlement until the seven-year FWS study of the river is complete, and the tribe may be unable to use its water if the fish are still considered threatened.

The San Juan species have also negatively impacted the Navajo Nation's attempts to complete construction of the Navajo Indian Irrigation Project. The project's Block 9 cannot be built unless a finding of no-jeopardy or a reasonable and prudent alternative is found under the Endangered Species Act.[19] The Navajo Nation has also encountered ESA concerns in its ongoing negotiations to settle its rights in the Little Colorado River, another Colorado River tributary. This has resulted in considerable frustration for tribal officials representing the affected area.[20]

Tribes that have had their water settlements stymied by the ESA feel the act has a disproportionate impact on Indian water development for a variety of reasons. First and most fundamentally, tribal waters may be more likely affected by the ESA because they are undeveloped or underdeveloped.[21] The Colorado River and many of its tributaries, for instance, are heavily developed. The remaining undeveloped stretches are likely to be found on or near Indian reservations and are home to several endangered plant and animal species. Over one-third of the area designated as habitat for the humpback chub is tribal land.[22]

Another, more serious problem lies in the difference between Indian reserved water rights and state appropriative rights. Under the prior appropriation system the priority of rights was determined by who appropriated first. Under the Winters Doctrine, tribal water rights date from the establishment of each reservation (see Glossary). For tribes with negotiated settlements, the priority date of the water right and a quantified amount of water they can use are usually specified in the settlement legislation. Unlike appropriative rights, Winters rights are not lost through nonuse.

As part of a species' recovery plan, the FWS must determine the environmental baseline of the critical habitat, which includes the past and present impact of human activity in the area—including water use.[23] Indian reserved rights have rarely been put to use because of a lack of funding and support from the federal government and opposition by non-Indian water users.[24] In environmental baseline calculations, reserved rights are not considered, since they are usually not past or present uses of water. Although tribes are legally at the front of the line in determining who has rights to the water, in practice Indian reserved rights have often been pushed to the rear. The ESA then blocks development of senior Indian reserved rights while considering junior non-Indian state appropriative rights as part of the existing environmental baseline.

Although tribes have water rights that predate almost all claims of surrounding non-Indian users, the politics of Western water makes it extremely unlikely that tribes will be able to "bump" non-Indian users and move ahead in line, especially in the Colorado Basin. A basic decision rule in negotiations is that the settlement of Indian claims must not infringe on current uses of water by non-Indians. Affected tribes, although sympathetic to the ESA's goals, have watched hard-won settlements unravel at the discovery of endangered fish. The tribes in the San Juan River Basin—the Colorado Ute tribes, the Jicarilla Apache tribe, and the Navajo Nation—feel they are being forced to shoulder most of the burden of preserving species threatened by other users' water development.[25] Rather than view the ESA as an ally, as in the case of Pyramid Lake, these tribes view it as a significant threat to their water settlements.

The Upper Colorado River tribes argue that the FWS has failed to uphold the federal trust responsibility in its enforcement of the ESA. As a federal agency, the FWS is required to act in the best interest of tribes in making any decisions that may impact the tribes' well-being. Some tribal representatives feel the FWS has failed in this regard and needs to be better educated about the federal trust responsibility and about FWS's role in fulfilling that trust.[26]

Instream Flow

In recent years water policymakers have been expanding their concept of beneficial use to include uses that do not depend on diversion. These instream uses include fishing and habitat preservation, aesthetics, recreation, water quality, and in the case of some Indian tribes, religious protection.[27]

Some tribes have attempted to protect instream flows in their settlements. The Fort Hall Shoshone-Bannock Tribes of southern Idaho, the Pyramid Lake Paiute Tribe, and the Northern Utes of Utah sought to ensure adequate instream flows for the protection of fish species and habitat important to the tribal culture.

As discussed earlier, the Pyramid Lake Tribe sought to protect the cui-ui and the Lahontan cutthroat trout. The Fort Hall Tribes wanted to restore the chinook and sockeye salmon. And the Northern Utes wanted to protect a blue-ribbon fishing stream. All of these tribes found support from environmentalists because they sought to preserve a water resource rather than develop it. Each of these three settlements is discussed in greater detail later.

In the Fort Hall Indian Water Rights Act of 1990,[28] a marketing provision entitles the Shoshone-Bannock Tribes to lease all or part of their federal contract storage water within the state of Idaho. Additionally, the tribes may transfer or lease their tribal water right within the reservation. The purpose of this marketing provision was to protect instream flows and the chinook and sockeye.[29] If the storage water is marketed to downstream users, it will remain within the reservation river systems for the benefit of the salmon rather than being diverted for irrigation. According to tribal attorney Candy Jackson, environmentalists were not involved in the settlement process. Several representatives of local environmental groups, however, told Jackson informally how pleased they are with the settlement, especially the instream flow protections.[30] The tribes' settlement was finalized with a court decree in September 1996.

In the case of the Pyramid Lake Paiutes, the overriding goal of the tribe's settlement was to maintain sufficient flows within the Truckee River to restore Pyramid Lake. Rather than marketing, however, the settlement relies on improved management, more efficient use, conservation, and voluntary reallocation of water through a federal purchasing plan.[31]

The Pyramid Lake settlement is considered an environmental victory. Numerous groups were involved in the process, including the Environmental Defense Fund, the Nature Conservancy, the Audubon Society, and a variety of sports groups and wetlands preservation groups.[32] These groups, however, initially had an adversarial relationship with the tribe. To increase Truckee River flows into Pyramid Lake to protect the cui-ui, the federal government enacted an Operating Criteria and Procedures (OCAP) for the Newlands Project in 1988. The OCAP mandated improvements in the project's delivery system to increase efficiency and decrease diversion from the Truckee.

Environmental groups initially opposed the OCAP because increased efficiency of the Newlands Project would dry up more than 14,000 acres of wetlands in the Lahontan Valley that relied on Newlands returns and spills for survival. Concerns about water quality, however, finally convinced environmentalists to side with the tribe and pressure the federal government to acquire other water sources. According to Robert Pelcyger, the attorney who represented the Pyramid Lake Tribe, the tribe and the environmental groups ended up working together, but it was an uneasy relationship.[33]

Instream flow was also an issue in the Northern Ute settlement. The CUP diverts a substantial amount of water out of the Uinta Basin, which is the location of the Uintah and Ouray Reservation of the Northern Ute Tribe. Pressure from environmentalists[33] and the tribe forced the Bureau of Reclamation and its successor, the Central Utah Water Conservancy District, to guarantee a minimum of 44,000 acre-feet of CUP water in the basin for "the preservation of minimum stream flows."[35] Of particular concern were the waters of Rock Creek. The construction of Upper Stillwater Dam on that creek threatened to dewater several miles of premier fish habitat. Initially, the bureau proposed to solve the problem by constructing a giant pump-back system that would permit water to run down the stream, then pump it back up to the dam where it could be diverted to the heavily populated Wasatch Front. This scheme was later abandoned in favor of a guaranteed minimum flow during the summer season.[36]

In sum, instream flow protection is one aspect of Indian water settlements where considerable cooperation has existed between tribes and environmental groups. The motives of these two groups may be different, but they have found common ground when tribes seek to protect watercourses from further development and diversion.

Marketing

One of the most contentious issues in negotiated settlements is whether tribes have the right to sell or lease their water off reservation. Most settlements have dealt with this issue by permitting limited marketing in local areas but attaching significant restrictions or outright prohibitions on marketing beyond the local area.

Traditional Western water policy was designed to protect early water users—principally irrigators—from the vagaries and competition of the open market. Thus it is very difficult, and in some cases illegal, to market water. This is especially true for the Colorado River Basin, where the "law of the river" makes it nearly impossible to set up a basinwide market for water. If Indian tribes could negotiate settlements that permit open water marketing, it would establish a significant exception—some would say a direct threat—to the existing water regime.

If tribes leased their water to downstream water users, principally cities, it would reduce the need for more dams to meet municipal water demand. For example, Las Vegas has been discussing water purchases with a number of Colorado River Basin tribes. For many tribes, off-reservation leasing may be much more attractive economically than attempting to use the water for irrigation, which often yields little if any return on the investment.[37] In addition, marketing water, rather than diverting it on the reservation, usually results in the water remaining in the stream much longer and thus serves the goal of instream use. Thus marketing provides more revenue for tribes, cities do not have to build additional dams to increase supply, and more water is available for instream flow, which pleases environmentalists.

all off-reservation transfers must also comply with state law, applicable federal law, interstate compacts, and international law.

The role of water marketing in the settlements continues to evolve. The original Colorado Ute settlement provided for local water marketing under Colorado state water law. Because of the difficulties in implementing the settlement, however, the Department of the Interior's inspector general has suggested the tribes should explore "water marketing alternatives" in lieu of waiting for water from the Animas–La Plata Project.[47] The Northern Ute settlement established a marketing arrangement between the tribe and the Central Utah Water Conservancy District, but the accompanying compact has yet to be ratified. The tribe's refusal to ratify the compact means in essence that the district has been diverting tribal water without a contract. In January 1994 the Northern Ute Tribe sent a bill to the district for $33 million for "unauthorized diversion" of tribal water "pending resolution of the tribe's water claims."[48] In early 1996 the tribe held public hearings on its water settlement funding but has yet to schedule a referendum on the compact.[49]

Another evolving marketing relationship concerns the Fort Peck Compact. The compact negotiated between the tribe and the state of Montana (Fort Peck–Montana Compact, 1985) had a transfer provision more permissive than most settlements. In recent years the tribes and the state have sought congressional confirmation of the water marketing provisions in that compact and a $50 million economic development fund for the tribes. Opposition from downstream states to the water marketing provisions, however, has prevented legislation from passing.[50]

In sum, tribes and environmental groups often have common interests on the issue of tribal water marketing. Tribal marketing will reduce the need for new water development. It also means water will remain in the natural watercourse for a greater distance rather than being diverted further upstream. This will help meet instream flow requirements and increase the recreational and aesthetic value of streams and rivers. Water marketing will also make it easier for tribes to meet the requirements of the Endangered Species Act. Widespread tribal water marketing is still resisted by a host of economic and political interests, however. It will take a prolonged effort by tribes and environmentalists to fundamentally change water marketing policy. If such a change occurs, it could provide tribes with a significant new source of income while protecting the environmental value of many watercourses.

Conclusion

The complex relationship between environmentalists and Indian tribes in the water negotiation process reflects a larger problem: the federal government is pursuing two contradictory goals that have manifested themselves in the negotiation process. First, federal natural resource management agencies have adopted a policy of ecosystem management that emphasizes the administration of environmental policy across multiple political jurisdictions.[51] If this policy is to be successful, each of the jurisdictions involved must surrender at least part of its autonomy to the common goal of protecting an ecosystem. This is a laudable goal and will dramatically enhance the effectiveness of environmental protection policies.

A second federal goal is to meet its obligations as trustee for American Indians. This treaty-based policy relies principally on the concepts of tribal sovereignty and Indian self-determination. As tribes develop their political, economic, and administrative structures, they are better able to function as independent, autonomous governments.

The conflict between these two goals is clear. When tribal policy coincides with the policies of natural resource management agencies and their environmental allies, they work well together in the water negotiation process. But if tribes prefer developmental priorities to environmental protection, their "natural allies" typically oppose them. In that situation it becomes exceedingly difficult to successfully implement a water settlement.

Currently twenty-four negotiations over Indian water rights are in progress. In those situations where environmentalists have a strong interest, it would make strategic sense for tribes and environmentalists to work out a side deal, much as environmentalists obtained side agreements in the North American Free Trade Agreement process. The tribes, which often face politically superior forces across the table, could then rely on the support of powerful environmental interests. This would enhance the probability of both successful negotiation and implementation of a settlement. Without environmental support and especially in the face of overt opposition from environmental interests, tribes go to the negotiation table with a large disparity in relative power. This reduces the possibility of reaching a fair settlement.[52] The reality is that negotiation is largely interest group politics, and when environmental interests happen to concur with tribal interests, it can change the outcome of the negotiation.

This concurrence of interests will only occur if environmental groups and natural resource management agencies recognize the legitimacy of tribal sovereignty. The recent record indicates that environmental organizations consistently demonstrate the last refuge perspective described at the beginning of this chapter.[53] Recent negotiations make it clear that American Indian tribes are sometimes not the "natural allies" of environmentalists. Tribes and environmentalists have a number of common goals, however, that can be addressed through existing procedures for negotiation and settlement when the federal government's trust responsibility is honored.

References

1. Gail Bingham, *Resolving Environmental Disputes: A Decade of Experience* (Washington, DC: Conservation Foundation, 1986); Douglas Amy, *The Politics of Environmental Mediation* (New York: Columbia University Press, 1987); Susan Moore,

"Defining 'Successful' Environmental Dispute Resolution: Case Studies From Public Land Planning in the United States and Australia," *Environmental Impact Assessment Review,* 16:3 (1996): 151–169.

2. Patricia Zell, minority counsel, Indian Affairs Committee, U.S. Senate, interview, Washington, D.C., June 12, 1996.
3. See, for example, Marjane Ambler, *Breaking the Iron Bonds: Indian Control of Energy Development* (Lawrence: University Press of Kansas, 1990); James Huffman, "An Exploratory Essay on Native Americans and Environmentalism," *University of Colorado Law Review,* 63:4 (1992): 900–920; National Indian Policy Center, "Survey on Tribal Actions to Protect Water Quality and the Implementation of the Tribal Amendments to the Clean Water Act," prepared by the law firm Gover, Stetson, and Williams, Albuquerque (New Mexico); Kristine Rogers, "Native American Collaboration in Cultural Resource Protection in the Columbia River Gorge National Scenic Area," *Vermont Law Review,* 17:3 (1993): 741–800; Jana Walker and Kevin Gover, "Commercial Solid and Hazardous Waste Disposal Projects on Indian Lands," *Yale Journal on Regulation,* 10:4 (1993): 229–262; Samuel Winder, "Recent Developments in Indian Legislation," paper presented to the Fourth Annual Conference on Natural Resources Management and Environmental Enforcement on Indian Lands, American Bar Association, Section on Natural Resources, Energy, and Environmental Law, Albuquerque, New Mexico, February 20–21, 1992.
4. 207 U.S. 564 (1908).
5. *Winters v. U.S.,* 207 U.S. 564 (1908); Daniel McCool, *Command of the Waters: Iron Triangles, Federal Water Development, and Indian Water* (Berkeley: University of California Press, 1987; reissued in paperback in 1994 by University of Arizona Press).
6. Daniel McCool, "Intergovernmental Conflict and Indian Water Rights: An Assessment of Negotiated Settlements," *Publicus,* 23 (winter 1993): 85–101; McCool, "Negotiating Water Settlements: Ten Common Themes," in Thomas McGuire, William Lord, and Mary Wallace, eds., *Indian Water in the New West* (Tucson: University of Arizona Press, 1993): 89–102; Jon Hare, *Indian Water Rights,* a Cooperative Project Between the Confederated Tribes of the Chehalis Reservation and the Office of Trust Responsibilities (Washington, DC: Bureau of Indian Affairs, 1996).
7. It states: "Our mission: To manage, develop, and protect water and related resources in an environmentally and economically sound manner in the interest of the American public." From "Reclamation's Strategic Plan," U.S. Bureau of Reclamation, June 1992.
8. Scott McElroy, "Implementing Settlements: A Case Study of the Colorado Ute Water Rights Settlement," paper presented to the Indian Water Rights Conference sponsored by the Stanford University Law School and the Native American Rights Fund, Stanford, California, September 9–10, 1994.
9. U.S. Congress, Hearings Before the House Subcommittee on Energy and Water Development, Committee on Appropriations, April 12, 1994, "Energy and Water Development for FY95," Testimony of Animus–La Plata Conservancy District.
10. *Farmington [NM] Daily Times,* July 27, 1997: 1; Ray Frost, former Tribal Council member, Southern Ute Tribe, interview, Ignacio, Colorado, May 17, 1997.
11. For example, Ak-Chin uses water from the Central Arizona Project (CAP) and the Gila Project, Fort Hall relies on water in Palisade Reservoir and American Falls Reser-

voir, Salt River Pima-Maricopa uses water from Roosevelt Reservoir and the Salt River Project, San Carlos Apache uses water from Coolidge Dam and CAP, Fort Peck Reservoir provides water for that settlement, Fort McDowell relies on waters stored behind Bartlett and Horseshoe Dams and the CAP, the Tohono O'odham settlement relies on CAP water, Jicarilla Apache uses water from both Navajo Reservoir and the San Juan–Chama Project, and Fallon Paiute Shoshone gets water from the Newlands Project.

12. Jason Whiteman, director, Natural Resources Department, Northern Cheyenne Tribe, interview, Lame Deer, Montana, September 5, 1996. The dam project still had to go through the National Environmental Protection Act process; the final environmental impact statement (EIS) was issued in March 1996. The enlarged dam will inundate some additional lands, which are primarily owned by a coal company. The company has given its consent to the settlement.
13. The compact must be approved by the state legislature and a tribal referendum. At this time the Northern Ute Tribe has not scheduled the required referendum, and the legislature is withholding a vote until after the tribe votes on the compact.
14. Daniel Beard, "Blueprint for Reform: The Commissioner's Plan for Reinventing Reclamation," Bureau of Reclamation, November 1, 1993.
15. *TVA v. Hill,* 437 U.S. 153, 174 (1978).
16. Leslie Fitzpatrick, telephone interview, November 16, 1994.
17. Stanley Pollack, "The Endangered Species Act: A Constraint on the Development of Indian Reserved Rights," paper presented to the Indian Water Rights Conference sponsored by Stanford University Law School and the Native American Rights Fund, Stanford, California, September 9–10, 1994.
18. Kate Berry, "Of Blood and Water," *Journal of the Southwest,* 39 (spring 1997): 79–111; Joe Ely, former chairman, Pyramid Lake Paiutes, interview, Phoenix, Arizona, March 26, 1996; David Yardas, telephone interview, November 16, 1994.
19. "Status of the Navajo Indian Irrigation Project" (Window Rock, AZ: Navajo Indian Irrigation Project Office, 1995).
20. Jack Colorado, Cameron Chapter representative, Navajo Nation, interview, Cameron, Arizona, March 26, 1997.
21. Pollack, "The Endangered Species Act"; Stanley Pollack, special counsel for water rights, Navajo Nation, interview, Window Rock, AZ, March 21, 1996.
22. Final Rule, Critical Habitat for the Colorado Endangered Fishes ("Fish Rule"), *Federal Register,* 59 (March 21, 1994): 13374, 13384.
23. 50 U.S.C.F.R. § 402.02.
24. McCool, *Command of the Waters.*
25. George Arthur, Congressional Testimony, Subcommittee on Water Power of the Senate Energy and Natural Resources Committee, Washingon, D.C., June 9, 1994; Pollack, "The Endangered Species Act,"; Pollack, interview.
26. Arthur, Testimony; Pollack, "The Endangered Species Act"; Les Taylor, telephone interview, August 30, 1994.
27. Michael Blumm, "Unconventional Waters: The Quiet Revolution in Federal and Tribal Minimal Streamflows," *Ecology Law Quarterly,* 19:3 (1992): 445–480; Ann Wechsler, "The Politics of Instream Flow," in Daniel McCool, ed., *The Waters of Zion: The Law, Policy, and Politics of Water in Utah* (Salt Lake City: University of Utah Press, 1995), pp. 134–156.

28. P.L. 101-602 (1990), Fort Hall Indian Water Rights Act.
29. Candy Jackson, telephone interview, November 22, 1994. Both species have subsequently been listed as endangered.
30. Ibid. During the negotiations the tribes made a considerable effort to protect the Fort Hall bottomlands along the Snake River. That area is now protected as a park and wetlands. See Gail Martin, former legal assistant, Fort Hall Indian Reservation, interview, Fort Hall, Idaho, September 10, 1996.
31. Yardas, interview.
32. Robert Pelcyger, paper presented to the Indian Water Rights Conference sponsored by the Stanford University Law School and the Native American Rights Fund, Stanford, California, September 9–10, 1994.
33. Pelcyger also represented the La Jolla, Rincon, San Pasqual, Pauma, and Pala Bands of Mission Indians in reaching the San Luis Rey Indian Water Rights Settlement Act (P.L. 100-675).
34. Forty environmental groups, ranging from the Utah chapter of the Sierra Club to the Stonefly Society, formed a coalition to influence the reauthorization of the CUP. See Daniel McCool, "The CUP [Central Utah Project] Completion Act of 1992," in McCool, ed., *The Waters of Zion,* pp. 180–196.
35. P.L. 102-575, 105 *Stat.* 4600, quote at 4653 (1992), Ute Indian Rights Settlement Act.
36. Ibid., p. 4654.
37. McCool, "Negotiating Water Settlements"; Lee Harold Storey, "Leasing Indian Water Off the Reservation: A Use Consistent With the Reservation's Purpose," *California Law Review,* 76 (January 1988): 179–220.
38. U.S. Congress, House, *Congressional Record,* 1988: 2527.
39. Ibid., 1988: 16251.
40. John Weldon, "Non-Indian Water Users' Goals: More Is Better, All Is Best," in McGuire, Lord, and Wallace, eds., *Indian Water in the New West,* pp. 79–88, quote on p. 83.
41. P.L. 97-293, 96 *Stat.* 1261 (1982), Title 3: The Southern Arizona Water Rights Settlement Act.
42. P.L. 102-497, 106 *Stat.* 3256 (1990), Section 8: Technical Amendments to Southern Arizona Water Rights Settlement Act of 1982.
43. Rule 1996. Note also Thomas R. McGuire, "Indian Water Rights Settlements: A Case Study in the Rhetoric of Implementation," *American Indian Culture and Research Journal,* 15:2 (1991): 139–169 [deals with San Xavier, Arizona].
44. P. L. 101-602, 104 *Stat.,* Fort Hall Indian Water Rights Act of 1990.
45. P.L. 100-512, 102 *Stat.* 2549 (1988), Salt River Pima-Maricopa Indian Community Water Rights Settlement Act.
46. P.L. 101-628, 104 *Stat.* 4480 (1990), Fort McDowell Indian Community Water Rights Settlement Act.
47. Office of the Inspector General, Department of the Interior, Audit Report: Development Status of the Dolores and the Animas–La Plata Projects, Bureau of Reclamation, Report No. 94-1-884, July 1994. The report concluded that neither the Dolores Project nor the Animas–La Plata Project was "economically justified," and under current policy it is not financially feasible to build the Animas–La Plata Project.

48. Correspondence of Stewart Pike, chairman, Business Committee, Ute Indian Tribe, to Don Christiansen, director, Central Utah Water Conservancy District, January 25, 1994.
49. *Ute Bulletin,* April 10, 1996: 1.
50. Reed Chambers, telephone interview, August 25, 1994; Chambers, interview, Washington, D.C., June 11, 1996.
51. William Weeks, *Beyond the Ark: Tools for an Ecosystem Approach to Conservation* (Washington, DC: Island Press, 1996).
52. Nina Burkardt, Berton Lee Lamb, and Jonathan Taylor, "Power Distribution in Complex Environmental Negotiations: Does Balance Matter?" *Journal of Public Administration Research and Theory,* 2 (1997): 247–275.
53. Huffman, "An Exploratory Essay."

Chapter 11

Traditional Knowledge and Tribal Partnership on the Kaibab National Forest with an Emphasis on the Hopi Interagency Management*

Lawrence M. Lesko and Renée G. Thakali

> It is the way of the Great Spirit for people to always have and show respect for all things and to give offerings to the spiritual value of all things. The more the Forest Service sees the ways of the Indian, the more the agency will begin to understand and respect Indian cultural values. It is good to see the Tribes and the Forest Service are continuing to work with each other.[1]

Many tribes today receive support from or participate in environmentally related projects or programs of federal land management agencies, which allows tribes to assume a leadership role in resource management decisions. Federal agency assistance has a long history, but its goals and efforts have been inconsistent and often contradictory. Today certain federal mandates have forced the U.S. Department of Agriculture (USDA) Forest Service (FS), National Park Service (NPS), Army Corps of Engineers (ACE), and other government agencies to involve tribes in cooperative resource management. Although the nature

---

*[Editors' note]: This chapter is based in part on two earlier articles: John A. Hanson and Lawrence M. Lesko, "Ancient Heritage: Walking the Land Together," *Inner Voice* (Forest Service Employees for Environmental Ethics) (March-April 1997): 12–23; and Renée Thakali and Lawrence M. Lesko, "Wisdom of the Ages: Traditional Knowledge and Forest Ecosystems," Kaibab National Forest (Williams, Arizona, 1998). The latter was presented at the Nineteenth Session of the North American Forest Commission, Villahermosa, Mexico, November 16–20, 1998. A number of the technical papers presented focused on traditional forest-related knowledge in Canada, Mexico, and the United States. The authors, as staff personnel of the Forest Service, often discuss ideas and facts from personal experience and interaction with the tribes, especially the Hopi.

of this cooperation differs among the agencies, the shift in policy toward tribal partnership has steadily advanced since the passage of the Indian Self-Determination and Educational Assistance Act in 1975. Such management of resources and physical environments can be characterized as dichotomous: (1) agencies may assist tribes and individual Indians on *trust* lands, as has been the case with the USDA Natural Resources Conservation Service, which has guided many Indian communities in the pursuit of farming and ranching; and (2) assistance to tribes may involve *public* lands, as has occurred recently with respect to NPS cooperation with the Timbisha Indian community of California and Death Valley National Park.[2]

Tribes seek involvement with agencies that manage former tribal territory because they still claim a traditional right, not always guaranteed by treaty provisions, to exclusive use and access to burial grounds and other culturally sensitive places but also to hunt and fish. Each involvement has a special nature, and some agencies, such as the Forest Service, have created tribal liaison officers who interact with tribal leaders regarding traditional places, which are outside reservations and over which the tribes have no direct management authority. Interaction works two ways: although the government pursues a more cooperative relationship, tribes themselves may initiate the effort to offer traditional knowledge as pertinent to the management of many different public lands.

This chapter describes the management relations of several American Indian tribes that have applied their traditional knowledge to the management of forest resources in the United States. As a result of tribal consultation, Forest Service officials in charge of managing the nation's national forests are beginning to recognize and understand the value of American Indian traditional knowledge. Some examples are cited of how forest management is changing when national forests and American Indian tribes work in partnership, applying new solutions using traditional knowledge. A case study of the Hopi Tribe outlines its unique relationship with nature and how the tribe has worked with the Forest Service and other federal agencies to provide traditional knowledge as they seek to become more effective in providing sustainable land stewardship. Emerging issues from a national perspective are discussed in the final section, including consultation guidelines, the need for policies for collection of forest resources for traditional uses by American Indians, and the need to seriously consider compensating tribes for their intellectual property rights and traditional knowledge.

American Indian Tribes and Forest Ecosystems

Many American Indian communities and Alaskan Native villages are located adjacent to forested lands that lie west of the 100th meridian or west of the Mississippi River. All or part of the former territory of countless tribes lies within national forest boundaries. Most of these forests are administered as national forests, and some are parts of other federal lands such as the National

Park Service, Bureau of Land Management, and state or private holdings. Today, tribally occupied lands form parts of private timberlands in eastern states. All U.S. forests represent one or more forest ecosystems (see Glossary)—from the vast ponderosa pine forests of the West, mixed coniferous forests of the Rocky Mountain states, and temperate rain forests of the Pacific Northwest to the mixed hardwoods of the eastern states and the tropical forests of Florida and Puerto Rico.

For centuries the forebears of various Indian tribes and, later, Euro-Americans played key roles in managing these forested ecosystems. The national forests, for example, are a legacy of human decisions and actions from early wood burning by American Indians,[3] and cutting of forests on a grand scale a century ago by early American settlers to contemporary forest ecosystem management that reflects human values of a heightened concern for natural systems, including restoration as a tool to reverse the trend of degraded ecosystems, loss of habitats, and the increasing threat of large-scale wildfire. Indigenous peoples may play a significant management role in future forest policy decisions.

A Brief Review of Law: National Forests and Rights of American Indians

A host of federal laws enacted since the early 1970s have changed the way the Forest Service interacts with Indian tribes, resulting in new working relationships, new exchanges of technical information, and new ways of managing forests by incorporating traditional knowledge from American Indian tribes. Aboriginal rights to occupy and use land American Indians have traditionally used stem from possession and use that predate the establishment of the National Forest System more than a century ago. Numerous treaties signed between Indian tribes and the United States led to tribal consolidation on limited reservation acreage; only a handful of these treaties guaranteed long-term fishing and hunting rights. During the past century some national forestland managers generally either ignored neighboring American Indian tribes or dealt with them as trespassers and lawbreakers, arresting American Indians for trespass or illegal hunting and fishing on national forests when members of the tribes asserted their traditional rights and uses.[4]

Laws such as the Forest Reserve Act of 1897 and the Transfer Act of 1905, which led to the establishment of national forests on land once inhabited by Indian tribes, direct forestland management responsibility but do not specifically consider tribal rights.[5] In recent years the Forest Service has begun to recognize some tribal rights and acknowledges that because these forests were part of traditional territory, federally recognized Indian tribes "have a unique government-to-government relationship with the United States Government. In some cases, tribal governments have reserved rights on what are present-day national forests or grasslands, that were retained when the tribes relinquished lands to the United States Government."[6]

Beginning with the National Environmental Policy Act (NEPA) in 1970, federal agencies began to invite Indian tribes to participate in forest management projects and activities that could affect Indians.[7] The National Indian Forest Resources Management Act of 1990 also ordered national forest managers to plan, consult, and coordinate activities with Indian tribes.[8] The National Historic Preservation Act of 1966, amended in 1992, states that "the historical and cultural foundations of the Nation should be preserved as a living part of our community life" and requires cooperation between federal agencies and American Indian tribes and Native Hawaiian organizations.[9] The Indian Self-Determination and Education Assistance Act of 1975 encourages tribes to assume responsibility of existing federally funded programs previously administered by the Bureau of Indian Affairs (BIA).[10] Since then most tribes now deal directly with other federal and state agencies and no longer rely on the BIA to speak on their behalf. The American Indian Religious Freedom Act of 1978 states that the policy of the United States is to protect and preserve religious rights, practices, and beliefs of American Indian, Eskimo, Aleut, and Native Hawaiian, which includes but is not limited to access to sites, including those sites located on national forests; use and possession of sacred objects; and the freedom to worship through ceremonial and traditional rites.[11]

The Archeological Resources Protection Act of 1979 requires a permit process for scientific study, including excavation of cultural sites on federal lands, providing for consultation with affected tribal governments.[12] The Native American Graves Protection and Repatriation Act of 1990[13] recognizes the federal government's responsibility to respect the cultural and religious beliefs of Native Americans, requiring consultation with tribes that may be affected by federally planned undertakings.[14]

In 1996 President William Clinton signed Executive Order 13007 ("Indian Sacred Sites"), directing federal agencies to accommodate access to and ceremonial use of Indian sacred sites and to avoid adversely affecting such sites.[15] Additionally, the two laws that apply specifically to Alaska—the Alaska Native Claims Settlement Act of 1971 and the Alaska National Interest Lands Conservation Act of 1980[16]—include among other provisions the recognition of subsistence hunting and fishing rights for Alaskan Natives.

These laws, along with their implementing regulations, have created opportunities for open dialogue and consultation between American Indian tribes and the Forest Service to work together to protect tribal resources on National Forest System lands. As a result of improved government-to-government relationships, Forest Service managers are now recognizing that many American Indian tribes have valuable traditional knowledge that can be applied to modern-day natural resource management.

American Indian Contributions to Forest Ecosystem Management

Collaboration on Ecosystem Management

Forest ecosystems extend far beyond land ownership boundaries, making cooperation and collaboration essential between the Forest Service and other federal land management agencies, tribes, states, and private landowners. Exchanging research, transferring technology, providing technical assistance, sharing skills, and implementing project activities are examples of workable cooperation and collaboration. Tribal ecosystem knowledge can be defined as a body of information and skills learned and passed down by clans, societies, and tribes through generations of living in a close relationship with the land and resources. It includes a framework for classification, a set of empirical observations about the local environment, and the methods employed in using the resources from the physical environment.[17]

Traditional knowledge is adaptive and dynamic and offers a means to evaluate new technologies and socioeconomic situations. It also offers a unique opportunity for sharing knowledge and expertise needed for land and resource restoration and management. Forest Service managers are realizing that traditional knowledge is valuable in forming land management goals and objectives and that it can be blended with Western science to benefit all.

With a long history of relations with the land, American Indian traditional knowledge contributes to a better understanding of our human relationship with all things within an ecosystem. Traditional knowledge can also be a guide for the maintenance of the natural resource uses and needs of American Indian and Alaskan Native peoples. Forest ecosystem managers from across the United States working on national forests, at research stations, and in state and private forestry are starting to consult with neighboring tribes to identify what forested ecosystems were like in the past and how they can be restored and maintained.[18]

Examples of Traditional Knowledge and Natural Resource Management

The Chippewa Tribe of the Lake States has off-reservation rights to gather miscellaneous forest products from national forests within the territories ceded by treaties signed in 1837 and 1842.[19] To ensure it has access to those resources, the Chippewa Tribe has developed a joint research and monitoring initiative with the Great Lakes Fish and Wildlife Commission and the Forest Service Northeast Research Station to "investigate acceptable harvest levels of wild plants and examine the effects of other management activities on these species; to properly monitor harvests; and to participate in long-range planning efforts to ensure that wild plant resources continue to be provided on Forest Service managed lands." Ginseng and club moss are species identified for this collaborative research effort, and both are relatively rare, with little available information on sustainable harvest levels.[20]

In Alaska, the Kenaitze Interpretive Site on the Chugach National Forest was established in 1992 with a cooperative agreement between the Kenaitze Tribe and the Forest Service to preserve, protect, and interpret the area's important natural and archaeological resources. Drawings, exhibits, and traditional tribal dancing by youth depict Dena'ina life, and tribal elders share family memories of living, hunting, and trapping on the land with visitors. Because the site is located on the Russian River, a very popular red salmon fishing area, the site and its resources suffered from overuse by the general public. Through this collaborative effort, this significant Alaskan Native cultural site on National Forest System land has now been protected and preserved.[21] Visitors to the site now experience a unique cultural and interpretive program.

Tribal–national forest interactions have provided important opportunities for tribes to share traditional knowledge.[22] For example, the Mendocino National Forest in northern California is studying the possibility of reintroducing bear grass (*Xerophyllum tenax*) in part of the forest so that local tribesmen can have access to the plant. Courses in traditional basketry are taught at Round Valley Indian Reservation adjacent to the forest, but no local populations of bear grass—an important basket-weaving plant—are known. This plant also has potential use for restoration efforts on highly erosive serpentine soils found in the forest. The Mendocino National Forest purchased all the available plants from a local nursery, and propagation efforts are continuing at the Forest Service Genetic Research Center in Chico, California.[23]

Members of the Karuk Tribe, also located in northern California, exchange information and participate in frequent meetings with staff of the Klamath National Forest, providing input to project planning—including the design and execution of timber harvest, prescribed burns to improve hazel and bear grass production, recreation site improvements, and special-use permits. As a result of these improved working relationships, tribal consultants participated as advisers during the Pony Wildland Fire, providing advice on tribal resource uses in the salvage recovery area and acting as monitors during field surveys. Celebrating Cultural Awareness Day brought Karuk elders and Forest Service employees together for a day of gathering and processing acorns and traditional cooking methods.[24]

On the Lake Tahoe Basin Management Unit, a botanical and ethnographic study was initiated to document the effects of Washoe tribal horticultural practices on bracken fern. Master Washoe basket makers participated in a series of field trips to identify suitable stands of bracken fern and documented the plant properties they sought to harvest. This pilot study was reported in 1995 at the annual meeting of the Society of Ethnobiology in Santa Barbara, California.[25]

Several workshops on traditional basket weaving have been held in recent years in the California Region of the Forest Service. As a result, basket weavers have acquainted others with various types of baskets they weave and the materials they need. The Forest Service has begun to compile lists of basketry plants and materials and to develop collection area maps. The agency in the Pacific Southwest Region now has a better understanding of the need for tribal access to these areas and no longer requires American Indian tribal members to obtain a permit for collection of traditional materials. Descendants of basket weavers also approve of the new cooperation.

The original forest plan for the Cleveland National Forest in Southern California did not address tribal traditional forest uses. Yet this is the traditional home of Kumeyaay, Luiseño, and other Indian groups. Today, basket weavers from eighteen reservations and even from Mexico have helped the Cleveland National Forest identify and locate plants needed for basket weaving. They have also shared management concerns related to the key plant species needed. The Cleveland National Forest is now more aware of traditional uses and has data to use in revising its forest plan, which will consider traditional forest uses of tribal members.[26]

The Hopi Tribe: A Case Study in Applying Traditional Knowledge in a National Forest

The Hopi Tribe has a population of about 10,000 and occupies twelve villages on three mesas on the Hopi Reservation in north-central Arizona. The village of Old Oraibi, located on Third Mesa, is considered the oldest continuously inhabited settlement on the North American continent.[27] Hopi ancestral lands cover a much larger territory—*Hopitutskwa*—that includes most of the Kaibab National Forest directly north and south of the Grand Canyon National Park. According to clan tradition various Hopi clans migrated through the area, made settlements, and constructed shrines. Archaeological evidence and ethnological reconstruction confirm ancestral Hopi occupancy considerably west, north, and south of the present-day reservation east of the Little Colorado River. Although the farthest extent of Hopi ancestral lands remains unclear, locations such as Bill Williams Mountain, the San Francisco Peaks, and the Little Colorado River Valley all represent areas of past occupancy until Hopi ancestors migrated to the Hopi mesas probably during the Great Drought at the end of the thirteenth century or later (Figure 11.1).[28]

According to oral tradition, Hopi clans emerged in this world—the Fourth World—and encountered the guardian of the world, *Ma 'saw.* A covenant was agreed on whereby the Hopi vowed to be the stewards of the earth and to place their footprints throughout the Fourth World while migrating on a quest to find their place in the center of the universe. During the migrations the clans established themselves throughout the land by cultivating the earth. The "footprints" they left behind consist of ritual springs, petroglyphs, pilgrimage trails, and shrines (Figure 11.2). Ancestral burials, potsherds, and ruins found on the landscape today are further evidence that they vested the land with their spiritual stewardship as they fulfilled the promise of *Ma 'saw.*[29]

This covenant forms the basis for the responsibility the Hopi Tribe feels for the land of their ancestors and where their ancestors still rest. The particular clans in the migration history are still responsible for maintaining and protecting the sites of their ancestors. This responsibility forms the obligation for the Hopi to share stewardship decisions with national forest managers. The Hopi

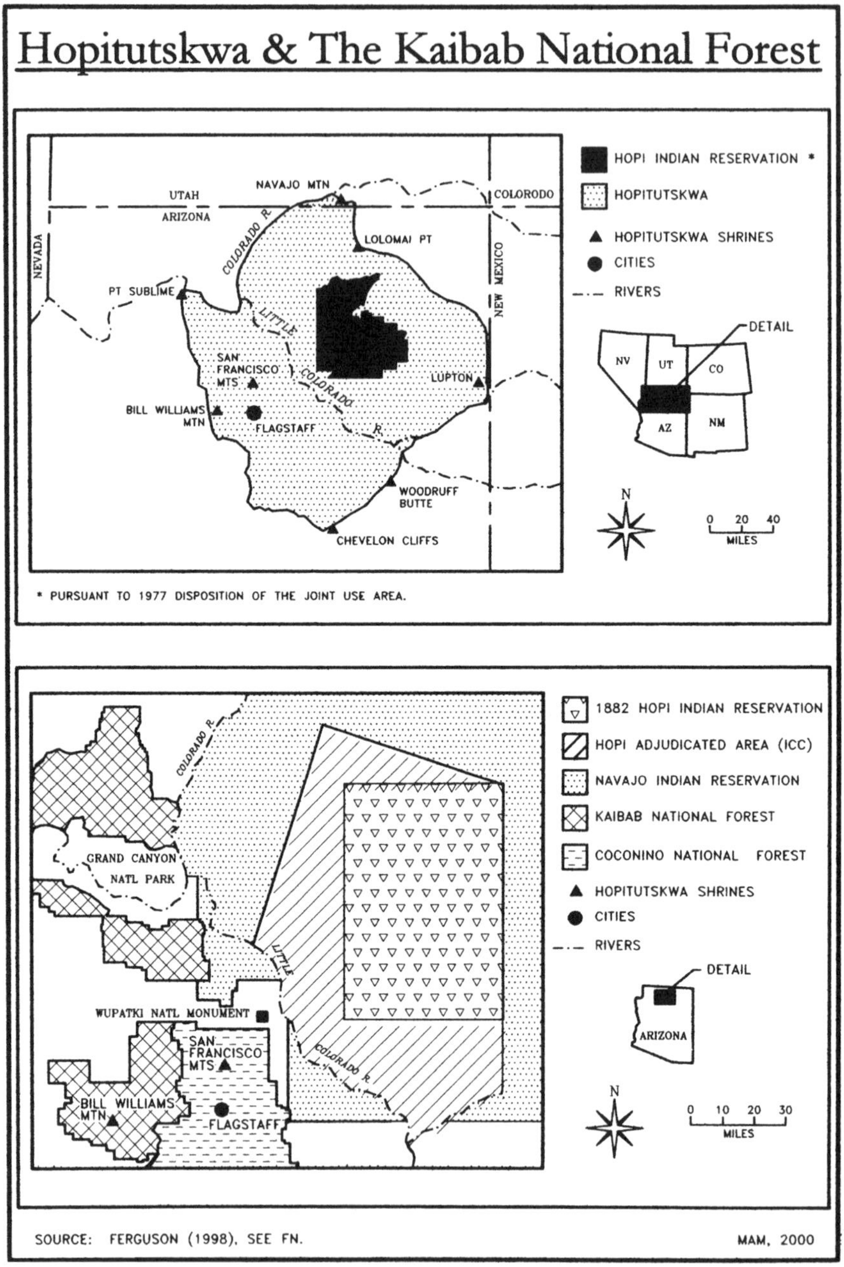

Fig. 11.1 Hopitutskwa and the Kaibab National Forest (Arizona). Hopi ancestral lands extend west, north, and south of the current Hopi Indian Reservation (Arizona) and embrace an area many times the size of the area adjudicated by the Indian Claims Commission in 1974.

Fig. 11.2 Hopi Petroglyphs Located Within Kaibab National Forest. The Hopi Indians vowed to be the stewards of the earth and to place their footprints throughout the Fourth World while migrating on a quest to find their place in the center of the universe. The footprints they left behind consist of ritual springs, petroglyphs, pilgrimage trails, and shrines. Photo by Lawrence Lesko, staff archaeologist, Kaibab National Forest, U.S. Forest Service, Williams, Arizona.

have told representatives of the Kaibab National Forest that "you are the present physical caretakers of the Forest, but we are the spiritual caretakers and we must work together."[30] Because land management decisions can affect historical as well as future footprints, the Hopi Tribe created a Cultural Preservation Office to interact with the various federal and state agencies and private organizations that make land use decisions over the Hopi ancestral lands. Federal laws such as the National Historic Preservation Act (NHPA) and NEPA require consultation with affected tribes during the federal decisionmaking process. As a result, the Hopi Tribe has found a way to integrate traditional knowledge during consultation with the Forest Service and other federal agencies by using the Hopi Cultural Preservation Office and the Cultural Resource Advisory Task Team.

Keepers of the Knowledge

The Hopi Cultural Preservation Office forms a connection among the Hopi government, the keepers of the knowledge, and federal agencies. This is not an easy task, as Hopi culture is unique and complex. The traditional histories are long and complicated, involving many individuals and Hopi clans. These multiple histories at multiple levels are rooted in religious beliefs, giving this knowledge an esoteric nature that becomes guarded and sacred.[31] Although there is general agreement on the basic tenets of Hopi religion, considerable variation is found among clans, religious societies, and villages. Each clan and society has a unique tradition that is not shared with other clans or societies, so information gathering can be difficult.

The ten staff members of the Cultural Preservation Office (CPO) cannot represent the views of each of these individual clans, but they have devised a way to reach consensus with the formation of the Cultural Resource Advisory Task Team. This advisory team guides the Hopi CPO staff in management recommendations and research efforts.[32]

Advisory team members often hold positions of authority within the traditional village structure, but their team participation is separate from their ritual duties. The advisory team meets once a month, but special meetings are also called to address immediate issues. Frequent field trips help clarify specific projects and identify sites and features that are important to the Hopi Tribe but that are not likely to be found by archaeologists or known by others outside the tribe. Through this process the Hopi Cultural Preservation Office has been able to identify traditional cultural places (TCPs; places specific and important to maintaining a cultural identity), evaluate potential impacts to these places, and recommend mitigation measures for some land management projects on the federal, state, and private lands in the Four Corners area. This information is then used during consultation with appropriate agencies.[33] Often the advisory team suggests projects or activities that benefit wildlife that will be hunted or plant species that are traditionally collected. For example, the use of fire can encourage the growth of many plants important to wildlife and to the Hopi

Tribe. The advisory team has supported and suggested such projects as well as others that improve overall forest health.

Former Hopi Tribal Chairman Ferrell Secakuku once said, "All land should be respected and all land is used only for survival, whether it be physical, spiritual, or mental. Our religion does not teach us to subdue the earth. Our religion teaches us to take care of the earth in a spiritual way as stewards of the land."[34] Taking this wisdom into consideration, meaningful dialogue takes place among the Hopi Tribe, the Forest Service, and other federal agencies. The Hopi people understand that the land is to be used by people but used respectfully.

Traditional Knowledge Is Living and Dynamic

The Hopi have accepted many scientific concepts and technical land management strategies and have applied them to their own lands on the Hopi Reservation. It is important to understand that traditional knowledge is living and dynamic and also must respond to present-day problems that were unknown in the past. When the Hopi Tribe decided to close and obliterate several roads on the Hopi Reservation, it requested a training session with Forest Service experts to learn the current techniques of closing roads and restoring natural conditions. Likewise, the Hopi Tribe consulted with the Coconino National Forest to develop a comprehensive integrated plan to manage piñon-juniper woodlands covering 79,757 hectares (approx. 197,000 acres) of the Hopi Reservation.[35] This plan recognizes Hopi cultural, ritual, and subsistence uses of these woodlands while employing Western silvicultural tools to manage and protect the forests, watersheds, and soils and, at the same time, addressing wildlife, recreation, range, and other concerns.[36]

Holistic View of Ecosystems

Science-based suggestions for managing land are essential, but philosophical attitudes are also paramount. When Hopi tribal members were surveyed to identify problems in the woodlands on the Hopi Reservation, the most common replies were sacred area desecration, artifact theft, and religious interference. Fuelwood theft, overgrazing, and lack of fuelwood were secondary issues.[37] It is interesting that the first three problems involve the spiritual realm rather than physical natural resources. This is not surprising when one understands that the Hopi view the spiritual and physical realms as intertwined. Spiritual matters affect physical matters, and vice versa, in the Hopi world.[38] For the Hopi the past is still living, and the future is directly connected to the present. Since everything we do is connected and affects the future, a holistic view of the ecosystem results in responsible stewardship.

Shared Stewardship: The Basis for the Partnership

The shared stewardship approach to forest management is relatively new. In the past, relationships between the Hopi and the Kaibab National Forest were often strained or even nonexistent. Interaction with all tribes was sporadic and usually confined to bureaucratic letters sent to satisfy legal requirements. These poorly developed relationships became more stressful as confrontations over a proposed ski area expansion and uranium mines went to federal court. Although the courts upheld the Forest Service for following the letter of the law, goodwill was compromised and mistrust prevailed.[39] It became evident that dissimilar worldviews and other cultural differences could not be overcome without really listening to each other and engaging in face-to-face dialogue.

This realization has helped foster a new era in forest-tribal relationships. Many changes have taken place within the forest itself, a tribal liaison was appointed from the heritage resource staff, and a new forest supervisor and a progressive management team have promoted a new vision for the forest. Forest management is no longer commodity driven, and there is an increasing emphasis on providing public service, forging partnerships, and promoting rural economic development.

Sharing stewardship responsibilities with the tribes is an important concept. The tribes are committed to this policy for the long term. Even if the Forest Service manages the land effectively in the present, the tribes believe they have a responsibility to ensure that the land is managed well for the future. Additional political changes further strengthen the Kaibab National Forest's tribal relationships. The Native American Graves Protection and Repatriation Act (NAGPRA) provides direction for the protection and return of American Indian human remains, grave goods, and sacred objects. New guidelines outlined ways National Register of Historic Places criteria can be applied to tribal cultural places, which are rooted in ethnic history and important in maintaining the continuity of a community's traditional beliefs and practices. These and other laws have increased the influence of American Indians in federal land management. Nowhere is this new awareness more evident than in the relationship of the Hopi Tribe and the Kaibab National Forest, who together have reinvented the way tribes and federal agencies can work together toward common goals.

Memorandum of Understanding

In 1999 the Hopi Tribe signed a Memorandum of Understanding (MOU) with the Kaibab National Forest that formalized the relationship that had existed on an informal basis since 1986. This was the first comprehensive MOU the Hopi had signed with a federal agency. The document establishes that the Kaibab National Forest will carry out government-to-government consultations with the Hopi Tribe under NEPA, the Archaeological Resources Protection Act (ARPA), NHPA, the American Indian Religious Freedom Act (AIRFA), NAGPRA, and Executive Orders 13007 and 13084. Among the highlights of the MOU are provisions for the Kaibab National Forest to:

- Provide NEPA and other project information to the tribe in a timely manner that provides for adequate consultation time. This information is exchanged both by mail and through scheduled face-to-face meetings.
- Allow access to shrines and resources on the forest to Hopi people for traditional uses, including the collection of medicinal and ceremonial plants from traditional use areas. Such access is assured through the American Indian Religious Freedom Act and Executive Order 13007 (sacred sites).
- Maintain as confidential records, maps, photographs, and other information about places significant to the Hopi Tribe that are prehistoric or historic resources. The confidentiality of these places is assured through exemption number 3 to the Freedom of Information Act, ARPA, and the 1992 amendments to NHPA.
- Send copies of proposals necessary for the issuance of ARPA permits to the Hopi Tribe for review and comment. Additional topics of interest to the Hopi Tribe may be identified at that time for incorporation into the proposed archaeological project.
- Refer independent researchers to consult directly with the Hopi Tribe on matters specific to the Hopi people.

This MOU also establishes areas of mutual interest and concern that can be pursued jointly to maintain the cordial relationship between the Hopi Tribe and the Kaibab National Forest. Some of these topics specified in the MOU are:

- Forest assistance to the Hopi to obtain wooden beams from the forest for village and kiva building and for restoration projects
- Forest Service technical assistance to the Hopi Tribe in natural resource management activities on Hopi tribal lands such as range, timber, soils, or wildlife as time and funding permit
- Forest Service consultations with the Hopi Tribe to reintroduce or foster conditions in the forest that encourage natural regeneration of plants that have traditional importance to the Hopi[40]
- Collaboration among the Hopi Cultural Preservation Office, Kaibab National Forest, and traditional Hopi people to determine topics of interest (e.g., clan migration traditions) that can be learned through the use of ethnographic, ethnohistoric, or archaeological research and to ensure that archaeological projects conducted on the forest make an effort to address these topics in the final project report

A true relationship extends beyond that required by law. As neighbors, the Hopi and Kaibab help and support each other. For example, the Hopi regularly link oral tradition with specific places on the landscape. They often seek out special locations with religious significance such as shrines or collecting areas that have been lost from memory through decades of acculturation. Forest Service staff often possess valuable knowledge of such places and of plant distribution that may help in these quests. In turn, the Hopi have helped the forest personnel by providing input and interpretation for a few heritage resource sites that are open to the public. This oral tradition provides an important and contemporary human tie to the past.

NAGPRA, the Hopi, and Kaibab National Forest

Other provisions specifically address the sensitive subject of the discovery and disposition of American Indian human remains:

- The forest maintains a policy of prohibiting the purposeful excavation of human remains for educational purposes such as research or field schools.
- The forest agrees to notify the Hopi Cultural Preservation Office as soon as possible of any emergency or discovery involving human remains so NAGPRA consultations can be made to determine appropriate disposition of the remains.

NAGPRA-related issues are often contentious. Sometimes there are conflicting claims of cultural affiliation. Sometimes conflicts occur between archaeologists who value the scientific information contained in burials and American Indian groups that view all disturbances of graves as desecration. The Kaibab National Forest has repatriated and reburied all the known human remains that had once been removed from the forest or discovered inadvertently. This has not been an easy task because in the past tribes have disagreed over the cultural affiliation of the remains. After years of discussion and negotiation, it was decided that the Hopi Tribe would take possession of the remains on behalf of the clans associated with the region and the other interested tribes.

Fortunately, the *Forest Service Manual* of the Southwest Region of the Forest Service has a directive that authorizes the reburial of human remains on national forestland if the remains were recovered from Southwest Region lands. This has facilitated reburials because all of the tribes involved expressed the belief that human remains should be reburied where they were originally interred. Burials exposed by erosion were reburied as close as possible to the original location. Moreover, although not required by existing law, the Kaibab National Forest has agreed with the Hopi and other tribes that purposeful excavation of human remains for educational purposes is inappropriate, and it is prohibited on Kaibab National Forest lands.

Acknowledgment of Partnership Successes

The Hopi Tribe recognized the efforts of the Kaibab National Forest in developing a unique intergovernmental relationship by awarding the forest staff with the annual Hopi Cultural Awareness Award in 1999. Also, Vice President

Gore's National Performance Review for government re-invention has recognized the Kaibab National Forest as a Reinvention Lab. The review reads:

Reinventing Tribal Relationships

To demonstrate innovative approaches to fostering respectful and mutually beneficial government-to-government relationships with our tribal neighbors:

- Sharing stewardship in land management
- Providing customer service and economic opportunities to underserved communities
- Engaging in face-to-face dialogue and "walking the land together"
- Forging partnerships for interpreting the past
- Using traditional knowledge to assist in the restoration and maintenance of forest health

It is a rare relationship that has no stumbling blocks or growing pains.[41] The first chief forester, Gifford Pinchot, summarized the multiple-use mandate of the Forest Service stating forests should be managed for the greatest good for the greatest number in the long run.[42] Some multiple uses conflict with tribal values. Ski area expansions and other developments on Bill Williams Mountain—or *Tusaqstomo,* as the mountain is known to the Hopi—have been a test of the relationship, as have other multiple-use issues through the years (Figure 11.3). Despite these problems the relationship is strong, and disagreements are dealt with in a collaborative and respectful manner. The Forest Service has undergone significant changes in the way it does business. Collaborative stewardship is a principle exemplified by forging mutually beneficial relationships with the Indian people who are the living embodiment of the clans who once called this forest home.

Emerging Issues from a National Perspective

The examples we have discussed represent only a small portion of the evolving partnerships between American Indian tribes and National Forests or other public land units where tribal knowledge is being applied to the management of forest resources on reservations and federal lands. As the partnerships develop, new issues emerge, and several old issues remain unresolved.

Consultation Procedures

Without uniform guidelines to define consultation with Indian tribes, federal agencies take a highly variable approach, from a notification that an action or decision affecting the tribe has already been made to a sincere effort to elicit the advice and opinions of the tribes and their religious leaders. This has created a confusing situation for a number of tribes. The Hopi Tribe has made the following recommendations to the federal government to improve the situation:

Fig. 11.3 Bill Williams Mountain (Arizona). Considered sacred to the Hopi, Bill Williams Mountain, or *Tusaqstomo,* is today the site of conflict between ski enthusiasts and the tribe. Photo by Lawrence Lesko, staff archaeologist, Kaibab National Forest, U.S. Forest Service, Williams, Arizona.

- Systematically review national, regional, and local consultation procedures to assess current interpretation and implementation of applicable federal laws and policies
- Develop formal policies and procedures for federal agencies dealing with tribes
- Initiate consultation with a formal letter describing the federal undertaking being proposed; follow up with telephone calls and face-to-face meetings with tribal officials
- Conduct on-site visitation of the proposed project or activity
- Compensate tribes to develop technical information needed by federal agencies
- Provide for longer response time, and initiate consultation early in project development
- Understand that a "cookbook" approach may not accommodate the cultural diversity of all Indian tribes, yet that a strong need exists for more uniform guidelines and principles to guide the consultation process[43]

Accessibility to Traditional Forest Resources

For many American Indians, community identity and survival are dependent on continued access to national forests and use of certain landscapes that possess key locations or contain unique resources. Certain plants are meaningful for renewal of the world by ensuring the passage of a child into adulthood and for health and social well-being. A particularly acute issue for American Indian and Alaskan Native peoples is the maintenance of traditional gathering, hunting, and fishing rights and other activities when there are changes in the access or availability of these important resources.

Gathering rights and permits have also been a source of frustration and confusion for many American Indians. Many harbor a deep resentment for even having to fill out a Forest Service permit to gather in their traditional areas or for being told they cannot gather at all. Some national forests are now entering into agreements with tribal government representatives so tribal members may gather "miscellaneous forest products for personal use," replacing the permit process and thus allowing them to freely gather native resources.

Intellectual Property Rights

American Indian communities are also beginning to deal with intellectual property and indigenous rights as they realize that tribal knowledge is unique and of value. Tribes may consider their input to be professional services, as true consultants who supply information not available elsewhere and thus worthy of compensation. Many large projects, such as the Bureau of Reclamation's Glen Canyon Environmental Studies, provide funding for ethnographic and traditional cultural place research that is paid directly to the appropriate tribes.

The confidentiality of information is another tribal concern. Traditional places and materials can be misused by others; therefore it is important that conditions of confidentiality are understood by all parties during the consultation. Although most information is freely available from federal agencies, some safeguards can be used to protect sensitive information such as provisions in the Freedom of Information Act, the National Historic Preservation Act [section 304(a)], and the Archeological Resources Protection Act.

Lessons Learned

By officially recognizing American Indian tribes on a formal government-to-government basis, streamlining the process for American Indians to gather traditional resources, actively promoting indigenous management strategies, and developing and protecting traditional gathering areas, national forests across the country are enriching the concept of multicultural land management. As tribes become more experienced with federal consultation laws, policies, and regulations, it will be become paramount for federal agencies to speak with one voice, clearly interpreting the laws and policies to eliminate confusion and frustration. Intellectual property rights may become increasingly important, and unless this issue is taken seriously it may become a roadblock to future collaboration and consultation efforts between federal land managers and tribal officials. By working cooperatively with American Indian tribal governments, the Forest Service will be able to identify more specific, traditional, and sustainable forest management strategies.

New efforts in ecosystem restoration may be more successful after they carefully combine conventional Western scientific principles with the traditional, more holistic view of ecosystem management embraced by many U.S. tribes. Incorporating traditional knowledge expands human understanding and may enhance biodiversity and resource sustainability for future generations. For generations, American Indians have employed a body of knowledge and a variety of management tools to enhance the production and quality of key plants and animals in selected locations and at predictable times. Landscapes were created and maintained by burning the land. A complex system of ritual and harvest practices influenced the use of plants and foods. Applying traditional knowledge today may not only improve the Forest Service's understanding of national forest ecosystems but may also guide the maintenance of forest resource uses and needs of American Indian and Alaska Native peoples for generations to come.[44]

References

1. Gaylan Azbill (silviculturalist, Mendocino National Forest) and Nomlaki Tribe, "Traditional Use and Living With the Land," *Working Together: California Indians and the Forest Service,* Annual Report, San Francisco, September 1993.
2. See Rebekah C. Beatty Davis, *Conservation and Culture: The Soil Conservation Service, Social Science, and Conservation on Tribal Lands in the Southwest,* Historical Notes 6 (Washington, DC: Natural Resources Conservation Service, 1997); Steven J. Crum, "A Tripartite State of Affairs: The Timbisha Shoshone Tribe, the National Park Service, and the Bureau of Indian Affairs, 1933–1994," *American Indian Culture and Research Journal,* 22:1 (1998): 117–136.
3. Cf. Henry T. Lewis, "Patterns of Indian Burning in California: Ecology and Ethnohistory," in Thomas C. Blackburn and Kat Anderson, comps./eds., *Before the Wilderness: Environmental Management by Native Californians* (Menlo Park, CA: Ballena, 1993): 55–116.
4. See discussion of northern California Indians and the Six Rivers National Forest: Nancy Akins, "New Direction in Sacred Land Claims: *Lyng v. Northwest Indian Cemetery Protective Assn,*" *Natural Resources Journal,* 29 (1989): 593–605.
5. 30 *Stat.* 34 and 33 *Stat.* 628, respectively.
6. U.S. Forest Service, *Forest Service National Resource Book on American Indian and Alaska Native Relations,* FS-600 (Washington, DC: U.S. Department of Agriculture, 1997).
7. National Environmental Policy Act, 42 U.S.C.A. § 4321 (1970); for a discussion of NEPA and related laws, see David H. Getches, Charles F. Wilkinson, and Robert A. Williams Jr., *Cases and Materials on Federal Indian Law,* 4th ed. (St. Paul: West, 1998): 620–635.

8. National Indian Forest Resources Management Act, 104, part 6 *Stat.* 4532 (1990).
9. U.S. Forest Service, *National Resource Book.*
10. Indian Self-Determination and Education Assistance Act, 90 *Stat.* 585 (1975).
11. American Indian Religious Freedom Act, 91 *Stat.* 469 (1978).
12. Archaeological Resources Protection Act, 93 *Stat.* 721 (1979).
13. Native American Graves Protection and Repatriation Act, 104, part 4 *Stat.* 3048 (1990).
14. Kurt E. Dongoske, Leigh Jenkins, and T. J. Ferguson, "Disparate Ambassadors: A Tribal Perspective on the Federal Agency Approach to Consultation With Native Americans," paper presented to the symposium Tribal Perspectives on Cultural Resource Management, Annual Meeting of the Society for Applied Anthropology, Cancun, Mexico, April 14, 1994.
15. President William J. Clinton, Executive Order 13007, "Indian Sacred Sites," W. Comp. *Presidential Documents,* 32: 942–943 1 (May 27, 1996).
16. The Alaska Native Claims Settlement Act of 1971, 43 U.S.C.A. §§ 1601–28; Alaska National Interest Lands Conservation Act, 16 U.S.C.A. §§ 3101–33 (1980); U.S. Forest Service, *National Resource Book.*
17. Cf. Dean B. Suagee, "Tribal Voices in Historic Preservation: Sacred Landscapes, Cross-Cultural Bridges, and Common Ground," *Vermont Law Review,* 21 (1996): 145–224; Lydia T. Grimm, "Sacred Lands and the Establishment Clause: Indian Religious Practices on Federal Lands," *Natural Resources and Environment,* 12:1: (1997): 19–24, 78.
18. U.S. Forest Service, *National Resource Book*; Dennis Martinez, "Back to the Future: Ecological Restoration, the Historical Forest, and Traditional Indian Stewardship," paper presented to the conference "A Watershed Perspective on Native Plants," Olympia, Washington, February 26, 1993.
19. Ronald A. Janke, "Chippewa Land Losses," *Journal of Cultural Geography,* 2:2 (1982): 84–100.
20. U.S. Forest Service, *National Resource Book.*
21. Ibid.
22. A series of reports account for Forest Service activities in California; U.S. Forest Service, Pacific Southwest Region, *Working Together: California Indians and the Forest Service: Accomplishment Reports* (San Francisco: U.S. Forest Service, 1993–1996).
23. Ibid., 1994. On California basketry, see Albert B. Elasser, "Basketry," in Robert F. Heizer, ed., *California,* Vol. 8, *Handbook of North American Indians* (Washington, DC: Smithsonian Institution, 1978): 626–641; also Bev Ortiz, "Contemporary California Indian Basketweavers and the Environment," in Blackburn and Anderson, comps./eds., *Before the Wilderness,* pp. 195–212.
24. *Working Together,* 1996.
25. "Lake Tahoe Basin Management Unit," in *Working Together,* 1995.
26. Cari VerPlanck, "Basketry Plants Field Trip" [Cleveland National Forest], in *Working Together,* 1995; see also Nathan Craig and L. Pfeiffer, "A Discussion of Native California Basketry Plants Found Growing in the Cleveland National Forest: Uses and Management," in *Working Together,* 1995.
27. Arnold Taylor Sr., "Importance of Woodlands to Hopi Culture and Religion," in Final Proceedings, Nineteenth Annual National Indian Timber Symposium, Yakima, Washington, April 24–28, 1995 (Portland, OR: Intertribal Timber Council, 1995):

80–81. For general ethnographic as well as legal background on the Hopi, see John W. Ragsdale Jr., "Law and Environment in Modern America and Among the Hopi Indians: A Comparison of Values," *Harvard Environmental Law Review,* 10 (1986): 417–465; Louis A. Hieb, "Hopi," in Mary B. Davis, ed., *Native America in the Twentieth Century: An Encyclopedia* (New York: Garland, 1994): 240–243; and several chapters on the Hopi in *Southwest,* ed. Alfonso Ortiz, Vol. 9 of *Handbook of North American Indians* (Washington DC: Smithsonian Institution, 1979); on Hopi land claims, see 39 *Indian Claims Commission* 204, 223 (1976); Florence Hawley Ellis, "The Hopi: Their History and Use of Lands [Docket 229]" in *Hopi Indians,* American Indian Ethnohistory, Indians of the Southwest Series (New York: Garland, 1974): 1–233.

28. See especially Ellis, "The Hopi," pp. 114–118, 140–141, chart, p. 65, list of shrines, pp. 222–227. Figure 11.1 is based on several sources, including Indian Claims Commission, *Final Report* (Washington, DC: Government Printing Office, 1979), map of "Judicially Established Areas"; and T. J. Ferguson, *Öngtupqa niqw Pisisvayu* [Salt Canyon and the Colorado River]: *The Hopi People and the Grand Canyon,* Final Ethnohistoric Report for the Hopi Glen Canyon Environmental Studies Project (Third Mesa, AZ: Hopi Cultural Preservation Office, 1998), figure 10, "Hopi *Tutskwa,*" p. 66.
29. T. J. Ferguson, Kurt Dongoske, M. Yeatts, and Leigh Jenkins, "Hopi Oral History and Archaeology, Part I: The Consultation Process," *SAA Bulletin,* 13:2 (1995): 12.
30. Dalton Taylor, personal communication.
31. Kurt M. Dongoske, M. Yeatts, R. Anyon, and T. J. Ferguson, "Archaeological Cultures and Cultural Affiliation: Hopi and Zuni Perspectives in the American Southwest," *American Antiquity,* 63:4 (1997): 600–608.
32. T. J. Ferguson, Kurt M. Dongoske, L. Jenkins, M. Yeatts, and E. Polingyouma, "The Roles of Archeology and Ethnohistory in Hopi Cultural Preservation," *CRM* (National Park Service), 16 (1993): 27–37, quote on p. 28. Most Hopi villages as well as a number of prominent clans, priesthoods, and religious societies have a representative on the Cultural Resource Advisory Task Team. Although there are Hopi villages that remain autonomous and refuse to recognize the Hopi Tribal Council as their government, they nevertheless participate with the Cultural Preservation Office by having representatives on the advisory team.
33. Ferguson et al., "Hopi Oral History." [Editor's note: The "P" in TCP usually refers to "property," but Hopi prefer the word "place."]
34. Ferrell Secakuku, "The Hopi View of Wilderness," excerpted from an article in *Proceedings of the National Interagency Wilderness Conference,* Tucson, Arizona, May 17–21, 1993.
35. B. K. Koyiyumptewa, "Spiritual Values of the Pinyon-Juniper Woodland: A Hopi Perspective," in *Managing Pinyon-Juniper Ecosystems for Sustainability and Social Needs,* General Technical Report RM-236 (Fort Collins, CO: U.S. Forest Service, Rocky Mountain Forest and Range Experiment Station, 1993): 19–20.
36. Ibid.; for an interpretation of another agency's role in piñon-pine country, see Richard O. Clemmer, "The Pinon Pine: Western Shoshone Indians vs. the Bureau of Land Management," *Environmental Review,* 9:2 (1985): 131–149.
37. Ronald K. Miller, "Cultural Uses of the 'Forgotten Forest,' " *Journal of Forestry,* 95:11 (November 1997): 26–27.

38. Koyiyumptewa, "Spiritual values."
39. See discussion of Arizona Snow Bowl in Chapter 7; and see Kimla McDonald, "Sacred Land in Environmental Planning," *Environmental Professional,* 9 (1987): 27–32; Lydia T. Grimm, "Sacred Lands and the Establishment Clause: Indian Religious Practices on Federal Lands," *Natural Resources and Environment,* 12:1: (1997): 19–24, 78. The uranium mine was located near Red Butte on the Kaibab. In 1990 the Havasupai filed suit against the Forest Service, alleging that the agency failed to uphold requirements of an EIS as it sought to determine if the Canyon Uranium Mine should be established at a site declared to be sacred but lying outside lands restored to the tribe. John Martin, an anthropologist, observed of the location near Red Butte about 40 miles east of the eastern boundary of the current reservation: "Whether or not Red Butte was sacred in the past, it is now, and the tribe holds an annual politico-religious gathering there, maintaining it is the locus of an 'earth navel' through which ancestors climbed to the present world." The record shows that the Forest Service went to great lengths to determine if environmental constraints should prohibit mining operations and found none. Moreover, the agency did examine religious circumstances of the site. The tribe contends that the site is located near the center of aboriginal territory, yet it did not formally argue for its inclusion when Congress sought to determine boundaries of the land restoration under the GCEA. See *Havasupai Tribe v. Robertson,* 943 F. 2d 32 (9th Cir. 1991), *cert. denied,* 503 U.S. 959 (1992); Imre Sutton, "Not All Aboriginal Territory Is Truly Irredeemable," *American Indian Culture and Research Journal,* 24:1 (2000): 148; John F. Martin, "Havasupai," in Davis, ed., *Native America in the Twentieth Century,* pp. 231–233.
40. For a thorough documentation of Hopi ethnobotany, see Harold S. Colton, "Hopi History and Ethnobotany," in *Hopi Indians,* pp. 279–386.
41. All federal agencies are requested to cooperate with the Kaibab National Forest within the constraints of statutes as set forth in the president's April 21, 1998, memorandum to all executive departments and agencies.
42. On Pinchot, see Chapter 4 in this book; also Gary A. Klee, *Conservation of Natural Resources* (Englewood Cliffs, NJ: Prentice-Hall, 1991): chapter 7; Roderick Nash, *From These Beginnings: A Biographical Approach to American History* (New York: Harper and Row, 1973): chapter 8.
43. Jenkins et al., "Disparate Ambassadors." On consultation, see also the Prologue to this book, pp. xxxi–xxxii.
44. U.S. Forest Service, *National Resource Book.*

CHAPTER 12

Indigenous Planning and Resource Management

THEODORE S. JOJOLA

> What we ask of America is not charity, not paternalism, even when benevolent. We ask only that the nature of our situation be recognized and made the basis of policy and action.[1]

Origins

Two generations have passed since the convocation of mostly young, idealistic native scholars and activists at the American Indian Chicago Conference in 1961.[2] Organized by anthropologist Sol Tax and his assistant, Nancy O. Lurie, its purpose was to involve Indian leaders in updating the 1928 Meriam Report on the conditions of and federal policies toward American Indians. A year later a Declaration of Purpose was presented to President John F. Kennedy in a formal White House ceremony. Unbeknown to anyone, this conference would usher forth the era of Indian self-determination.

Another irrefutable aspect of the Chicago conference was that its deliberations consigned nonnatives to a "consultancy" status. This meant nonnatives were allowed to speak only after the native participants had recognized them. Unlike any major academic forum up to that time, the indigenous voice was allowed to preside. In a manner of reckoning—and considering that the University of Chicago's Department of Anthropology had convened the conference—this went against the grain of meetings that had been controlled by academics and nonnative policymakers. This style of participation was repatriated back to Indian Country and something truly amazing began to occur. Rather than tolerate a situation where Bureau of Indian Affairs (BIA) paternalism had basically consigned native people to a passive role, the indigenous voice began to assert its own mode of self-rule. In particular, a host of questions were raised, many of which pertained to the management of their most critical community resources—the human and natural resources.

The synchronicity of the event also brought together a critical mass of young and educated activists. Feeling their voices had not been given full recognition at the Chicago Conference, they regrouped later that year and founded the National Indian Youth Council (NIYC). Among the first of the campaigns the NIYC waged were the "Fish-ins" in Washington state. In 1964 native people asserted their fishing rights along the banks of the Columbia, Green, Nisqually, Puyallup, Quillayute, and Yakima Rivers.

The NIYC aligned itself with other civil rights movements under the banner of "Red Power" activism and by the 1970s expanded its efforts into the arena of environmental justice. The group's legal actions paved the way for bringing the injustices of coal strip mining, uranium mining, and milling in Indian Country to the public's attention.

The discourse that emerged from this activism led to the formation of a philosophical movement whose notions, like those of Plato, presumed that ideas originate from a person's direct experience. Because indigenous people were nurtured in a tradition of collective action, tribal community development had to be based on ideals that could arise only from a history of shared experiences. This is known as an indigenous worldview, and it not only served to unite native people, but it also distinguished them from non-Indians, who did not share the same common history. Furthermore, the discussion sparked life into indigenous scholarship. It was a fledgling movement that was not entirely invested in learning and scholarship but was rooted in idealism. The process was not based entirely on a strict rule of "analysis"—as in the objectified sense of the social science paradigm—but was based on "deconstructionism." Here the whole was taken apart and then pieced back together again. Much in the manner of a curious child taking apart a wind-up clock to explore its mechanism, the attention of this exploration was diverted from the "why" to the "how."

When I got involved in this movement, there had been some short-lived attempts to create a community of native scholars. I was fortunate to have participated in several organizing attempts during my directorship of the Native American Studies Center at the University of New Mexico. The first was an initiative that was a spin-off of a Ford Foundation grant to establish a Native American Studies Association (NASA). Interestingly, my first duty as a neophyte acting director was to coordinate the conference in 1980.[3] Unfortunately, the deliberations never advanced beyond the separate programmatic ego(s). NASA was eventually transplanted to the American Indian Studies Program at UCLA. There a series of annual conferences helped to keep the organization alive but also provided an important venue for the discussion of natural resources development. In 1983, for example, forty-one presenters convened for the Conference on American Indian Issues, Energy Independence—A Challenge for Native American Communities.

The most interesting forum, though, emerged out of an informal but strategic initiative among a select group of native activists and scholars from the United States and Canada. Organized as the Wayfinding Indigenous Multiversity of the Americas, the group was assembled in Oneida, Wisconsin, through the organizing efforts of the En'owkin Center, Penticton, British Columbia, in 1994. The discussions were intended to cross-fertilize the organizing efforts of of like-minded natives with the goal of establishing an alternative curriculum—one that manifested itself in both the classroom and the field.

The gathering was funded by revenue generated through tribal gaming at Oneida. More important, such independent funding assured that the free-wheeling discussions were totally unaffected by any outside sponsor's agenda. Although the forum itself never advanced beyond a group-think, it tied together some disparate threads that had been revealed elsewhere.

For example, in 1992 a planning session conducted under the auspices of the Community Fellows Program in the Department of Urban Studies and Planning at the Massachusetts Institute of Technology led to a "postmodernist discourse" among students from "communities of color" that pertained to grassroots activism and culture.[4] The result was the formulation of a new theory of action that would be called indigenous planning. Some of its fledgling ideas called for a radical reexamination of contemporary planning practice through long-term learning, the empowerment of a community voice, and the advocacy of culture and tradition. In 1995 the movement formulated its five basic principles:

1. People thrive in community.
2. Ordinary people have all the answers.
3. People have a basic right to determine their own future.
4. Oppression continues to devastate people.
5. The people are beautiful already.[5]

Another initiative was the Indigenous Planning Network (IPN), which had been seeded at the annual conference of the American Planning Association in Chicago in 1995. At the conference, planners who worked in native communities embarked on reestablishing a professional organization modeled after the defunct United Indian Planners Association (UIPA).[6] Influenced by the 1994 UN pronouncement on the International Decade of the World's Indigenous People, the Geographic Land Information Systems Department of the Oneida Nation of Wisconsin took the lead role in convening this "indigenous" initiative.[7] A newsletter titled *Indigenous Planning* was disseminated periodically with the stated goal of "forming a new division within the APA [American Planning Association] for native/indigenous planning."[8] Since its inception, the IPN has successfully convened tribal community development panels at the annual meetings of the APA, which in the spirit of the American Indian Chicago

Conference of 1961 are composed primarily of native planners practicing indigenous principles.

Currently, several faculty at the University of New Mexico, including myself as a representative of the IPN, are collaborating on creating the academic counterpart of the IPN.[9] The collaboration is centered on a course entitled "Indigenous Planning," which brings together students from the American Indian Law Program, the Anderson School of Management, and the Community and Regional Planning program in an interdisciplinary seminar. Recently, a philanthropist granted an endowment to support this interdisciplinary effort by establishing graduate fellowships in the three colleges.[10]

The seminar uses a case study approach. Students are not only subjected to concepts pertaining to Indian law, planning, and management, but these ideas are used to help model an analytical framework that deconstructs a real-world Indian community development problem. Students use not only the skills they learn from the mainstream disciplines but also their own experiential knowledge in working as interdisciplinary teams. In that way, their interactions are a microcosm of the complex interactions among planners, lawyers, and business managers that are played out daily in Indian Country.

Indigenous Planning

Although it can be argued that the indigenous planning paradigm is a new concept, its principles are actually a reformulation of planning practices used by "traditional" communities for millennia. Before traditional authority had been wrested away or usurped by Euro-Western agencies, tribal societies planned their own communities. And unlike the Western approach that bases its planning primarily on land use, the indigenous planning approach was formulated on practices associated with land tenure.

Land tenure is distinguished by long and sustained patterns of ownership. In the case of indigenous communities, such ownership was sustained over successive generations. Land became the embodiment of collective groups whose intent was to sustain the productivity of the land for those who would inherit it. As such, land became a birthright, and stewardship was the primary vehicle for maintaining it. Given a legacy of land tenure, it becomes easier to understand how traditional communities evolved distinctive worldviews. Those worldviews embodied values that were essential to attain a balanced and symmetrical interrelationship between humankind and the natural environment. A worldview functions much like an ontological blueprint. Its collective concepts supersede an individual's lifetime.

Take the case of the Pueblo Bonito ruin located at Chaco Canyon National Park in northeastern New Mexico. It stands as one of the finest examples of Anasazi ingenuity and is an archetype of prehistoric Pueblo Indian architecture. Yet from the perspective of the Euro-Western mind, such an edifice could have been accomplished only through the genius of a singular mind commanding a legion of builder slaves. What this interpretation fails to consider, however, is that Pueblo Bonito was built over a period of approximately three centuries and was constructed in seven phases.[11] Yet at no time during this extended period did it vary in form and function. There was no singular genius, simply a collective one. This is a testament to the power of the worldview.

Worldviews are endowed with ideals that integrate the past, the present, and the future. Because it is experiential, there is a certain tolerance for change. As collective societies explored the peripheries of their territories they would interact with other groups. When they experienced new ideas, they adapted them. This was contrary to the notion of invention. Rather, change was a process of transformation tempered by the need to assure the community that new ideas were mindful of the past, cognizant of the present, and suitable for the future.

The overall impact of such deliberations was a distinctive style of consensus making. I have discussed this in detail in another publication.[12] For the sake of brevity, it is important mainly to know that consensus making was a long process deliberated over by a strict clan protocol and repeated until there was unanimous agreement. As a result, tribal communities were far from reactionary governments. In fact, tribal proceedings frustrated Western observers used to making on-the-spot decisions based on simple majorities. Consensus became the root source of Westerners' frustration with tradition and deliberation. It left the short-term impression that indigenous societies were unyielding in the face of modernization, when in fact they were fairly adaptive in the long term.

To distinguish the Western from the indigenous paradigm in this manner is critical. Land use as applied in traditional Western planning practice is both temporal and corporal. It gives form and shape to communities by upholding the privileges associated with private property rights. Land use becomes the embodiment of the individual who develops it with the primary intent of raising its capital valuation. When it is maximized, it is then resold. There is little incentive to hold land as property longer than necessary, especially if it becomes unproductive. This behavior leads to slash-and-burn economics.

One can see how such behavior conflicts with indigenous tribal community development values. One such arena is Indian gaming. For a few lucky tribes, Indian gaming has become a panacea that has not only resulted in breaking away from the cycle of dependency on treaty reparations but has given tribal governments a renewed ability to make decisions for themselves. At the same time, it has forced tribal governments to adopt new models of management and to embark on strategic planning.[13]

This is a change from the comprehensive planning model. That process had been enabled on Indian reservations in the early 1960s and 1970s by the U.S. Office of Economic Opportunity.[14] Strategic planning, on the other hand, was a development model created by corporations for determining reinvestment goals. Whereas comprehensive planning was based on an inventory approach—that is, what can you do with the resources you currently have—strategic planning was based on crafting a futuristic "vision statement." That vision was strategic in setting into motion how the organization would plan.

The difference between comprehensive planning and strategic planning can be easily demonstrated by a simple analogy. Suppose a group of individuals decided to go to lunch together. One choice would be to select from the restaurants in the immediate vicinity, thereby tempering one's appetite with what was available. This is the comprehensive planning approach. Another strategy would be to agree on the type of cuisine everyone wanted and then figure out the resources necessary to get everyone to a restaurant that served such fare, even if it meant going across town. This is the strategic planning approach.

Many well-meaning comprehensive tribal planning approaches fell out of disfavor principally because they limited tribal governments to choosing enterprises within their meager resource bases. The process essentially left the tribal governments feeling bankrupt and impoverished. It was only after a few gaming tribes received windfall profits that they began to craft vision statements with the intent of diversifying. And when the resource base did not exist on their lands, tribes expanded their capital by acquiring resources on the outside. Thus strategic planning unwittingly hastened the transformation of Indian policy away from paternalism and toward self-determination.

It remains to be seen, however, if such visioning will be limited to the accumulation of capital. Simply "putting more eggs into the basket" does not necessarily solve the enormous social and political problems contemporary tribes face. In particular, will the exercise of visioning return tribes to doctrines that incorporate vestiges of their worldviews? My hunch is that it will. A few vestiges of community development have already been crafted that are based, at least in part, on traditional worldview values.[15]

It is becoming clear that some unifying ideological factors serve as the foundation of a long overdue paradigm shift such as indigenous planning. Although the following tenets are by no means definitive, I offer them as a way to begin deconstructing the past and present toward a future of indigenous planning.

1. Indigenous people are not minorities. The territories of indigenous people are characterized by a social and cultural geography in which the outsider or nonnative is the minority. Indigenous communities and lands exist where the presence of outsiders and nonnatives is almost nonexistent. As long as indigenous communities continue to unconsciously ply the notion that their power is insolvent because they are demographic majorities, the collective will continue to be marginalized and made to appear invisible and insignificant.

2. The essence of indigenous scholarship is native self. True indigenous scholars and activists do not suffer from cultural amnesia. In the spirit of idealism, indigenous people adapt their ideas from experience. As proven time and again, indigenous people excel in the process of deconstruction as characterized by reflection and introspection. Indigenous people are not afraid to be a part of their own community research, and the role of the expert is tempered by the collective experience.
3. Indigenous voices need no translation. Rather, indigenous people are educated and trained in the best of traditional and Western traditions. Their voice is neither revisionist nor elitist. Instead, it empowers the collective mind by challenging those who attain their expertise solely through individualism and privilege. Native people are poised to take their rightful role as enablers and empowerers of their own communities. This is accomplished through mutual respect, participatory styles of consensus making, and adherence to traditional protocols.
4. The indigenous planning process is informed by the indigenous worldview. Central to that worldview are values associated with territory, land tenure, and stewardship. It represents a philosophical construction of humankind's relationship to the natural world and is demarcated by territories that balance human needs with ecologically viable and sustainable development. Worldviews are endowed with ideals that integrate the past, the present, and the future.

Indian Affairs and the Environmental Movement

The Confederated Salish and Kootenai Tribes in Diane Krahe's Chapter 8 on environmental philosophy and the Mission Mountains Tribal Wilderness describe wilderness as "where our people walked and lived, lands and landmarks carved through the minds of our ancestors through coyote stories and actual experiences." As demonstrated in the Salish and Kootenai situation, the Indian and non-Indian worldviews of "wilderness" clashed principally because the tribes recognized that humans were in fact the "changeling" guardians of the forest. That responsibility meant humans did intervene and that their actions did affect and change some aspects of the resource for the better. In abeyance of that role, the Western concept of wilderness was implemented as the "roadless" approach, which was the extreme exercise of private property rights shrouded under the cloak of public guardianship. The policy was designed to systematically exclude anyone from touching the area and, in a manner of speaking, eventually resulted in the entire area falling into disrepair.

The importance of a tribal worldview is also evident in another instance mentioned in Richmond Clow and Imre Sutton's Prologue. The Northern Utes' worldview pitted their animate beliefs in the physical environment against the propensity of their white neighbors to commodify water. Western concepts of property and resource management presented the flip side of that tribal worldview. Resources were inanimate units that could and can be severed from the environment as a discrete and titled property right. The notions of water, mineral, and timber rights, for instance, were alien principles that befuddled native people even more than land titles. Property rights were further advanced by laying down the Cartesian grid. Ecological zones and watersheds were segmented into unnatural and unsustainable parcels.

Of course, the legacy that befell many tribal communities was banishment to the most unsuitable of such parcels—unsuitable, that is, from the eighteenth- and nineteenth-century notions of cultivated lands. No amount of education in the agricultural trades was enough to make up for the unsuitability of reservation lands for cultivation. That, in turn, virtually guaranteed that the treaty reparations would be plied inordinately to undermine tribal self-determination by creating an endless cycle of listless dependency.

Such was also the situation with those resources held in "reserve" by the federal benefactor. The pretense of assimilation as a means to disempower native people was evident in the Winters Doctrine. As Clow and Sutton concede in the Introduction to Part I, irrigation was just another strategy to impound water rights while bureaucrats sat around and thought hard about Indians as farmers. And when it came time to make public concessions on behalf of their tribal wards, they were just as apt to give away the entire proverbial henhouse by designating "national sacrifice areas."

The same fundamental schism is apparent in Clow's discussion of treaty subsistence hunting and the Northern Utes (Chapter 1). Whereas for the Utes hunting was a matter of subsistence, for the local whites hunting became a sport. As public policy was formulated, its regulations were predicated on the concept of game conservation as necessary to maintain a high standard of recreational amenity for sports hunters. Deer carcasses went unclaimed, and the spoilage caused by excessive thrill killers did more to decimate the deer population than anything previously witnessed.

Much of the disquiet between native people and the outside was artificially mitigated by the designation of reservations. Reservation lands of themselves were not designated by rational ecological principles. Instead, they often represented the last stands for indigenous communities against outside encroachment. Territoriality, on the other hand, was linked to the concept of land tenure, which in turn was integrated into the concept of sustainability as applied to an ecologically viable geography. In particular, unlike private property, reservation lands were not subject to the dynamics of slash-and-burn economic cycles. Land tenure, most simply applied, meant natives were there to stay.

That simple premise more than any other has helped to shape the worldview of native people. Their values and beliefs—the very essence of their ontological belief systems—are a direct outcome of knowing that what you and your progeny have inherited will not be going anywhere soon. That was the case related in Peter Booth's chapter on the Tohono O'odham's resistance to New Deal conservation. In the face of eleven disparate village complexes, the glue that bonded the communities together was the shared ties, loyalties, and values. Decisions were reached through consensus making, and a confederation of sorts was met with mutual preservation of one another's ecological territories.

That approach, ironically, fit the New Deal's purpose to a tee. Livestock depletion and land conservation were unwittingly met by the Indian agency's inability to create one tribal government entity and, conceivably, one territory. Such an arrangement would have allowed all livestock to be culled irrespective of the cultural, social, and political ramifications to the villages. Only after the Indian agency deferred and allowed the fence boundaries to run contiguous with the traditional territories of each village was a semblance of sustainable self-government attained and the disquiet mitigated. On the other hand, had the same consolidation scheme befallen the tribe, as in the case presented by Clow of the Rosebud Sioux and their Tribal Land Enterprise, it would have doubtless have met with the opposite fate.

Terry Anderson's essay on land tenure and agricultural productivity (Chapter 2) provides more proof that ecological territory was linked to stewardship. The crucial aspect of such stewardship was the maintenance of a resource base that optimized capacity and yield. Certainly, it came as a surprise that native people could assert some individualism and resourcefulness as a collective group. Communal property or usufructuary rights to common lands may exist in an idealized sense, but at some juncture layers of usage are understood and used to regulate the interplay of actions among tribal or clan members. Play by the collective rules or forfeit your individual right of inheritance. As Anderson points out, it was the imposition of a Western concept of stewardship that most disrupted those rules. That concept came in the form of individual or tribal trust lands. The designation carried a bureaucratic liability: stewardship was all or nothing. Individual rights were superseded for common shares. Bureaucrats impeded the consolidation of the shares to single owners, resulting in a morass of heirs who were happy to see someone else take charge of their minuscule share. As long as tribal trust lands were being regulated in the same manner, inefficiency was not far behind.

Fee simple allotments were perhaps the most catastrophic of all. They allowed individuals to consign all their rights to non-Indians. Many fee simple allottees opted for this route, probably because their allotments carried little or no sense of stewardship in the first place. To them, they were abstract deeds of entitlement severed from any collective enterprise. This was also somewhat the case with the Rosebud Sioux and their Tribal Land Enterprise project. Without an overarching worldview ideology, individual avarice and local politics inevitably unravel land tenure.

Of course, privatization was not the operative goal; rather, it was to determine how tribes would link land ownership back into the collective fold. That can occur only with a strong sense of purpose or stewardship. As Alan McQuillan points out in Chapter 4 on Indian timber management policy, the earliest formulation of public timber policy was predicated on the belief that tree cutting was good for agriculture. In other words, felling trees to open land for farming was a necessary step in civilization. What such practices did not foresee, however, was that settlers would metamorphosize into avaricious developers and that the forests in Indian Country would become fair game for the timber industry. Naturally, Indian agents deferred to this lobby and justified it on the same basis as the Jeffersonian "yeoman farmer" policy.

Stewardship took precedence only after the Menominee Indians were granted important concessions in 1891. That allowed both the employment of an Indian labor force and the creation of a tribal discretionary fund. By the time of the Indian New Deal, Congress had adopted language mandating that forest resources on Indian lands be managed according to the principle of sustained yield. A full century after that fateful legislation, ecosystem management finally allowed managers to embrace principles that encompassed spiritual and aesthetic values.

Yet a certain amount of cynicism remains. Albeit, McQuillan concludes that there were "no significant differences between Indians and white people" in their approach to forestry. Such a revelation is a bit pretentious considering that historically tribes had never been allowed to exercise management policies, much less to formulate an approach based on their own ideologies. The Menominees were on the right track, but the termination of their Federal Indian status in the 1950s—predicated largely on their timber concession successes—undermined any chance to wed ideology with forest management. Termination essentially disassembled generations of creative management.

American Indian people and their lands have always been the sacrificial lamb when it comes to the national resource agenda. Nowhere was this more evident than in the flooding of Indian lands to create water reservoirs. As Katherine Weist points out (Chapter 3) about hydroelectric dams, "the greater good for the majority" became the mobilizing credo for appropriating even more Indian resources. Moreover, the concessions involved more than land and water. They included the ability of Indians to govern the resource use and allocation of benefits arising from these massive projects. Underwriting this effort was a distinct ideology that held that demographic minorities were insignificant. Of course, tribal people fell immediately into the trap in spite of the fact that they held hundreds of thousands of acres. As Weist indicates, the collaborations intended to undermine tribal authority were solidified when overt racism and assimilationist attitudes were allowed to enter policymaking. Especially because political considerations appeared to be the primary impetus behind river basin initiatives, tribes as minorities were ousted from playing any significant role.

It follows, therefore, that minorities in the demographic sense can be usurped of their power and authority when their resources are leveraged against the will of the majority. As Imre Sutton (Chapter 7) notes of Indian cultural, historical, and sacred resources, this is precisely why land tenure and jurisdiction go hand in hand. Establishing a clear line of jurisdiction better enables the principal stakeholders (regardless of their size) to protect and manage their resources. Unfortunately, the legacy the tribes have inherited through tribal self-determination has been to mend the damage wrought by generations subjected to paternal jurisdiction and the lack of a direct voice in managing their own human and natural resources.

This runs contrary to the popular Western interpretation that tends to characterize tribal leadership as a banal and static state of affairs. It is euphemistically referred to as "traditional rule," and it has been the bane of policymakers since interrelations among native people began. Static tradition was the underlying excuse for Western assimilation. What the process did not acknowledge was that tribal people and their societies did have a tradition of dynamic change—it occurred through the selective adaptation of concepts and goods and furthermore entailed with a consciousness that assured their survival.

Summary

This is an interesting time for indigenous communities. As seen in the discussion here, tribal governments have had to cope not only with the impacts of a legacy of paternalism and outside imposition but also with their basic community needs. In the arena of natural resources, trust as played out within the guise of conservation has alienated tribes from their worldviews and sapped the ideological soul of the indigenous communities. Many generations have ensued since colonial practices began to infringe on indigenous rights and self-reliance. In indigenous communities, understanding of the traditional worldview has been lost; in others it is fragmented and in others secularized. In spite of this, indigenous people have always held to the basic belief that their collective responsibility is to be the principal stewards of the land.

As long as they are able to sustain their territories, the values associated with land tenure should allow indigenous people to harbor a sense of identity. On the other hand, this will rest on the ability of the collective society to bring clarity and cohesion to its planning process through its timeless worldview. This is both the essence and the challenge of indigenous planning.

References

1. "Declaration of Indian Purpose," American Indian Chicago Conference Proceedings, Chicago, Illinois, June 20, 1961. [Editors' note: Professors Sol Tax and Nancy Lurie brought together different Indian groups at this conference: "Four hundred and sixty Indians from ninety tribes . . . issued [the declaration], which sought to preserve traditional values and rights in the face of steady encroachment of white economic power and law." See Wilcomb E. Washburn, *Red Man's Land/White Man's Law: A Study of the Past and Present Status of the American Indian* (New York: Charles Scribner's Sons, 1971): 229.]
2. Proceedings reprinted in *New Directions in Indian Purpose* (Chicago: Native American Educational Services, 1988).
3. *Proceedings of the Roundtable of the Native American Studies Association,* Native American Studies, University of New Mexico, Albuquerque, New Mexico, September 1980.
4. John Friedmann and Carol Kuester, "Planning Education for the Late Twentieth Century: An Initial Inquiry," *Journal of Planning Education and Research,* 14:1 (fall 1994): 55–64.
5. Sean Robin, "The Story of Indigenous Planning With Its Basic Principles," *Indigenous Planning Times,* premier issue (June 1995): 3–18.
6. The UIPA was organized in the 1970s as a response to the comprehensive tribal planning agenda of the U.S. Office of Economic Opportunity.
7. Several individuals at Oneida have also participated in these forums, as well as having regularly attended the annual meetings of the APA.
8. *Indigenous Planning,* 2 (August 1995): 1. Produced by the Sovereign Oneida Nation of Wisconsin, Oneida Planning Department.
9. They include Kenneth Bobroff, associate professor of law, and Helen Muller, professor of management.
10. New York philanthropist Ed Cohen.
11. See "High Noon in Old Bonito," John Stein, et al., in Baker H. Morrow and V. B. Price, eds., *Anasazi Architecture and American Design* (Albuquerque: University of New Mexico Press, 1997), pp. 133–148.
12. Theodore S. Jojola, "Indigenous Planning: Clans, Intertribal Confederations, and the History of the All-Indian Pueblo Council," in Leonie Sandercock, ed., *Making the Invisible: Insurgent Planning Histories* (Berkeley: University of California Press, 1998), pp. 100–119.
13. Eve L. Baron, "Public Participation and the Choice of Casinos as Development Strategy in Iroquois Nations," Ph.D. diss., Rutgers University, New Brunswick, New Jersey, 1998.
14. Theodore S. Jojola and Herman Agoyo, "One Generation of Self-Determination: Native American Economic Self-Reliance in New Mexico," in *Proceedings of the Annual Conference* (Western Rural Development Center, Oregon State University, 1993), pp. 56–61.
15. Research is under way to develop three case studies of such developments; the Turtle School of the Oneida Nation in Wisconsin has been completed.

EPILOGUE

Despite a century of resource management, tribes still have not fared well. Some Indian communities have gained selectively from the larger theoretical framework of the conservation and environmental movements. If some conservation measures have led to beneficial results, gains in one area do not compensate for losses in another whether the trustee or the tribes were in charge. For example, improvements in forestry do not offset declines in agriculture. Productive tribal management of the tribes' own parks does not compensate for the tremendous loss of former lands now part of the national parks and national forests where tribal access means less than full restoration of sites to the tribes.

More consistent conservation practices would have made a difference as long as one does not overlook the long-term social as well as environmental costs. To be sure, soil conservation efforts have abetted some tribal agricultural enterprises, and tribal park management has encouraged a tourist economy. Yet allotment's failure to prevent complex heirship and its attendant problems of fragmented idle and erosion-ridden lands argue that the original reforms of the New Deal did not go far enough. Tourism, especially associated with Indian gaming, has led to traffic congestion and inadequate infrastructure, and lucrative tribal enterprises such as waste disposal have threatened several reservations with environmental hazards.[1] At one time officials as well as many champions of the Indians' cause perceived assisted relocation of Indians from reservations to towns and cities as a productive employment opportunity and a means to reduce population density and pressure on marginal trust resources. Still, the tragic story of urban Indian poverty, although stemming from multiple causes, must also be understood in terms of environmental conditions on reservations.[2]

The inability of countless Indians to earn a living utilizing reservation resources must be addressed in terms not just of the paucity of resources but also of the inadequacies in the management of trust resources and realty. The poverty of reservation Indians and, to a degree, the plight of urban Indians are linked in part to many failures of resource management. For example, even if tribes were to overcome deficiencies in soil quality and insufficient water resource development, fragmented landholdings and subsequent idleness of land preclude many options for individual Indians and their families. To overcome poverty, tribes have elected many options. To date, despite difficulties, many tribal leaders have secured appropriate talent among their members and have encouraged the return of members who offer expertise and skills. Other tribes such as the Menominee and the Navajo have developed on-reservation courses of study and training or sent youth off to college to develop the skills needed to manage their home environment.[3] Tribes also vary in their utilization of non-Indian talent. Under self-determination, as we have seen, a selective number of tribes have chosen to secure the advice and assistance of many public agencies and environmental organizations. These are among the more positive steps taken by Indian communities.

Efforts of tribes to improve and diversify resource management on reservations will not alone displace tribal need for the involvement of public agencies. Frankly, it is the trusteeship that sustains the reservation system and tribal culture regardless of whether the living environment itself always sustains its residents. Sustainability of a livelihood on many reservations continues to depend on multiple sources of income, and grants from the federal government still play a significant role in tribal life. Many observers remind us of the element of dependency, without which many tribes could not sustain on the marginal lands they occupy. As Francis Paul Prucha notes:

> The Indian drive for self-determination and sovereignty, in many ways so fruitful and successful and, most importantly, accepted as the official goal of the United States, carries within it the contradictory seeds of dependency. Even the government's trust responsibility in regard to land and other Indian assets . . . entails an element of paternalism.[4]

This is not to say that absent paternalism and the implications of dependency, tribes under rigorous resource management cannot improve their lot and even encourage, as many choose to do, the return of members. There is a certain negativism in presuming that Indian communities cannot overcome some of the least desirable aspects of resource management dependency. The white majority that farms, ranches, mines, runs tourist facilities, and the like also gains from public grants and other financial support. Tribes perhaps must make a choice, as Terry L. Anderson states: "If Indians choose to retain trusteeship over their natural resource assets, they must accept the position of the weaker party dominated by the stronger guardian. . . . This implies less than sovereignty . . . and rules out the prospect for real self-determination."[5]

The contributors in this book are not of one mind as to the potential success of self-determination and resource management. Tribes may now willingly welcome the policy of self-determination but too soon become distressed if, as in past administrative practice, another policy supplants the current one of government-to-government relations. Just as critics of the land claims litigation process warned, self-determination may predicate a harbinger of termination, an end to trust status.[6] Also, no one has stated that self-determination denotes economic independence, for tribal reliance on financial support for various environmental programs will and must continue to implement the purposes of self-determination.

As noted earlier, tribal leaders perhaps perceive self-determination to include their right to seek greater support from agencies such as the Environmental Protection Agency, the Administration for Native Americans (ANA), the National Park Service, and the Forest Service—perceiving them as surrogate trustees. Tribes report progress based on grants from other agencies, as Michael T. Pablo, former tribal chairman of the Confederated Salish and Kootenai of the Flathead Reservation, reported in 1991 of an ANA grant:

> Our reservation implemented a broad and far-reaching study involving our land and future use and developments. . . . Maps were created showing: wildlife, environmental, and cultural protection zones; natural resource zones; land status/land use; and zones-of-influence delineating jurisdictions of off-Reservation lands in the area concerning water quality, air quality, etc.[7]

Stanley G. Jones Sr., chairman of the Tulalip Tribes of Washington, emphasized that the Indian Environmental Enhancement Act of 1990 [P.L. 101-408] "holds promise for tribal groups to better manage their environments, including land, air, water, etc."[8] These and other tribal observations speak well of the self-determination movement despite the criticism that dependency—paternalism—persists.

The conservation programs that were established and are still operative on trust lands represent trustee paternalism that continues to encourage dependency. Only when the tribes and individual Indians are financially and technically able to assume control of resource management and conservation programs will dependency diminish. On the other hand, as historian Rebekah Davis notes, "Conservation programs designed without regard for the beliefs and practices of the human population occupying the land are fruitless at best, and at worst increase the level of mistrust and misunderstanding that has historically plagued Federal Government–American Indian relations."[9] Changing sensitivities of the Forest Service and the National Park Service suggest a better direction for improved resource management between tribes and public land agencies. This new era of cooperation does not assume that tribes will always be the beneficiaries.

At the same time we praise newer policy directives undertaken by public land agencies—as in the instances of supporting land restoration for the Timbisha in Death Valley National Park and participating in a partnership with the Hopi in Kaibab National Forest—we must express disappointment with several conservation organizations for opposing tribally related resource concerns. Many tribes do not yet possess the resources to manage complex environments. At the same time, some tribes, although seeking expanded tourism—such as the Mescalero Apache, who are developing the Ski Apache area yet voted to develop a nuclear waste site—continue to encourage environmental changes that may run counter to modern environmentalism. On the other hand, Navajo management of Monument Valley and general environmental management on the Warm Springs Indian Reservation (Oregon) exemplify the potential tribes offer for managing their own resources. In time, with cooperative assistance rather than interference or objection by conservation groups, it is hoped Indian communities will develop the capacity to create sustainable resource management programs on reservations.

There is a negative factor that tribes cannot overlook when managing reservation resources. Sun Prairie Partnership of Nebraska had entered into a lease with the Rosebud Sioux Tribe to build 288 hog barns for pork production. Subsequently, the tribal council reversed the lease and the Rosebud Sioux tribal court stopped the construction. Sun Prairie sued in a South Dakota federal court to continue construction and U.S. District Judge Charles Kornmann agreed, writing: "I'm not going to stop Sun Prairie from proceeding under a lease which I held was valid. . . . If anyone gets the idea a contract with a tribe is worth less than a contract with General Motors . . . that's a serious matter." The tribe has appealed to the 8th U.S. Circuit Court of Appeals,[10] but the case reveals that tribes too must operate in good faith just as they would expect others to do. Tribal council resource decisions require careful pre-contract planning and they should inform all tribal members of all plans. Hopefully, tribal governments would not have to resort to litigation in either tribal or federal courts. For tribes to sustain autonomy over their resources, it is essential that they function in the marketplace like other entities.

These chapters make a strong case for the limitations of reservation resource management that will sustain Indian economies. By examining tribal resource management concerns, the contributors have chronicled the conservation movement's role in the management of Indian trust lands. Beginning with this idea, the authors progressed readily toward providing interpretations of the changing focus in the resource management of tribal lands. Although no one collective statement speaks for us all, the editors perceive an underlying belief that ecology and economics must come together to enhance the lives of Native Americans.

The geography of Indian Country is even less a bounded world today than in the past: tribes live in a real world where conservation is too often addressed only in spirit and is not applied. Indians left to themselves have developed viable management programs even if they are denied by court decisions the option to embrace a holistic ecomanagement approach. For the long term, the tribes must combine their energetic means with supportive public and private organizations if they hope to sustain a home environment—the reservation—as the locus of Indian culture.

References

1. See Ward Churchill and Winona LaDuke, "Native North America: The Political Economy of Radioactive Colonialism," in M. Annette Jaimes, ed., *The State of Native America: Genocide, Colonization, and Resistance* (Boston: South End, 1992): 241–266; Churchill, "A Breach of Trust: The Radioactive Colonization of Native North America," *American Indian Culture and Research Journal,* 23:4 (1999): 23–69; Donald A. Grinde and Bruce E. Johansen, *Ecocide of Native America: Environmental Destruction of Indian Lands and Peoples* (Santa Fe: Clear Light, 1995).
2. On facets of Indian urban living that bear on our discussion, see Susan Lobo and Kurt Peters, eds., "American Indians and the Urban Experience," *American Indian Culture and Research Journal,* 22:4 (1998): 1–440. When an Indian leaves a reservation for longer than 180 days, his eligibility for federal health benefits expires. Also, urban communities that have no federally recognized tribes are denied federal health care funds for native people resident in the community. See Hector Becerra, "UCI Program Will Assess Indian Health," *Los Angeles Times,* May 21, 2000: B1, B5.
3. Cf. Jack Hunt, "Land Tenure and Economic Development of the Warm Springs Indian Reservation," *Journal of the West,* 9:1 (1970): 93–109. Hunt discusses the successful aspects of tribal efforts to utilize claims award monies to establish long-term management for the reservation. The efforts of this Indian community represent an example of self-determination before the policy was in place.
4. Francis Paul Prucha, *The Indians in American Society: From the Revolutionary War to the Present* (Berkeley: University of California Press, 1988): 101. Cf. the observations of Richard White, *The Roots of Dependency: Subsistence, Environment, and Social Change Among the Choctaws, Pawnees, and Navajos* (Lincoln: University of Nebraska Press, 1983).
5. Terry L. Anderson, *Sovereign Nations or Reservations? An Economic History of American Indians* (San Francisco: Pacific Research Institute for Public Policy, 1995): 168.
6. Cf. Clayton R. Koppes, "From New Deal to Termination: Liberalism and Indian Policy, 1933–1953," *Pacific Historical Review,* 46:4 (1977): 543–566; Imre Sutton, ed., *Irredeemable America: The Indians' Estate and Land Claims* (Albuquerque: University of New Mexico Press, 1985): 214.
7. U.S. Senate, *Reauthorization of the Native American Programs Act—Administration for Native Americans,* Hearings before Select Committee of Indian Affairs, 102nd Cong., 1st sess. (Washington, DC: Government Printing Office, 1991): 329.
8. Ibid., pp. 322–323.
9. Rebekah C. Beatty Davis, *Conservation and Culture: The Soil Conservation Service, Social Science, and Conservation on Tribal Lands in the Southwest,* Historical Notes 6 (Washington, DC: Natural Resources Conservation Service, 1997): 53; cf. earlier

observations by an Indian scholar in Ward Churchill, "American Indian Lands: The Native Ethic Amid Resource Development," *Environment,* 28:6 (1986): 13–17, 28–32.

10. Terry Woster, "Tribe Loses Bid to Stop Hog Farm," *Argus Leader* (Sioux Falls, SD), Sunday, May 13, 2001, 7B.

Bibliographical Note

Although each chapter includes documentation, some of the literature and documents dealing with Indian environmental affairs cut across the subject matter and the tribes, thus deserving separate comment. Citations here are grouped by subject matter rather than according to the subjects of the chapters. We have also added some reference materials.

1. Bibliographical Sources, Encyclopedias, and Guides

Most reference works include some citations and data referring to trust lands, resources, and environmental management. Francis Paul Prucha's *A Bibliographical Guide to the History of Indian-White Relations in the United States* (Chicago: University of Chicago Press, 1977) includes a brief listing of sources on land and economic development; Imre Sutton's *Indian Land Tenure: Bibliographical Essays and a Guide to the Literature* (New York: Clearwater, 1975) discusses land utilization in section C. Although geographers are much less represented in the literature on the Indian, Stephen C. Jett's (comp.) *A Bibliography of North American Geographers' Works on Native Americans North of Mexico, 1971–91,* Haskell Indian Nations University Studies in the Geography of the American Indian, 1 (Lawrence: Haskell Indian Nations University, 1994) contains a wealth of studies relevant to land, resources, and environmental management. The following volumes also contain discussions of resources, land utilization, and related economic activity: Duane Champagne, ed., *The Native North American Almanac* (Detroit: Gale, 1994; 2d ed. due in 2001); Mary Davis, ed., *Native America in the Twentieth Century: An Encyclopedia* (New York: Garland, 1994); Veronica E. Velarde Tiller, comp./ed., *Tiller's Guide to Indian Country* (Albuquerque: BowArrow, 1996).

2. Periodicals (with sample symposia)

Only a few periodicals are specific to the Indian field; most relevant are *American Indian Culture and Research Journal*, *American Indian Quarterly*, and *American Indian Law Review*. From time to time these and other periodicals include relevant articles and symposia on Indian affairs; for example, Tracy J. Andrews and Castle McLaughlin, eds., "Farming and Ranching in Reservation Economies," *American Indian Culture and Research Journal*, 22:3 (1998): 1–138; David R. Lewis, "Native Americans and the Environment: A Survey of Twentieth-Century Issues," *American Indian Quarterly*, 19:3 (1995): 423–450; [a water symposium], *Natural Resources Journal*, 20:1 (1980): 1–158; "Symposium: Issues in Native American Law," *Stanford Environmental Law Journal*, 8 (1989): 174–291; "Developing Resources on American Indian Lands," *Natural Resources and Environment*, 7:4 (1993); "American Indian Environmental History," Richard White, ed., *Environmental Review*, 9:2 (summer 1985): 101–170; J. E. Thorson, ed., "Proceedings of Symposium on Settlement of Indian Water Rights Claims," *Environmental Law*, 22 (1992).

3. Legal-Governmental Sources and Legal-Environmental Studies

The standard casebook on Indian affairs is David H. Getches, Charles F. Wilkinson, and Robert A. Williams Jr., *Cases and Materials on Federal Indian Law*, 4th ed. (St. Paul: West, 1998), which includes relevant chapters on reservation economic development, water rights, and fishing and hunting. An older basic legal treatise is: Felix S. Cohen, *Handbook of Federal Indian Law* (Washington, D.C., 1941); see also Rennard Strickland, editor-in-chief, *Federal Indian Law*, rev. ed. (Charlottesville: Michie Bobbs-Merrill, 1982). Theodore W. Taylor's *American Indian Policy* (Mt. Airy, MD: Lomond, 1983), although somewhat older, provides data on government agencies that have served tribes. The interface of law and environment has become an important arena of research for scholars in different fields; for example, Imre Sutton, ed., "The Political Geography of Indian Country," *American Indian Culture and Research Journal*, 15:2 (1991): 1–169; N. Bruce Duthu, ed., "Symposium: Stewards of the Land: Indian Tribes, the Environment, and the Law," *Vermont Law Review*, 21:1 (1996).

4. Native Geography, Resource Management, and Environmental Perception

The study of Indian affairs is dominated by non-Indian interpretations and environmental perspectives. Yet several studies have sought to bring together native experiences and perspectives: Christopher Vecsey and Robert W. Venables, eds., *American Indian Environments: Ecological Issues in Native American History* (Syracuse: Syracuse University Press, 1980); Thomas C. Blackburn and Kat Anderson, eds., *Before the Wilderness: Environmental Management by Native Californians*, Anthropological Papers no. 40 (Menlo Park, CA: Ballena, 1993). The controversy over whether it is appropriate to identify the Indian as an environmentalist has many critics, including Shepard Krech III, *The Ecological Indian: Myth and History* (New York: W. W. Norton, 1999).

5. Historical Studies and Impact of the Reservation System

Historical studies usually include some discussions—however brief—of Indian lands, resources, and conservation. Here we cite general historical accounts as representative: Donald L. Parman, *Indians and the American West* (Bloomington: Indiana University Press, 1994); Wilcomb E. Washburn, *Red Man's Land/White Man's Law* (New York: Scribners, 1971). The reservation system reduced Indian livelihoods to a limited space that was and remains ecologically inadequate and has made tribes dependent on government assistance. Richard White's *The Roots of Dependency: Subsistence, Environment, and Social Change Among Choctaws, Pawnees, and Navajos* (Lincoln: University of Nebraska Press, 1983) demonstrates to what degree three tribes lost most of their independence to subsist. But the vast changes in territoriality brought a new system of land tenure that led to diminishment of tribal acreage and other problems, most of which to the date of each publication are considered by J. P. Kinney, *A Continent Lost, a Civilization Won: Indian Land Tenure in America* (Baltimore: John Hopkins University Press, 1937); Lewis Meriam et al., *The Problem of Indian Administration. Studies in Administration,* no. 17 (Baltimore: Brookings Institution for Government Research, 1928) [Meriam was technical director; his staff included Ray A. Brown, Henry Roe Cloud, Edward Everett Dale, Emma Duke, Herbert R. Edwards, Mary Louise Mark, Fayette Avery McKenzie, W. Carson Ryan Jr., and William A. Spillman]; William Brophy and Sophie Aberle, *The Indian: America's Unfinished Business* (Norman: University of Oklahoma Press, 1966); U.S. National Resources Board, *Indian Land Tenure, Economic Status and Population Trends,* Report no. 10, Land Planning Committee (Washington, DC: Government Printing Office (GPO), 1935). By far, the Meriam report had the greatest impact on Indian policy development during the New Deal years. Janet A. McDonnell's *The Dispossession of the American Indian, 1887–1934* (Bloomington: Indiana University Press, 1991) examines the negative impact of federal land management policies up to the years of the New Deal.

6. Contemporary Assessments of Resources and Environments

There is only one full-length geographic study: Klaus Frantz, *Indian Reservations in the United States: Territory, Sovereignty, and Socioeconomic Change,* Geography Research Paper 242 (Chicago: University of Chicago Press, 1999). Several surveys focus more on economics and law; for example, Americans for Indian Opportunity, *Survey of American Indian Environmental Protection Needs on Reservation Lands: 1986* (submitted to the Environmental Protection Agency, Washington, DC, September 1986). The following two books are proactive approaches written mostly by Indian scholars: Kicke Kickingbird and Karen Ducheneaux, *One Hundred Million Acres* (New York: Macmillan, 1973); Donald

A. Grinde and Bruce E. Johansen, *Ecocide of Native America: Environmental Destruction of Indian Lands and Peoples* (Santa Fe: Clear Light, 1995).

7. Economic Development on Reservations

There are a number of newer economic analyses: Stephen Cornell and Joseph P. Kalt, eds., *What Can Tribes Do? Strategies and Institutions in American Indian Economic Development,* American Indian Manual and Handbook Series no. 4 (Los Angeles: American Indian Studies Center, UCLA, 1992); Terry L. Anderson, *Sovereign Nations or Reservations? An Economic History of American Indians* (San Francisco: Pacific Research Institute for Public Policy, 1995).

8. Agriculture

Most published materials are government documents, including House and Senate reports. Although there are numerous articles and a few books on farming and ranching, Rebekah C. Beatty Davis's *Conservation and Culture: The Soil Conservation Service, Social Science, and Conservation on Tribal Lands in the Southwest,* Historical Notes 6 (Washington, DC: Natural Resources Conservation Service, 1997) is a critical evaluation of the successes and failures of government policy as applied to one region yet offers advice of general utility. Leonard A. Carlson, in *Indians, Bureaucrats, and the Land: The Dawes Act and the Decline of Indian Farming* (Westport, CT: Greenwood, 1981), successfully demonstrates the link between policy affecting the distribution of tribal lands and the decline of farming by Indians.

9. Water and Related Environmental Problems

Most book-length studies review broad water policies, including the implication of the Winters doctrine, development of irrigation, and the like: Daniel McCool, in *Command of the Waters: Iron Triangles, Federal Water Development, and Indian Water* (Berkeley: University of California Press, 1987), discusses the conflicts of interest that arise among sister agencies such as the Bureau of Indian Affairs and the Bureau of Reclamation; John A. Folk-Williams's *What Indian Water Means to the West: A Sourcebook* (Santa Fe: Western Network, 1982) reviews prevalent cases up to the 1980s; see also, Thomas R. McGuire, William B. Lord, and Mary G. Wallace, *Indian Water in the New West* (Tucson: University of Arizona Press, 1993). We include two case studies—for the northern Great Plains and for the upper Allegheny River in New York: Michael Lawson, *Dammed Indians: The Pick-Sloan Plan and the Missouri River Sioux, 1944–1980* (Norman: University of Oklahoma Press, 1982); Joy A. Bilharz, *The Allegany Senecas and Kinzua Dam* (Lincoln: University of Nebraska Press, 1998). (See Fishing for an additional study.)

10. Forestry and Conservation

J. P. Kinney's *Indian Forest and Range: A History of the Administration and Conservation of the Redman's Heritage* (Washington, DC: Forestry Enterprises,

1950) was written by a forester-lawyer who was the first director of Indian forestry. For a more comprehensive reexamination of policy, practice, personalities, and litigation, see Alan S. Newell, Richmond L. Clow, and Richard N. Ellis, *A Forest in Trust: Three-Quarters of a Century of Indian Forestry, 1910–1986,* for Bureau of Indian Affairs, Litigation Support Services (Missoula: Historical Research Associates, 1986).

11. Fishing Rights and Treaties

The biggest controversy and litigation over treaty fishing rights has occurred in the Pacific Northwest, associated mainly with the Columbia River; two studies focus on the controversy and the impact of dams and impoundment on the fishery itself: Fay G. Cohen, *Treaties on Trial: The Continuing Controversy Over Northwest Indian Fishing Rights* (Seattle: University of Washington Press, 1986); Roberta Ulrich, *Empty Nets: Indians, Dams, and the Columbia River* (Corvallis: Oregon State University Press, 1999). See also Robert Doherty, *Disputed Waters: Native Americans and Great Lakes Fishery* (Lexington: University Press of Kentucky, 1990).

12. Energy, Mining, Hazards Management

Much has been written on the Council of Energy Resources Tribes; for example, Marjane Ambler, *Breaking the Iron Bonds: Indian Control of Energy Development* (Lawrence: University Press of Kansas, 1990). Ward Churchill has written a number of articles focusing on hazards, most recently "A Breach of Trust: The Radioactive Colonization of Native North America," *American Indian Culture and Research Journal,* 23:4 (1999): 23–70. Others have taken a proactive approach to abuses of the tribal environment: Donald A. Grinde and Bruce E. Johansen, *Ecocide of Native America: Environmental Destruction of Indian Lands and Peoples* (Santa Fe: Clear Light, 1995); Donald L. Fixico, *The Invasion of Indian Country in the Twentieth Century: American Capitalism and Tribal Natural Resources* (Niwot: University Press of Colorado, 1998).

13. Tribal Resources and Public Lands

Policy changes have occurred toward indigenous tribes that formerly occupied what became federal public lands and later formed the bases for national parks or forests. To date there is no comprehensive review of Forest Service or Bureau of Land Management policies, but three studies examine National Park Service policies: Theodore Catton, *Inhabited Wilderness: Indians, Eskimos, and National Parks in Alaska* (Albuquerque: University of New Mexico Press, 1997); Robert H. Keller and Michael F. Turek, *American Indians and National Parks* (Tucson: University of Arizona Press, 1998); and Mark D. Spence, *Dispossessing the Wilderness: Indian Removal and the Making of the National Parks* (New York: Oxford University Press, 1999).

14. Land Claims, Rights, and Restoration

The loss of land by various means reduced native ecology and hence impaired subsistence. Adjudication of claims forms part of the relevant story of environmental matters, in part because many tribes have been utilizing award monies to improve their environment and economic opportunities. Basic reviews of litigation include Russel L. Barsh, "Indian Land Claims Policy in the United States," *North Dakota Law Review,* 58 (1982): 1–82; Ward Churchill, "The Earth Is Our Mother: Struggles for American Indian Land and Liberation in the Contemporary United States," in M. Annette Jaimes, ed., *The State of Native America: Genocide, Colonization, and Resistance* (Boston: South End, 1992): 139–188; Imre Sutton, ed., *Irredeemable America: The Indians' Estate and Land Claims* (Albuquerque: University of New Mexico Press, 1985); Sutton, ed., "The Continuing Saga of Indian Land Claims," *American Indian Culture and Research Journal,* 24:1 (2000): 129–198; Harvey D. Rosenthal, *Their Day in Court* (New York: Garland, 1990). A classic volume reporting treaty provisions and including countless maps of land cessions is C. C. Royce, comp., *Indian Land Cessions in the United States,* 18th Annual Report, 1896–1897, part 2 (Washington, DC: Bureau of American Ethnography): 521–997.

15. Preservation of Cultural Heritage

Tribes are concerned over access to as well as protection of cultural resources, including sacred sites and burial grounds; in litigation, they have invoked the American Indian Religious Freedom Act and "The Native American Graves Protection and Repatriation Act [NAGPRA]" [symposium], *Arizona Law Journal,* 24:1 (1992). With reference to the application of NAGPRA, see Devon A. Mihesuah, ed., "Repatriation: An Interdisciplinary Dialogue," *American Indian Quarterly,* 20:2 (1996): 153–307. On preservation, see Dean B. Suagee, "Tribal Voices in Historic Preservation: Sacred Landscapes, Cross-Cultural Bridges, and Common Ground," *Vermont Law Review,* 21 (1996): 145–224; Christopher Vecsey, ed., *Handbook of American Indian Religious Freedom* (New York: Crossroad, 1991). A newer, broader study is Andrew Gulliford, *Sacred Objects and Sacred Places: Preserving Tribal Traditions* (Boulder: University Press of Colorado, 2000).

GLOSSARY[1]

Aboriginal title—Also called original title. Refers to Indian land not identified with land cessions documented in treaties and agreements. Generally, a title to territory of considerable square miles reconstructed from Indian informants, ethnographic and historic research, and other sources.[2]

Acknowledgment—A contemporary process by which an Indian community is recognized by the federal government; Indians must prove that their tribal affiliation and association have persisted to present; sometimes called *recognition.* When secured, usually grants a tribe and its members eligibility for federal funds and services; may also make possible the acquisition of trust land.[3]

Agreements—A legal instrument defining specific relations between a state (or local government) and a tribe that is normally recognized and holding trust land or reservation. Currently, these agreements involve the operation of casinos subject to the Indian Gaming Regulatory Act (1988). Such agreements require the signature of the state governor and tribal chair and may even require vote of the state legislature or be based on enactment of a general law granting the governor the power to negotiate with tribes. Sometimes called *compacts.*

Alienation—The more legal term for sale; refers to "the voluntary and absolute transfer of title and possession" of property. In nonlegal context as applied to Indian affairs, often connotes less than satisfactory alternative because it leads to the loss of trust lands.[4]

Allotment—A parcel of land inside or outside of reservations, authorized usually by congressional legislation and distributed in severalty to individual Indians. When beyond reservation borders and located on the public domain, often referred to as Indian homesteads. The allotment is held in trust by the United States but can be alienated through sale. Allotments cover at least 50 percent of all reservations, mainly in Western United States. On average, they are 80 to 160 acres but may be as small as 5 acres or as large as 640 acres. Although established selectively prior to 1887, the General Allotment Act provided the mechanism for most allotments. Allotments are subject to the devisement or inheritance laws of the state in which they are found. Complex heirship problems have resulted from allotments left when the owner dies intestate, which thus encumbers long-term use of such lands. See also *land consolidation.*

Autonomy; see *sovereignty*

Boundaries—Sometimes called *borders,* delimited and delineated on paper and demarcated on the ground, representing the limits of tribal territory and individual Indian allotments. In Indian affairs there are many kinds of boundaries, those diminished by congressional legislation that opened so-called surplus lands for non-Indian purchase. Such boundaries are fluid with respect to non-Indian landowners and operators within reservations. See also *closed and open areas.*

Burial grounds; see *repatriation*

Cadaster—Generally, the keeping of records of property boundaries and other documents relating to real estate. Identified in the past with the General Land Office of the federal government; today a function of the Bureau of Land Management. The Bureau of Indian Affairs maintains its own cadastral facility.

CERT—The Council of Energy Resource Tribes, a nonprofit organization established in 1976 by twenty-five tribes; it had grown to forty-three tribal members by 1993. "CERT's founders were determined to take control of the management of energy resources on their lands to enable their tribes to build healthy self-sufficient communities." In 1993 CERT members had access to professionals in such fields as economics, engineering, law, energy management. CERT member tribes supported the passage of landmark energy legislation in 1982—the Mineral Leasing Act—which reflects increased self-determination of the tribes. Many coal leases have been renegotiated because, among other factors, they did not embrace environmental demands of tribes. National environmental laws were also amended to affirm tribal primacy over trust resources.[5]

Closed areas—Pursuant to *Brendale v. Confederated Tribes of the Yakima Nation* [109 S. Ct. 2994 (1989)], the U.S. Supreme Court determined that those areas of the reservation mostly held in trust for the tribe and occupied by most tribal members were closed in terms of tribal authority to zone. Although specific to this tribe, the ruling has potential application elsewhere in Indian Country, for it bears on tribal authority over non-Indian ownership and lease utilization of lands within the borders of a reservation. See also *Devils Lake Sioux Tribe v. North Dakota Public Services Commission* [U.S. District Court, Dist. of N.D.—Southwestern Div., no. A1-90-179, February 3, 1993]. See also *open areas.*

Compacts; see *agreements*

Conservation—*Webster's* defines conservation as a "careful preservation and protection of something; especially planned management of a natural resource to prevent exploitation, destruction, or neglect." Raymond Dasmann defines "environmental conservation as the use of the environment to sustain the greatest possible diversity of life while insuring for humanity the physical basis for continued well-being. . . . It is based on a recognition that in any environment all things are tied together, and actions that change one part of that environment will have effects on all parts." Environmentalism, characterized by Gary Klee as the new conservation, emphasizes broader issues of environmental quality.[6]

Dispossession; see *land cessions, treaties*

Ecological Indian—Recent contention by scholars and other observers of Indian culture that Indians are nature-bent conservationists and have lived in harmony with nature. This view is now contested. It is not a universal fact that Indians deal entirely with nature in ways different from Euro-American culture.[7]

Ecosystem—No single definition satisfies everyone. Raymond Dasmann, biologist and environmental author, suggests that "ecosystems are subdivisions of the biosphere. They consist of communities of plants, animals, and microorganisms along with the air, water, soil, or other substrate that supports them. . . . Ecosystems may be very simple, such as those supporting a community of lichens growing on a hard rock in the high Arctic; or very complex, such as a tropical rain forest or a coral reef in tropical seas." John M. Blair and others define an ecosystem as "a biological community [all of the organisms in a given area] plus its abiotic [nonliving] environment . . . ecosystems occupy a given area, and that they therefore have boundaries [at least conceptually]. . . . The concept of the ecosystem as real physical entity sometimes presents problems, especially in terrestrial habitats, where it is often difficult to say where one ecosystem ends and another begins."[8]

Edaphic—Of or relating to the soil rather than to climate; refers to the role of soil in the growing of plants and crops.

Extraterritorial—In the nineteenth century meant "being beyond or without the limits of a territory or particular jurisdiction." Then tribes occupied areas extraterritorial to the newly formed territories or states; even Indian Territory was at first extraterritorial and later became part of Oklahoma.

The inference is that tribes originally were independent and treated as sovereigns. Today, extraterritorial has a modified meaning in international law and applies to an embassy. It does not apply to reservations or other trust lands; they are fully within state boundaries even though they are semiautonomous units mostly responsible to federal authority.[9]

Federal Indian law—Countless laws, treaties, agreements, and court decisions that involve tribes and individual Indians. Much of it may be located in Title 25, *U.S. Code,* but it also applies to other federal agencies, states, and local governments. It is not a separate body of law ordained by the Constitution or by Congress.[10] Federal Indian law is not tribal law, which is unique to each tribal nation.

GIS—Geographic Information Systems, a relatively new, sophisticated technology focusing on gathering and analyzing environmental data. It utilizes a number of methods, including satellite and ground technology, traditional maps, computer graphics.[11]

Government-to-government; see *self-determination*

Heirship; see *allotment*

Holism—Applied to nature, refers to whole multitude of related systems rather than their parts and implies that man and nature are part of a single system.

Indian Claims Commission; see *land claims*

Indian Country—The legal meaning of Indian country (lowercase c) embraces all Indian communities, reservations, allotments, and public domain trust lands for Indians. A broader meaning, based on political geography, embraces the state and local governments within which trust lands are found. Although not having specific legal force except in criminal law (Title 18, *U.S. Code*), it recognizes that tribes interact with non-Indian citizens and governments in the hinterland, and many legal interactions result from agreements over casinos and jurisdictions over civil and criminal matters.[12]

Indigenous planning—A planning process involving the full participation of indigenous peoples or tribes such as American Indians, Native Hawaiians, Eskimos. It focuses often on traditional environmental interpretations and culture ways. Today, it is closely linked to self-determination.

Iron Triangle—An "informal political alliance that forms to influence a specific public policy to its advantage. Consisting of congressional committees and subcommittees, administrative agencies, and interest groups, these tripartite coalitions influence the allocation of government goods and services. . . . Thus the triangle works in a symbolic fashion that creates advantages for all three participants."[13]

Jurisdiction; see *Indian Country*

Land cessions—Resulted from treaty provisions in negotiations between tribes and the federal government. Some tribal lands were ceded by formal treaties and others without formal agreement, but most resulted from written agreements, even if the tribes were at a disadvantage to oppose conditions. Such cessions were mapped based on the treaties.[14]

Land claims—Tribes have laid claim to lands acquired by treaties, agreements, and conquest and dispossession for which they were not properly compensated. Early claims were argued before the U.S. Court of Claims, but after 1946, when the Indian Claims Commission Act was passed, tribes brought their claims to that commission (acting as a tribunal). A large percentage of the claims were adjudicated in favor of the tribes, but the commission rejected any restoration of land and awarded a net number of dollars based on adjudicated acreage. Claims embraced major categories of tribal territory: original title (reconstructed with tribal informants and the work of anthropologists, geographers, and historians) and recognized title based on the C. C. Royce compilation (see *land cessions*).[15]

Land consolidation—Refers to grouping several Indian allotments encumbered by complex inheritance patterns into a larger single unit to prevent the land from sitting idle. Tribes have been encouraged to link separate allotments in an effort to meet the needs of an economy of scale in which larger acreage holdings facilitate production from the land. The Land Consolidation Act of 1982 [P.L. 97-459, 96 *Stat.* 2517] opened the way to such tribal efforts as part of tribal planning, but in recent years the Supreme Court has ruled that tribes could not take by escheat allotments under given concerns.

Land tenure—Refers to the nature of land holding whether tribal, communal, fee simple, or private ownership. It also embraces arrangements for utilization of the land such as agreements wherein all members of a group may use a commons, that land may be used by informal agreement or lease, or that land may be sold or alienated. Indian land tenure is complex and involves more than just tribal and individual ownership, for it does embrace the issue of trusteeship and heirship. It also includes the leasing of trust land and the sale of such land to non-Indians, who tend either to operate the land or live on former trust lands within the borders of a reservation. On nonallotted reservations individual Indians and families may occupy areas by long-term consent (understood) and by what is called tenancy-in-common or a tribal assignment.[16]

Measured separatism—Based on law, "the reservation system was intended to establish homelands for the tribes, islands of tribalism largely free from interference by non-Indians or future state governments. This separatism is measured, rather than absolute, because it contemplates supervision and support by the United States. . . . The measured separatism was subsequently modified by federal legislation."[17]

National sacrifice areas—Defined as tribal lands that have been or are today subjected to environmental abuse such as the dumpage and disposal of hazardous waste materials, mining, and other environmentally degrading activities for the good of the nation as a whole.[18]

Open areas—The counterpart to closed areas as applied to the Yakama Indian Reservation in Washington state pursuant to *Brendale v. Confederated Tribes of the Yakima Nation* [109 S. Ct. 2994 (1989)]. Such areas are defined mostly as non-Indian fee simple and would be outside the planning jurisdiction of the Yakama and, by extension, other tribes. Cf. *closed areas.*

Public Law 280—Enacted in 1953, transferred civil and criminal jurisdiction from the tribes and federal government to select states. Ultimately, all states that enclose trust lands gained some jurisdictional authority over activities on reservations but not over the land itself. Controversy arose when states and local governments sought to tax, zone, or plan for the utilization of trust lands. The Indian Civil Rights Act, 1968 [82 *Stat.* 77 (1968)] permitted tribes to retrocede from P.L. 280 and required a tribal vote before states could assume jurisdiction over reservations.[19]

RARE—The U.S. Forest Service term meaning roadless area review and evaluation; is applied to forest management areas to be protected.

Recognition; see *acknowledgment*

Relocation—A program of assisted relocation, instigated by the United States in the early 1950s for Indians who sought employment and housing away from reservations in urban settings. Chicago, Dallas, Denver, Detroit, Los Angeles, Oakland, and Seattle were destinies of countless Indians, many of whom and their descendants retain tribal affiliation. Relocation necessitated the creation of Indian urban centers, many of which received federal funding, but these centers are not divisions of the BIA.

Repatriation—In the context of Indian affairs, the process whereby tribal burial remains and other artifacts are returned to a tribe or an individual Indian. Tribes today have been invoking the Native American Graves Protection and Repatriation Act to secure the return of such remains from public lands and certain private lands. Several tribes have established museums to house repatriated artifacts.[20]

Reservation—Defined as a tract of land, from a few acres to hundreds of thousands of acres, actually has two definitions. It is correctly land tribes did *not* cede by treaty or other agreements, and it is also land the federal government established for tribes from the public domain that became federal pursuant to treaties or conquest. Other terms that carry the meaning of reservation include *colonias* in New Mexico and *rancherias* in California. Allotments are reserved parcels, held in trust but smaller than a reservation—they are found within a reservation or as public domain allotments elsewhere on federal lands.

Restoration—Applies to the return in status of tribes formerly terminated, such as the Menominee of Wisconsin and rancherias in California, as well as to the return of certain lands, such as sacred sites, back to tribes. This includes the sacred site of Kolhu/wala:wa of the Zuni and the much larger acreage restored to the Havasupai. See *land claims* for further discussion.

Sacred places and sites—Whether on existing trust lands, public lands, or other former tribal territory, including private holdings, sacred places and sites include culturally significant resources identified by Indian literature and culture history. Such sites include Bear Lodge, known as Devil's Tower.[21]

Self-determination—For most of the history of Indian affairs, tribes have been treated as dependent wards, and the government has been both trustee and guardian. Although some tribes assumed or were granted greater autonomy to run their own affairs, today's freedom to function in an autonomous way came with the Indian Self-Determination and Education Assistance Act of 1975. As a result, many tribes negotiate grants and contracts nearly free of interference from the BIA and often seek funding from other agencies such as ANA and EPA. Self-determination makes possible tribal planning of conservation projects. The law specifically calls for "an orderly transition from federal domination of programs for and services to effective and meaningful participation by the Indian people" [88 *Stat.* 2203–04 (1975)].

Severalty—A term referring to the distribution of allotted lands to individual Indians.

Sovereignty—American Indian sovereignty is characterized as inherent but is less than that of other nations such as the United States and Canada. Tribes have some autonomy within their borders, and this suggests the limited meaning of sovereignty. Tribes have no meaningful foreign affairs even if they address the United Nations and other international tribunals. Existing tribal sovereignty is being challenged by cases that seek to diminish tribal authority or jurisdiction over areas within tribal borders dominantly non-Indian in ownership and occupation.

Surplus lands—A phrase identifying tribal lands that remained inside reservation boundaries following the allotment of land to individual Indians. So-called surplus lands were made available to homesteaders, which was the beginning of creating mixed Indian Country, itself part of a policy of bringing Indians into closer contact with the majority culture. See discussions of *allotment.*

Termination—Pursuant to laws passed after the end of World War II and essentially abrogated or not enforced after 1961, termination sought legislatively to end the political status of tribes and to remove the trust status over reservation lands. Many Indian communities were terminated; some were later restored by laws, but only after several tribes suffered the loss of land and a decline in standard of living.

Territoriality—A loose term identifying the perceptive or legal basis for occupation and utilization of a given area. Hunting-and-gathering communities functioned within a broader lingually related territory but occupied smaller areas to which they laid claim. More settled communities could identify with larger territory measured in hundreds of square miles. Expressions of territoriality may imply the existence of a tribe in the political sense of knowingly occupying and claiming a given area and defending it.

Tribal law—Is not federal Indian law but may be interlocked as law codes, although the boundaries between tribal justice and that of the majority culture—federal and state courts—are sometimes difficult to determine.[22]

Trusteeship—By treaty, statute, and interpretation of the Constitution, the United States is the trustee for all federally recognized tribes and their trust lands. Today as in the past, several states also assume such a role, as on the eastern seaboard. The designated trustee's agency is the Bureau of Indian Affairs, formerly the Office of Indian Affairs. In fact, any federal agency involved in providing funds and services to the tribes acts on behalf of the trustee.

Watershed—The gathering ground of a single river system, that is, many streams flowing to a common dominant river. Size of a watershed will vary—the entire Mississippi-Missouri drainage is the largest watershed in the nation, but each of its components constitutes a watershed in its own right, such as the Yellowstone River.

Winters doctrine—Established in 1908, pursuant to *Winters v. United States,* a U.S. Supreme Court ruling that recognizes inherent water rights to tribes. The court determined that the United States pursued a policy of encouraging agriculture on allotted and tribal lands within a reservation and that necessitated the protection of water rights to guarantee that public policy will flourish. The doctrine in recent years has called for quantification of water rights, measured in acre feet—the equivalent of about 325,000 gallons of water—and the determination of whether tribes and individual Indians must use the water for agriculture or permit non-Indians to lease the water or even transport the water off reservation.[23]

References

1. Three volumes provide a wealth of definitions and discussions of terms related to Indian affairs: Duane Champagne, ed., *The Native North American Almanac* (Detroit:

Gale Research, 1994; 2d ed. due in 2001); Mary B. Davis, ed., *Native America in the Twentieth Century: An Encyclopedia* (New York: Garland, 1994); Imre Sutton, *Indian Land Tenure: Bibliographical Essays and a Guide to the Literature* (New York: Clearwater, 1975).

2. See discussion in Imre Sutton, ed., *Irredeemable America: The Indians' Estate and Land Claims* (Albuquerque: University of New Mexico Press, 1985).
3. Stephen L. Pevar, *The Rights of Indians and Tribes,* 2d ed. (Carbondale: Southern Illinois University Press, 1992): 261–263.
4. Steven H. Gifis, *Law Dictionary* (Woodbury, NY: Barron's Educational Series, 1975): 10.
5. A. David Lester, "Council of Energy Resource Tribes," in Davis, ed., *Native America in the Twentieth Century,* pp. 144–145.
6. Raymond F. Dasmann, *Environmental Conservation,* 5th ed. (New York: Wiley and Sons, 1984): 6; Gary A. Klee, *Conservation of Natural Resources* (Englewood Cliffs, NJ: Prentice-Hall, 1991): 14.
7. Readers should see Shepard Krech, *The Ecological Indian: Myth and History* (New York: W. W. Norton, 1999).
8. Dasmann, *Environmental Conservation,* p. 11; John M. Blair, Scott L. Collins, and Alan K. Knapp, "Ecosystems as Functional Units in Nature," *Natural Resources and Environment,* 14:3 (winter 2000): 150–155, quote on p. 151.
9. Cf. Imre Sutton, "Sovereign States and the Changing Definition of the Indian Reservation," *Geographical Review,* 66:3 (1976): 281–295, quote on p. 286.
10. See David H. Getches, Charles F. Wilkinson, and Robert A. Williams Jr., *Cases and Materials on Federal Indian Law,* 4th ed. (St. Paul: West, 1998). The original compilation and analysis of federal Indian law was Felix Cohen, *Handbook of Federal Indian Law* (Washington, DC: Government Printing Office (GPO), 1941; reprinted University of New Mexico Press, 1971).
11. Bryan Marozas, "The Role of Geographic Information Systems in American Indian Land and Water Rights Litigation," *American Indian Culture and Research Journal,* 15:3 (1991): 77–93.
12. See Vine Deloria Jr. and Clifford M. Lytle, *American Indians, American Justice* (Austin: University of Texas Press, 1983), chapter 3; see also Imre Sutton, "Preface to Indian Country: Geography and Law," *American Indian Culture and Research Journal,* 15:2 (1991): 3–36.
13. Daniel McCool, *Command of the Waters: Iron Triangles, Federal Water Development, and Indian Water* (Berkeley: University of California Press, 1987): 5.
14. C. C. Royce, comp., *Indian Land Cessions in the United States, 18th Annual Report, 1896–97,* Bureau of American Ethnography (Washington, DC: GPO, 1899): part 2, pp. 521–997.
15. Sutton, ed., *Irredeemable America.*
16. Sutton, *Indian Land Tenure.*
17. For more discussion, see Charles F. Wilkinson, *American Indians, Time, and the Law* (New Haven: Yale University Press, 1987): 14–19, quote on p. 14.
18. For a discussion with maps, see Ward Churchill and Winona LaDuke, "Native North America: The Political Economy of Radioactive Colonialism," in M. Annette Jaimes, ed., *The State of Native America: Genocide, Colonization and Resistance* (Boston: South End, 1992): 250–255; see also Churchill, "A Breach of Trust: The Radioactive

Colonization of Native North America," *American Indian Culture and Research Journal,* 23:4 (1999): 23–69.

19. Carol Goldberg-Ambrose, *Planting Tail Feathers: Tribal Survival and Public Law 280* (Los Angeles: UCLA–American Indian Studies Center, 1999).
20. See "The Native American Graves Protection and Repatriation Act" [symposium], *Arizona Law Journal,* 24:1 (1992).
21. See, for example, Andrew Gulliford, *Sacred Objects and Sacred Places: Preserving Tribal Traditions* (Boulder: University Press of Colorado, 2000). For a general treatise that includes Indian discussion, see Thomas F. King, *Cultural Resource, Laws, and Practice: An Introductory Guide* (Walnut Creek, CA: Altamira, 1998).
22. Cf. Frank Pommersheim, *Braid of Feathers: American Indian Law and Contemporary Tribal Life* (Berkeley: University of California Press, 1995).
23. See McCool, *Command of the Waters.*

Index to Cases

Index

IR = Indian Reservation
NF = National Forest
NHP = National Historic Park
NP = National Park

Page numbers in italics indicate illustrations.